ESSAY'D 3

ESSAY'D 3 // 30 DETROIT ARTISTS

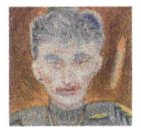 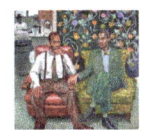 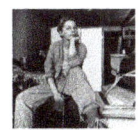 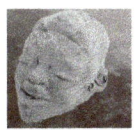 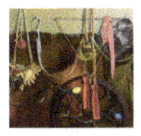 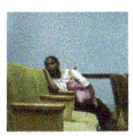

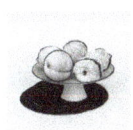 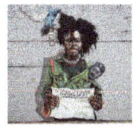 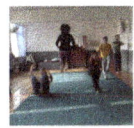 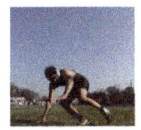 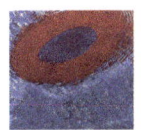 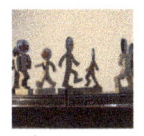

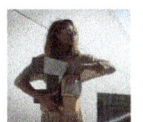 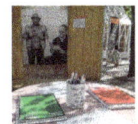 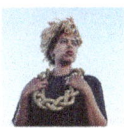 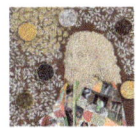 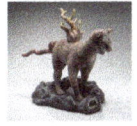 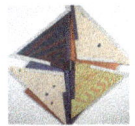

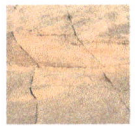 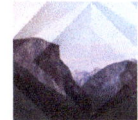 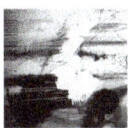 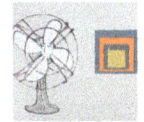 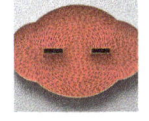 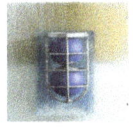

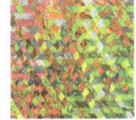 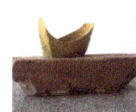 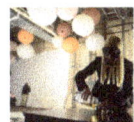 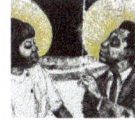 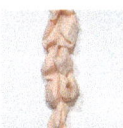 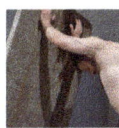

Edited and Compiled by
Dennis Alan Nawrocki,
Steve Panton, and
Matthew Piper

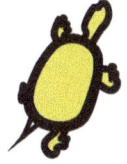

A Painted Turtle book
DETROIT, MICHIGAN

Ed Fraga

Richard Lewis

Donita Simpson

Matthew Angelo Harrison

Jeanne Bieri

Oren Goldenberg

Cynthia Greig

Sydney G. James

The Hinterlands

Billy Mark

Allie McGhee

Gary Schwartz

Maya Stovall

Andrew Thompson

Tiff Massey

Yvette Rock

Susan Aaron-Taylor

Gary Eleinko

Carla Anderson

Millee Tibbs

Lauren Semivan

Timothy Van Laar

Sharon Que

Tom Phardel

Carole Morisseau

Laith Karmo

Nicola Kuperus

Sabrina Nelson

Sophie Eisner

Eli Gold

ISBN: 978-0-8143-4587-0

Library of Congress Control
Number: 2018953472

Painted Turtle is an imprint of
Wayne State University Press

Wayne State University Press
Leonard N. Simons Building
4809 Woodward Avenue
Detroit, Michigan 48201-1309

Visit us online at wsupress.wayne.edu

CONTENTS

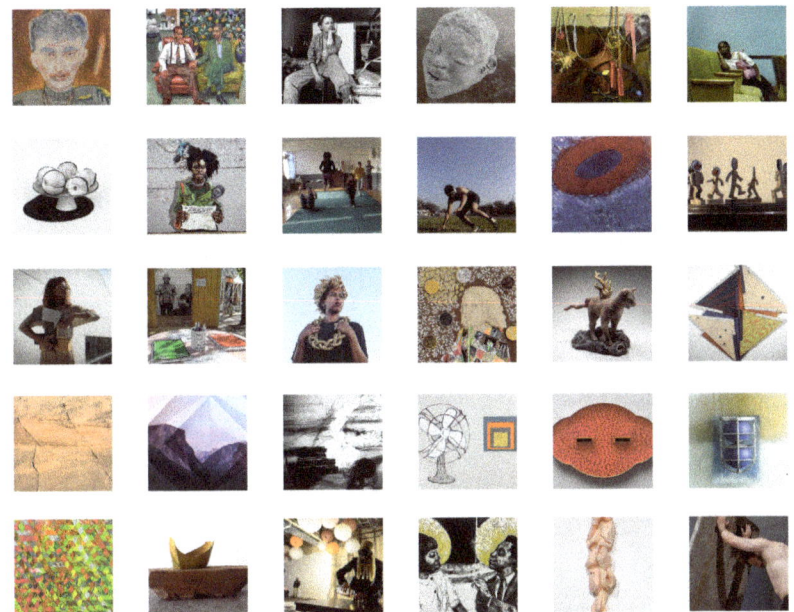

ACKNOWLEDGMENTS

We remain grateful to Wayne State University Press for their continued enthusiasm and support for our project. Thanks to their vision and care, the words and images that follow have been transformed from pixels on a webpage to the beautifully designed book that you hold in your hands.

As Essay'd continues to grow, we find new reasons to thank our partners at the Anton Art Center and the Birmingham Bloomfield Art Center, with whom we organize a series of rotating Essay'd artist talks; the Detroit Symphony Orchestra, where we regularly mount exhibitions of work by Essay'd artists; the Museum of Contemporary Art Detroit, where we host workshops and book launches; and Allied Media Projects, which provides continued support as Essay'd's fiscal sponsor, grant guru, and, lately, workshop partner as well.

For their financial support, we wish to thank the Knight Foundation and the Erb Foundation, without whom the ongoing expansion of our efforts would be, frankly, impossible.

For his dedication to our project and invaluable technical assistance, we thank, always and forever, our attorney, Noel French, who has learned more than he ever could have imagined about art, and who has taught us, in turn, more than we thought we needed to know about the law.

With profound gratitude, we tip our hats to the twelve (!) guest writers whose words are featured here alongside our own. Thanks to their passion, participation, and patience with our process, our imperfect survey of contemporary Detroit artists grows ever more diverse, inclusive, and truly representative of the flourishing art community that calls Detroit home.

To that community—artists, curators, gallerists, writers, and enthusiasts alike—we offer our sincere appreciation for creating the conditions under which Detroit art continues to thrive and offer inspiration.

Finally, we acknowledge our families, partners, and friends. Our names are on the cover, but it is thanks to your love, support, and encouragement that we are able to do what we do. Thank you.

D.A.N., S.P., M.P.

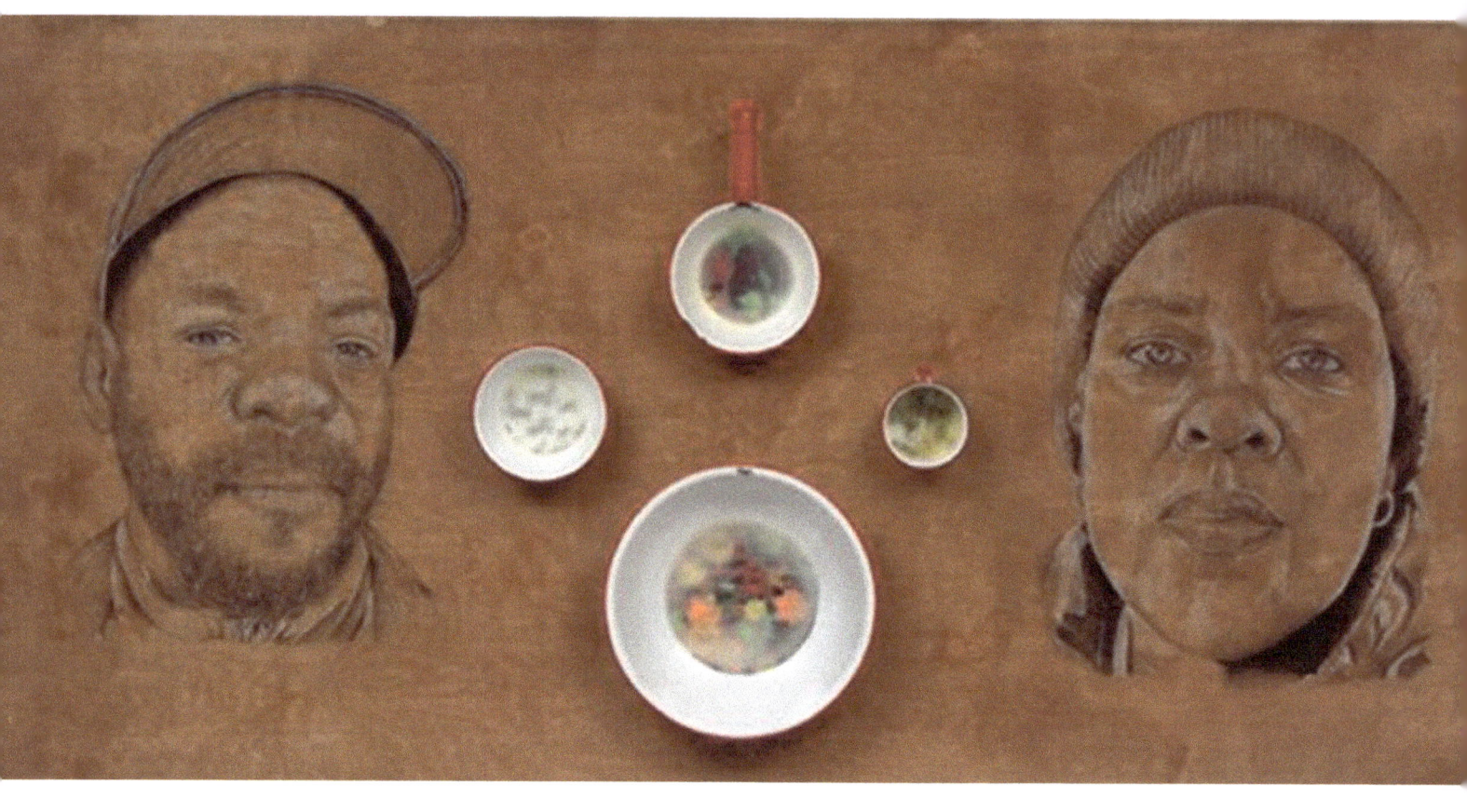

INTRODUCTION

The word "essay" comes to English via the French *essai*: a trial, an attempt. To essay an artist, then, is to attempt to relate an understanding of that artist's work. Where does it come from, and where is it going? How is it made? Why? (The answer to that one is, perhaps, ever elusive but occasionally fleetingly glimpsed.) What notions, states, or intuitions does it provoke in the participant? What forces—personal, political, social—lie beneath it? What does it *mean*?

At Essay'd, we ask these questions about artists currently living or working in or around Detroit, a place where artists proliferate. The collection that follows continues our ongoing attempt to answer these questions, artist by artist, in a format that is clear, concise, and accessible to the common reader. We make this attempt because

we believe in Detroit art—its richness, its cultural value, its power to touch, humanize, and inspire—and because we believe that it is worthy of attention, documentation, and study. We make it, furthermore, because we believe in a general *inclusivity* of contemporary art, not its much-purported exclusivity—that, in other words, curious people of all walks can and should experience, read about, and think about the art that's being made around them, so that they might understand, more deeply, the time and place in which they live.

The art that is made in Detroit today resists being fit into any given narrative. The solid story passed down to us from the heady days of the Cass Corridor movement—that Detroit art is about deindustrialization and its discontents—is, necessarily, overgrown by a flowering,

twenty-first-century multiplicity. There are, we are happy to say, as many kinds of Detroit art as there are Detroit artists, and even if certain themes and methods recur, they are handily contradicted or obviated by any number of others. Consider, for instance, in this volume, the accomplished figurative oil paintings of Richard Lewis and the layered mystery of Ed Fraga's watercolor "time logs," both of which emerge from deeply personal relationships in each artist's life. Or the sociopolitical and economic concerns of Oren Goldenberg and Maya Stovall, in whose performance and video-based practices marginalized Detroiters are given expressive voice. Experience a recent performance by The Hinterlands that refracts contemporary national anxieties about violent extremism through a rich, historical prism,

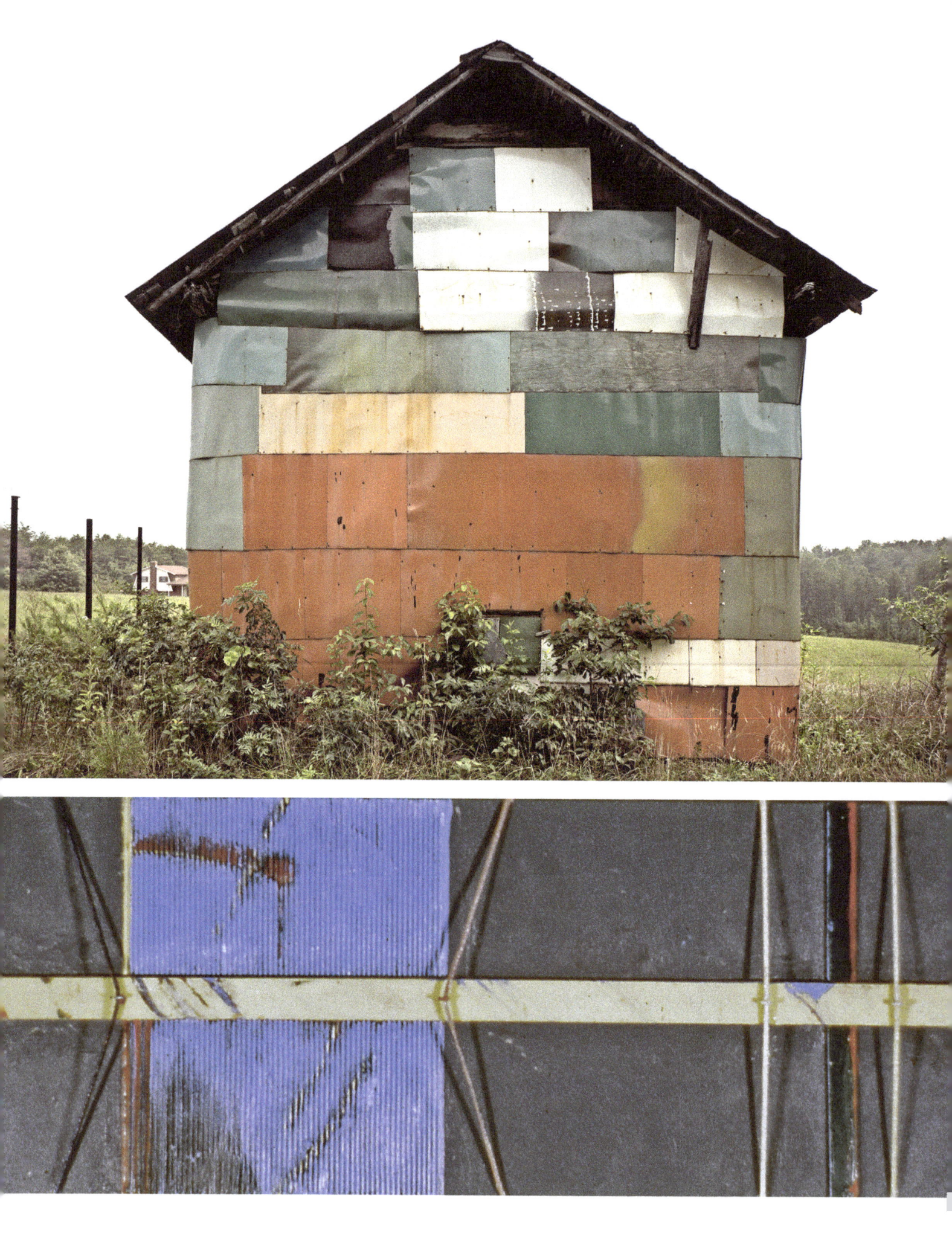

or the elegant, postminimal sculptures of Matthew Harrison that embrace recent advances in fabrication technology. . . .

A diverse population of artists, such as we have in Detroit, is perhaps best explored by a varied cohort of writers, and this third volume in the *Essay'd* series marks a seismic shift in that direction. While the small team of core writer-editors has contracted from four to three since the 2017 publication of *Essay'd 2*, the number of guest writers here swells to twelve—twelve additional voices, all making their own attempt to understand artists in whom they, personally, find interest and inspiration.

While the format of our essays is intentionally brief, their gestation period is not. Each writer pays each artist one or more studio visits, followed by many hours of study, review, clarification, analysis, image selection, and, finally, writing. Each draft is then peer-edited before it is published (originally on our website, essayd.org, where new essays continue to be released regularly). We do this work, collectively, to continue a conversation, or to start one (in many cases, these essays are the first piece of critical writing undertaken about a given artist), and because we believe the artists deserving of this attention and care.

Ours, however, is a fundamentally nonhierarchical pursuit; Essay'd seeks not to rank artists, nor to promote a canon of "the best" Detroit artists, but simply to give our audience opportunities to critically engage with art that our growing pool of writers finds compelling. As we continue our efforts and reach, incredibly, toward our one hundredth essay, we are well aware that our project is actually nowhere near complete. The field in which we labor is too fertile, the scene too storied and ever changing. There are too many artists whose work we love and long to understand better but whose essays remain as yet unwritten.

For now, we are pleased to present this latest collection, essays #61–90, in which thirty remarkable artists come to the fore. We hope that you find in these passionately prepared pages something that stimulates, challenges, or wakes you up—something that complicates, complements, or clarifies your own understanding of art, and of Detroit, today.

DAN, SP, MP

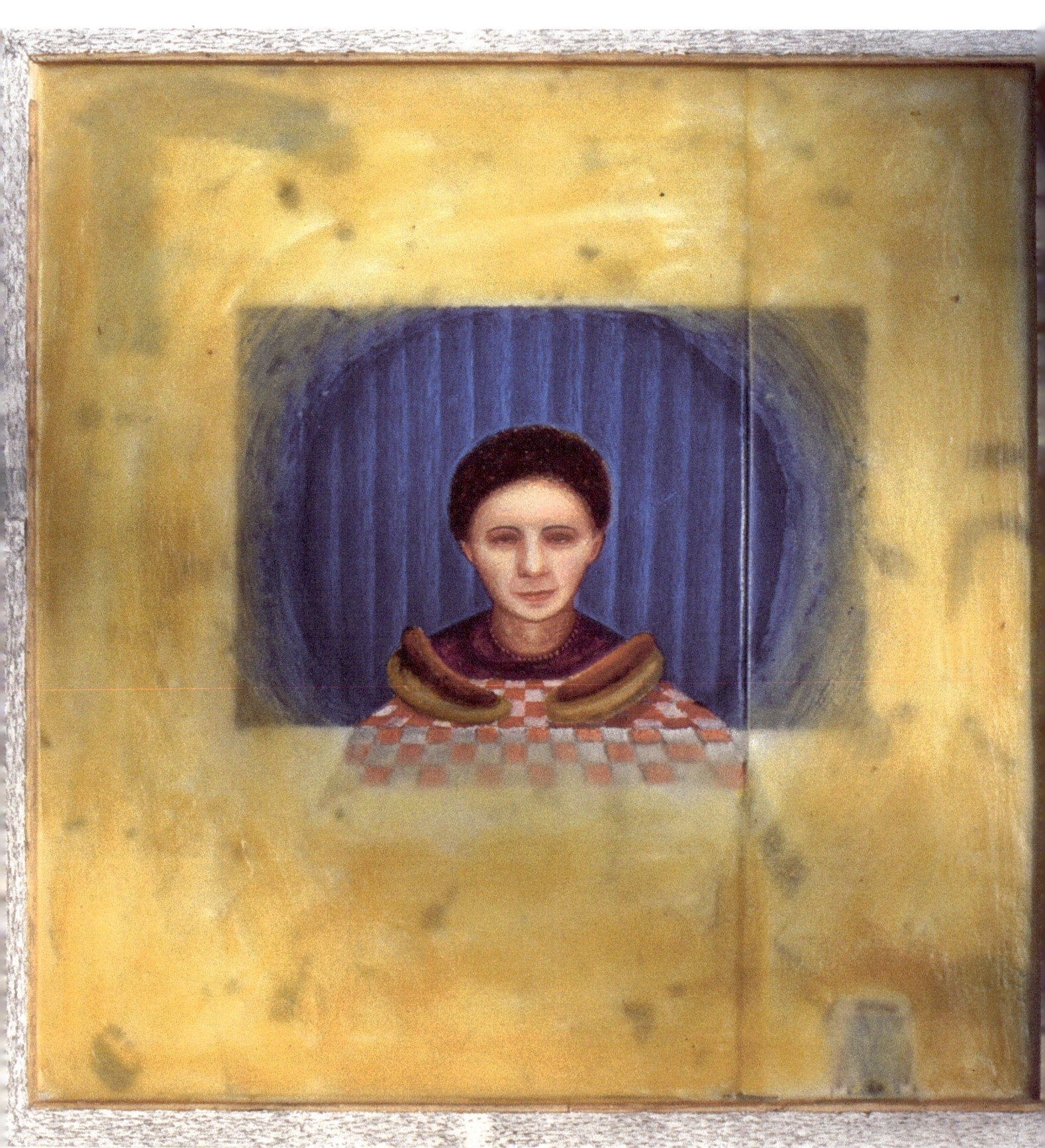

Geenie's Weenies. 1983. Oil pastel, wax, glass, paper, wood, 20 x 20 x 2 in.

Born Imlay City, Michigan, 1956
BFA, Wayne State University
Lives in Troy, Michigan

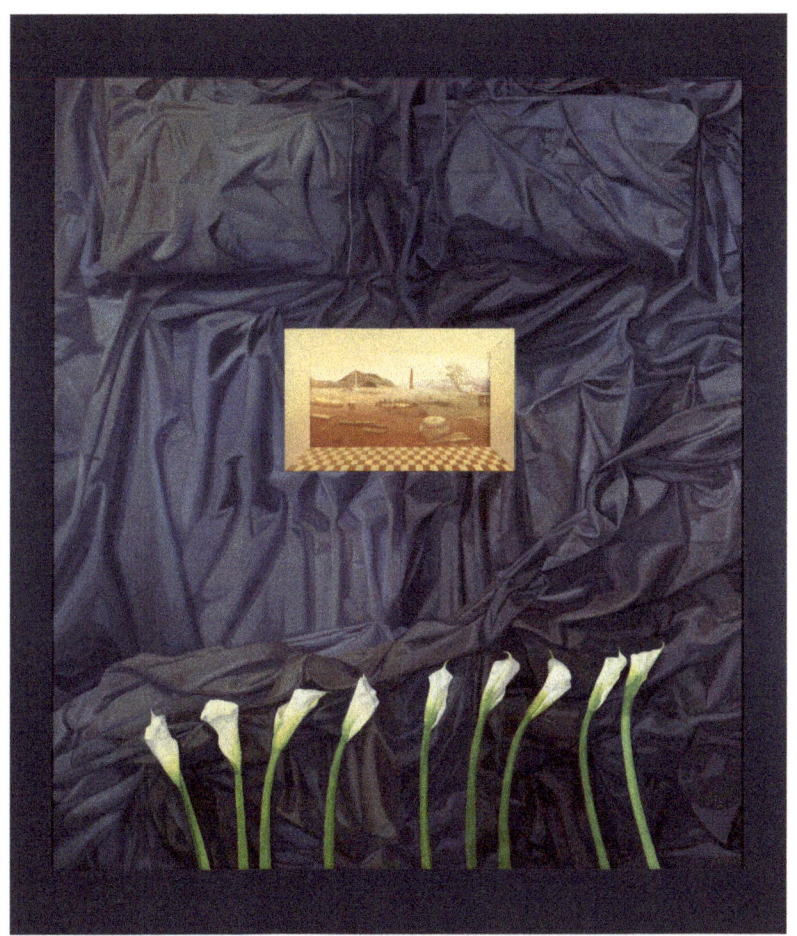

La Santa E Gloriosa Carne. 1994. Oil on wood, 84 x 72 x 4 in.
Courtesy of the Detroit Institute of Arts.

Ed Fraga remembers as a child taking a sheet of cardboard, folding it into a box, and looking at it, being thrilled to realize he'd created a small but powerful object. Later he started to populate the box, with dioramas, stage sets, magic shows for neighborhood kids, and other constructs of his imagination. "In a way," he says, "I'm still trying to fill the box."

Mostly Fraga fills the box with material that speaks to the human condition. In a seminal early work, **Memory Portrait Book** (1982–83), he created over thirty small-scale oil pastel portraits of "everyday saints" he encountered while living in Detroit's Cary Building. The portraits were compiled into an artist's book covered in asphalt peeled directly from the street. In a later solo show at Detroit's Feigenson Gallery, Fraga presented a series of figurative works (for

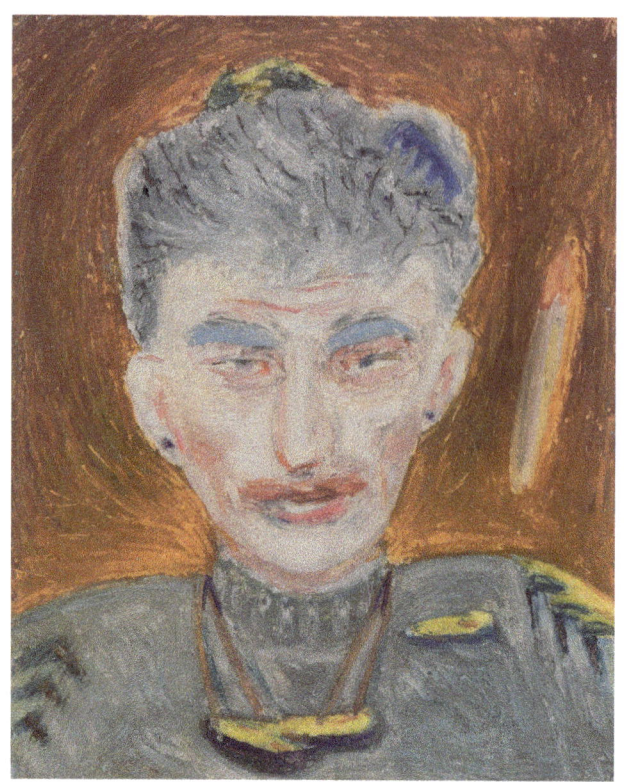

Stella (from *Memory Portrait Book*). 1982. Oil pastel on paper, 7 x 6 in.

example, 1983's ***Geenie's Weenies***), each surrounded by a meticulously detailed box/frame, assembled from, and often containing, found objects. The two series reveal Fraga deeply absorbed with life's anomalies, but looking at them through a lens that feels closer to Joseph Cornell than Diane Arbus.

Subsequent works—e.g., 1986's ***Summer*** or 1989's ***Sinking Man***—show Fraga moving into unequivocally spiritual and psychological terrain. The overall construction of *Summer*, with its clear references to forms such as the altar and the baptismal font, indicates Fraga's lifelong dialogue

Time Log 21. 2008. Watercolor on paper, 6 1/2 x 8 in.

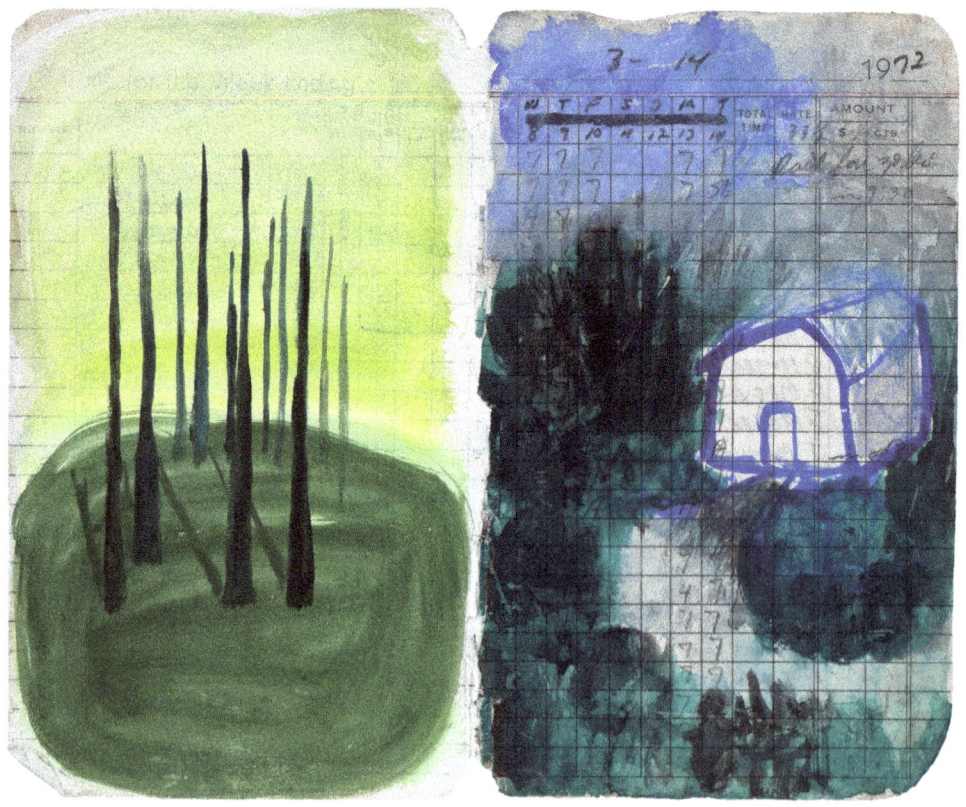

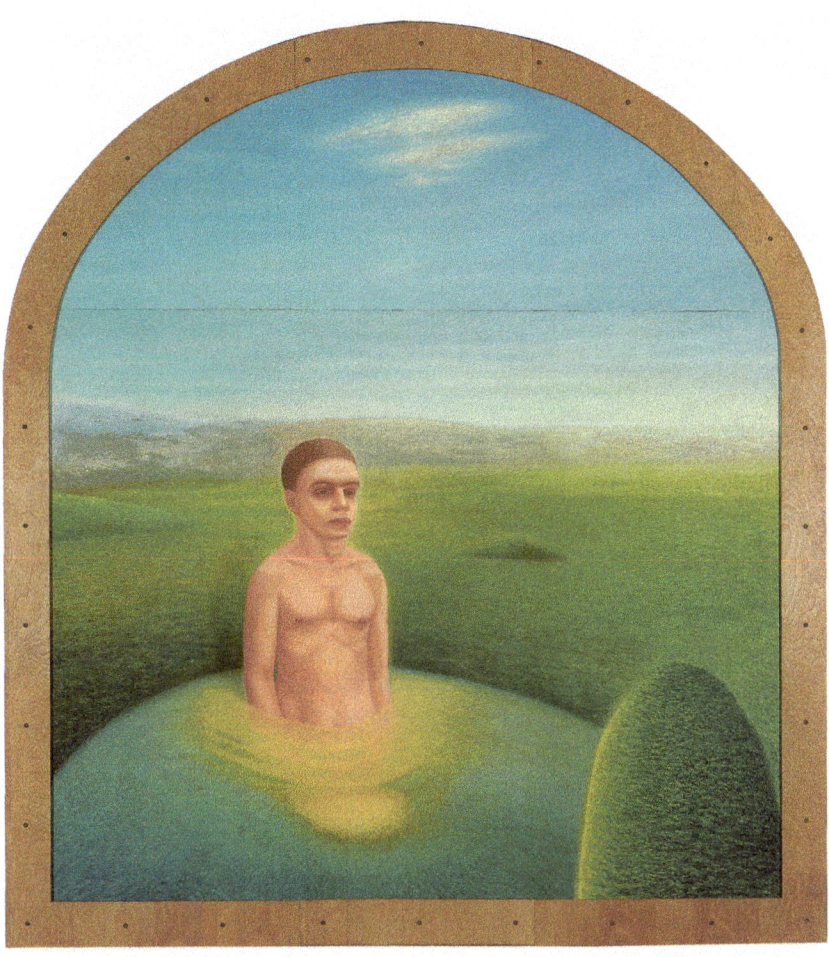

Sinking Man. 1989. Oil on wood, 75 x 67 in.

with Christianity. Religion is a constant subtext for Fraga, but he is adamant that his art should be open and free of specific messaging. Works such as *Sinking Man* hover just on the edge of narrative, inviting viewers to create their own interpretation. This is Fraga's intention. While he undoubtedly sees the artist as having a responsibility to the viewing public, it is difficult to find the precise metaphor for this relationship. Certainly it is not the preacher and the flock, nor

is it the teacher and the class or the storyteller and the audience. Perhaps at times it is closer to the artist as magician, encouraging the viewer to suspend disbelief and see more mystery in the world.

Other constants in Fraga's work are craft and composition. His studies with teachers such as John Hegarty and Louise Nobili provided him with the rigorous education typical of Wayne State's art program of the late seventies. As he puts it, these aspects of art object-making are

now so deeply engrained that he can't escape them. One of his best known works is *La Santa E Gloriosa Carne* (1994), a large elegiac painting that was exhibited in the Detroit Institute of Art's early medieval gallery during the institute-wide *Interventions* exhibition (1995) and subsequently purchased and placed on permanent display. Fraga considers it a culmination of his efforts to that date, both in terms of its technical fluency and the directness with which it addresses his core themes of birth, death, and resurrection.

In the early/mid-2000s, Fraga began to focus his drawings and paintings on themes of childhood memory and innocence. Simultaneously he developed a looser, more intuitive style than the meticulous rendering exemplified by *La Santa E Gloriosa Carne.* An important literary touchstone was William Blake's collection of poems *Songs of Innocence.* Shortly afterward he also started an important body of work that was physically based on time logs that his father had kept as part of his electrical contracting business back in the 1970s. Fraga considered his artistic mark-making in this series to be a collaboration with the work

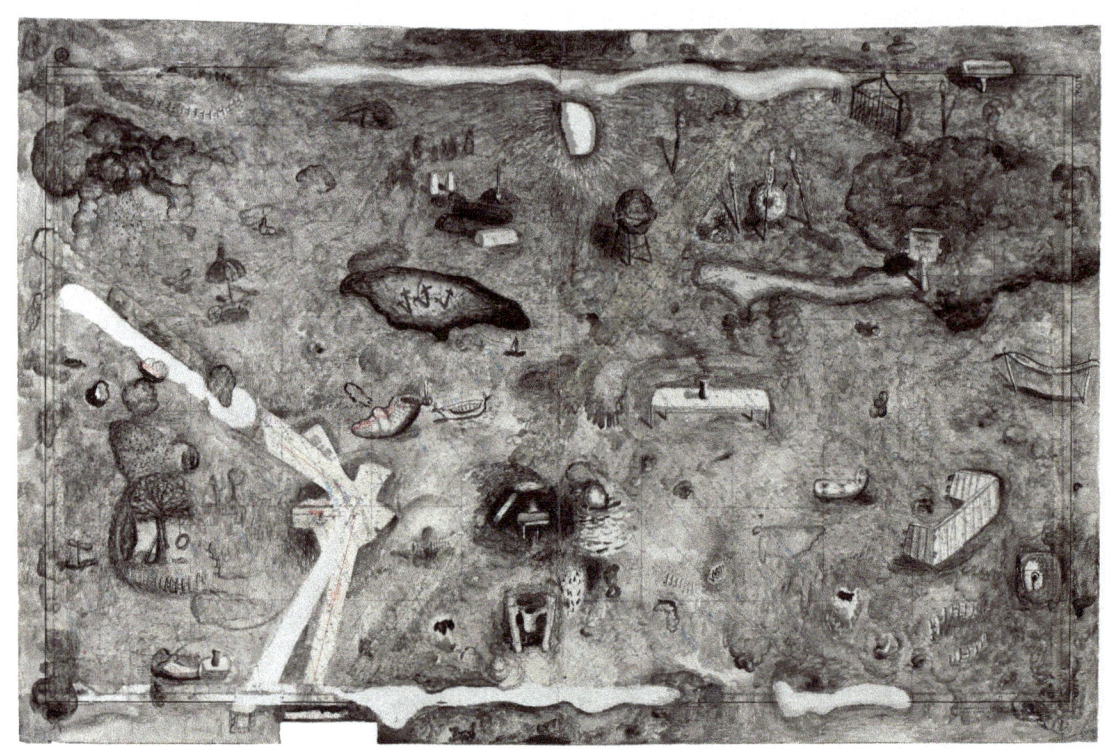

Map: Allegory of Childhood. 2008.
Watercolor on water table map, 36 x 54 in.

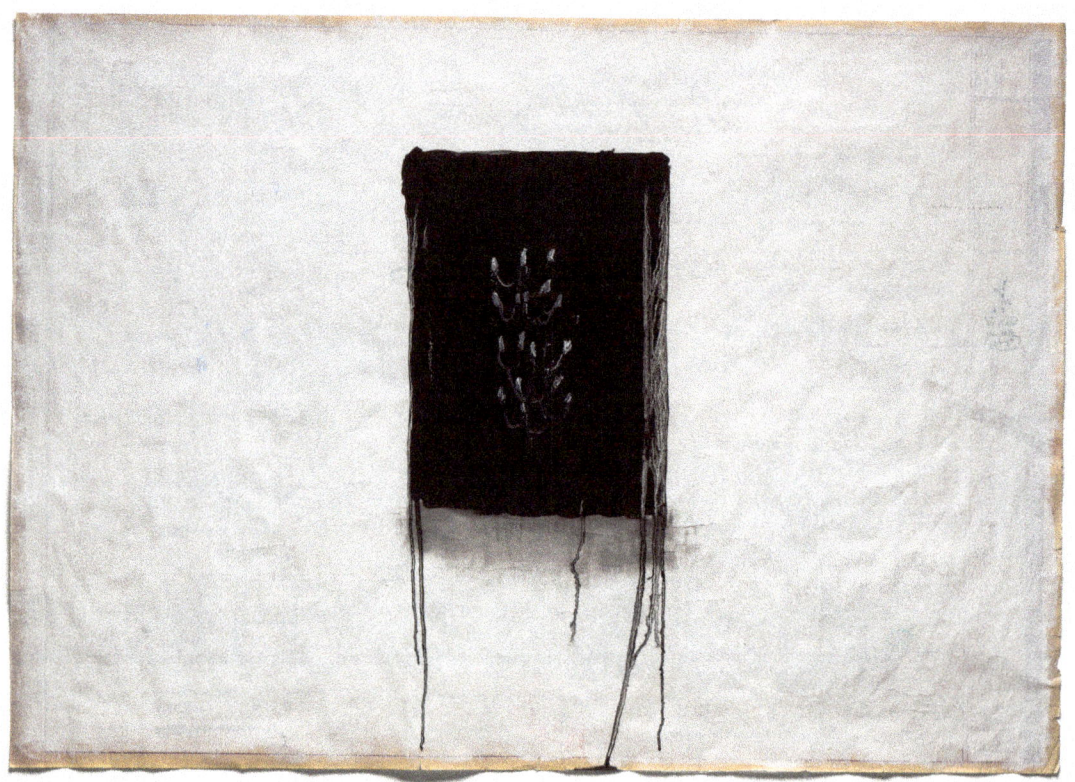

Tablet. 2015. Gesso, oil on blueprint, 30 x 42 in.

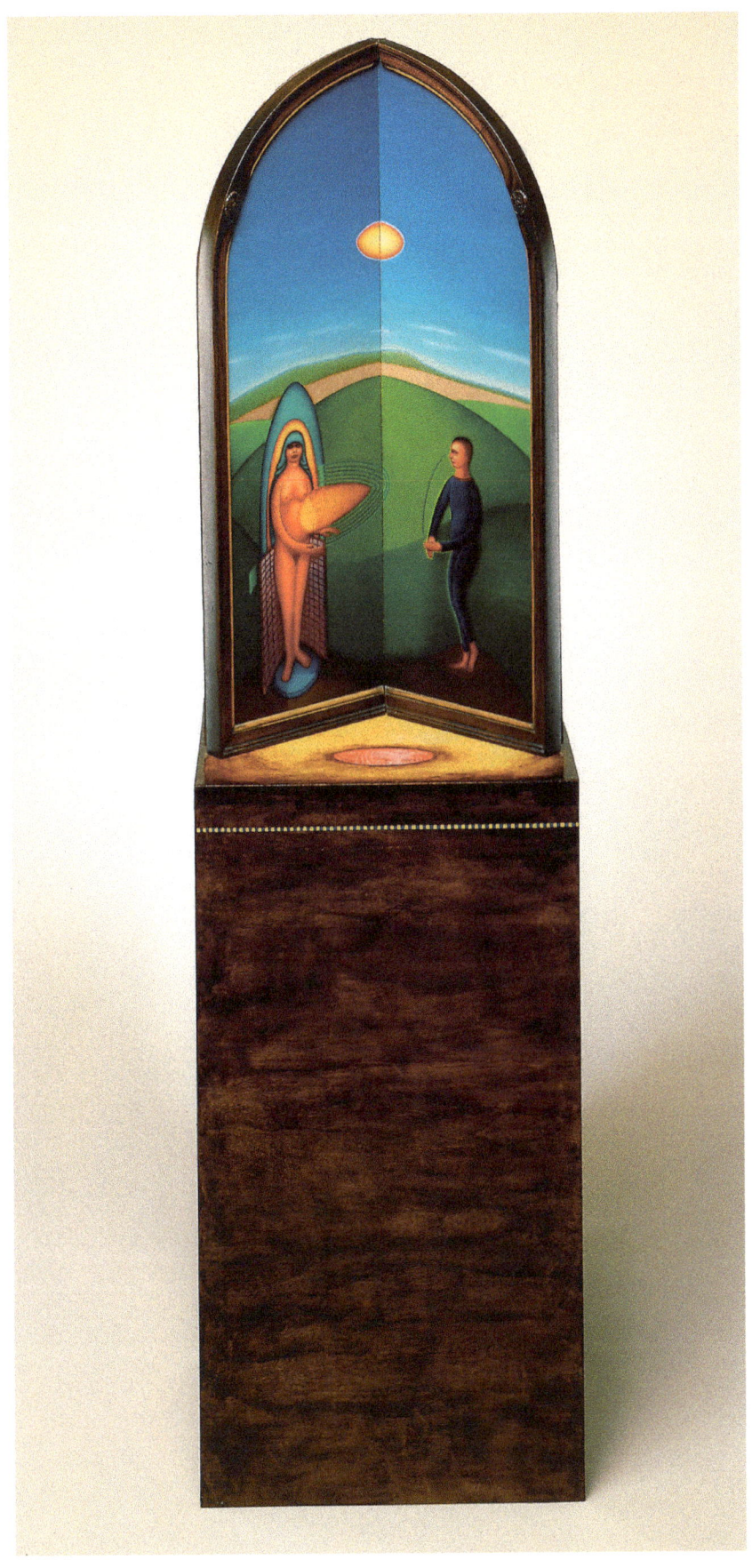

of his deceased father. Much of the art from this period, including **Book of Time Logs** (2008) and **Map: Allegory of Childhood** (created in 2008 on a bathymetric survey of the Caribbean that Fraga found in his father's possessions), was exhibited at the Flint Institute of Arts in 2009.

In recent years, Fraga has continued to draw and paint on ephemeral materials that arrive with their own history. Since 2014 he has been working on *Sanctuary*, an extended series of paintings that are presented on blueprints for a nondenominational sanctuary in Ann Arbor drawn by an architect friend. The blueprints are first painted in gesso, which give individual works (e.g., **Tablet**, 2015) a distinctively ethereal quality. Ultimately, Fraga sees the completed series as an installation configured for a specific location. His objective is that viewers will experience the work in a transcendent manner. In a sense, the gallery will become another iteration of the box he started to fill as a child—and we will all be able to enter into it.

STEVE PANTON, DECEMBER 2016

Summer. 1986. Oil on wood, 67 x 18 x 14 in.

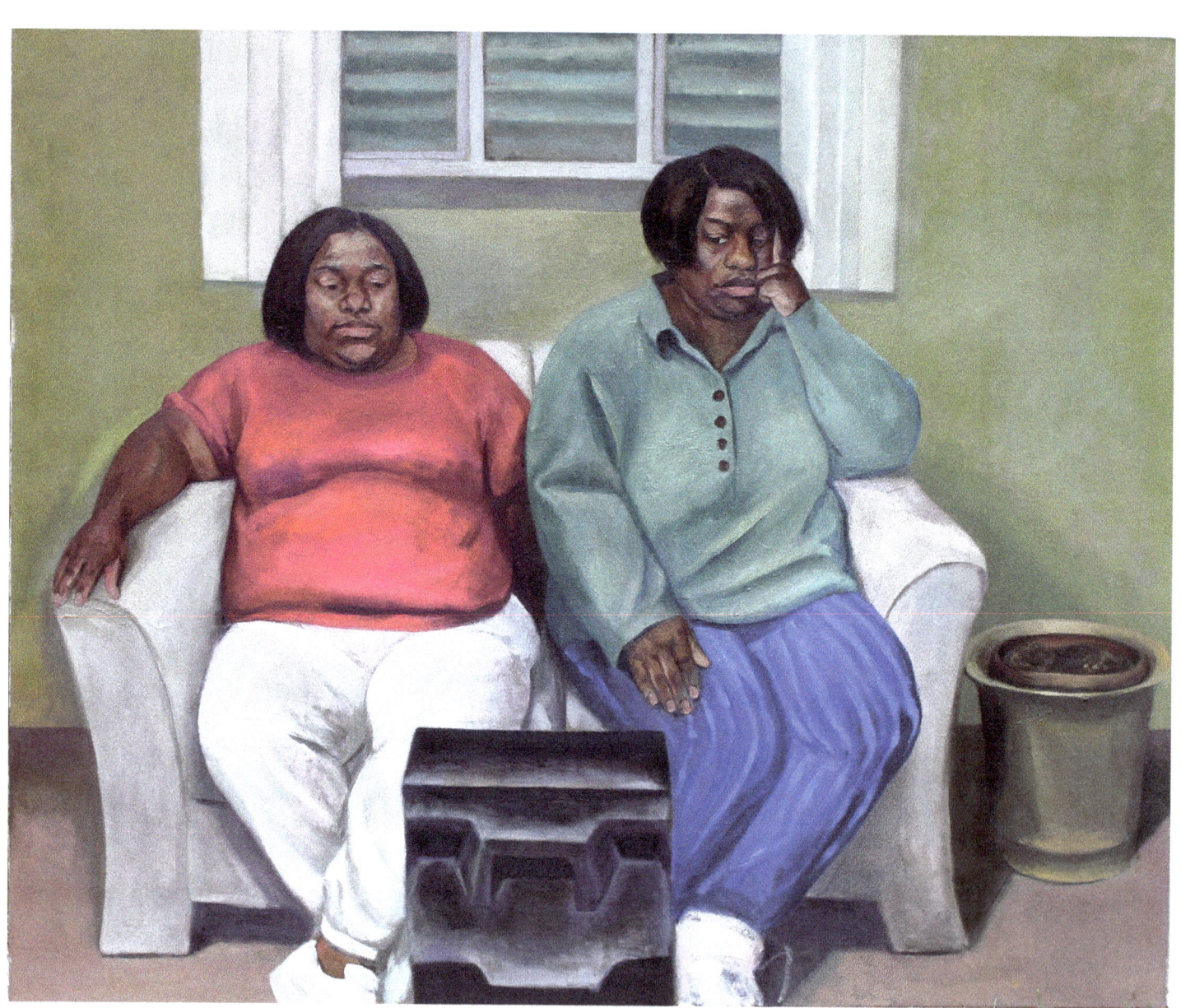

Kim and Tonya Watching T.V. 1998.
Oil on canvas, 60 x 72 in.

Born Detroit, 1966
BFA, College for Creative Studies;
MFA, Yale School of Art,
New Haven, Connecticut
Lives in Detroit

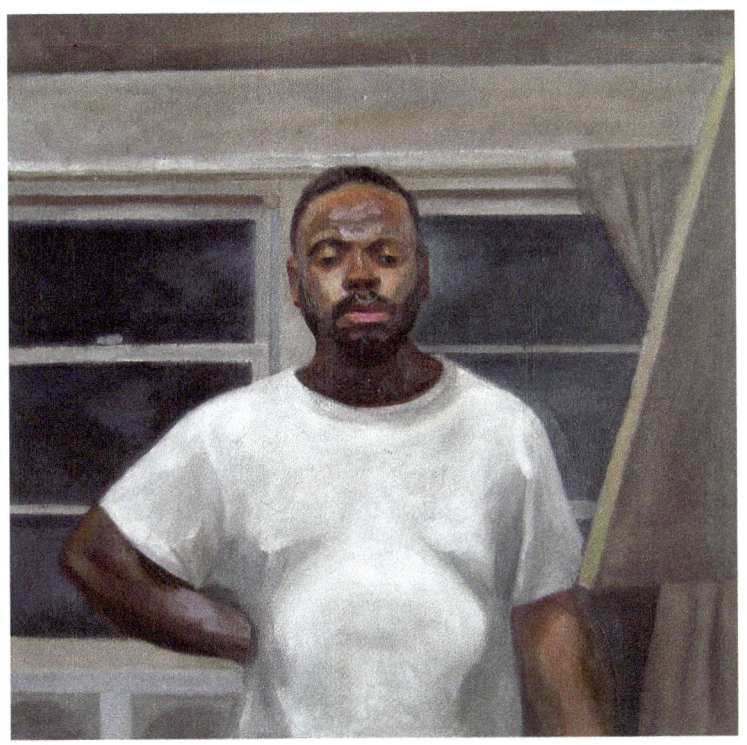

Self Portrait in White Shirt. 2004. Oil on canvas, 36 x 36 in.

Richard Lewis's stark, striking *Self Portrait in White Shirt* (2004) establishes at a glance the mode of bold, arresting portraiture he has practiced over the last decade and a half. Here, his own half-length, life-size visage dominates a shallow space wherein he reveals himself at a terse, decisive moment. Though a stretched canvas at right appears primed for action, he stands stock still, his flushed face charged with emotion. In particular, the emphatic swabs of thick red and white pigment slashing across his forehead augur a deep-seated determination. Another angsty portrayal of 2004 represents *Anthony*, a friend whose parted lips and wary glance imply concern and vulnerability in equal measure.

Painted about a year and a half after a six-year sojourn in New York (1996–2002),

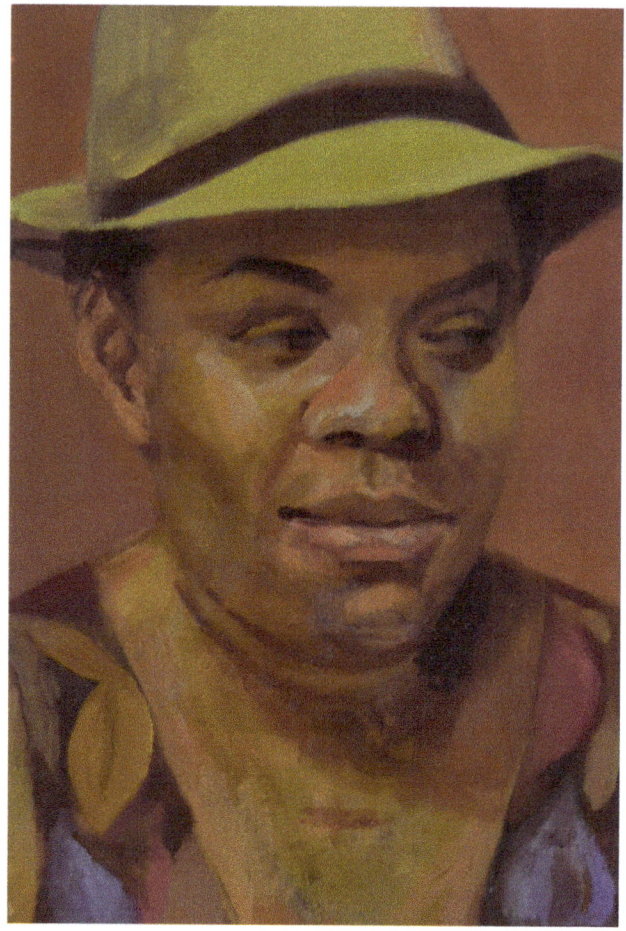

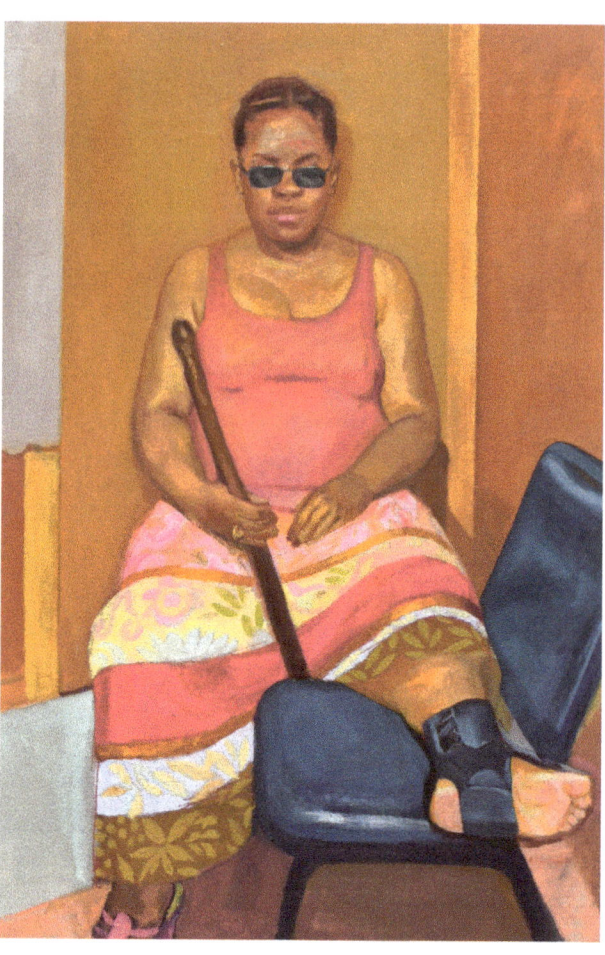

Tracey Wearing a Hat. 2011. Oil on canvas, 22 x 15 in.   *Tracey.* 2009. Oil on canvas, 72 x 60 in.

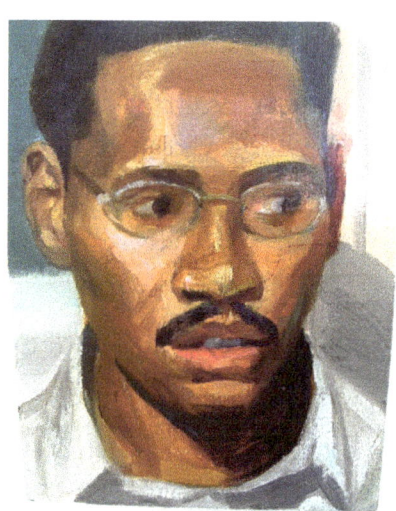

Anthony. 2004. Oil on canvas, 11 x 8 in.

these bare-knuckled portraits suggest Lewis's affirmative resolve to reengage with his art and natal environs. In fact, his 2002 reappearance was his second repatriation to his Detroit roots; earlier, after graduation from Yale in 1993, he had relocated to his hometown but stayed only a year and a half before decamping for his six-year residency in Gotham.

Resettled in the D post-2002, one of Lewis's favorite—and reliably available—models became his cousin Tracey, who has posed for a number of transformative likenesses or "takes," ranging from a cool, composed *Tracey* (2009), undaunted by a sprained ankle, to the professionally attired, "all-business" *Tracey* in a bright red blazer (2010) and a rakish, summer-attired *Tracey Wearing a Hat* (2011). In these images, as in many of Lewis's solo portraits, the figure is centralized and confronts the viewer directly, as in classical European portraiture, stoical African sculpture, and iconic religious pictures. Insisting

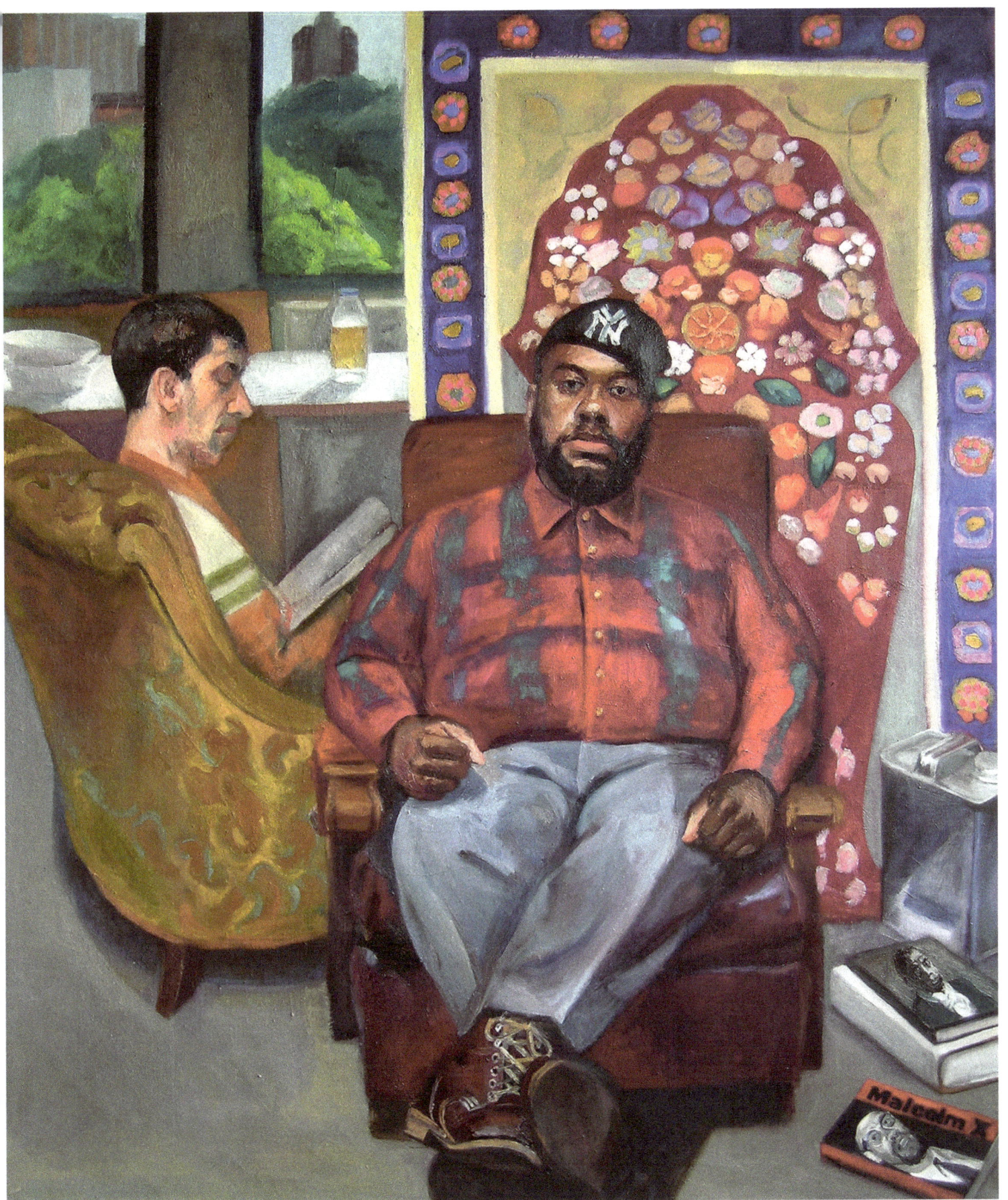

Study Group. 1997. Oil on canvas, 72 x 60 in.

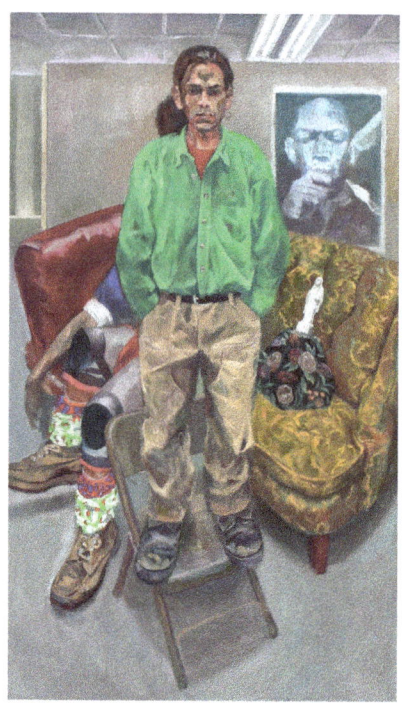

Nelson. 1996. Oil on canvas, 84 x 48 in.

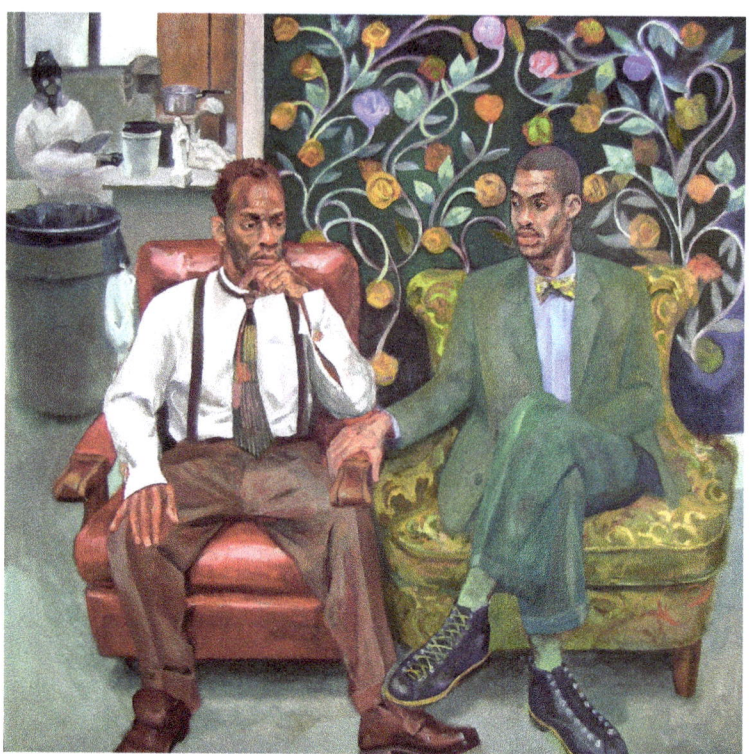

James and Kelly. 1996. Oil on canvas, 72 x 72 in.

that "to be a realist painter" is a moral imperative, Lewis devises "makeshift classical paintings" inhabited, paradoxically, by contemporary subjects rendered "like African sculptures—regal and enveloped in thought."

Notable as well is a raft of ambitious double portraits that caught the attention of critics during his multiyear New York residency. In *James and Kelly* (1996), two men, seated side by side, face forward and avert eye contact. Yet their gazes in opposite directions intersect, and James, on the right, grasps the arm of his lover's chair, if not his lover's arm. A masked person at

the rear, preoccupied and wearing a respirator, constructs a sculpture. In another dual depiction, *Study Group* (1997), Lewis presents himself and a studious friend, the former facing forward, fists clenched, and the latter in profile, opposites ostensibly "studying." A large, red-figured carpet backdrops and visually augments the seated Lewis (a decorative device that also enlivens *James and Kelly*), while the rapt reader is set against a green, hilly cityscape. But what are they studying? Revolution perhaps, given the gasoline can and books by James Baldwin and Malcolm X scattered on the floor. A third example, *Nelson* (1996),

the largest at eighty-four by forty-eight inches, is daringly surprising in that the towering Nelson, front and center, overshadows the second figure partially visible behind him, almost as if the portrayal represents a dueling couple—as a John Coltrane poster looms behind.

Closer to home—to both Motown and family—are two affecting double portraits of Lewis's sisters. Painted more than a decade apart, each conveys the pair's closeness and separateness. In the 1998 depiction, *Kim and Tonya Watching T.V.* are scrunched together on a loveseat, directing their full attention to

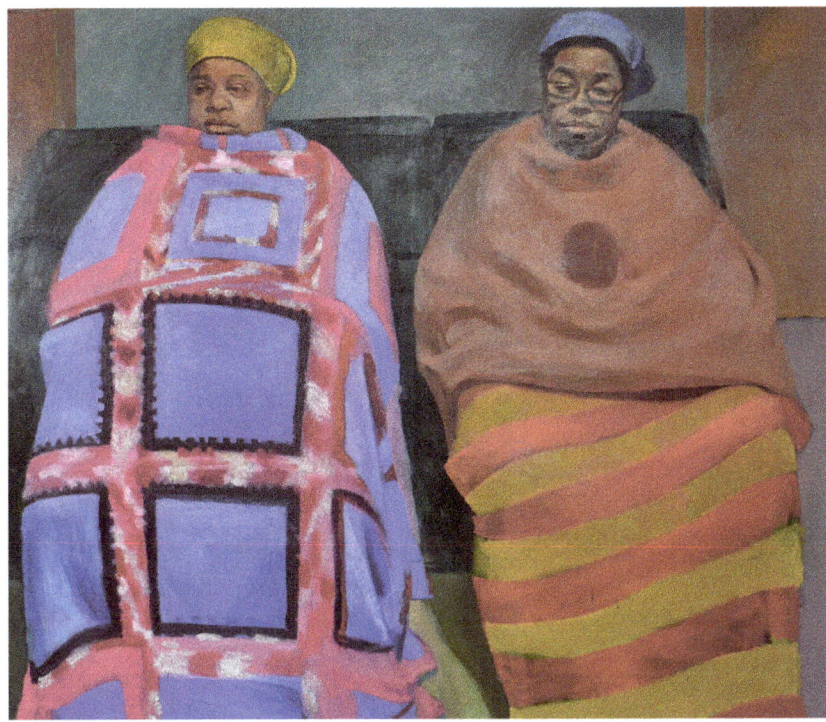

Kim and Tonya (in progress). 2015–16. Oil on canvas, 72 x 84 in.

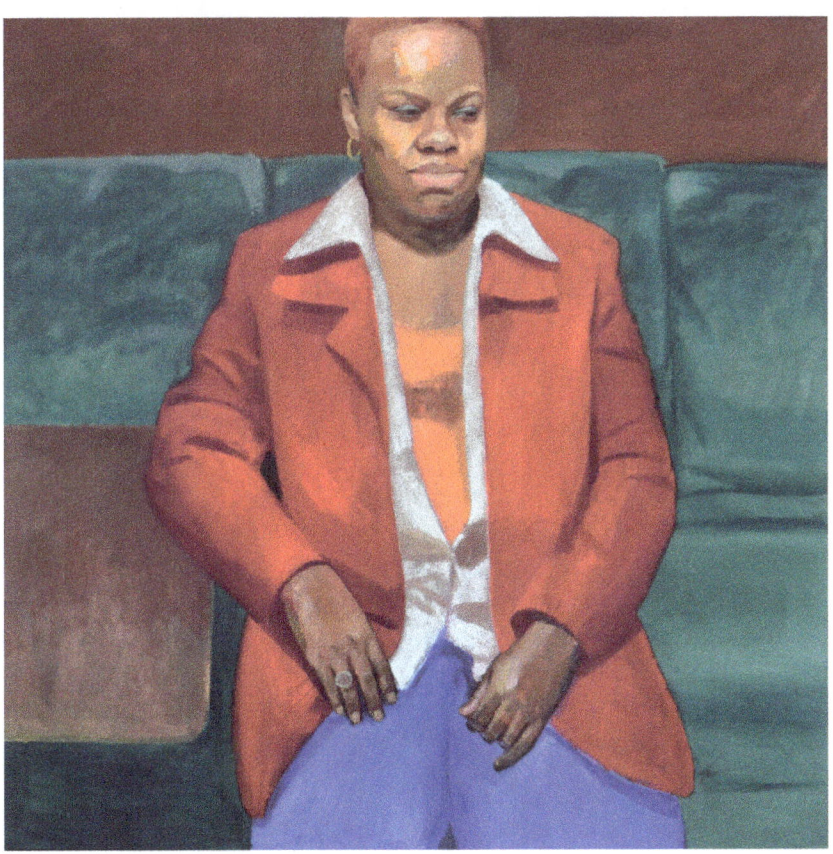

Tracey. 2010. Oil on canvas, 60 x 60 in.

the television set in the foreground. Tonya, on the right, turns slightly away from her sibling as well as from whatever is transpiring on the screen; her sidelong glance, as well as her sib's bland expression, suggests their less than enthralled interest in the unfolding program. Yet the soft, muted palette contributes a measure of intimacy to the scene. In the later, 2015–16 view, titled at present ***Kim and Tonya (in progress)***, the duo, once again settled in side by side, are snugly swaddled in colorful blankets and shawls, their eyes riveted along parallel tracks. This time, despite the clash of gridded pattern and vivid stripes, their immobilizing cocoons convey filial contentment.

Thus Lewis, keen-eyed explorer of souls and their discontents (figures barely crack a smile in his scenarios) focuses on what is truly important—his subjects' resilient humanity. For this peripatetic artist, whether in New York or Detroit, some modicum of connection between individuals seems as inevitable as isolation, whether they dwell amidst a cohort of blood relatives or a band of like-minded outliers.

DENNIS ALAN NAWROCKI,
DECEMBER 2016

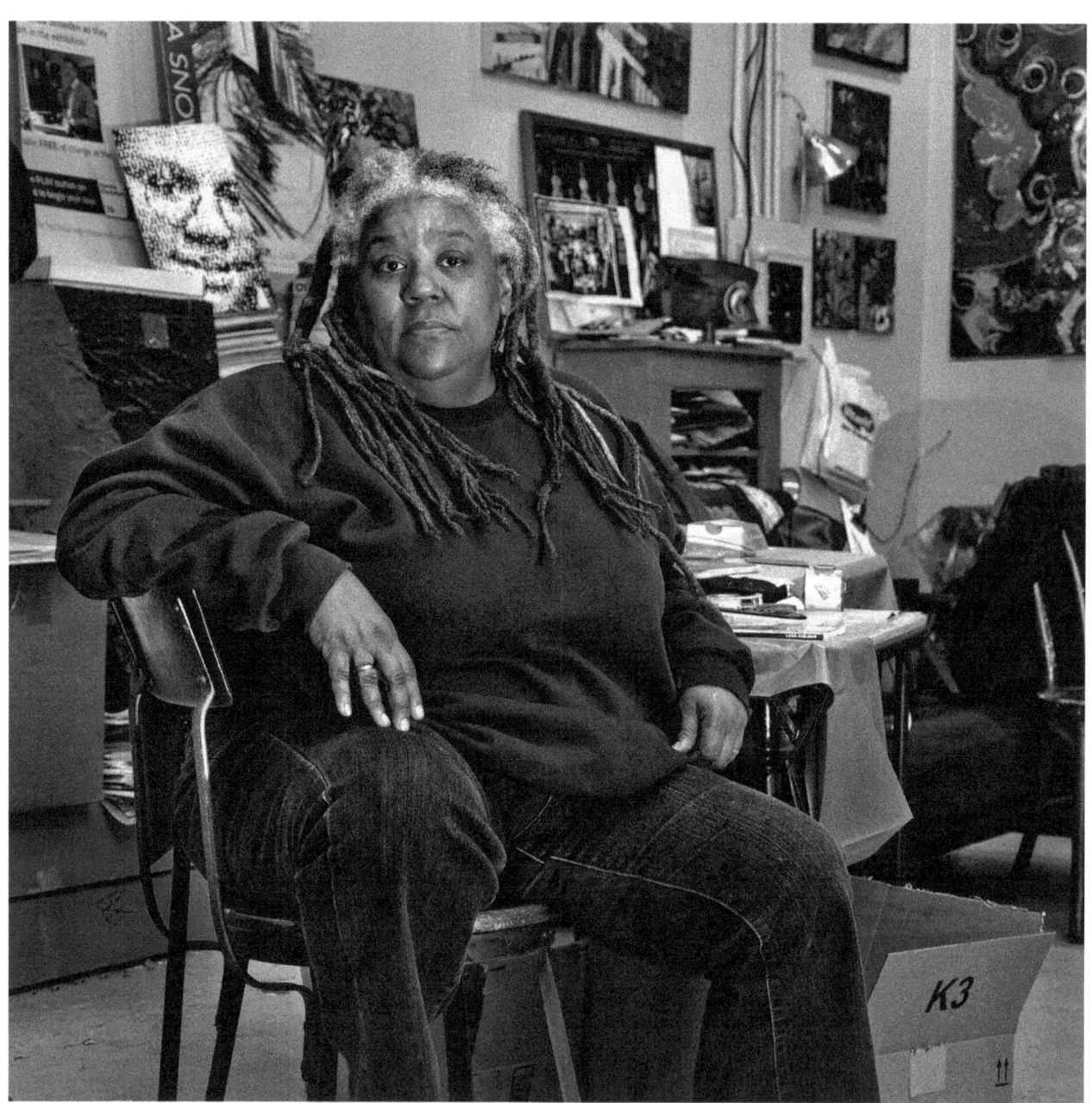

Gilda Snowden. 2014. Black-and-white archival pigment print, 19 1/2 x 19 1/2 in.

Born Detroit, 1948
BFA, MFA, MEd, Wayne State University
Lives in Royal Oak, Michigan

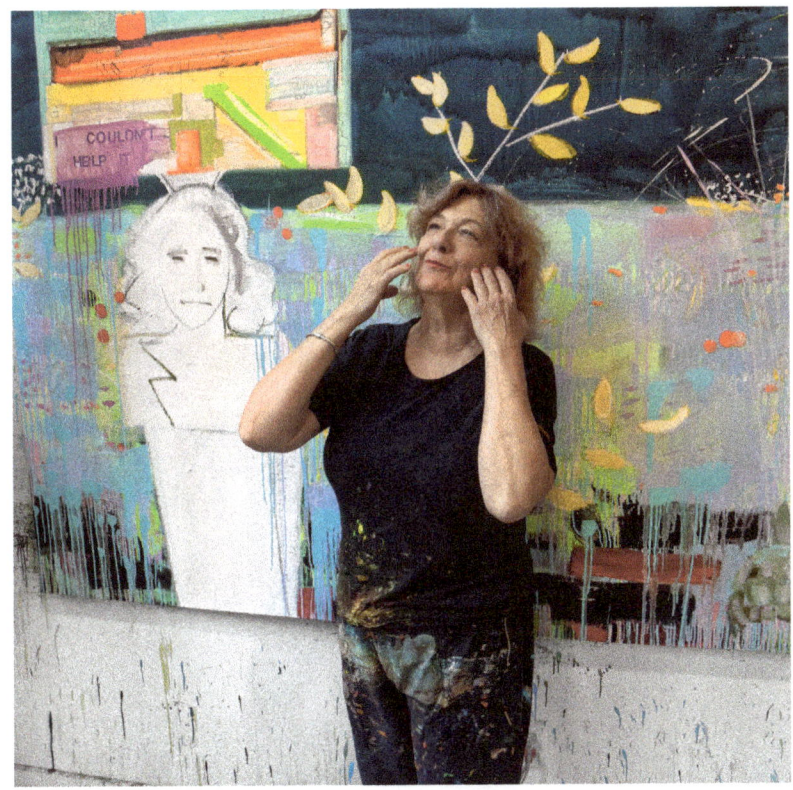

Nancy Mitchnick. 2014. Color archival pigment print, 19 1/2 x 19 1/2 in.

Donita Simpson's regal portrait of **Gilda Snowden** (2014) is a commanding example of her ongoing series of photographs of Detroit artists. In Snowden's pose, as if athwart a throne—as one respondent opined—Simpson nails her fellow artist's magnetic, larger-than-life persona as painter, teacher, and indefatigable arts activist. Casually dressed and ensconced amidst a cluttered studio, Snowden (1954–2015) all but bursts into the viewer's space, dominating both pictorial field and spectator's territory. Snowden's open-armed enthusiasm vis-à-vis the metro art community is mirrored in Simpson's brace of photographic studies—and, one might add, Essay'd's ongoing profiles too. Such expansive efforts, including canvassing and connecting with an array of area artists,

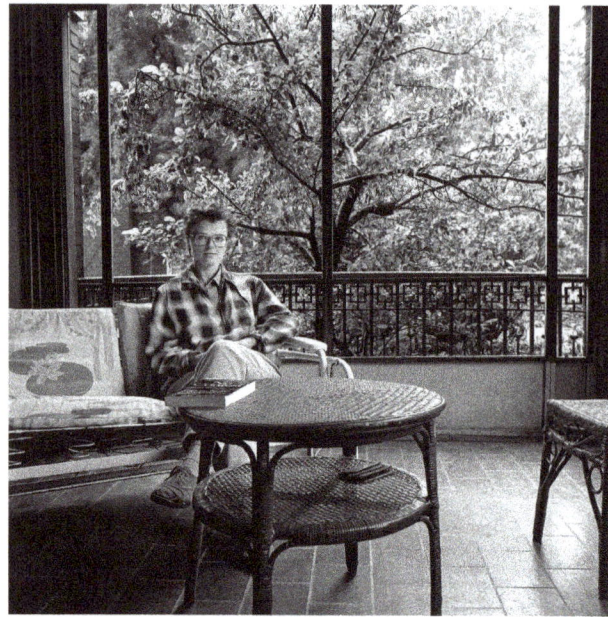
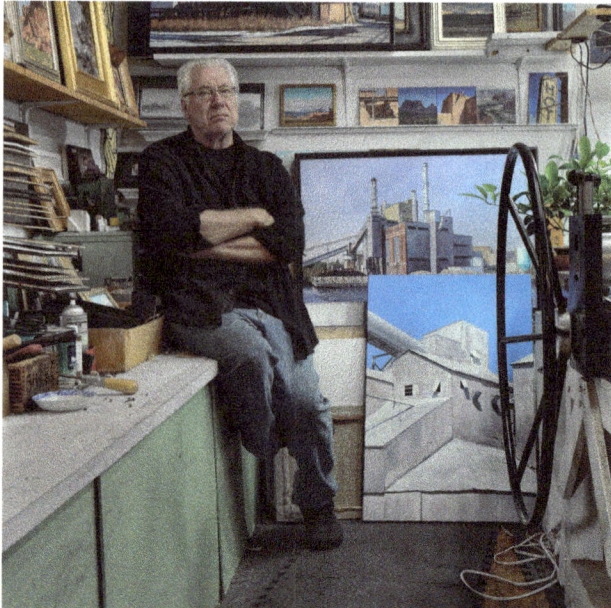
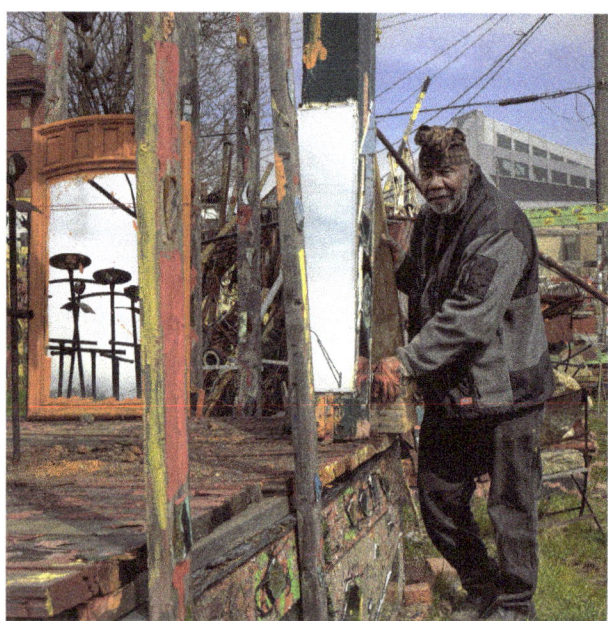
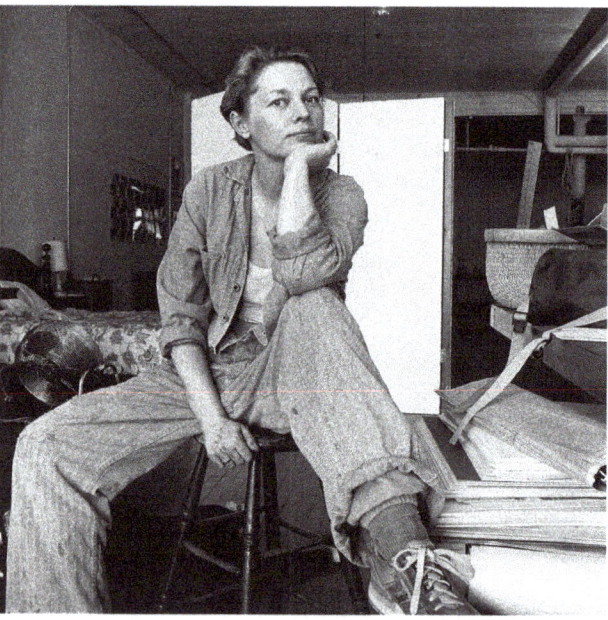

(Clockwise) Coco Bruner. 1989. Black-and-white archival pigment print, 19 1/2 x 19 1/2 in. *Stephen Magsig.* 2016. Color archival pigment print, 19 1/2 x 19 1/2 in. *Marilyn Zimmerman.* 1989. Black-and-archival pigment print, 19 1/2 x 19 1/2 in. *Olayami Dabls.* 2016. Color archival pigment print, 19 1/2 x 19 1/2 in.

inform Simpson's own creative practice.

Initiated in the late 1980s, her project has sought out "the artists of the city that have remained, endured, enlivened, and enriched a city that has otherwise been crushed," and she has titled two of her exhibitions *The Spirit of Detroit* to reflect "the pride and exuberance with which they share their art." Acknowledging the influence of such photographic luminaries as Dawoud Bey, Jeanne Hilary, and Arnold Newman, she follows her arrow in a metropolitan milieu where other limners of artists, albeit working *from* rather than making photographs—Matthew Hanna, Deborah Kashdan,

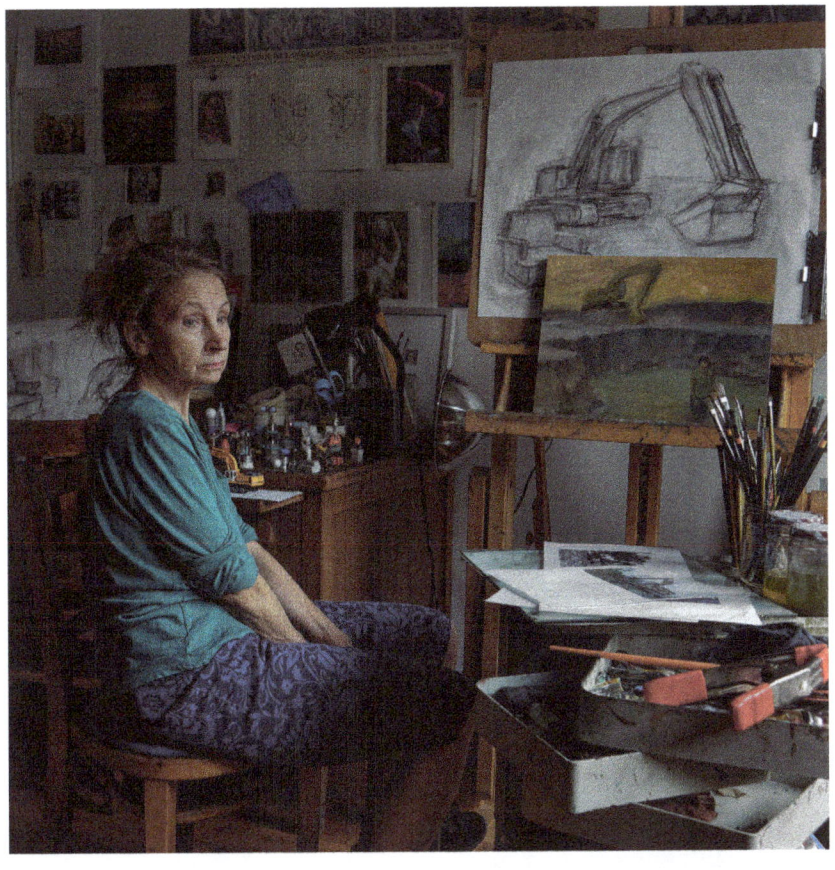

Ann Mikolowski—have plied their painterly visions.

Two of Simpson's early likenesses include the black-and-white portraits of multimedia artist **Coco Bruner** and photographer **Marilyn Zimmerman**, both from 1989. Bruner, preternaturally calm and self-possessed, gazes out from the middle of a high-ceilinged veranda, a full-leafed tree beyond the railing providing a lush, tapestry-like setting, while the table in the foreground serves to distance subject and observer from one another. Upfront and personal, the free-spirited Zimmerman, precariously perched on and straddling a high stool, appears on the verge of leaping out of the picture, an impulse subtly moderated by her cool, wary expression. An even closer close-up of painter **Bryant Tillman** (2013) merges one of his swirling, restless paintings with his tilted, go-with-the-flow pose and wavy brimmed hat. Photographed the next year, a full-length **Lynne Avadenka** greets us at the threshold to her work space, flanked by an orderly array

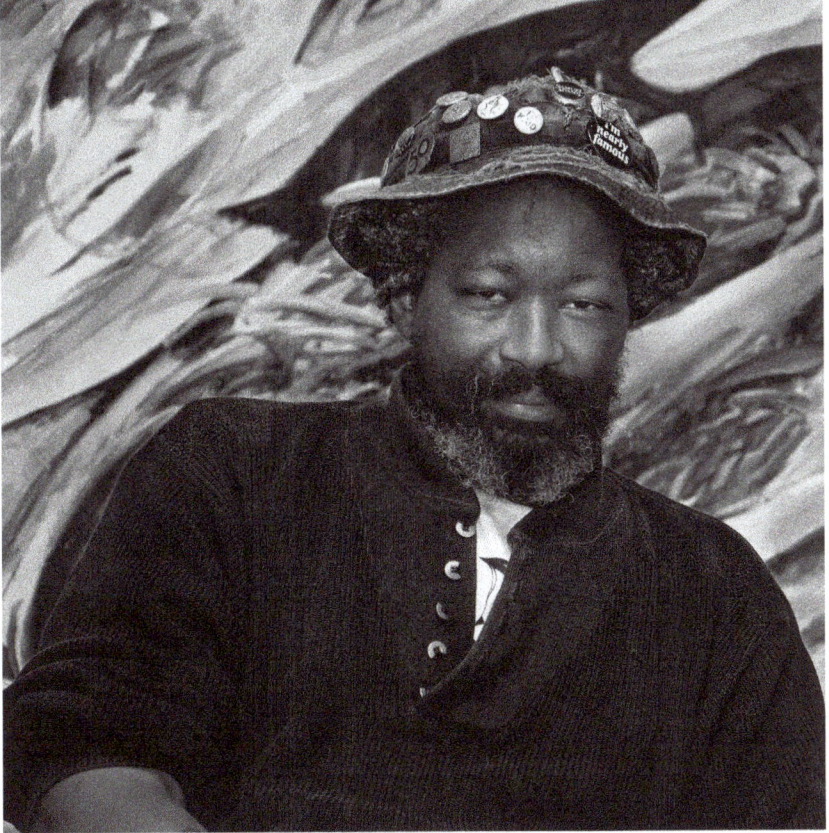

(Top) Jo Powers. 2016. Color archival pigment print, 19 1/2 x 19 1/2 in. (Bottom) Bryant Tillman. 2013. Black-and-white archival pigment print, 19 1/2 x 19 1/2 in.

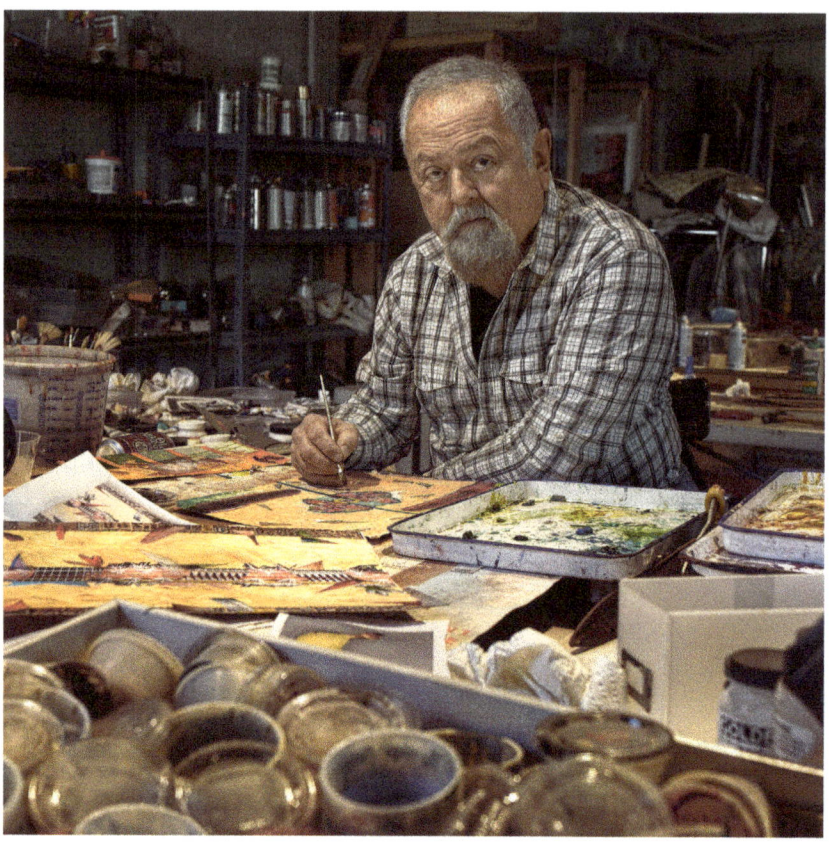

Gary Eleinko. 2016. Color archival pigment print, 19 1/2 x 19 1/2 in.

sheets of watercolors, as Eleinko, in midprocess, looks up, barely ruffled by the invading camera. Rather, immersed as he is in the midst of the creative chaos of his studio, he multitasks on several renderings in front of him. Dabls too is seen *in medias res*, as he perennially refines and adds to his magnum opus, a sprawling outdoor sculpture installation at his African Bead Museum.

Three other depictions present artists in various states of engagement with their art. Gesturing ecstatically, **Nancy Mitchnick** (2014) stands before the mural-scale painting in progress that eventually portrayed artist and mother at opposite poles of the composition. Here, Simpson snaps Mitchnick as she bares something of the intensity occasioned by the rendering of a fraught relationship. **Stephen Magsig** (2016), by contrast, backed into the corner of his studio, arms protectively crossed at his chest, forms a blocky, formidable silhouette as solid and substantial as his delineations of steel and concrete factories. Alone in her studio and surrounded by the utensils of her craft, **Jo Powers** (2016) seems bereft and stymied, momentarily

of rulers and pens to the left and cluttered bulletin board on the right. Behind and above, fluorescent light fixtures, like perspectival orthogonals, hasten one toward the marvels of her printmaking studio mere steps away.

In the course of Simpson's years-long project, facets of her practice have shifted, as she has traded small, portable cameras (one hundred photos per shoot to yield a keeper) for a large-format camera (fifty frames max from which to cull the defining image); or switched from posing artists in domestic environs to studio settings, and then segued from static studio spaces to incorporating examples of the subject's art or working process within the image; and most dramatically, recently eschewing canonical black-and-white impressions for the irresistible imperatives of color.

Among the recent color portraits, two 2016 compositions capture artists **Olayami Dabls** and **Gary Eleinko** at work. Compositionally, in the latter, Simpson propels the viewer front to back across a tablescape of cylinders and shifting tectonic

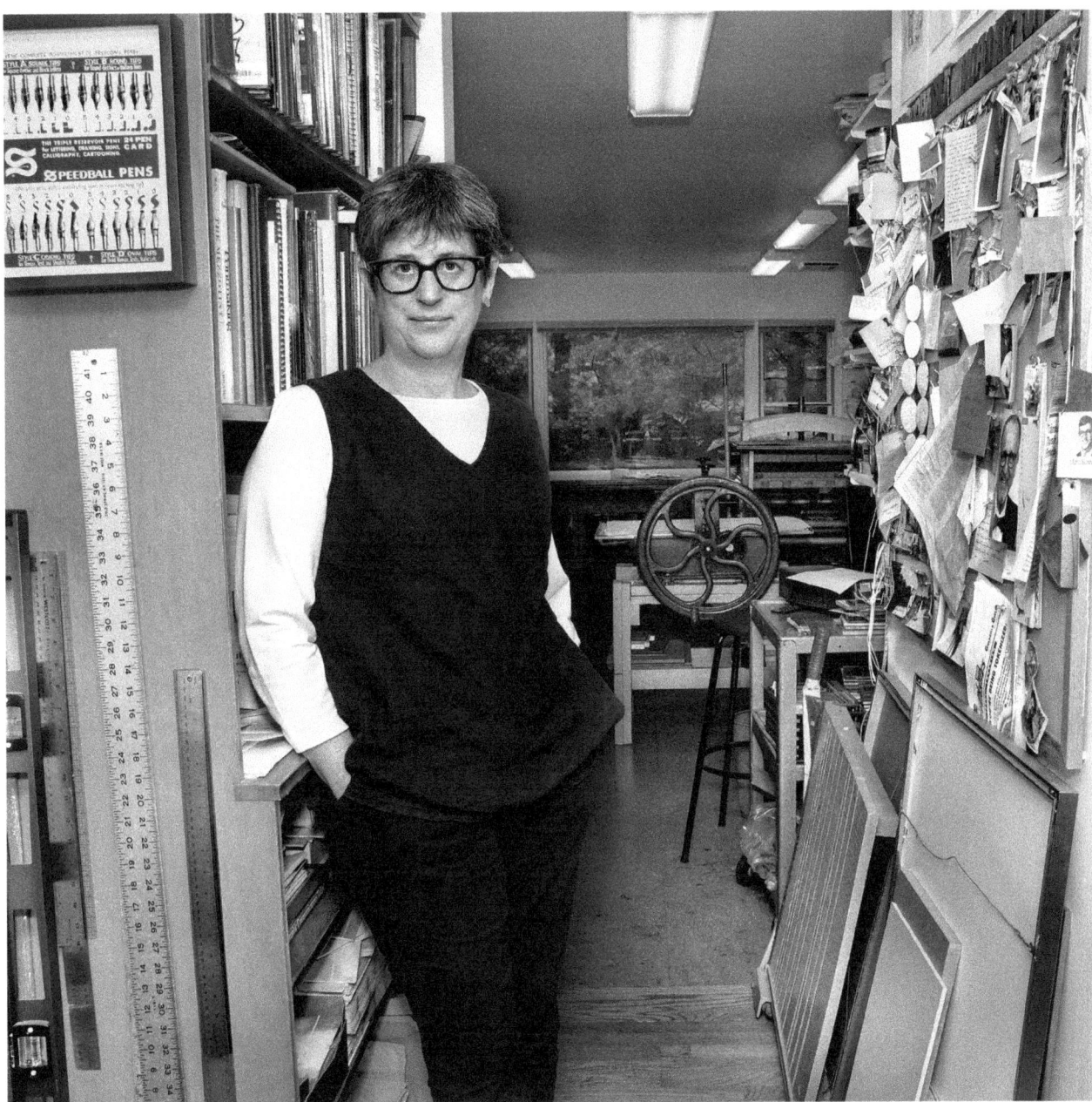

Lynne Avadenka. 2014. Black-and-white archival pigment print, 19 1/2 x 19 1/2 in.

overwhelmed by the sinister agent of upheaval drawn, painted, and displayed on her easel.

In these "photographic endeavors," Simpson, while gleaning both nuances and astonishments from collegial, one-on-one "conversations" with her subjects, also evinces something of the resilient pulse of the city's aesthetic life, no mean feat for artists as well as their photographer ally in these fractious, volatile times.

DENNIS ALAN NAWROCKI, JANUARY 2016

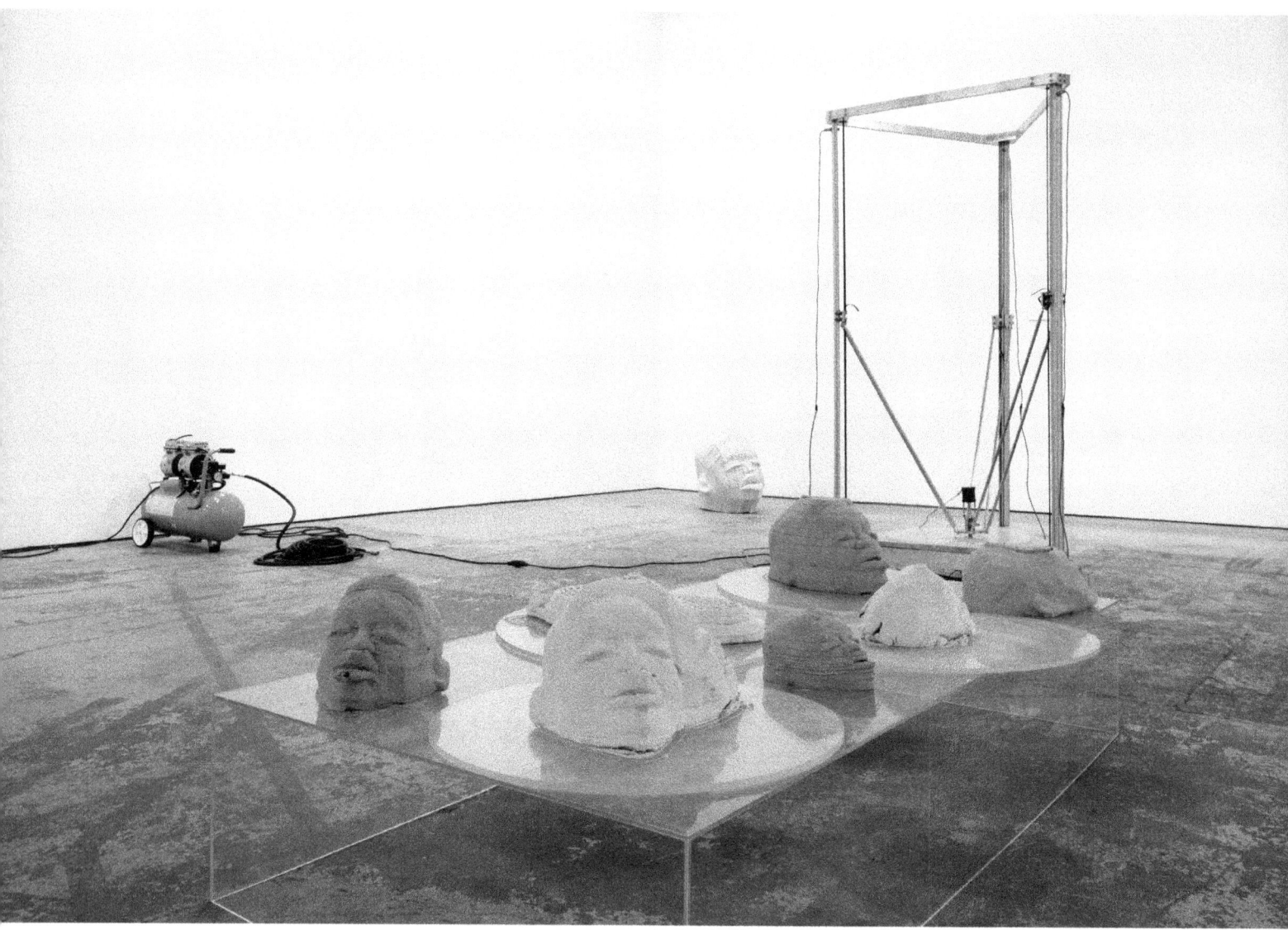

Installation view of MOCAD exhibition (part of the *Detroit City / Detroit Affinities* series). 2016.

Born Detroit, 1989
BFA, School of the Art Institute of Chicago
Lives in Detroit

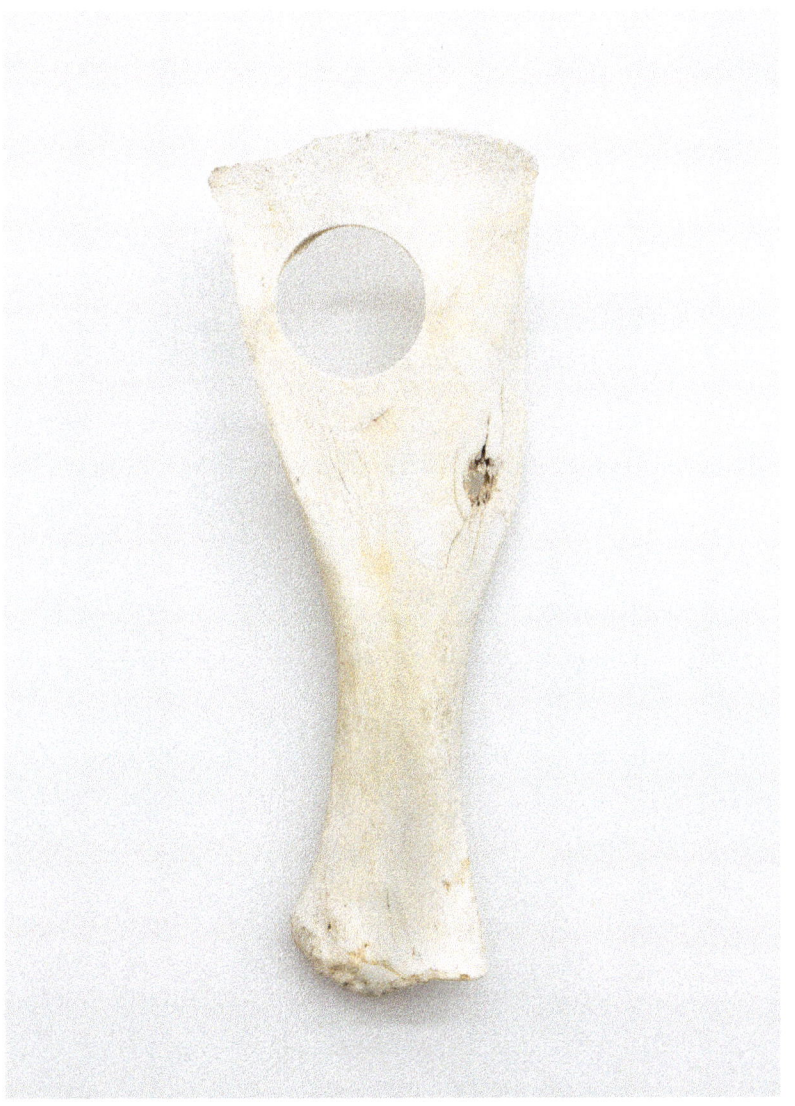

Untitled. 2015. Altered bone with bullet hole, 25 x 9 1/4 x 3 3/4 in.

Some time ago a camel was shot. Later, artist Matthew Harrison acquired the animal's right shoulder bone, complete with a ragged, preexisting bullet hole, and CNC cut a 130 mm diameter, cylindrical through-hole, creating the sculpture *Untitled* (2015). Harrison's simple intervention leads to a number of profound comparisons. First, the cut hole is jarringly precise, but still crude relative to the free-flowing shape of the bone. If the cut hole is a surrogate for man's technical prowess, then it is also a reminder of how unsophisticated our engineering skills remain in relation to those of nature. Second, and this may be closer to the artist's intentions, the physical violence of the gunshot hole seems archaic in comparison to the surgical symbolic-violence of the cut hole. If the gunshot hole symbolizes a period from the late

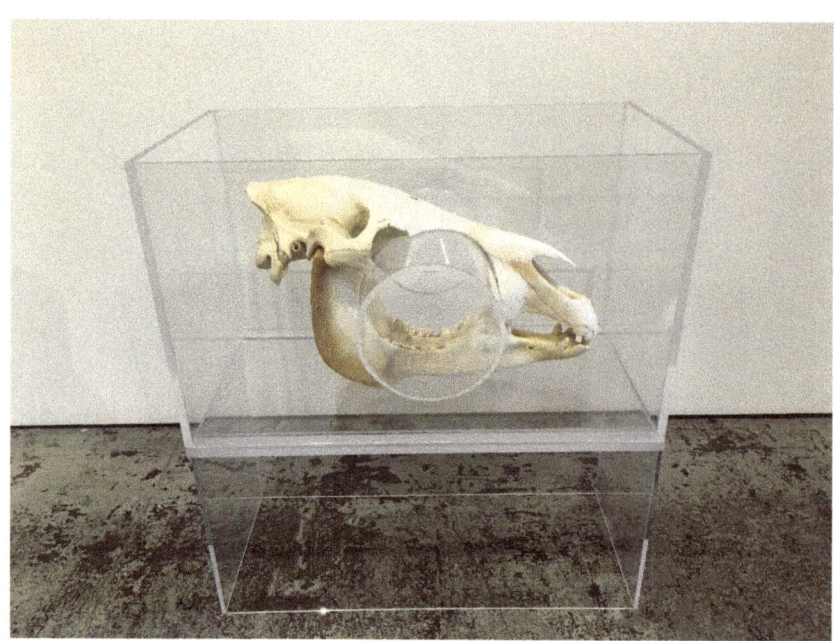

Hole 1.005. The Consequence of Synthetic Apertures. 2016. Zebra skull, automotive clay, acrylic, 23 ¾ x 14 x 12 1/2 in.

colonial era onwards, the cut hole can only point to the digital age.

In his sculptures, Harrison uses large-animal bones to symbolize the exotic, both in a general sense and more specifically for him as a twenty-something African American artist who grew up in Grosse Pointe. He is undoubtedly aware that exoticism has, historically, often been conflated with race, but seems to be making the point that it is more accurately a function of the viewer's perspective—and that race is irrelevant. Harrison's relationship to technology also shows an interesting perspective. He works in the design studios at Ford Motor Company,

and clearly this has been an important formative influence on his art practice, providing him with a working-level familiarity with advanced technological systems and processes that might seem abstract (or even exotic) to most artists.

An important overlap between Harrison's artistic life and his day job at the design studio is the idea of the prototype. In a concept that informs his artwork, he talks of "everything being a prototype—for something that follows." His worldview is an all-encompassing one of systems in constant flux, multiple perspectives on reality, and consequences

that result from both physical laws and socially constructed codes—including those that exist specifically for him as a black man in a society where race is not a negligible factor.

For his 2016 exhibition at the Museum of Contemporary Art Detroit, as part of the *Detroit Affinities* series, Harrison designed, built, and operated two 3-D printers, aka "rapid prototyping" devices. As an artist, he conceived the 3-D printers as sculptural objects, with form clearly following function. In operation, the printed object is built up from layers of clay, squeezed like toothpaste as the printer head is moved in three coordinate directions. The selection of clay as the printed material results in considerable dimensional variation and effectively prevents reproducible results. It is, as he puts it, "the weather" in the tiny worlds that he sets up—something out of his control.

In preparing for the installation/performance (which he titled *The Consequence of Platforms*), Harrison created an initial three-dimensional scan of a tourist-trade African mask. Then, over the almost

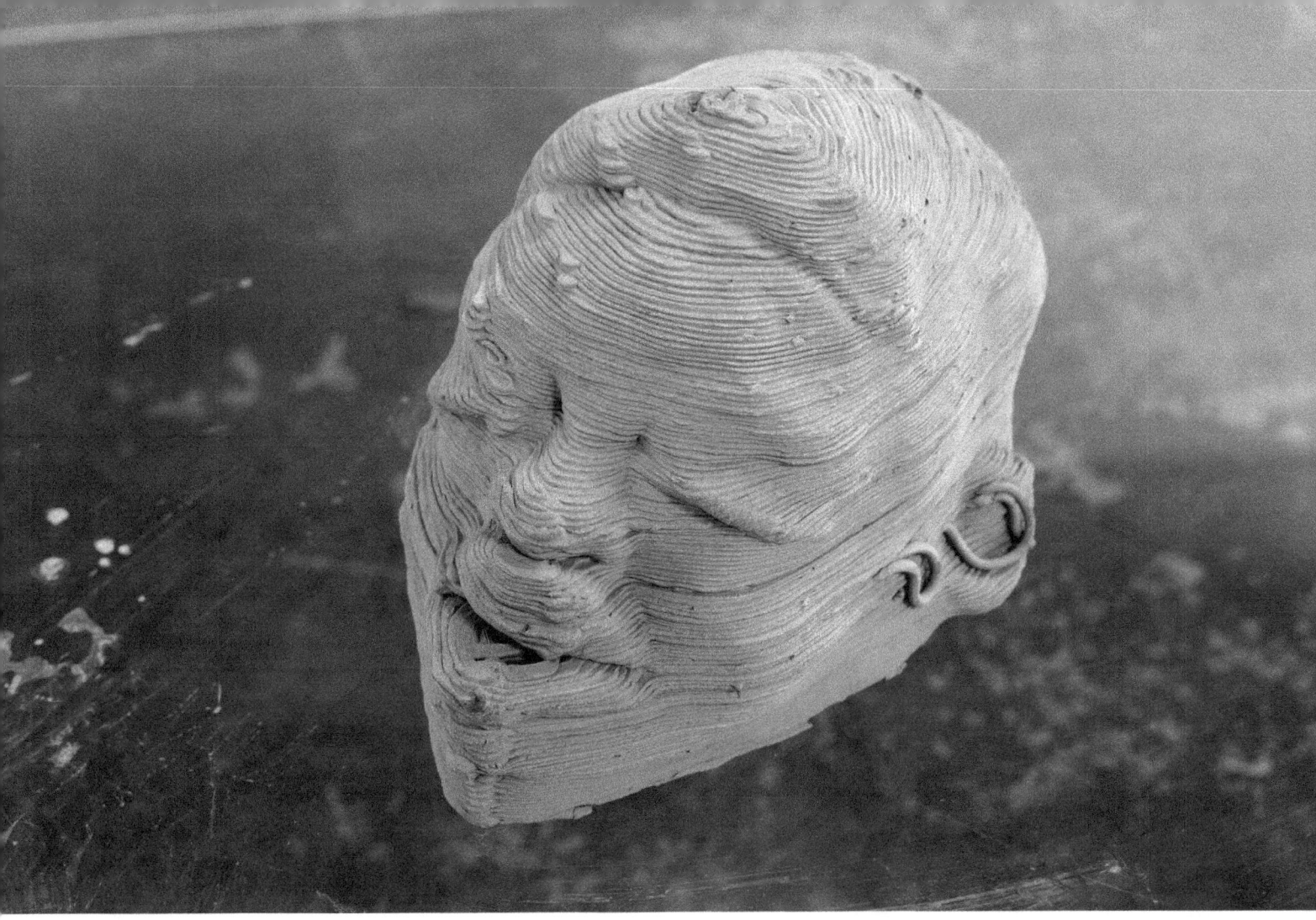

3-D printer used during the performance/installation *The Consequence of Platforms* at the Museum of Contemporary Art Detroit. 2016. Aluminum, stainless steel, ceramic, marble, 75 x 33 1/2 x 33 1/2 in.

four-month duration of the show, he went through a cyclic process of printing the mask, scanning the resulting object, and then reprinting the mask. Predictably, with each iteration the resulting shape diverged further from that of the original object. The overall process can be thought of as a metaphor for the attenuation of cultural memory with time. More specifically, for Harrison, it might represent a model for the divergence over time between African American and African culture.

Surrounding the 3-D printing machines, at close to ground level, were further modified large-animal bones. For example, **Hole 1.005. The Consequence of Synthetic Apertures** (2016) contains a zebra skull with a cut cylindrical hole mounted in an acrylic case. On closer inspection, there are small smears of automotive clay on the surface of the bone. These are not a gesture applied by the artist, but rather residues of the machining method that requires the bone

to be encapsulated for support during cutting. It is an example of Harrison's ethos of making his processes transparent—nothing hidden. It is hard to predict where his work will go from here, but it seems safe to assume that it will be ambitious, grounded in (his) reality, and, even if the evidence for it is sometimes subtle, imbued with more than a trace of idealism.

STEVE PANTON, JANUARY 2017

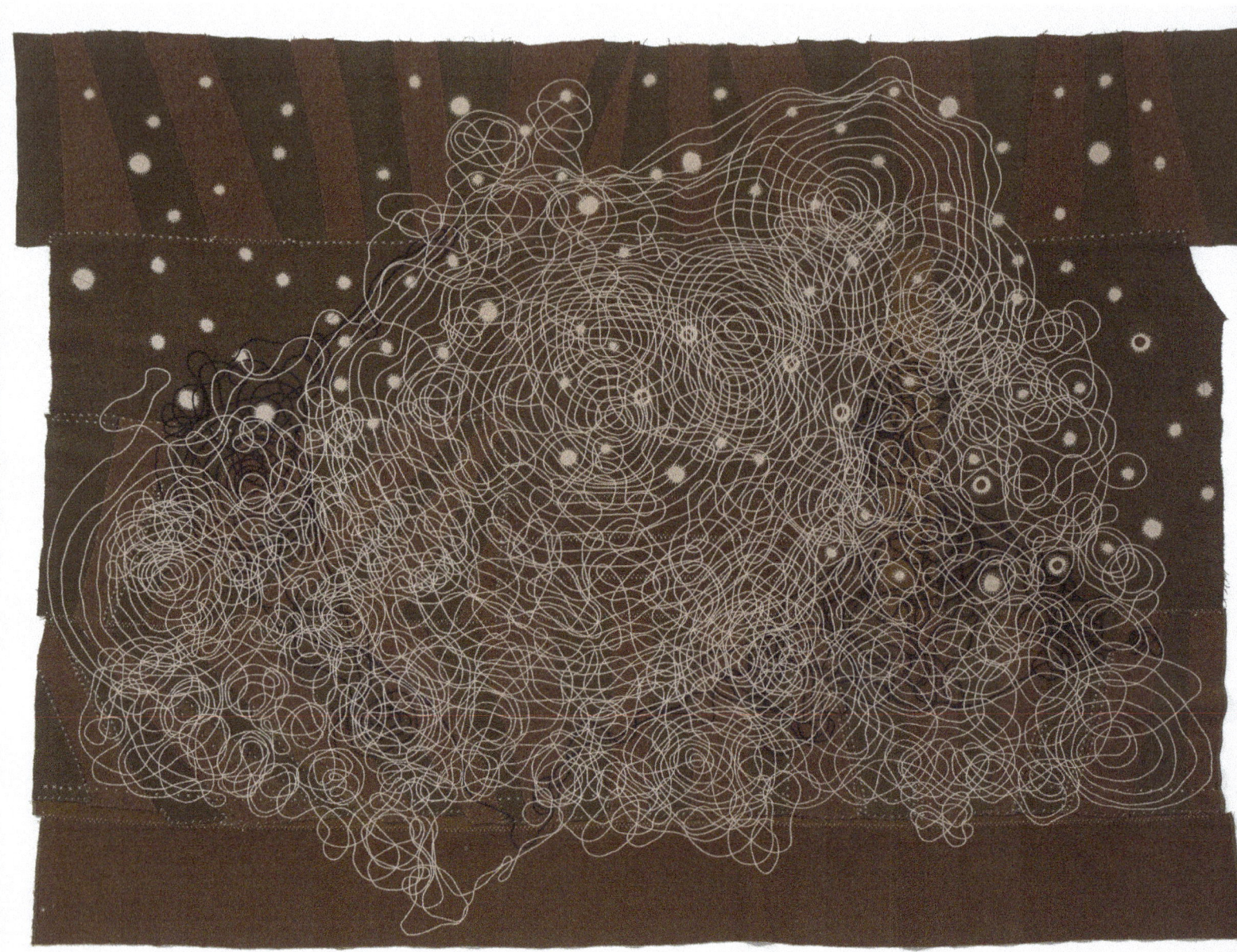

Seep. 2014. Army blanket, wool, silk, cotton, 48 x 73 in.

Born Ann Arbor, Michigan 1949
BA, Western Michigan University; MFA, Wayne State University
Lives in Grosse Pointe Farms, Michigan

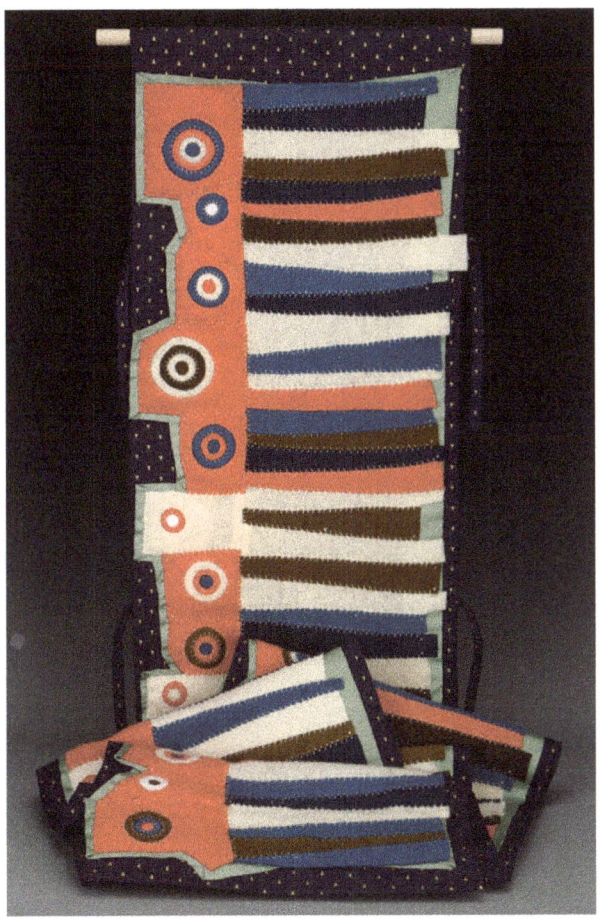 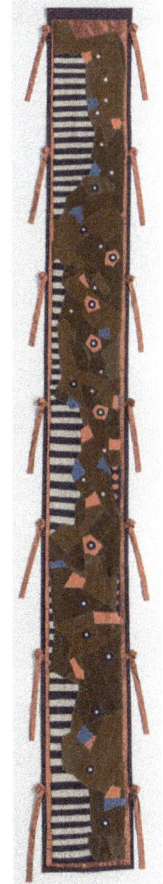

(Left) Young Street. 2016. Army blanket, wool, silk, cotton, 132 x 16 in.
(Right) Linda's Wish. 2016. Army blanket, wool, silk, cotton, 144 x 16 in.

Describing herself as the "compulsive collector that I am," Jeanne Bieri *is*, verily, a hunter and gatherer of assorted, throwaway "stuff," from which she occasionally assembles a one-of-a-kind grouping to render in oil. Other salvaged discards, chiefly textiles, accumulated by her and a cohort of friendly enablers, she restores, mends, sews, repurposes, "heals," and "makes whole" again. An example of the former, ***Christmas Lights*** of 2007, is a veritable compendium of rescued artifacts arrayed, not on a laden table, but sprawled like a frieze almost five feet in width. Suspended, swaged, and pushpinned to a wall, backdropped by a dun-hued army blanket, the ribbons, bones and skull, Christmas lights, spool of thread, jump rope, and vintage photograph are immobilized by pushpins as well as gravity.

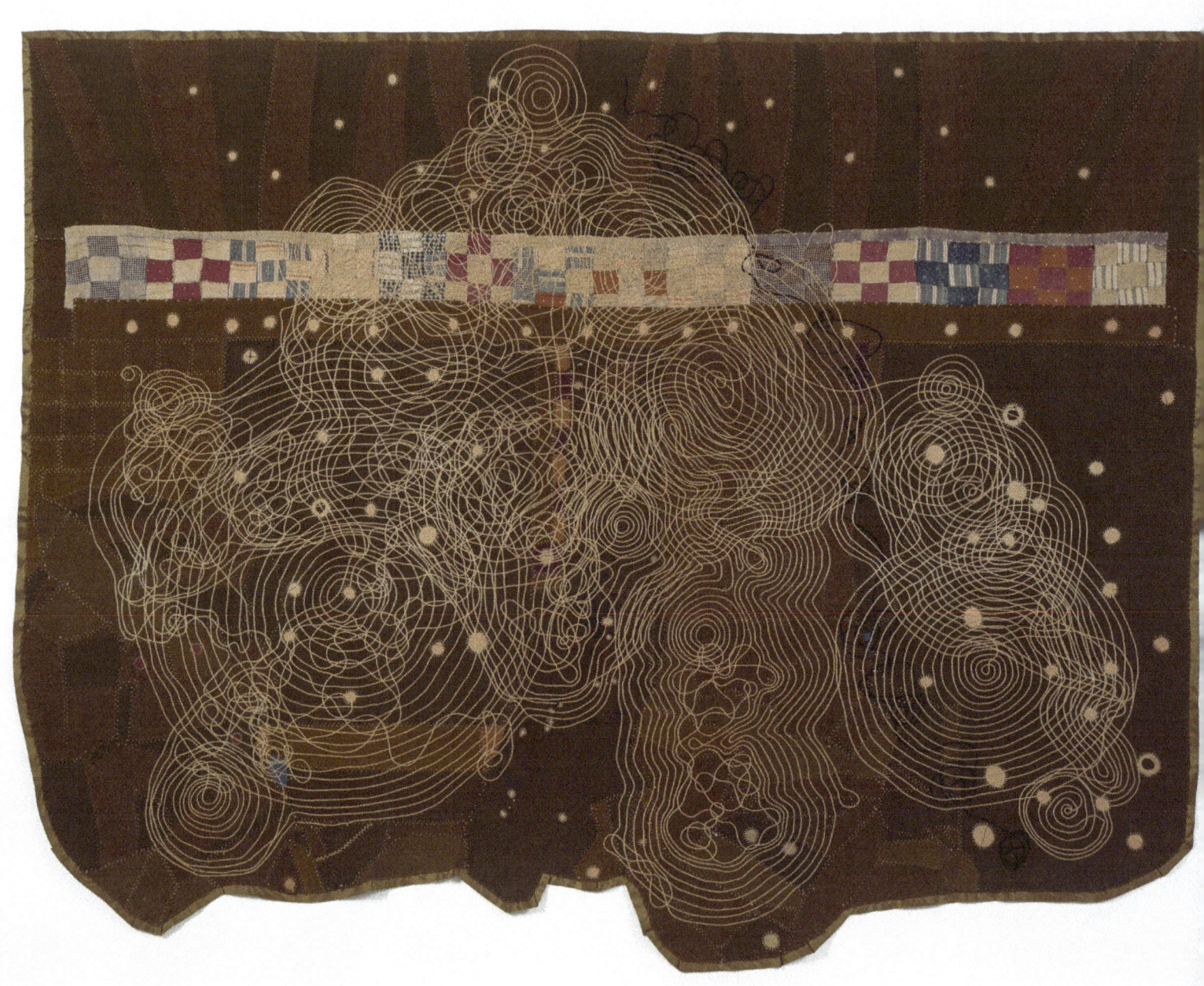

Mended Shirt Quilt. 2015. Army blanket, wool, silk, cotton, 48 x 73 in.

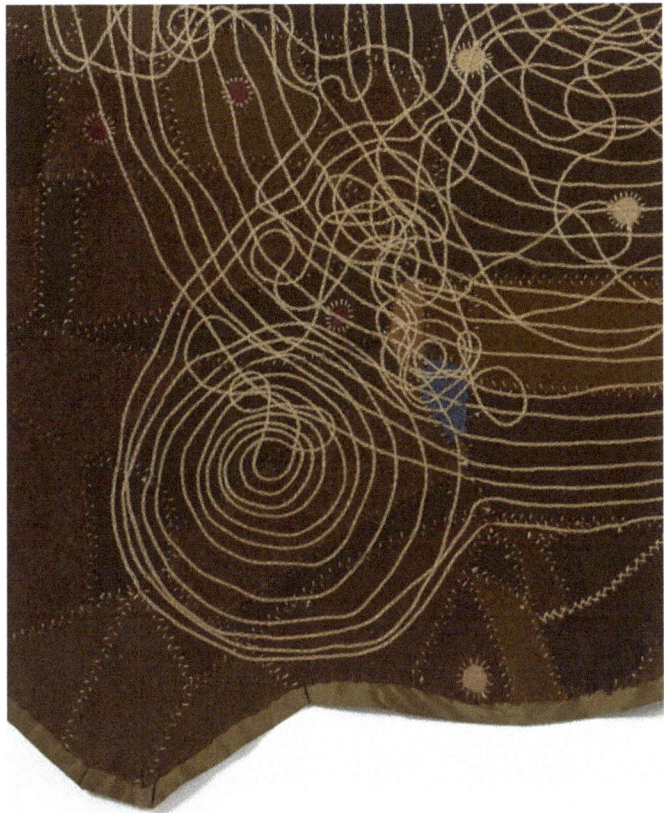

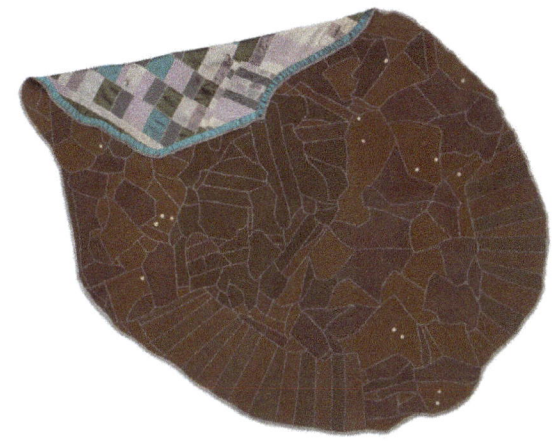

(Left) Mended Shirt Quilt (detail). 2015. Army blanket, wool, silk, cotton, 48 x 73 in.
(Right) Cape. 2014. Army blanket, silk, felt, cotton, 90 x 67 in.

Other subjects, drawn from Bieri's cache of vintage photos, represent the performative images that fill many a family album. They too are accorded the oil-on-canvas honorific that elevates, recalls, and fixes in amber such everyday frolics. Notable are two antic examples in which anonymous, but now reintroduced, individuals are clowning and showing off for the camera. Though both paintings mimic black-and-white photos, each scene is in fact drawn from the original snapshot, albeit enlarged, tweaked, and sparingly colorized: the surface of *Peek A*

Boo (2015) is glazed a pale yellow, while *Ta Da*, of the same year, is accented with a two-tone green door that underscores the unfurled body language of the blissfully oblivious danseuse.

A number of concurrent bodies of work populate Bieri's practice, from painting to multiple experiments with textiles, tacking in several directions within a given year. *Linda's Wish* (2016), a slender vertical form, fabricated of tattered quilt remnants, army blankets (scratchy cast-offs courtesy of her father's WWII service), and a passel of other

fabrics, towers fourteen feet, its frisky forms cascading top to bottom. For Bieri, these slender "boards" evoke human figures. When exhibited as a group, their personas and titles—Linda, Clara, Myrtle—intimate distinct individuals, much as the unrolling of a scroll, which they also evoke, discloses words or images unique to writer or artist. Here, as the ladder-like black-and-white forms on the left jostle with the bright-eyed circles and geometric forms on the right, dominance seesaws back and forth along its statuesque height.

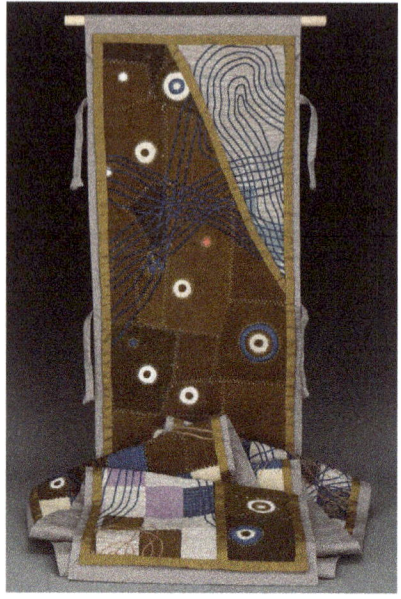

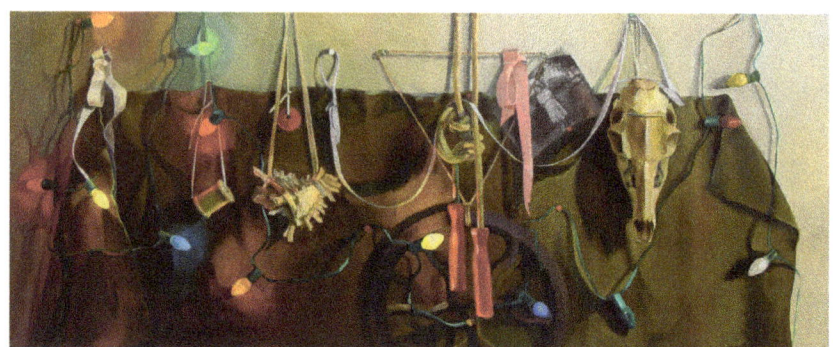

(Left) Clara's Ribbon. 2016. Army blanket, wool, silk, cotton, 144 x 16 in. Photography by Beth Steinkellner. *(Right) Christmas Lights.* 2007. Oil on canvas, 24 x 58 in.

Two other pieces (composed and sewn in 2016), ***Clara's Ribbon*** and ***Young Street***, illustrate an alternate mode of display that disrupts the smooth surface and plumb edges of Bieri's columnar forms. The artfully scrunched-up passage, about three-quarters down the length of the panel, resists the tug of gravity, proffering robust projections and transforming flatness into sculptural relief. The rumpled, bunched-up disturbance, serendipitously highlighting the artistry of piecing and stitching, then abruptly terminates, as upheaval (perhaps emotional?) swiftly reverts to bespoke order. These three-dimensional interruptions,

deployed by artist or preparator when a work is displayed in a low-ceilinged space, in fact contribute weight and substance to Bieri's signature mash-ups of geometric and organic forms. All's well that ends well.

Broad, encompassing, and spacious are qualities invoked by other models of Beiri's fiber art, as in ***Seep*** (2014) and ***Mended Shirt Quilt*** (2015). In both, the horizontal expanse of dusky-green, military-issue wool is blanketed by a looping stream of hand-wrought chain stitching conjuring a restive universe of whirling galaxies. At random intervals circular, star-like nodes wink and blink, especially in *Seep*, evoking

at once a starry night and expanding universe. In *Mended Shirt Quilt*, a multicolored bar, actually a repaired strip of a checkerboard quilt, hovers like a surreal sighting in the firmament. Bieri's meticulous stitchery preserves the frayed fragment—presumably the handiwork of an unknown woman—and revivifies it as a radiant emblem of her existence and the longevity of art.

Cape (2014), a somber, vertically oriented patchwork of brown and black fabric, registers as an austere anomaly of the dark ground group. Its sparse smattering of pinpricks of light and the suggestion of warmth and protection embedded in its

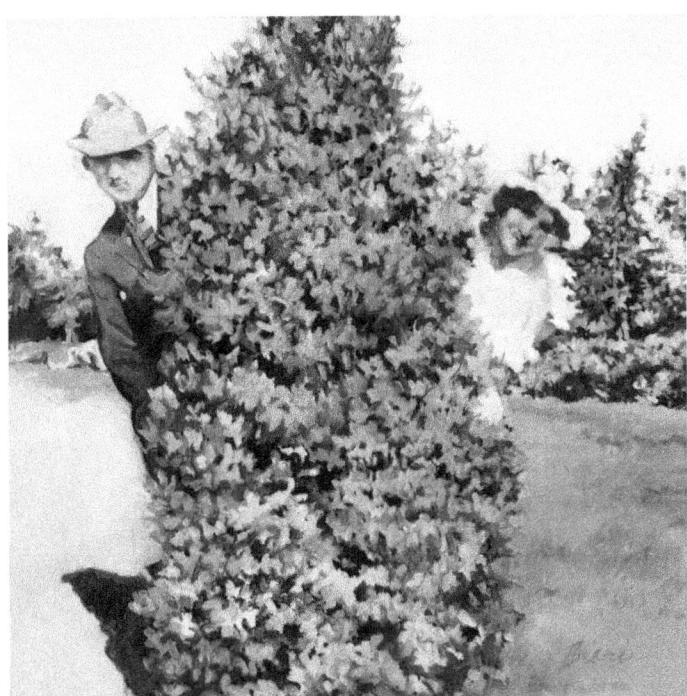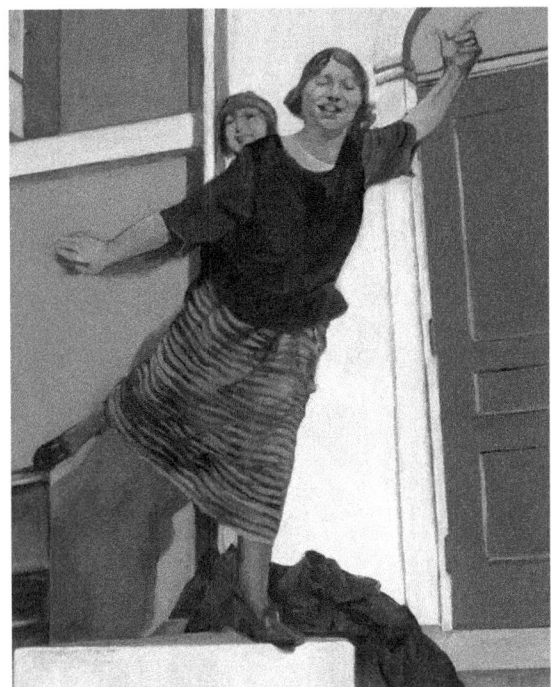

(Left) Peek A Boo. 2015. Oil on canvas, 8 x 8 in. (*Right*) *Ta Da.* 2015. Oil on canvas, 10 x 8 in.

title distinguish it from others in the series. It might be read as an aerial view of a topographical map of abutting plots of land and fabric (about 250 discrete pieces) whose irregular outline seems on the verge of imminent expansion.

So, Bieri collects, mends, pieces, assembles, and stitches to create wholes; converted into wholes, they constitute bulwarks against loss, dissolution, entropy, amnesia—and tender sustenance for the future. Summarizing this multistep process at the core of her practice, Bieri says, simply and disarmingly, "I create big piles of sewn ideas."

DENNIS ALAN NAWROCKI, MARCH 2017

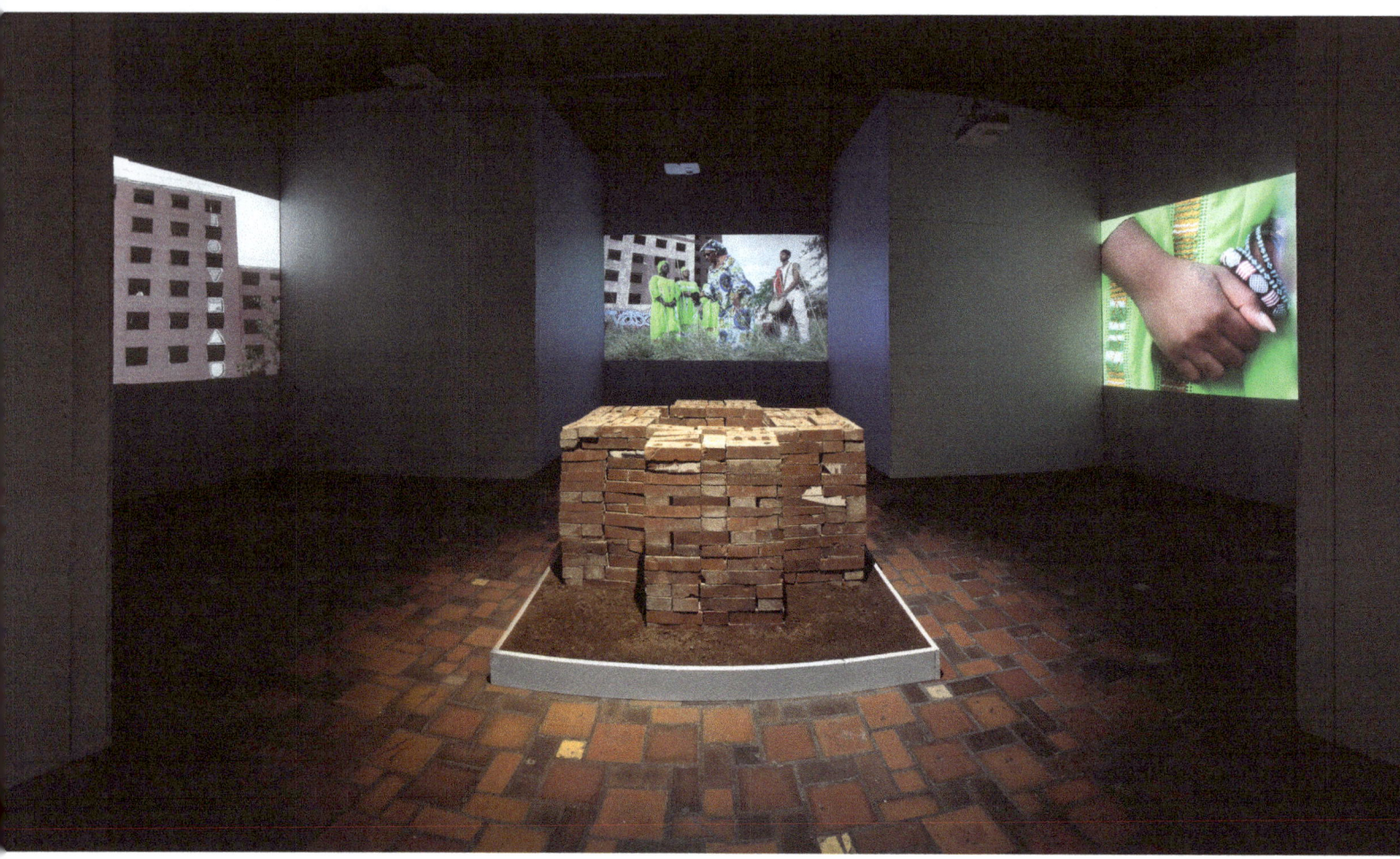

Still from the interactive installation *A Requiem for Douglass*. 2015.
Video and brick.

Born Detroit, 1983
BA (Film and Video), University of Michigan
Lives in Detroit

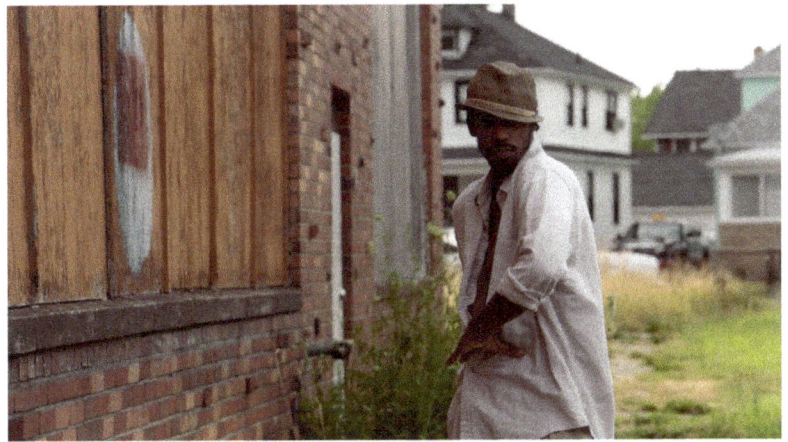

Still from the video *Time I Change*. 2012. 8 min., 3 sec.

Between 2013 and 2014, the four high-rise towers that were the last remnants of Detroit's Brewster-Douglass housing projects, the country's first federally funded public housing for African Americans, were demolished. While the towers had been officially cleared of residents in 2008, they were, in fact, still home to a handful of people up to the time of their demolition, as Oren Goldenberg's 2012 *cinéma vérité* short **Brewster Douglass, You're My Brother** reveals. The video opens with a two-minute montage depicting the derelict complex from a series of neighboring perspectives—evoking its omnipresence, both physical and psychic, in the Detroit landscape—set to the sound of a gospel crooner's insistent refrain that "Time don't wait for no one." Then the focus shifts to Darlene, a long-term resident

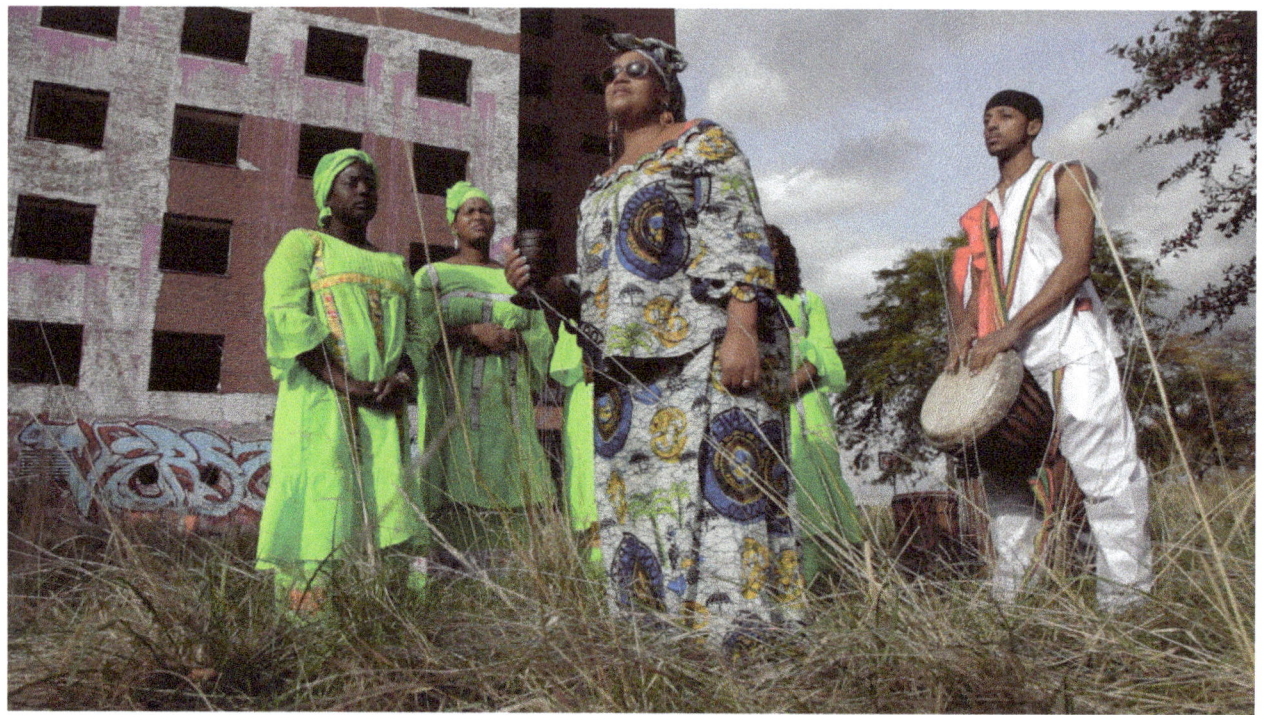

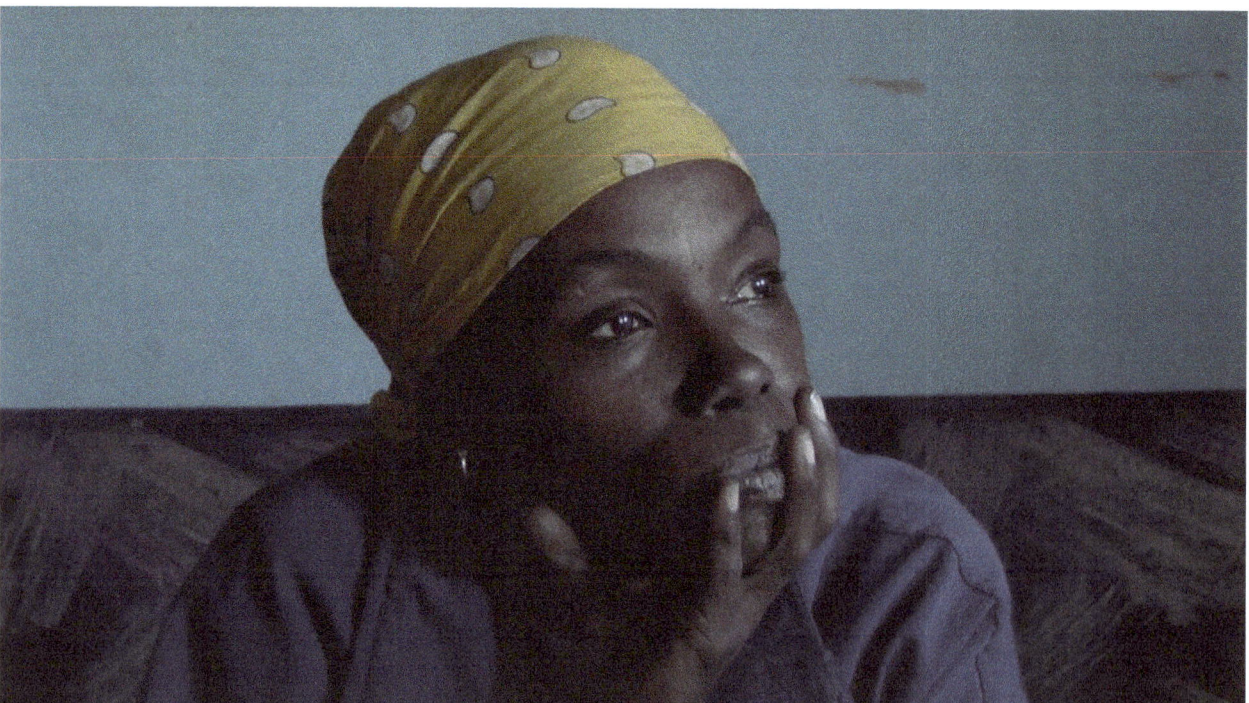

(*Top*) Still from the interactive installation *A Requiem for Douglass*. 2015. Video and brick. (*Bottom*) Still from the video *Brewster Douglass, You're My Brother*. 2012. 27 min.

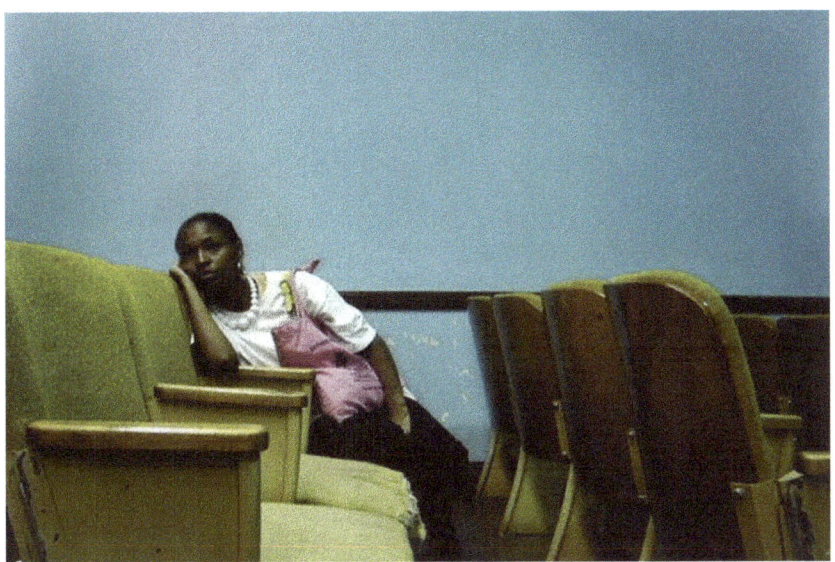
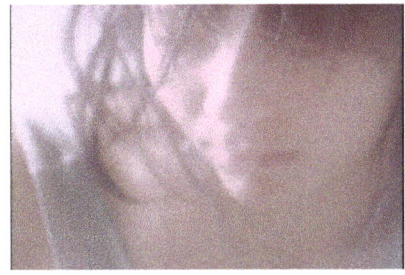
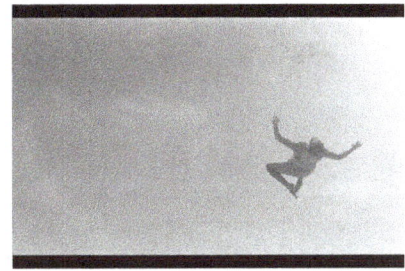

(*Left*) Still from the video *Our School*. 2009. 90 min. (*Top right*) Still from the film *Se Reveiller*. 2011. 1 min., 43 sec. (*Bottom right*) Still from the video *Genesis*. 2010. 3 min., 15 sec.

who says, as she reflects candidly on her hard life, that she survives by scrapping and that she hasn't seen her large family in years. At the end of the video, with the towers' demolition imminent, Darlene is seen leaving, her empty hands in her pockets. She's crossing the I-375 overpass, going—where? She doesn't say. Does she know?

Goldenberg's empathetic portrait of Darlene is typical of the video and installation artist's concern for what happens to people when the spaces around them change, and for what happens to Detroiters, in particular, when their public institutions collapse. Goldenberg, who grew up in Huntington Woods, is part of a generation of activists who

moved to Detroit in the middle of the first decade of the 2000s to promote social justice and to find, as he puts it, "healing and transcendence and the radicalization of our minds." He describes his Bush II–era realization that "the disparity in Detroit was linked with the privilege I grew up with in the suburbs," an awakening that led to his first short film out of college, a 2005 documentary about the Detroit Public Schools crisis (and a precursor to 2009's *Our School*, his intimate, feature-length meditation on the same subject). While there is ample room in Goldenberg's broad, ambitious, and technically accomplished practice for projects that do not deal explicitly with the effects of injustice—see,

for instance, *Genesis* and *Se Reveiller*, a pair of soulful short romances he made in 2010 and '11, or *Who Are You?* (2014), an absorbing, interactive exploration of teen identity formation—his work nevertheless remains fundamentally humanist, as deeply rooted in ethics as poetics.

One of his key concerns is the power of ritual as a form of catharsis. Goldenberg had a conservative Jewish upbringing, and after seeing friends and family use ritual to transcend hard times, he began to explore its application in Detroit, where life is "inextricably connected to loss," but where that loss is insufficiently grieved. First were the *Rituals for Spatial Transformation* (2012–14), conceived

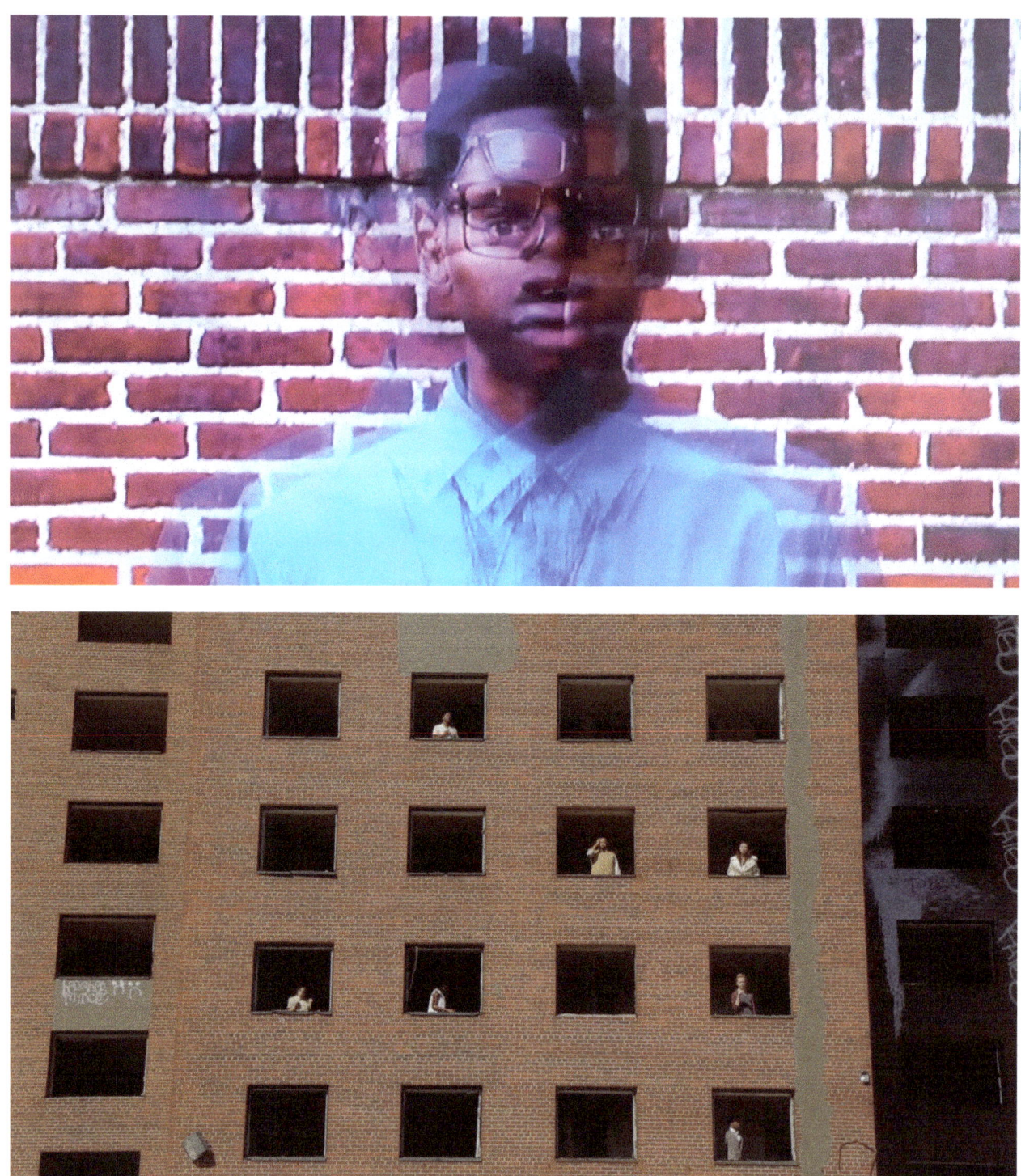

(*Top*) Still from the interactive video installation *Who Are You?* 2014. Video and motion sensors, 3 min., 23 sec. (*Bottom*) Still from the interactive installation *A Requiem for Douglass.* 2015. Video and brick.

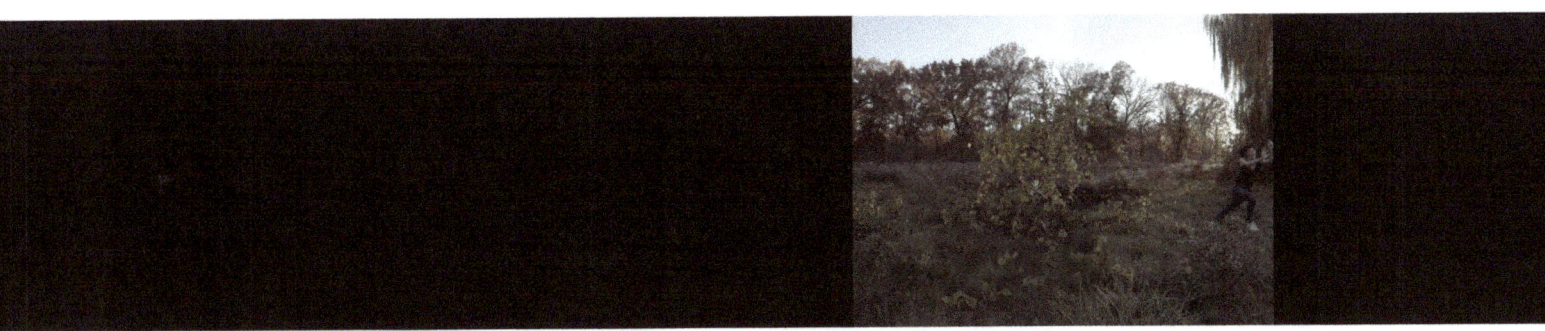

Still from the video installation *Untitled Experiment of the Modern Gaze.* 2016. 9 min.

to memorialize the Brewster-Douglass projects. These included on-site dance, music, poetry, and a lantern lighting and libation ceremony, as well as enthusiastically attended public conversations, screenings, and a live video performance. The series culminated in *A Requiem for Douglass* (2015), an installation at the Museum of Contemporary Art Detroit in which footage of the on-site rituals was triggered by a final ritualistic gesture, enacted by the spectator: the removal of a brick from a pile arranged in the distinctive cross shape of the Douglass towers (and sourced from the site itself).

In 2016, in partnership with William Danaher, rector of Christ Church Cranbrook, Goldenberg organized Art as Ritual,

a conference for artists, academics, and interfaith community members to explore the power of ritual and lamentation to bring people closer together. This gesture points to the instinctive generosity and inclusiveness of Goldenberg's practice, which typically finds him collaborating with and elevating others' work in the realization of his own creative vision.

Recently, inspired in part by a desire to rekindle the "magic" of video in our oversaturated age, Goldenberg has begun working with local performers to create vivid, nonnarrative performance videos, like *Time I Change* (2012), in which dancer/choreographer Haleem "Stringz" Rasul is tracked through a fragmented cityscape while

seemingly fighting for control of his beleaguered body, and *Untitled Experiment of the Modern Gaze* (2016), an immersive installation in which dance artist Biba Bell recognizes, rejects, flirts with, and penultimately performs for the camera before decisively (and spectacularly) obliterating the frame around her. Goldenberg used virtual reality technology to make *Untitled Experiment. . .*, and even then, he was thinking about place, connectedness, and the ideal of the public. In discussing the future of his chosen medium, he wonders aloud: "Virtual reality is here. How are we going to start experiencing it? Isolated, with goggles on? Or in spaces, together?"

MATTHEW PIPER, APRIL 2017

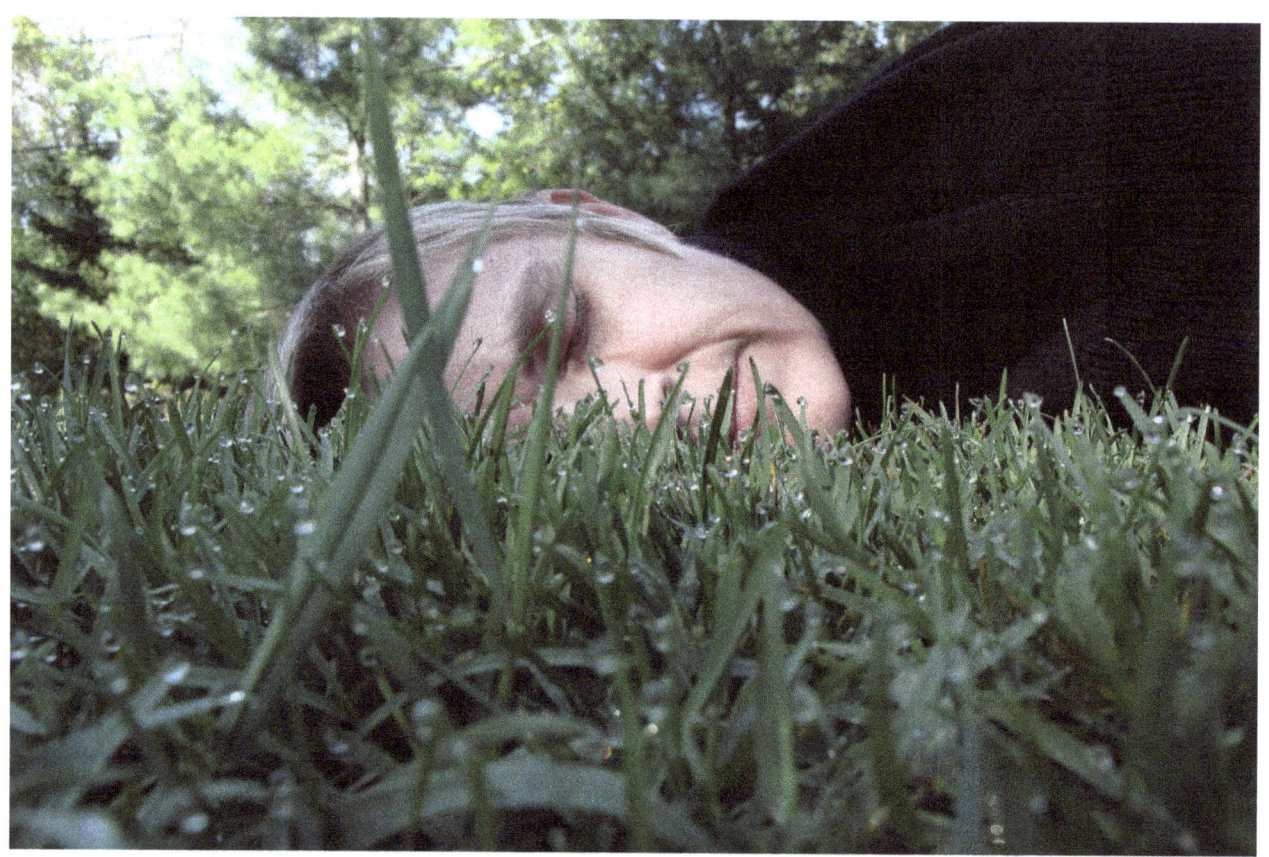

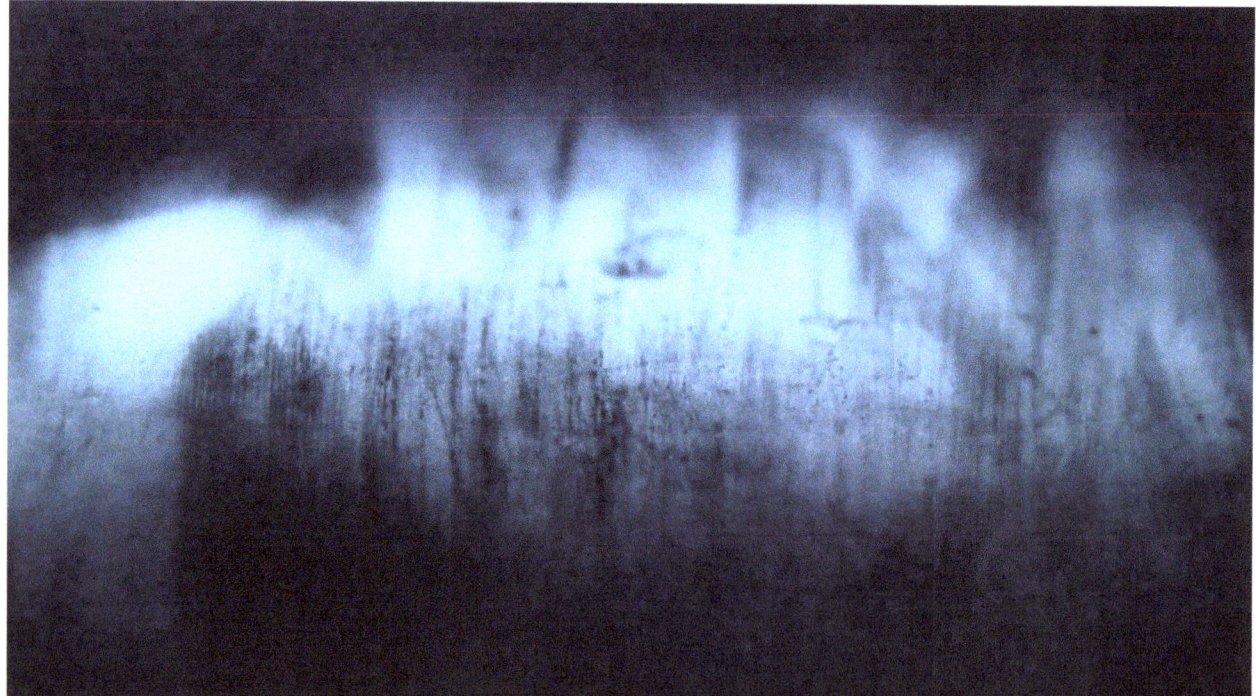

(*Top*) Still from the video *Growth Gravity*. 2010. 1 min., 15 sec. (*Bottom*) Still from the video *Breathscape*. 2015. 5 min., 26 sec.

67 // CYNTHIA GREIG

Born Detroit, 1959

BFA, Washington University, Missouri; MA, The University of Iowa;

MFA, University of Michigan

Lives in Bloomfield Hills, Michigan

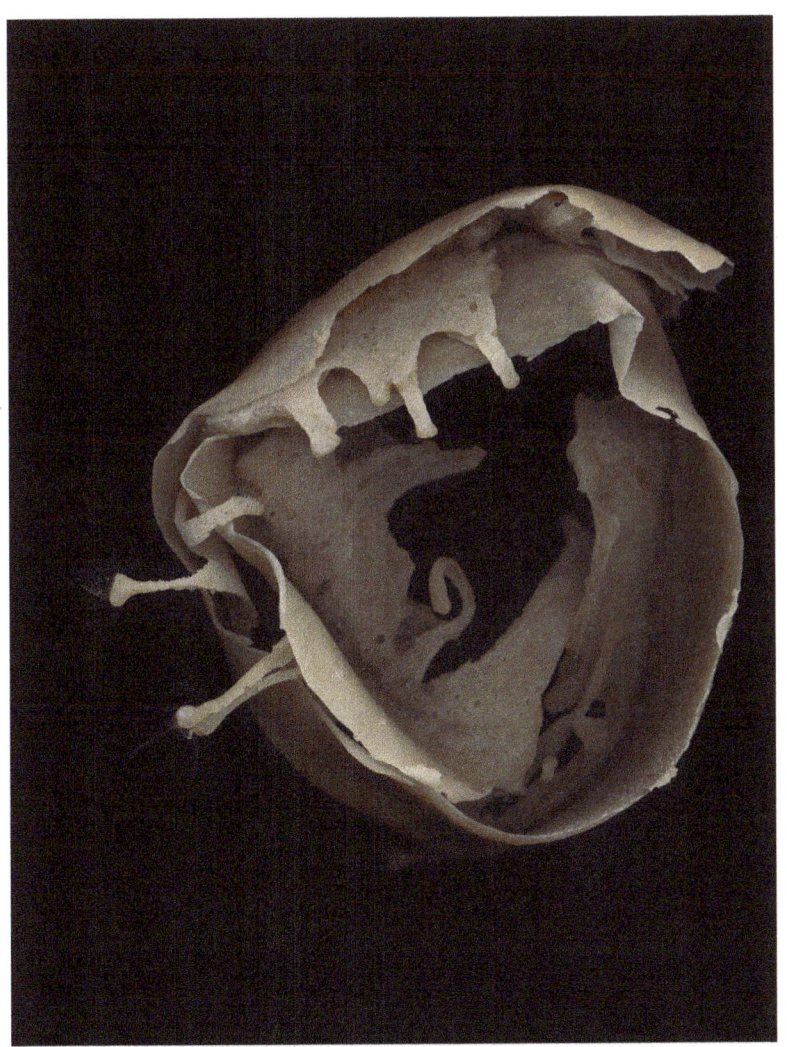

Studio Skin (Iris Eichenberg). 2013. Archival pigment print, 50 x 40 in.

Conceptual photographer Cynthia Greig admits to being uninterested in the mechanics of photography; rather, she is fascinated by the facts and fictions of the photographic image. She came to photography through studying art history and filmmaking after an undergraduate degree in printmaking and is a collector and published historian of nineteenth-century photography. Manipulated photographs, such as enhanced scenes of the Civil War and trick portraits of circus performers, hold a particular fascination. Inspired, in part, by these rudimentary red herrings, her own work as a photographer and video artist has centered on photography's ability to manipulate what we think we see. With sly wit underscoring elegant images, she explores the area between idea and belief, between the physical and the

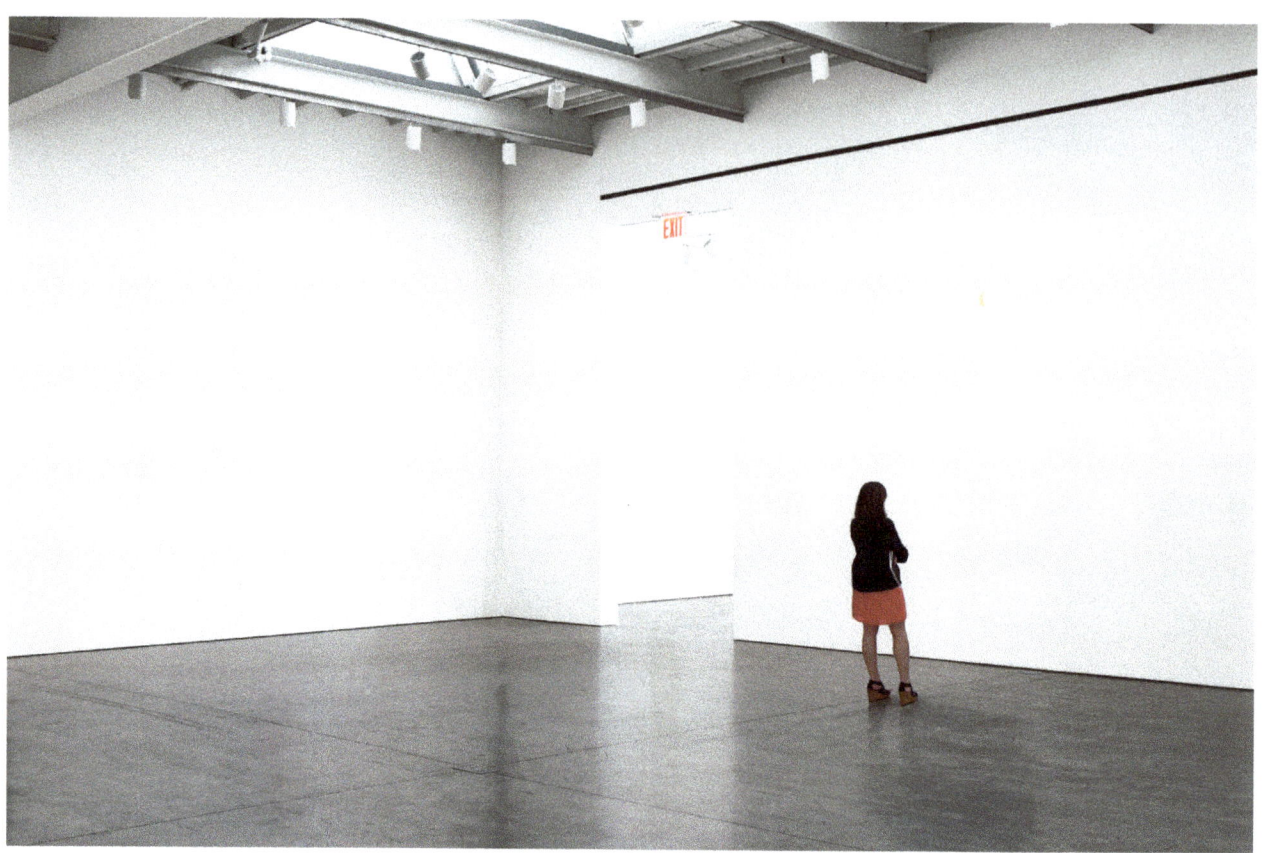

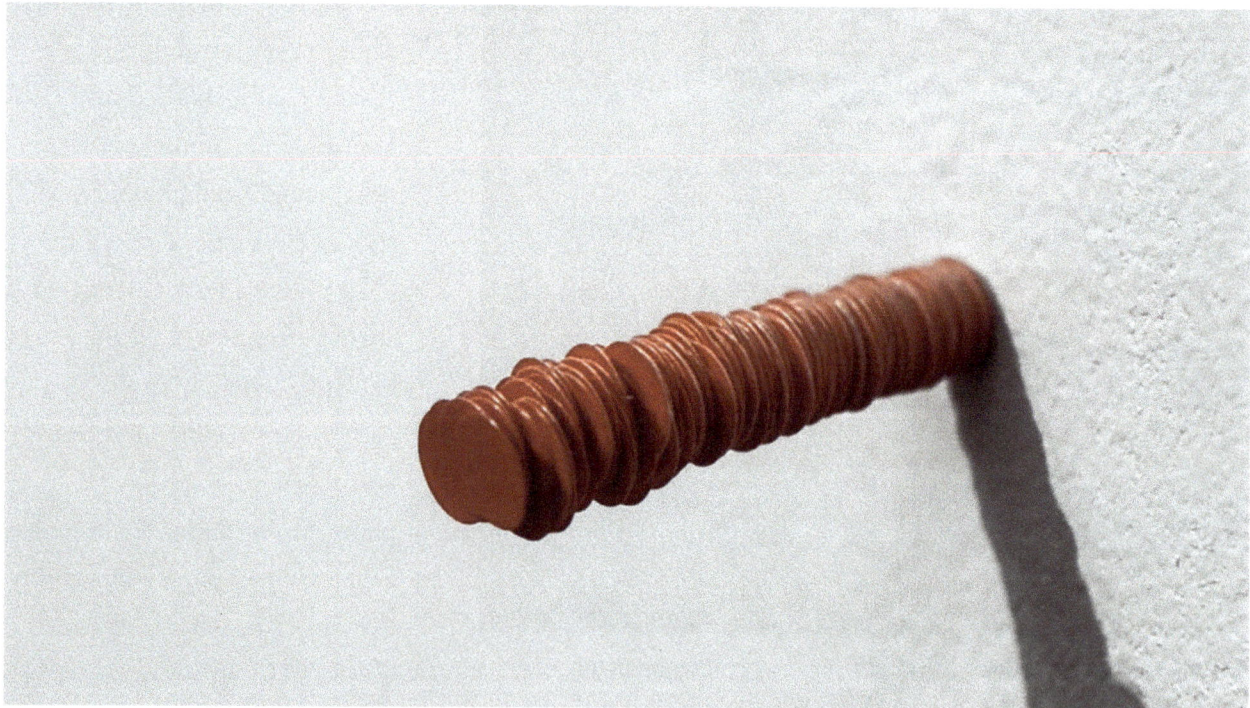

(Top) Threshold (Doug Argue/Haunch of Venison/Chelsea). 2016. Archival pigment print, 30 1/2 x 44 in. *(Bottom)* Still from the video *Too Big to Fail.* 2016. 1 min., 30 sec.

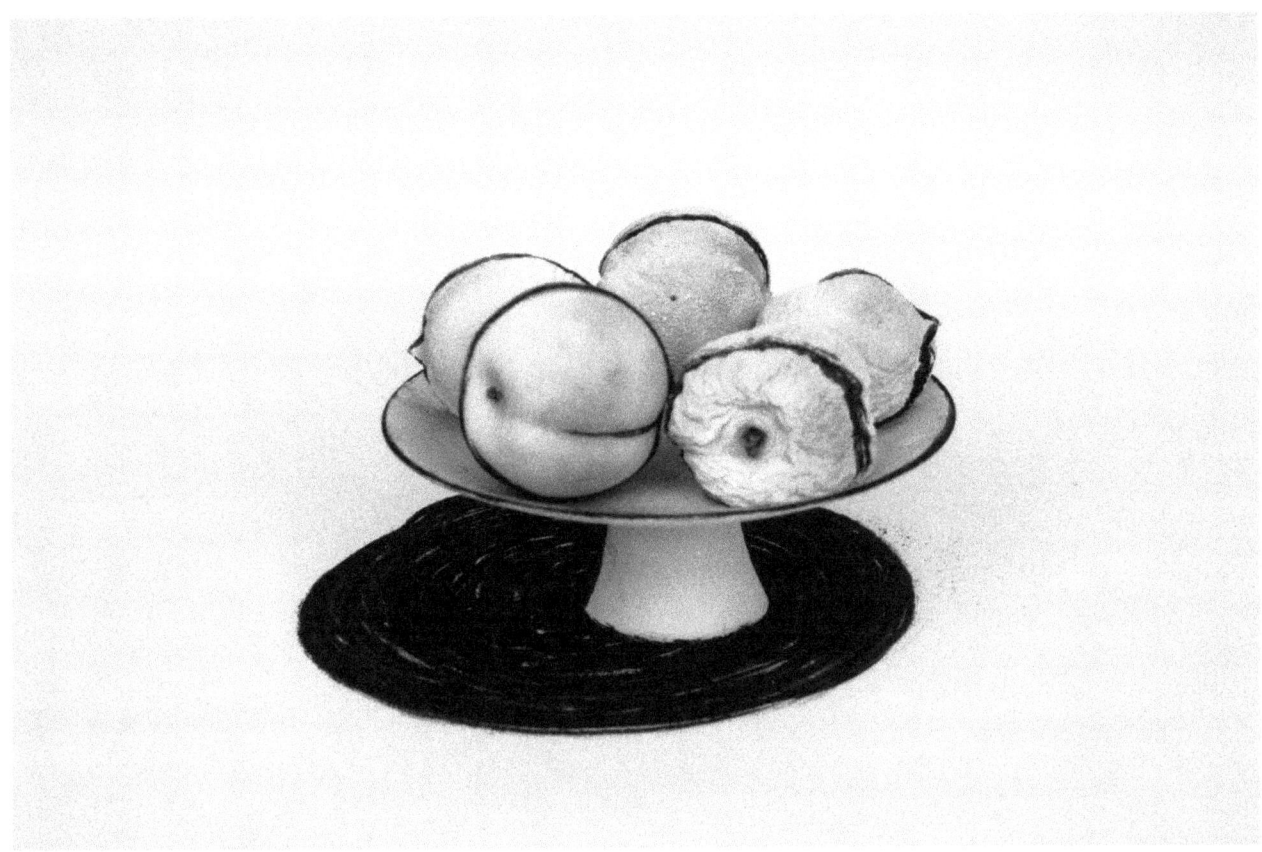

Still from the video *Still Life with Peaches (Sam Taylor-Wood)*. 2009–10. 1 min., 51 sec.

imaginary, between perception and reality.

Early 16 mm films, such as the short ***Death of a Postmodernist*** (1988), wink at the metaphysical, often campy, aesthetics of surrealist films while exploring the alteration of narrative through the manipulation of time. This film and other early works establish important tenets of her style: working in black and white; the evocation of the work of other artists or other styles; and subtle humor, as

well as an emphasis on deceptively simple compositions that gain from close looking.

In the series *Nature Morte*, she combines video with still photography, painting, and drawing. To reveal the "life" behind traditional still-life painting, Greig combined real and artificial fruit in a bowl and turned on the video camera; the resulting video, ***Still Life with Peaches (Sam Taylor-Wood)*** (2009–10*)*, documents the changes to the real fruit over time, contrasted

with the unchanging artificial one. Inspired by a 2001 video by the English artist Sam Taylor-Johnson, Greig's video posits the cycle of decay and regeneration, using video to both record and erase the hand of the artist. Similarly, ***Growth Gravity*** (2010), a time-lapse video filmed in her backyard over seven months, is a meditation on the change of seasons, growth, and aging.

An important recent group of photographs uses art galleries and studios as sites for intervention,

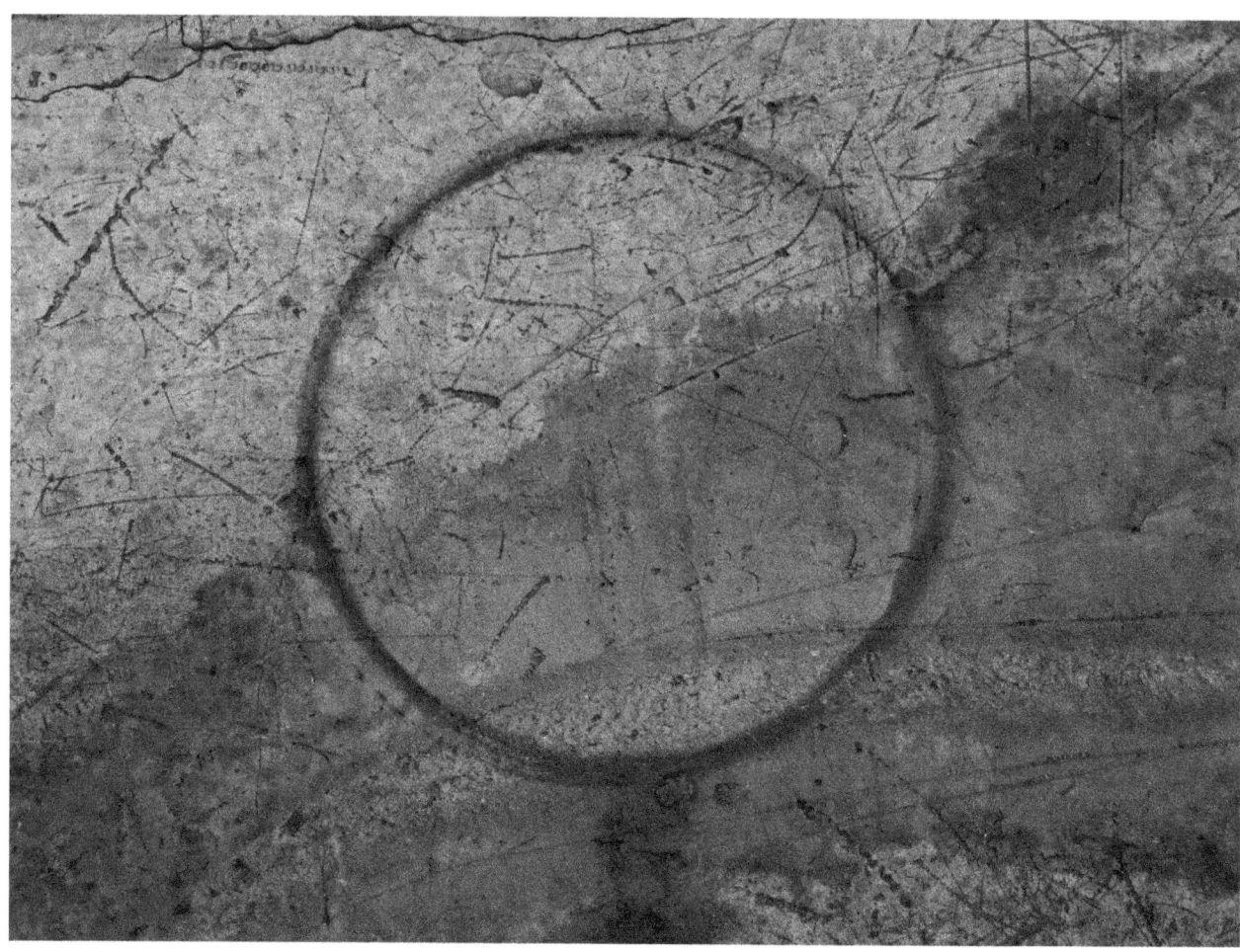

Gone (34° 1′53.2″N 118° 22′34.2″W—Culver City). 2014. Archival pigment print mounted on Dibond, 30 x 40 in.

observing and interpreting minute architectural details. The photographs in the series *Studio Skins* (2013) look ominously like flayed, scarred skin coiled against a dark background but are actually latex strips that exhibit the physical imprint of cracks in the concrete floors of artists' studios. Calling out this detail in the ordinary construction materials of these spaces lends each studio a unique identity, as well as hinting at its history. Her series *Gone* (2013–15) is a set of photographs depicting close-ups of small geometric shapes, often marks from the legs of furniture, on art gallery floors. The composition references geoglyphs such as the Nazca Lines, enormous designs on the desert plateau of southern Peru, documented through aerial photography. The visual link between the marks of an ancient culture and the traces of a contemporary one, inverted in size and scale, suggests a curious continuum. The intriguing series *Threshold* (2012–17) strands visitors in empty art galleries. Greig has digitally stripped away the works of art from the gallery walls, leaving only the human figures, dwarfed by a seemingly limitless white space. This simple premise, harking back to her early interest in manipulated photographs, renders the visual experience of the gallery space as abstracted, enigmatic, and often flattened in a cubist manner. The

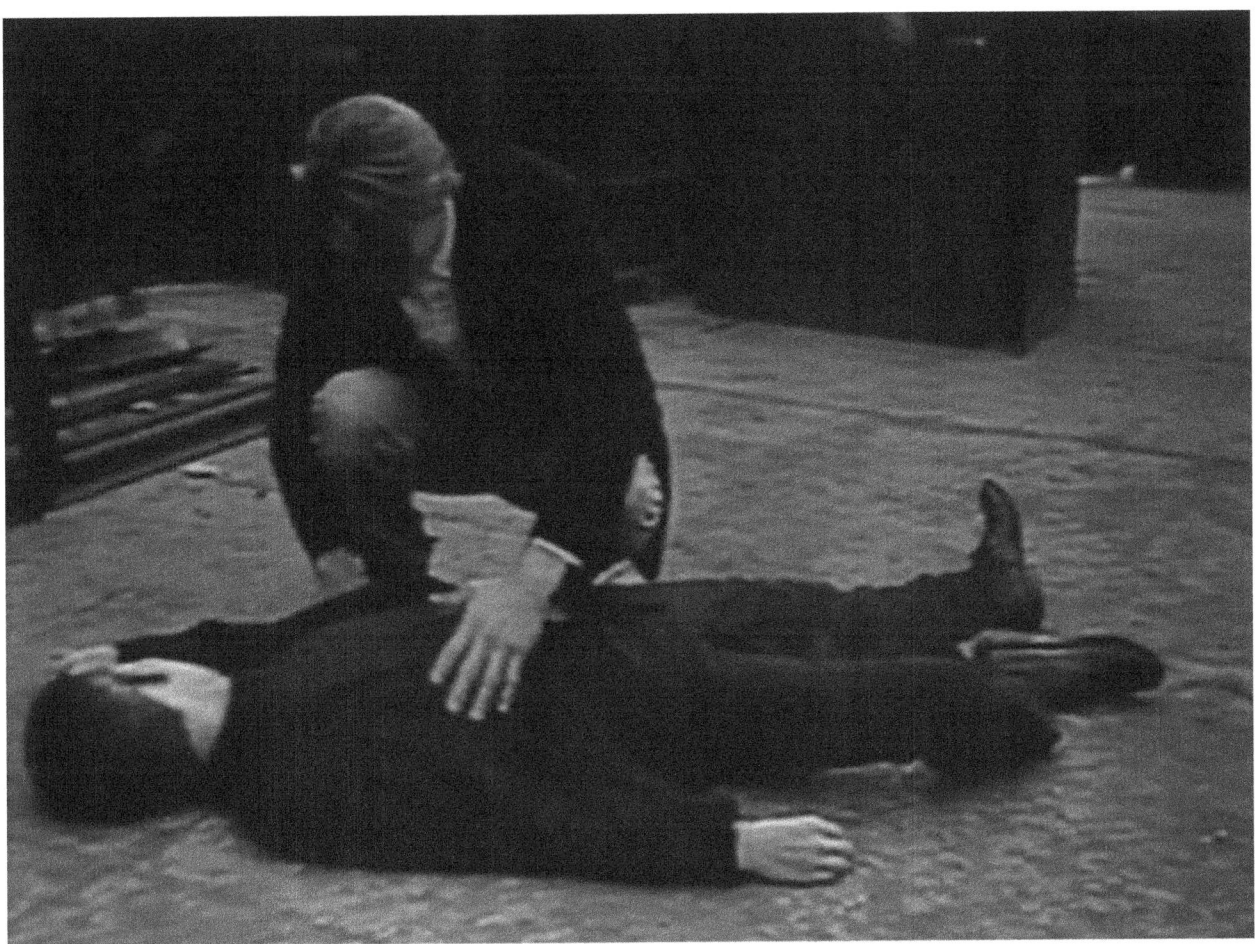

Still from *Death of a Postmodernist*. 1988. 16 mm film, 2 min., 43 sec.

quietly comical video ***Too Big to Fail*** (2016) explores the tyranny of the red dot, that marker of commercial success, with a close-up of red dots being stacked one on top of another until they fall off the wall. Greig's irreverent take on the obsession with sales harnesses the breathless anticipation of a fake dynamic.

The sound of breath exhaled onto glass, ***Breathscape*** (2015) posits the question "What does breathing look like?" This series is perhaps the purest expression of the conceptual thread of the paradox between knowing and seeing that runs through her work. By trying to capture the ephemera or the insignificant details that make up our world and confound them with the push-pull of two- and three-dimensionality, Greig's work does more than question photography's persistent reputation for factual objectivity. Through her focus, the ordinary and often overlooked is given monumental significance, drawing attention to photography's ability to manipulate, frame, highlight, and shape the way we perceive reality.

MARYANN WILKINSON, APRIL 2017

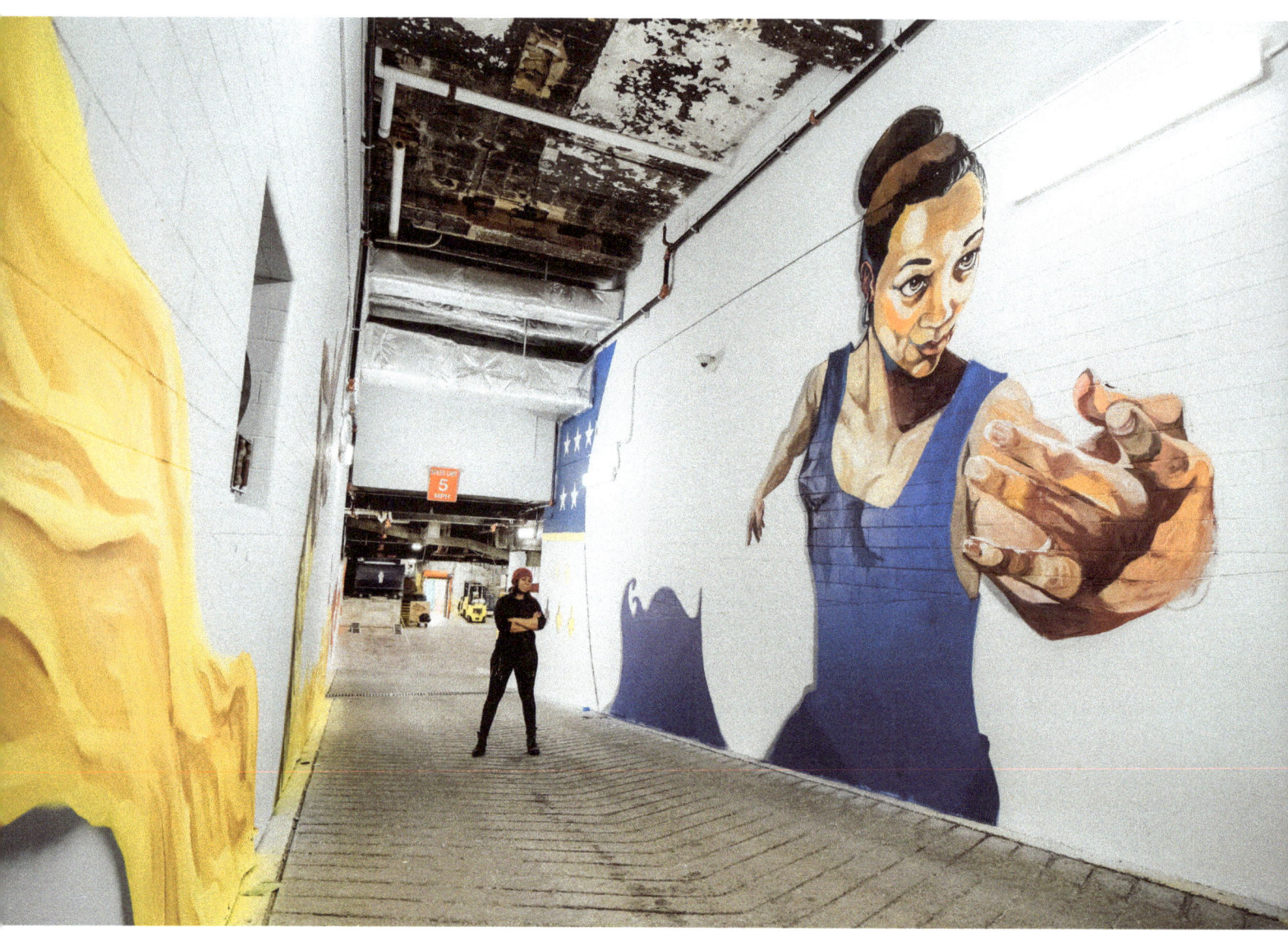

Out of the Ashes We Will Rise. 2016. Wall painting, two walls, 12 x 80 ft., 12 x 45 ft.

Born Detroit, 1979
BFA, College for Creative Studies
Lives in Detroit

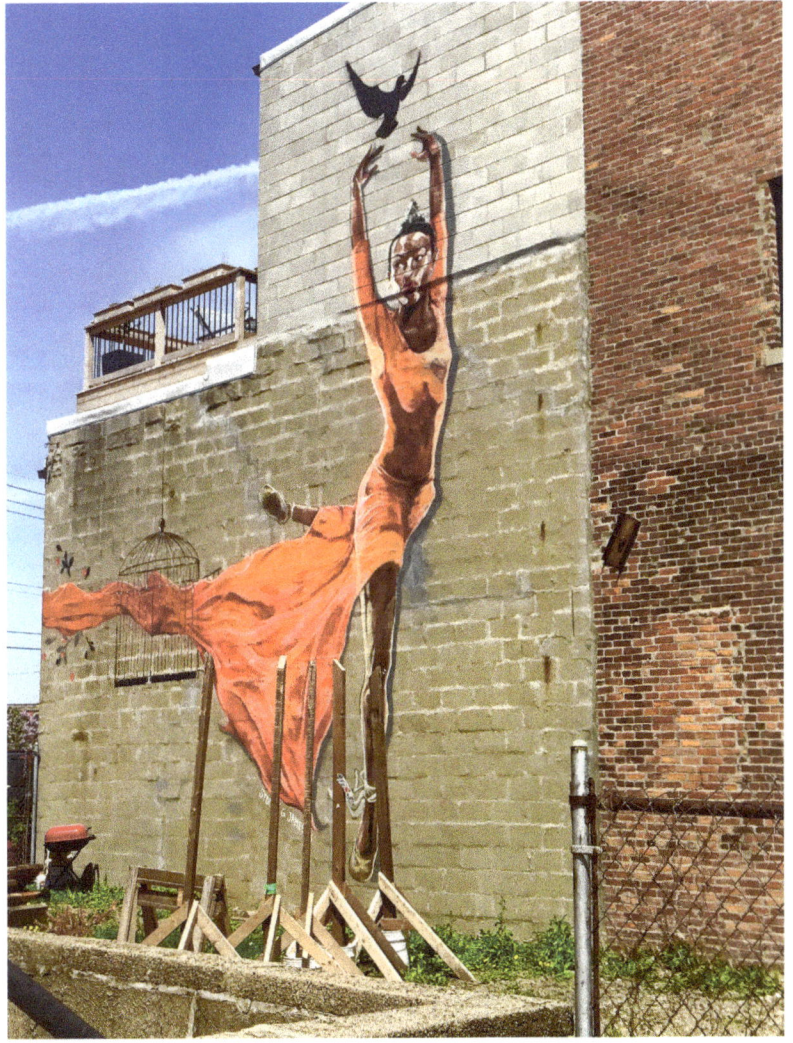

Precious Freedom. 2016. Wall painting, 33 x 26 ft.

"I'm not a street artist, but I can paint on anything," asserts Sydney James, prolific muralist, painter, and illustrator. After graduating from the College for Creative Studies in 2001, she forged ahead as designer, art director, and "ghost artist" (for television dramas), at first in Detroit and subsequently in Los Angeles. Reviewing the evolution of her practice up to that point, she recalls, "I was an illustrator, [but] when I took control of the stories, I became a fine artist." This epiphany coincided with her timely move back to Detroit in late 2011, where she encountered a burgeoning art community and street art stirrings, fueled in part by the Grand River Creative Corridor and Murals in the Market initiatives.

As a painter, she produced a number of portraits of family and acquaintances,

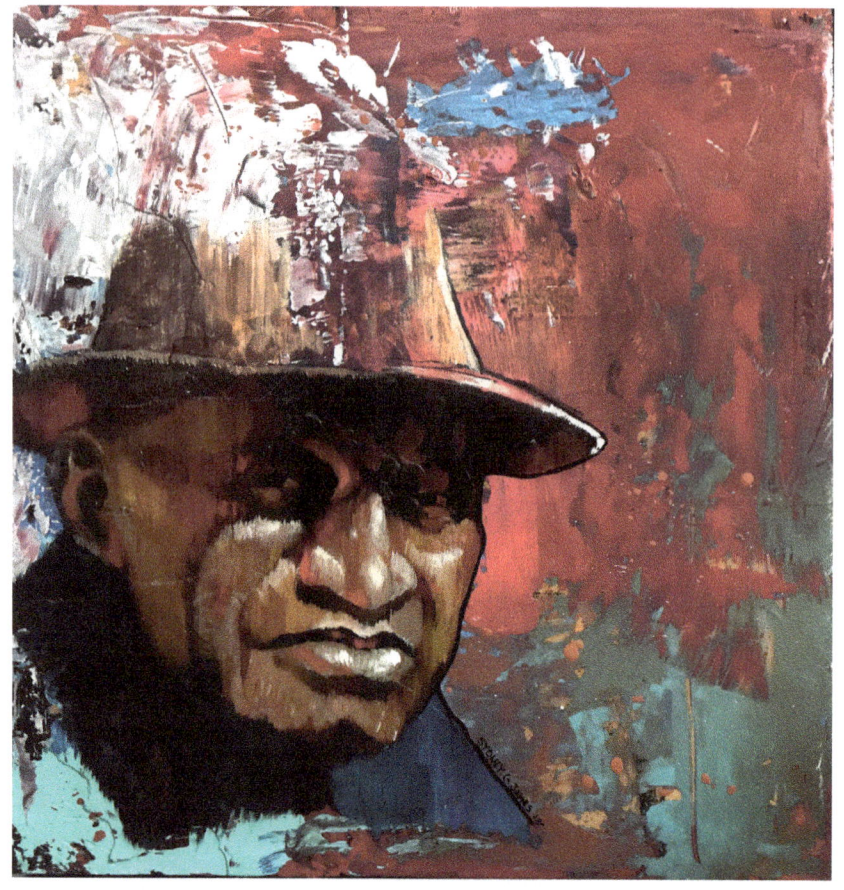

including a likeness of her grandfather, **American Dream?** (2012), and **The Purge** (2014), from a series titled *House of Mirrors*. Both imply something of the anxiety of their protagonists' predicaments; in the case of the former, the shadowed visage suggests the recognition of a dream deferred, ironically limned in an all-American palette of red, white, and blue. Many of the *House of Mirrors* images likewise focus on close-up studies of intimate, unguarded moments. Executed on medicine cabinet mirrors, a setting especially conducive to one-on-one probings of the self, these include *The Purge*, in which a woman boldly alters her appearance, a fraught decision heightened by the shattered glass just above her head. Implicit vulnerability also emerges in the installational *Appropriated Not Appreciated* series of 2016. Wall-mounted drawings of nude black women surround **Preach**, an acrylic-on-vinyl self-portrait displayed on the floor. Positioning her arms to protect her body, James hugs

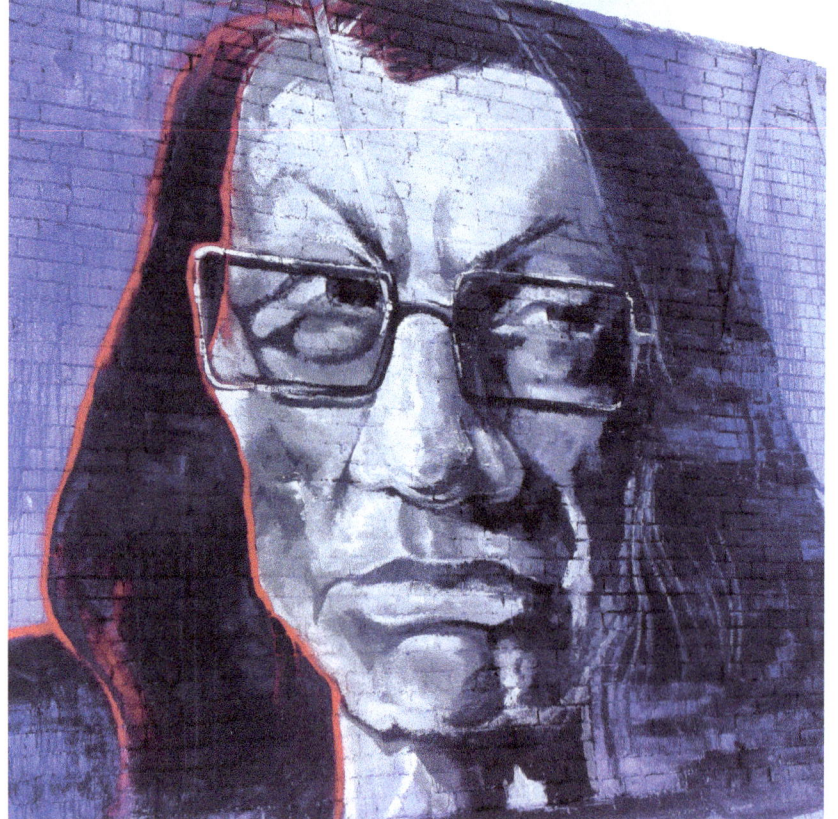

(Top) American Dream? 2012. Multimedia on wood panel, 24 x 24 in.
(Bottom) Rodriguez. 2014. Wall painting, 9 x 9 ft.

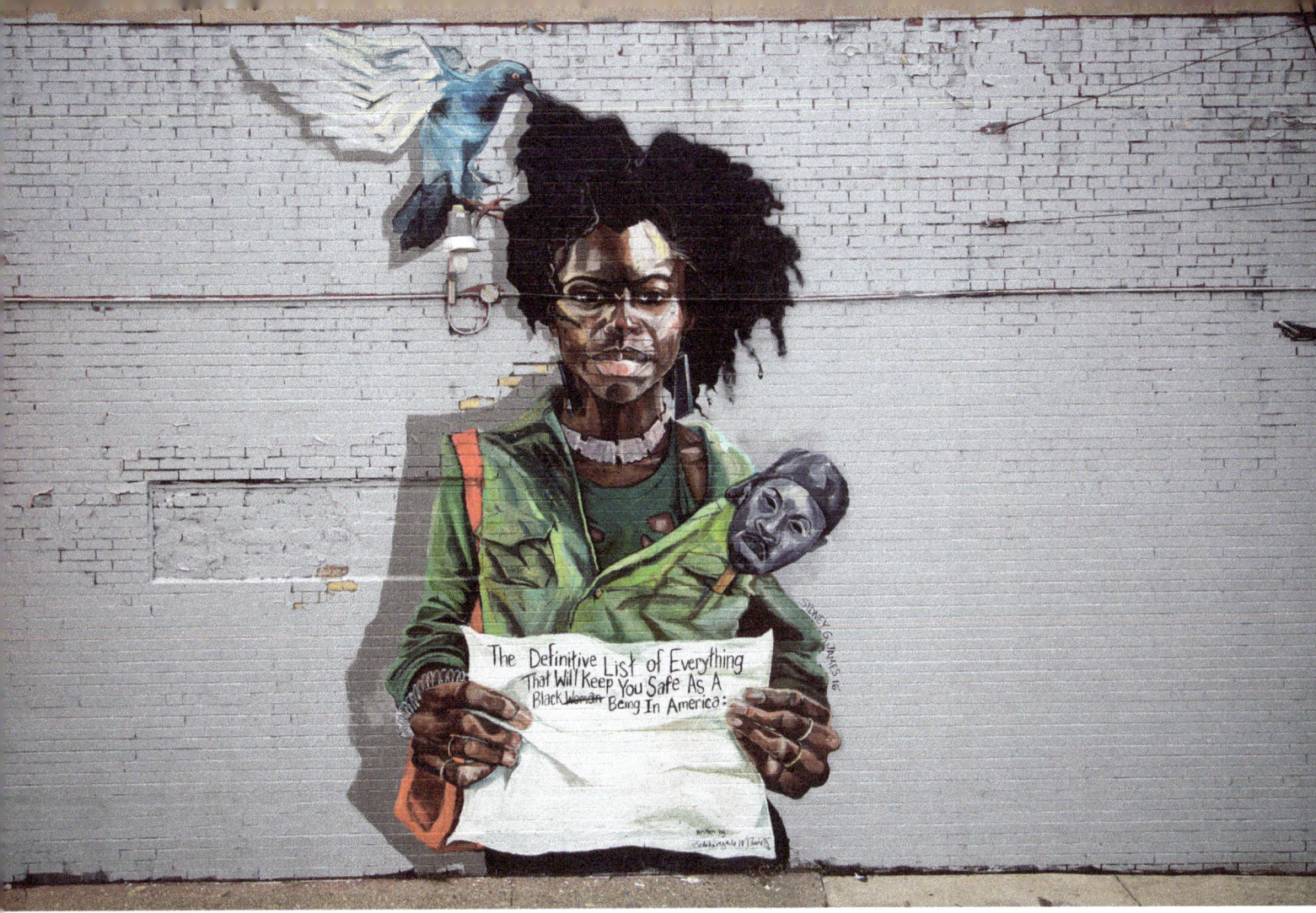

Black List. 2016. Wall painting, 15 x 25 ft.

the margin of the support as if to avoid the footsteps of passersby, to little avail, it would seem. This literal presentation of woman as doormat speaks to a societal climate that, James notes, can be as sexist as it is racist.

James's king-size visage of musician ***Rodriguez*** (2014), her first mural, measures approximately nine by nine feet. Ensconced on the second floor of the side wall of a building located at Grand River and Calumet, the grisaille countenance of

"Sugar Man" commands the blue-violet background against which he is silhouetted. His identifiable presence—long hair, accented in red, distinctive rectangular glasses, and intense expression—joins others nearby, also commissioned by the Grand River Creative Corridor to spruce up and personalize a shopworn stretch of Grand River.

Subsequently, in rather rapid succession, James produced several additional wall paintings in Detroit over the next few years.

Her ***Black List*** was commissioned by Murals in the Market in 2016. Located in Eastern Market at Division and Orleans, its "definitive list" is left "blank to symbolize the current state of racial injustice and attack that we are under in America." ***Precious Freedom***, of the same year, located in the Corktown neighborhood, addresses personal liberation in the guise of a tall, willowy, orange-gowned woman, nearly thirty feet in height, who has escaped the gilded cage of

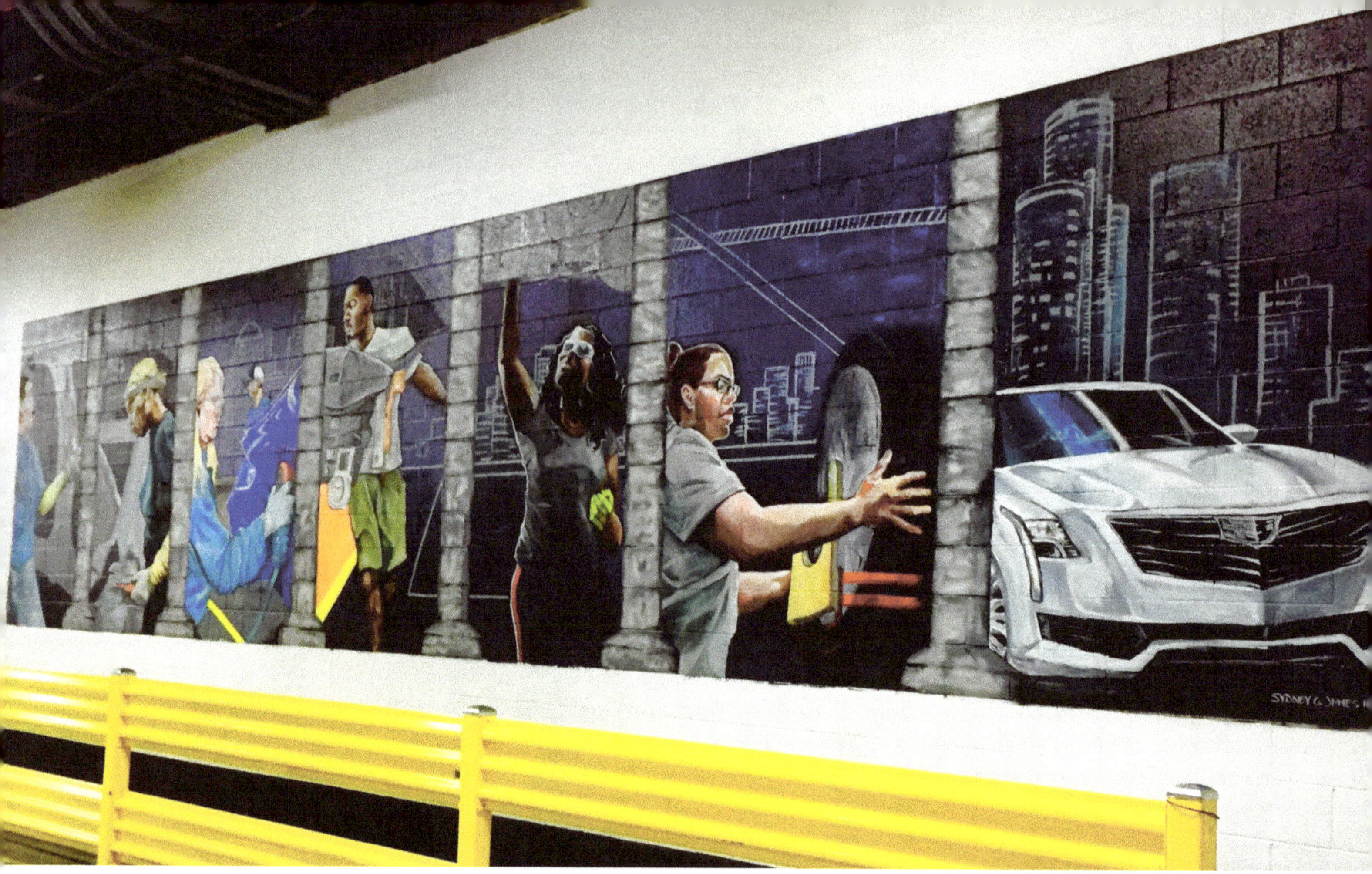
SYDNEY G. JAMES

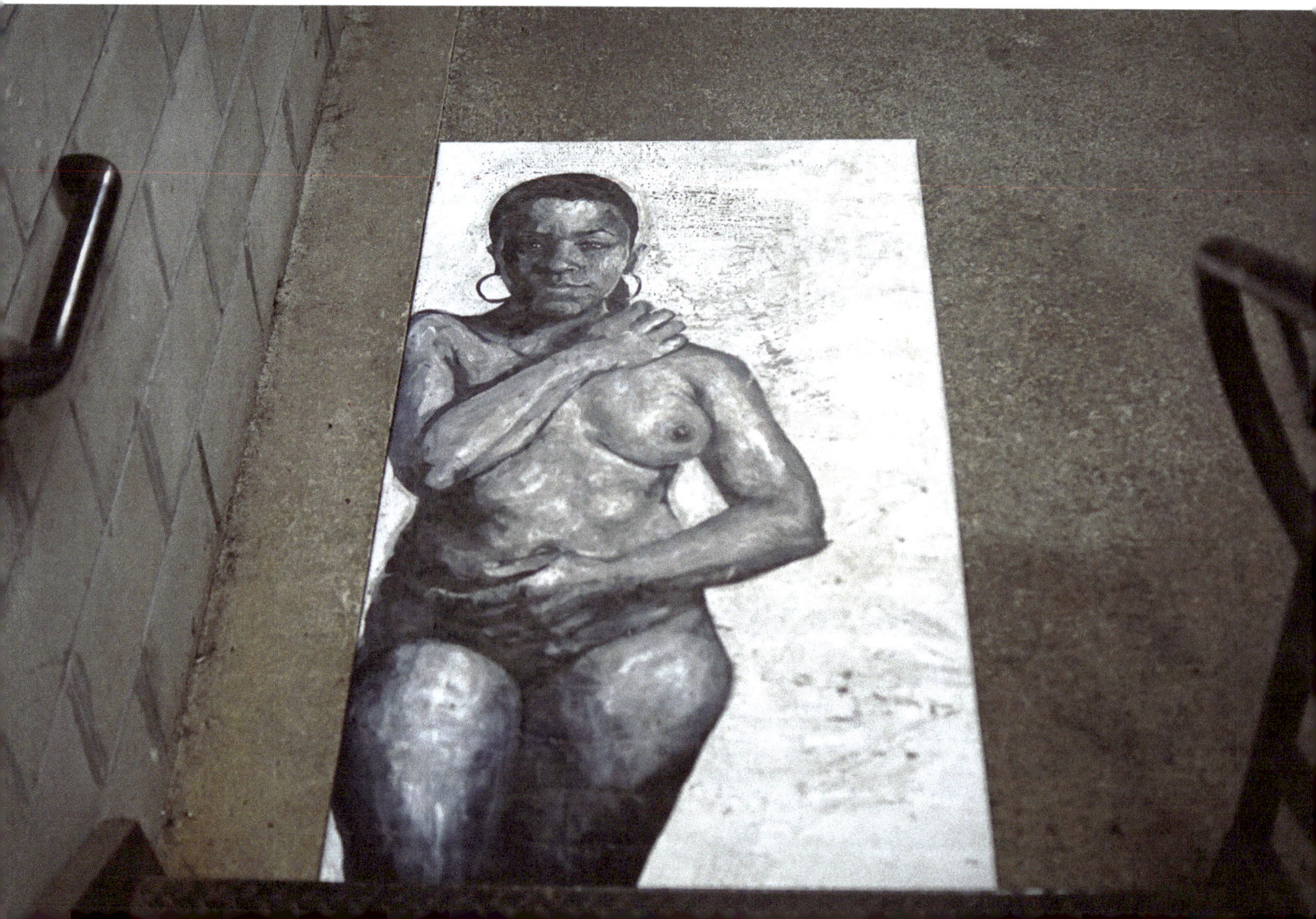

(Opposite, top) Methodical Harmony. 2016. Wall painting, 15 x 30 ft.

(Opposite, bottom) Preach (from Appropriated Not Appreciated: The State of Black Women in America series). 2016. Acrylic on vinyl, 60 x 30 in.

incarceration. The elongated train of her gauzy gown flows around the corner where it is surrounded by a flurry of flowers on a wall painted by fellow artist Ouizi.

Additional exemplars of James's muralist skills, conceived and realized in 2016, include two Detroit-themed designs. ***Out of the Ashes We Will Rise***, contracted by Bedrock Detroit, is comprised of two long walls leading to a loading dock in the Federal Reserve Building. Ballerinas on each side, leaping and pirouetting in primary-hued garb, represent the rising of Detroit. One, in blue, leans forward, beckoning and welcoming the viewer with outstretched arm and hand. And in the anthemic ***Methodical Harmony***, commissioned by GM, a diverse panoply of workers, mustered from the factory floor, stretches thirty feet in length. Albeit compartmentalized by stainless steel columns, they strive individually and in unison to produce the gleaming Cadillac CTS rolling off the assembly line. Harkening back to familiar emblems of Detroit—the city's 1805 credo, "We hope for better things; it will arise from the ashes" and the *Detroit Industry* murals by Diego Rivera introduced to the nascent artist during childhood visits to the DIA—James has reembraced her hometown with a Motor City mix of resolve and reality: "Grind is my brand. It's an acronym for Girl Raised in Detroit. . . . We all grind as artists. We had to grind to get here."

The Purge (from House of Mirrors series). 2014. Acrylic on medicine cabinet mirror, 20 x 16 in.

DENNIS ALAN NAWROCKI, MAY 2017

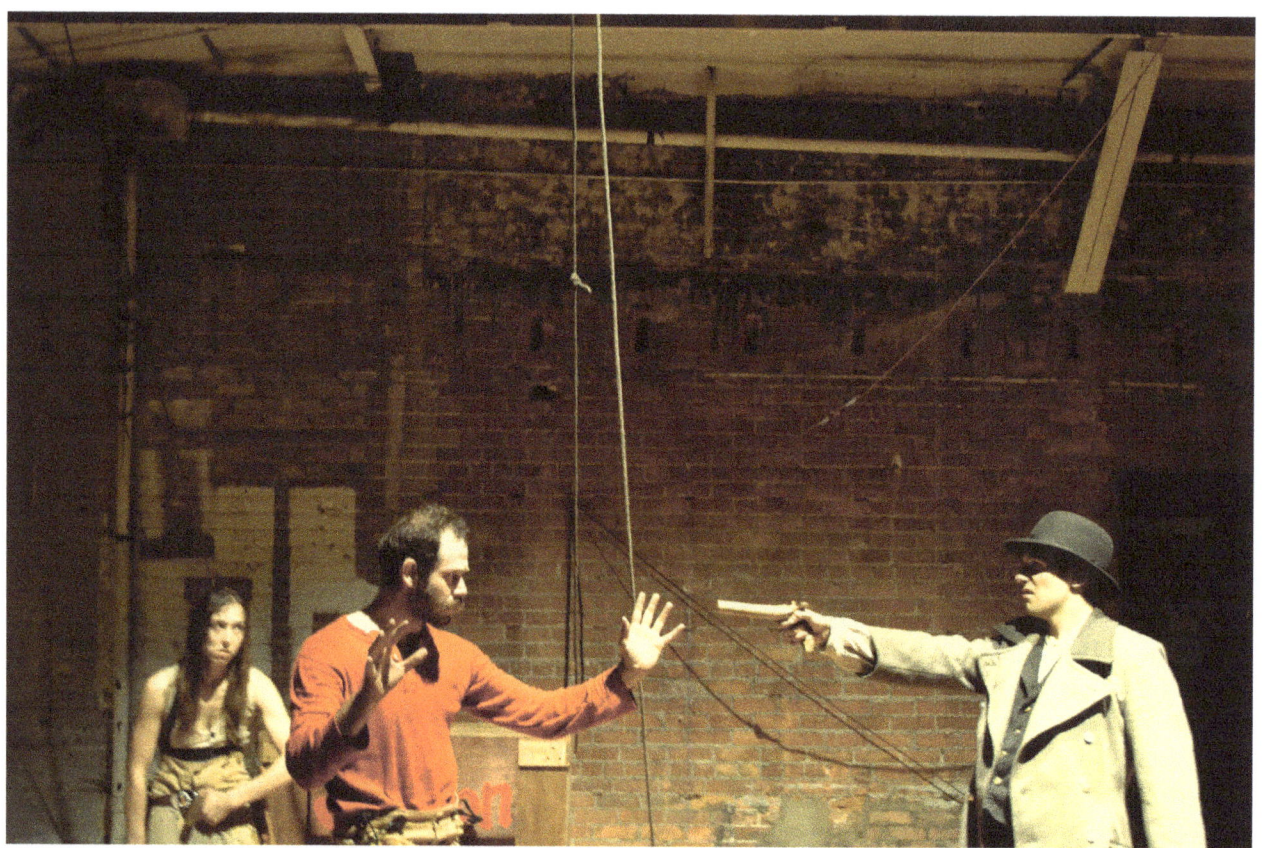

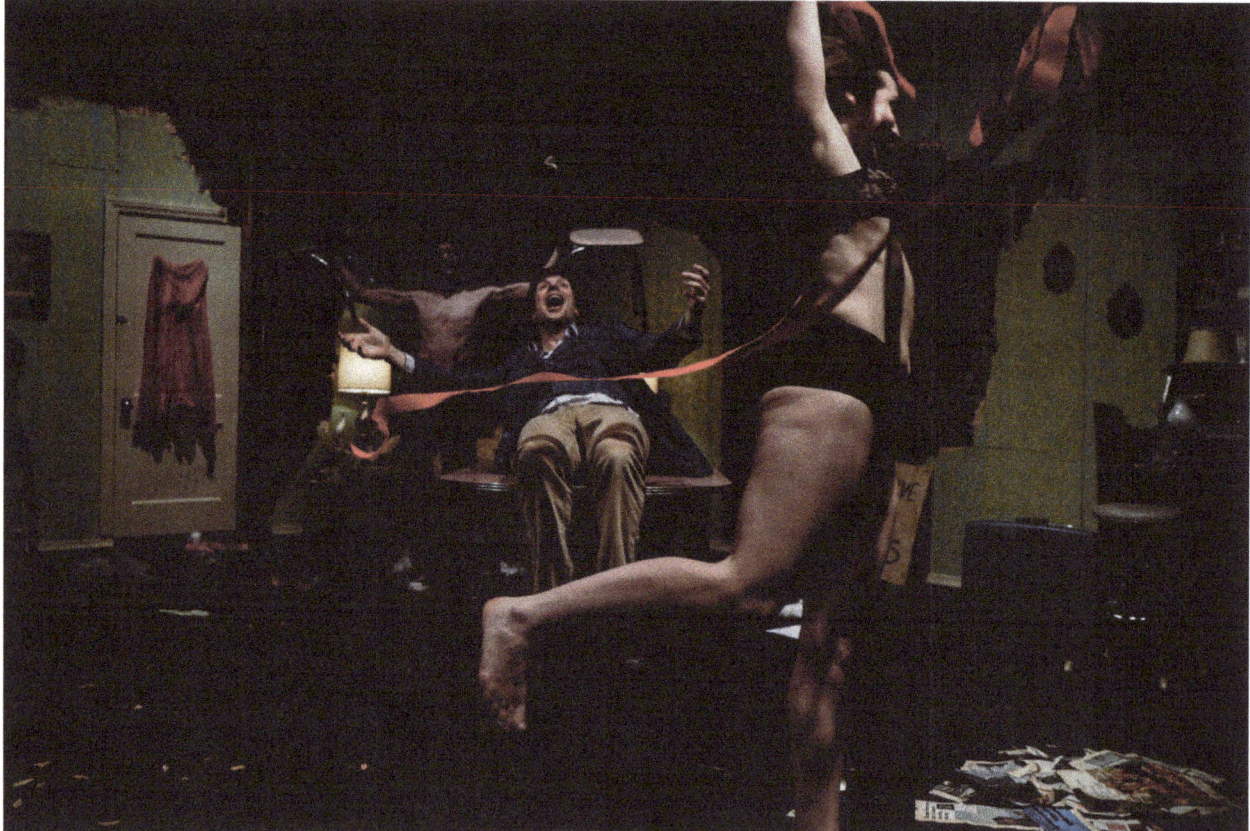

(*Top*) Performance of *Manifest Destiny*. 2011. Photography by Amanda Reintjes. (*Bottom*) Performance of *The Radicalization Process* at Alverno Presents, Milwaukee, WI. 2016. Photography by Kat Schleicher / Alverno Presents.

LIZA BIELBY

Born Flint, Michigan, 1980

BA, Kalamazoo College; MFA, Dell'Arte International, California

Lives in Detroit

RICHARD NEWMAN

Born London, England, 1980

BA, Greensboro College, North Carolina

Lives in Detroit

It's 1970. The sixties are over, but not yet past. In a townhouse in New York's Greenwich Village two members of revolutionary leftist group The Weather Underground are building a pipe bomb packed with nails and dynamite. They plan to use it to "bring the war home" to a dance for non-commissioned officers and their dates at Fort Dix, New Jersey. Casualties are inevitable. A third member of the cell is hammering out an accompanying statement on a typewriter, maniacally searching for inspiration in lines from Sophocles's *Antigone*—a play whose message of nonconformity in wartime has achieved renewed currency in the Vietnam protest era. The book he reads from is not just any version of the play, but one by the legendary New York–based anarcho-pacifist ensemble The Living Theater—which is in turn a

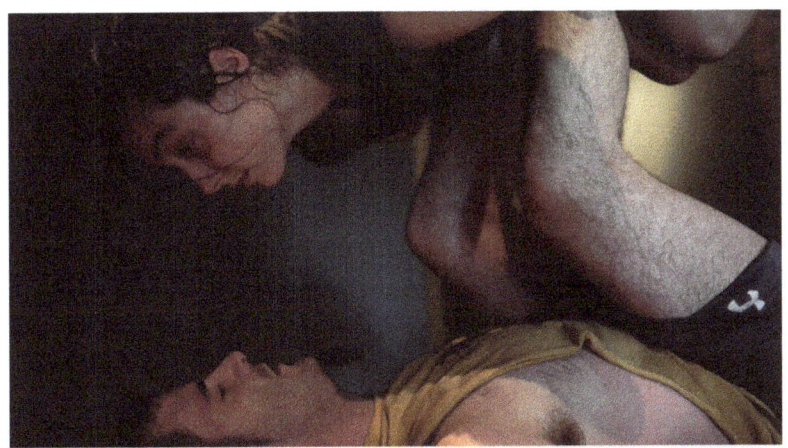

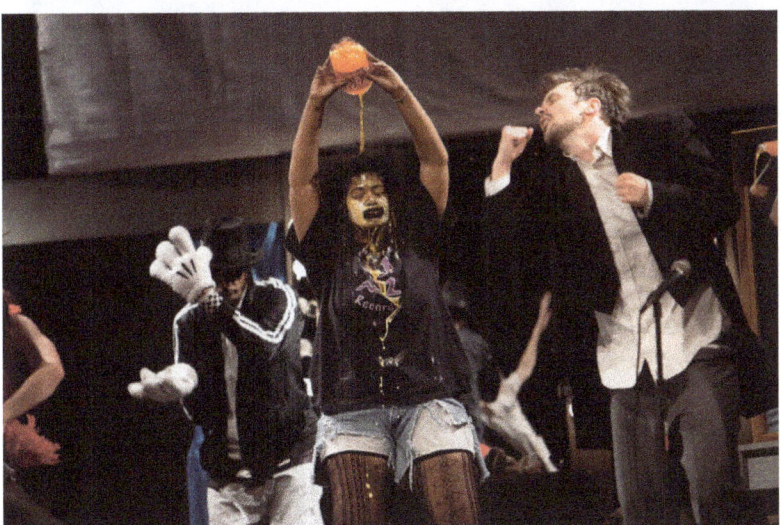

(*Top*) Open training, 2015. (Production still from Julia Yezbick's 2015 film *Into the Hinterlands*.) (*Bottom*) Performance of *The Circuit*. 2013. Photography by Erik Ljung / Alverno Presents.

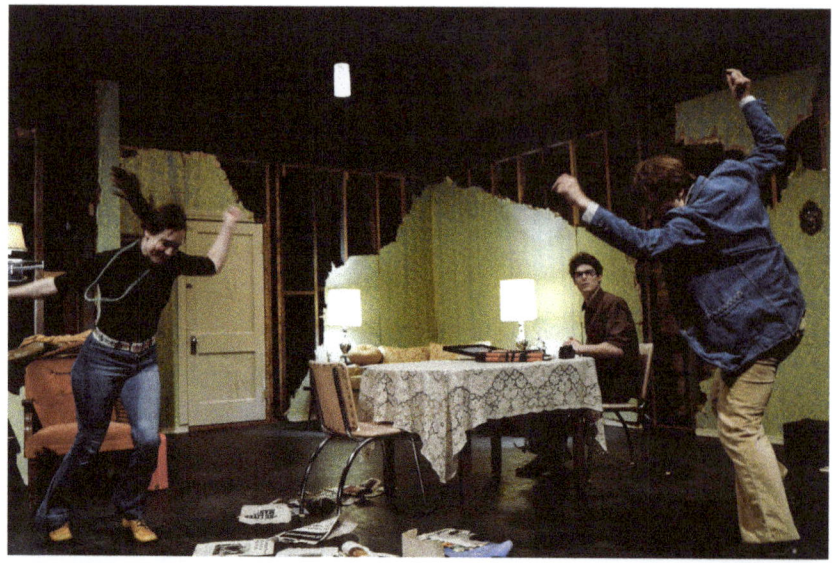

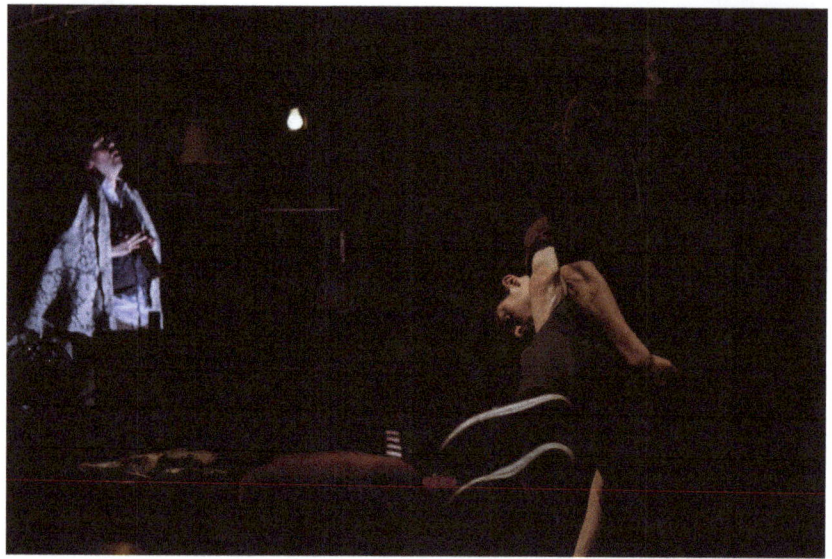

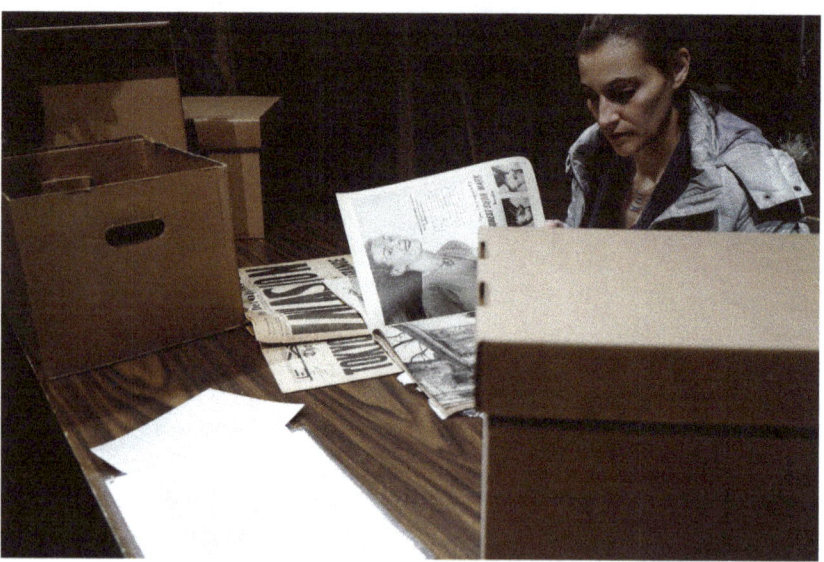

translation of a version by Bertolt Brecht. At that moment, the twin radical undercurrents of theater and far-left politics converge. Then the bomb explodes. So ends a pivotal scene in The Hinterlands' kaleidoscopic 2016 art/theater project *The Radicalization Process*.

Let's start again. It's 2004. Michigan native Liza Bielby is the only non-Chinese national enrolled to study *chuānjù*, a theatrical form of traditional Chinese opera from Sichuan. The training is almost absurdly arduous. In order to perfect the meticulous footwork that underpins professional performances, students are required to run in circles for hours, until the teacher gives

(*Top*) Performance of *The Radicalization Process* at Alverno Presents, Milwaukee, WI. 2016. Liza Bielby (left), Richard Newman (right), and the third cast member Dave Sanders (center). 2016. Photography by Kat Schleicher / Alverno Presents.

(*Center*) Performance of *The Radicalization Process* at Alverno Presents, Milwaukee, WI. 2016. Photography by Kat Schleicher / Alverno Presents.

(*Bottom*) *The Radicalization Process*—an audience member investigates the archive "discovered" in the basement of Play House. 2016. Photography by Kat Schleicher / Alverno Presents.

permission to stop. She stays for four years. Meanwhile, in rural New England, Bielby's future partner, Richard Newman, is pursuing a similarly committing path as part of Double Edge—a communal theater ensemble dedicated to simultaneously furthering the theatrical form and creating the conditions for their own self-sufficiency. His mentors are the veteran Argentinean actor and street-theater creator Carlos Uriona and iconoclastic feminist director Stacy Klein.

On Bielby's return from China, the pair meet at Dell'Arte International in California (Newman is artist-in-residence, and Bielby is a graduate student), and in 2009 they form The Hinterlands. The foundation of their joint artistic practice is daily, ongoing physical and vocal training. They see this as a platform for creating work through the continuous investigation of improvisation and form, a way of building their expressive capabilities, and a way of escaping the known and familiar. They use their training to explore the cultural forms of the Western (to create *Manifest Destiny* in 2011) and vaudeville (to create the contemporary variety show that is 2013's *The Circuit*).

Improvisation and form are in constant interplay as Bielby and Newman develop these works. In creating original content for *Manifest Destiny*, for instance, they may improvise for hours within the form of a pair of circling duelers, each hyperconscious of the other and probing for advantage. With time, the physical and psychological nuances of this characteristic "cowboy movie" form emerge. As they internalize the form, they start to improvise within it—for example, increasing the speed at which they circle each other to almost comedic effect, or training to the rhythm of a spaghetti Western soundtrack. They become conscious of how their body movements change to adapt to these new conditions. It is these meticulous details of body movement (or speech patterns), and how they relate to cultural memory, that is a defining feature of The Hinterlands' work, anchoring their lofty, and often frenetic, subject matter in precise details, humor, and a certain intimacy.

Another layer of Bielby and Newman's practice relates to place and community. In December 2010 they relocate to Detroit

and establish their base at 12657 Moran (aka Play House)—a former two-story residence that has been remodeled into an airy performance space. The surrounding area contains a large Bangladeshi population, and numerous artists/art projects. The pair connect easily with both communities. Neighboring artists become collaborators, and Bielby studies with the local Bengali music school. Training and community converge in monthly free-form *open training* sessions.

Let's start again. It's 2013. Two bombs explode near the finish of the Boston Marathon, killing three and injuring many more. The Tsarnaev brothers are identified as the perpetrators. A chance remark from Newman's father to the effect that he will never be able to understand how someone can do such a thing convinces Newman that we must understand why someone does such a thing. The training process begins. A mysterious archive is discovered in a basement, and the Play House starts to take on the appearance and spirit of a townhouse in Greenwich Village in 1970.

STEVE PANTON, MAY 2017

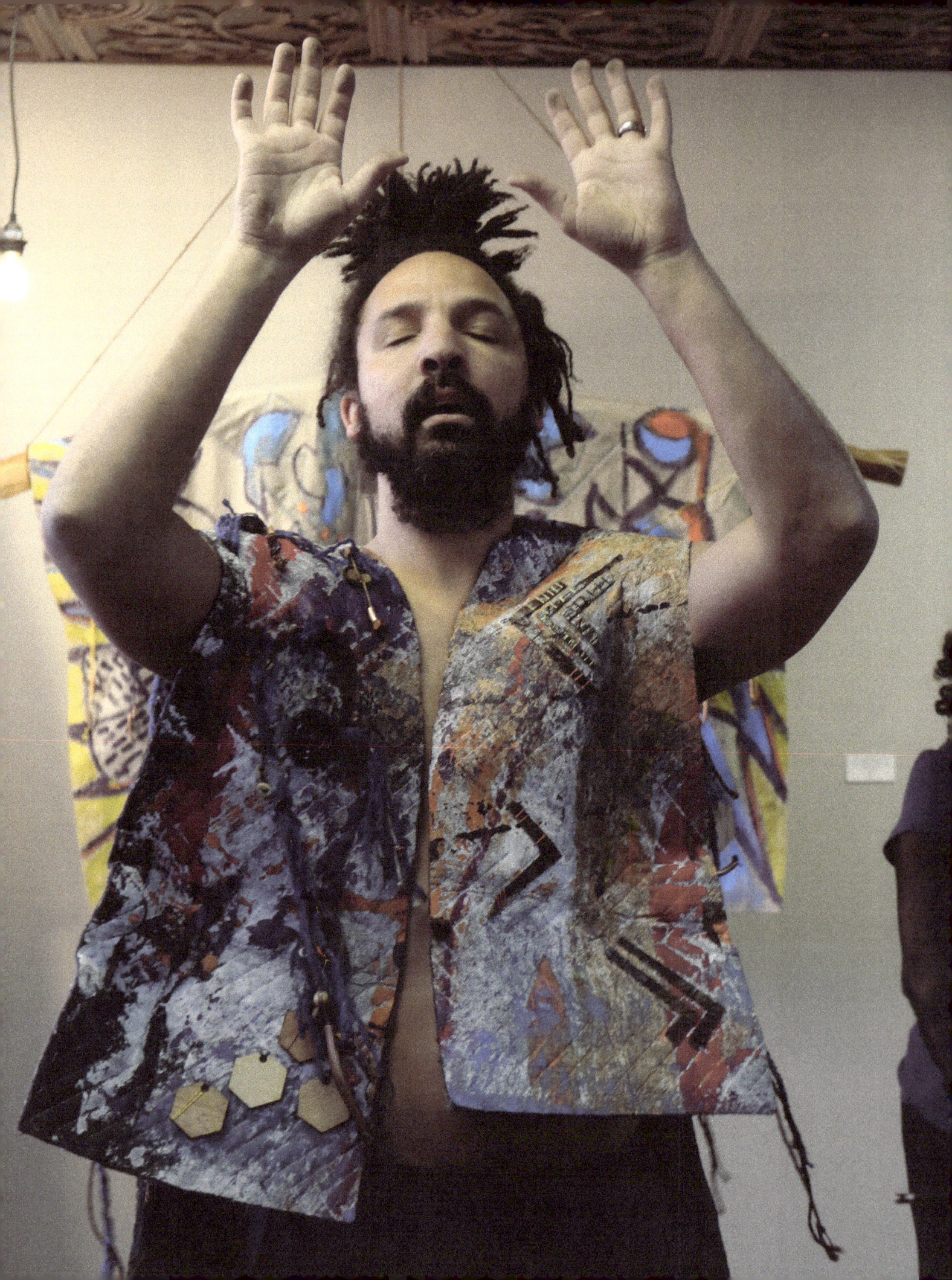

Born Rhinelander, Wisconsin, 1979
BFA (Music), California Institute of the Arts
Lives in Detroit

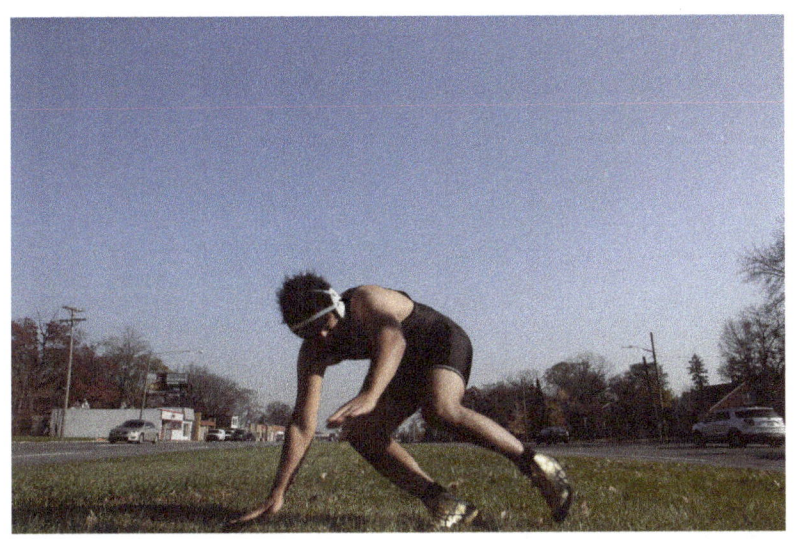

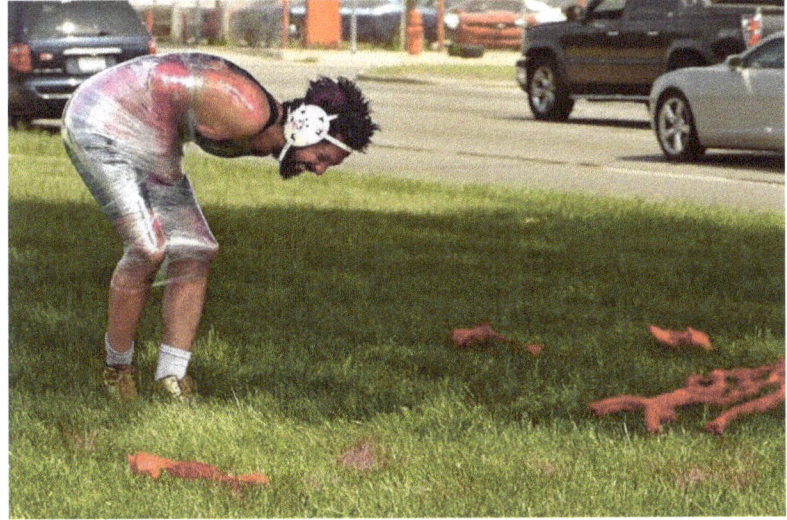

(Top) Wrestle. 2016. Performance. *(Bottom) Wrestle.* 2016. Performance. Photography by Jeff Cancelosi.
(Opposite) Primal Flash (collaborative garment pieces by Saffell Gardner and Sarah Mark). 2017. Performance. Photography by Arise Rock.

The artist Billy Mark intentionally messes with your head. He moves, he morphs, he mystifies. Watch him for even a moment, and it's soon clear that he embodies this trio of Ms and more—sometimes all at once.

In fact, Mark means to make you believe that the whole "artist" moniker—improvisational freestyle poet and installation artist, to be exact—is too confining for him or his multidimensional work, which spans and connects conceptual theater, performance, sculpture, poetry, music, movement, and even silence. Label him, if you must, but no longer will he narrow himself.

"I've had this revelation," he said during a visit to the North End two-family flat that doubles as his work and living space. (Mark lives with his wife, fiber artist Sarah Perry Mark, and their two young sons.) "After

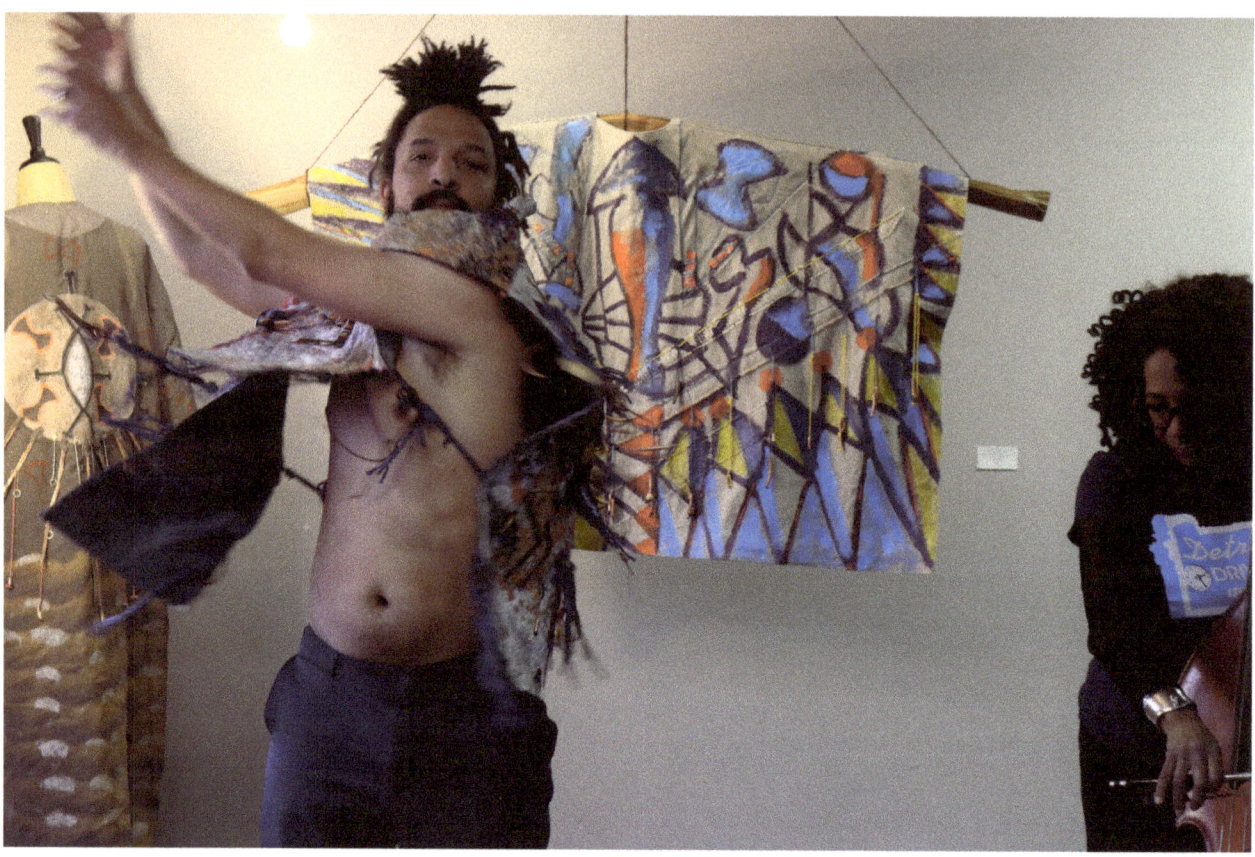

Primal Flash (collaborative garment pieces by Saffell Gardner and Sarah Mark). 2017. Performance. Photography by Arise Rock.

seventeen years of saying to people, at my core, I'm an improvisational poet and then watching eyes glaze over, I'm letting it go." Never mind that the very label Mark is releasing was the hook that earned him a coveted Kresge Arts in Detroit Fellowship (2015) and a visiting artist stint at the Cranbrook Academy of Art.

Mark sounds part mystic as he describes his journey away from defining himself and his work. "I found myself in a deep struggle trying to shape myself. I thought, 'Maybe you better identify yourself before somebody else identifies you.' I've felt this need to try to have some control over my own creativity so that maybe I'd be remembered long after I'm dead. But that's where the work gets lost, in the need to control. The naming of a thing sometimes blinds you, instead of letting the experience become an opening."

Opening: The dictionary describes it as a beginning. In Mark's lexicon it's a synonym for Detroit and a stark antonym for Los Angeles, the city where a Cal Arts degree was supposed to help him make his creative mark. "After going to art school I started to get all of these ideas from all of these different arts movements throughout history, trying to figure out how they applied to the work I do; I felt more encumbered than anything," he explained. "So much time was spent trying to find a tagline for my entire artmaking soul, because in LA you're always only one or two degrees away from someone who can get your face out to a million people." He continues: "I lost myself in the

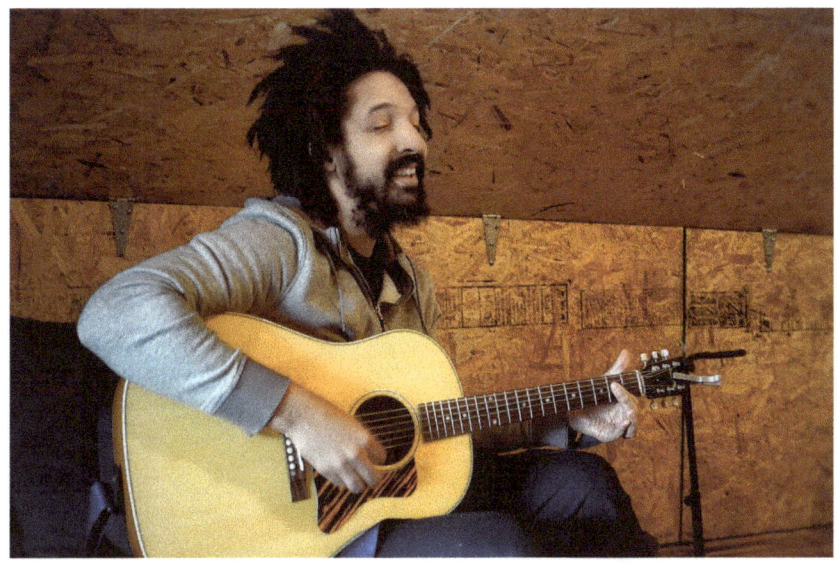

Artist Billy Mark shares a selection from a poem in progress that he's setting to music. 2017. Photography by Nichole M. Christian.

conversation of what art is supposed to be, rather than creating."

In the Bible, a book that Mark looks to for both its lyrical beauty and life application, to be lost is eventually to be found. This is the tale Mark tells to himself and to curious observers to make meaning of what's happened to his art-making since being led to a place where struggle itself is art. "Nobody is going to make your career in a moment here," he said. "For me the lack of that possibility, or even having a well-established creative infrastructure to look to, gave me a reason to reexamine why I even make work in the first place. It's been a frightening and wonderful experience, to really look at who I am instead of how I fit into the latest art trend."

Truth be told, Mark fits no more in Detroit than he did in LA. But here, he says, he's learning to allow his difference to multiply his curiosity. This is how Mark wound up, in 2016, in the middle of a grassy median on Eight Mile clad in a wresting singlet and eventually completely wrapped in cellophane. ***Wrestle*** was his live response to Detroit's stinging racial divides. Mark cast the infamous city/suburb dividing line as his stage and evil opponent. His body became the metaphor of what he likened to a spiritual battle for Detroit's heart and soul. Mark often uses his body as metaphor. For ***Primal Flash*** (2017), a traveling Live Coal Gallery exhibit, he and renowned jazz bassist Marion Hayden collaborated to

interpret the sounds of a series of vibrant handmade African hunting jackets. Mark's wife, Sarah Perry Mark, and painter Saffell Gardner, who is married to Hayden, designed each of the pieces. By fusing piercing rhythms and jagged movements, Hayden and Mark made the jackets speak, creating narrative where there was none.

Moments like *Wrestle* and *Primal Flash* now form exclamation points on Mark's vow never to leave Detroit. "I'm making work that I don't have to define or limit or shape in order to please people. I can embrace parts of myself out of sheer curiosity. That's a freedom and it feels more real here than in any city I've ever lived in."

NICHOLE M. CHRISTIAN, 2017

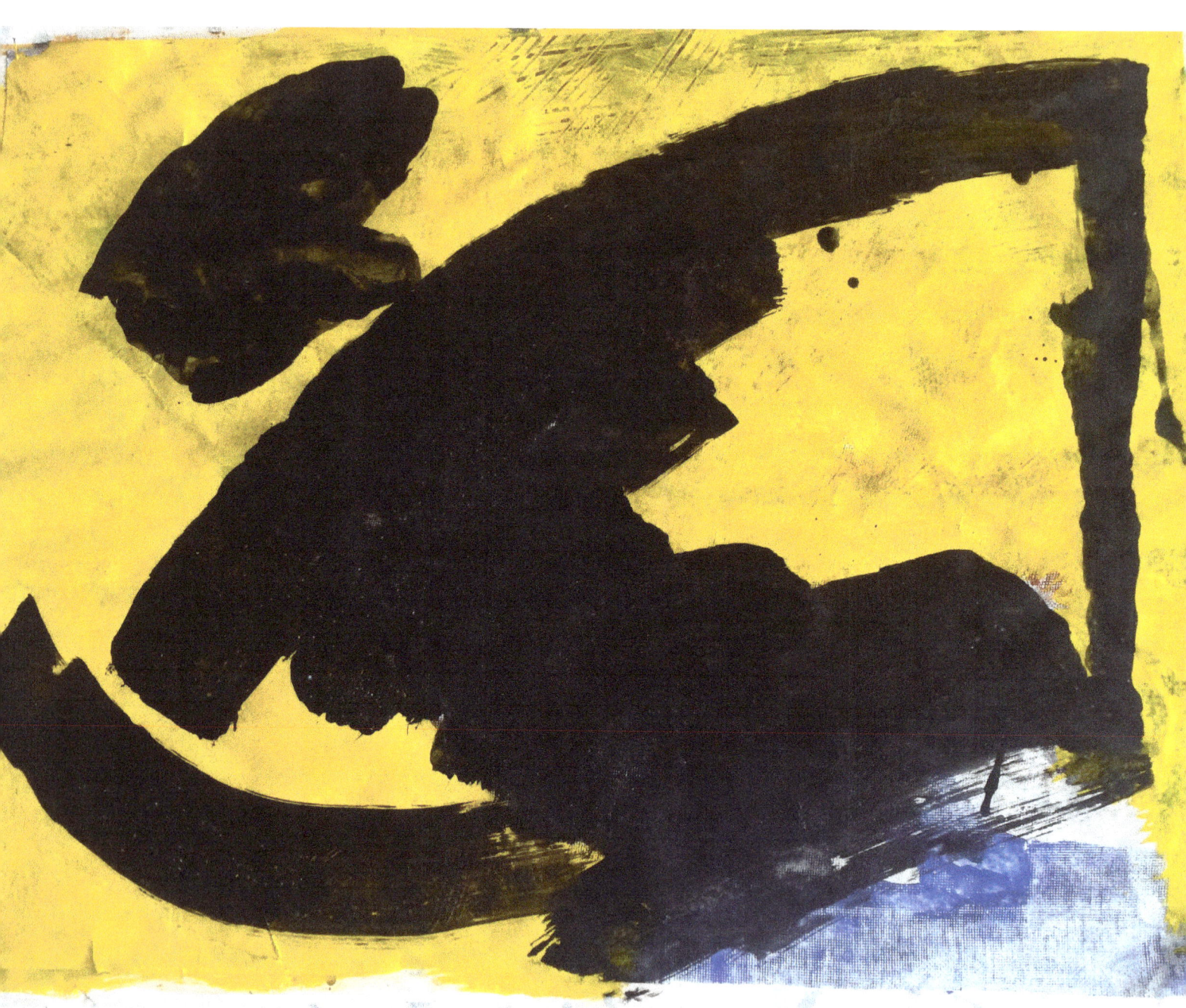

Swimmer. 2017. Mixed media on paper, 22 x 30 in.

71 // ALLIE MCGHEE

Born Charleston, West Virginia, 1941
BA, Eastern Michigan University
Lives in Detroit

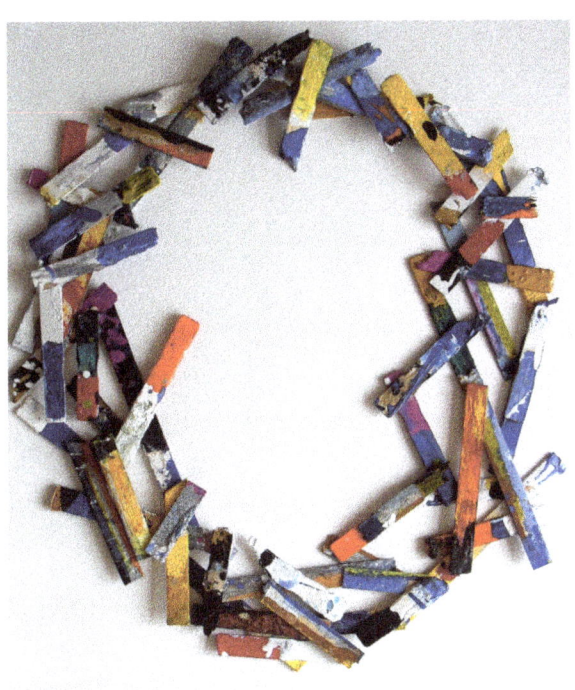

Ring of Fire. 2006. Mixed media on sticks, 44 x 40 in.

Allie McGhee is a seven-day-a-week, 360-plus-days-a-year abstract artist. He has, from early afternoon until the waning of natural light in the evening, followed this blue-collar schedule for decades. McGhee is also an experimenter. He is as intellectually and artistically restless as liquid in porous soil. The range of his curiosity and breadth of inquiry is all-encompassing. New directions pop up like spring flowers.

McGhee long ago gave up representational storytelling in favor of a jazz-like modal subversion of the pictorial. Music is an apt metaphor for his methodology. Miles Davis, one of the artist's heroes and a restless explorer of musical forms, gave up the conventional song form in favor of improvisational sound clusters. The content of a composition was no longer just

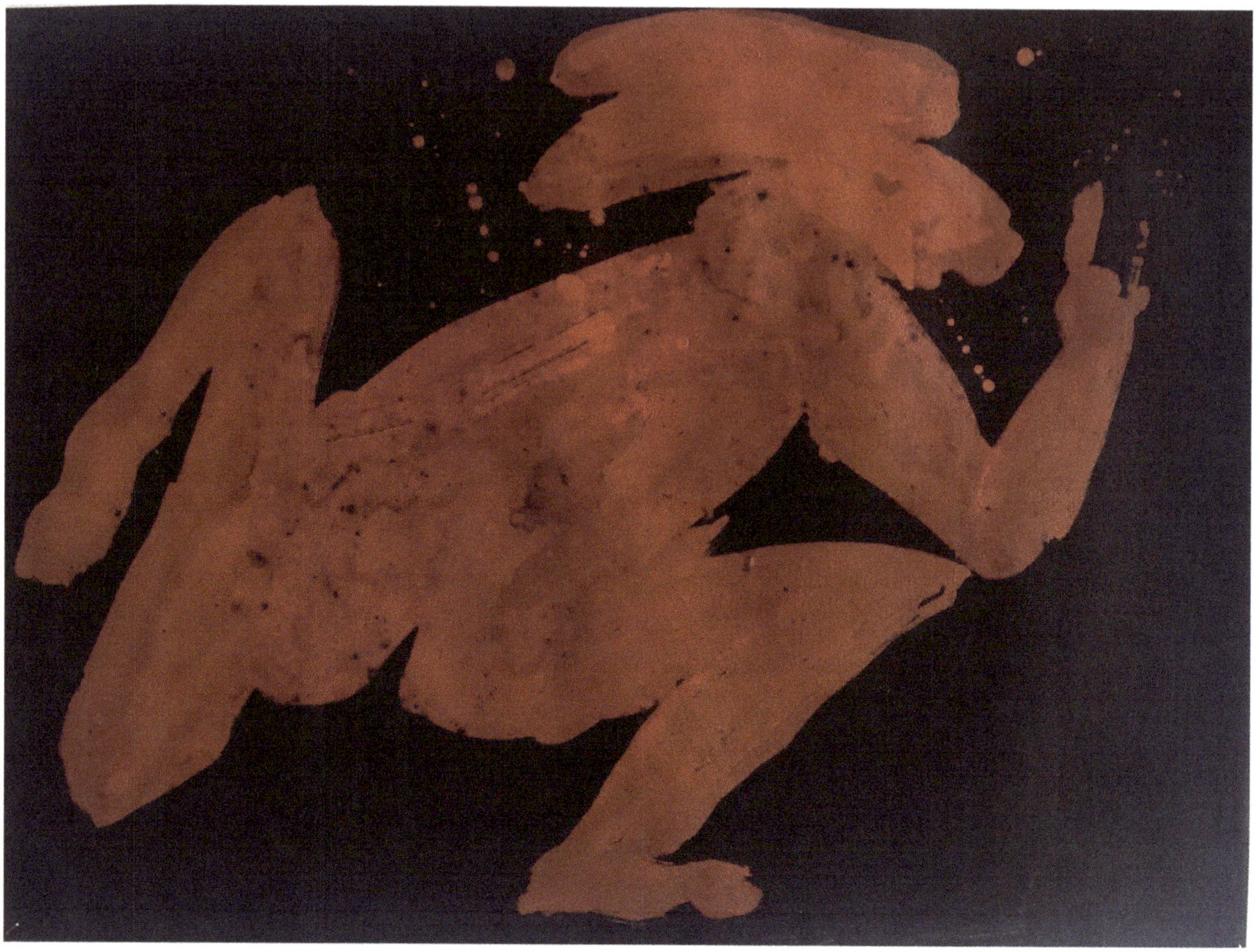

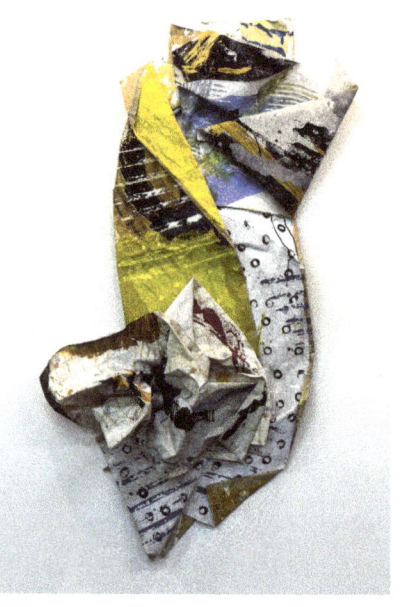

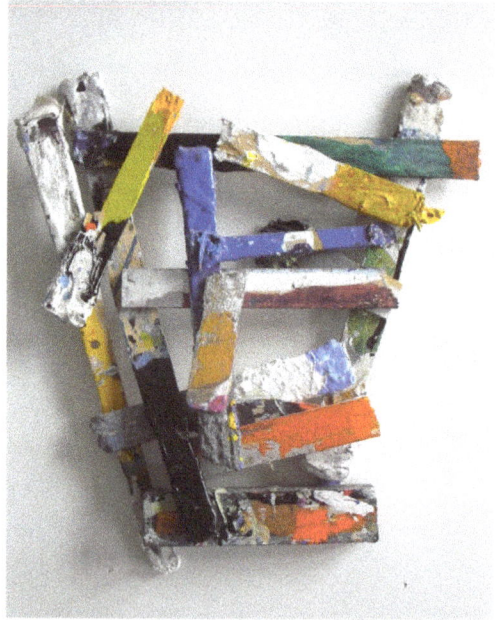

(Top) *Hush.* 2017. Mixed media on paper, 22 x 24 in.

(Left) *Similar Rhythm.* 2016. Mixed media on fiberglass and wallpaper, 59 x 35 x 10 in.

(Right) *Self Portrait.* 2008. Mixed media on sticks, 14 x 15 in.

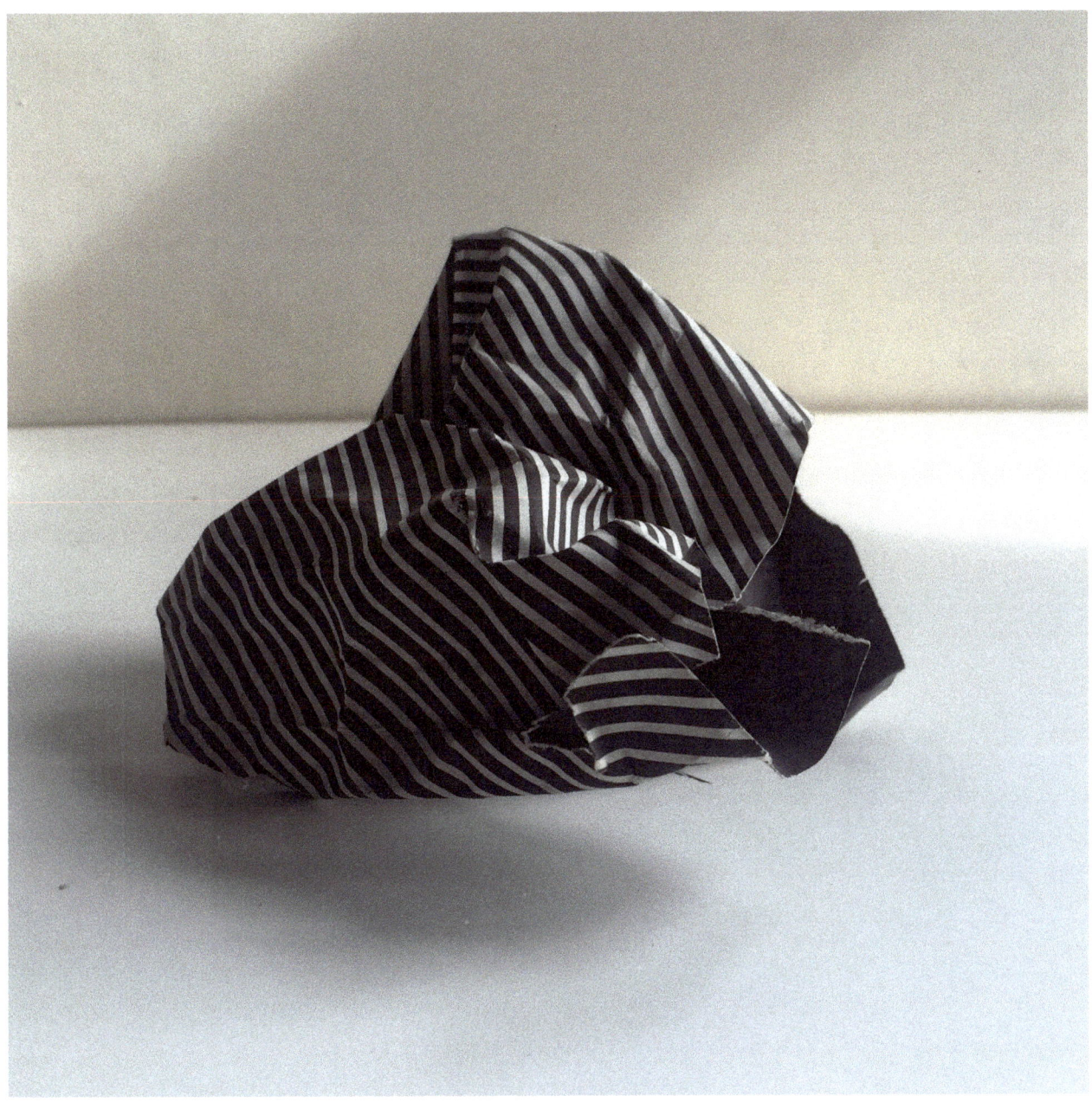

Floater. 2016. Maquette (mixed media on paper), 5 x 6 x 5 in.

variations on a melody in major and minor scales but an embodiment of the feelings evoked by the process of playing itself. Viewers of McGhee's finished work similarly experience the visceral nature of his creative process. In **Red Spinner** (2009), for instance, the vigorous strokes of blue, suggestive of water or sky, in tandem with the vibrating red oval evoke emanations of sounds vibrating across the water or across the cosmos.

Relief constructions, such as **Floater** and **Similar Rhythm** (both 2016) are the serendipitous products of his encyclopedic mastery and undermining of the techniques, intentions, and traditions of visual as well as musical world art. Although unbound by the Euro-Western rules of art-making, his process,

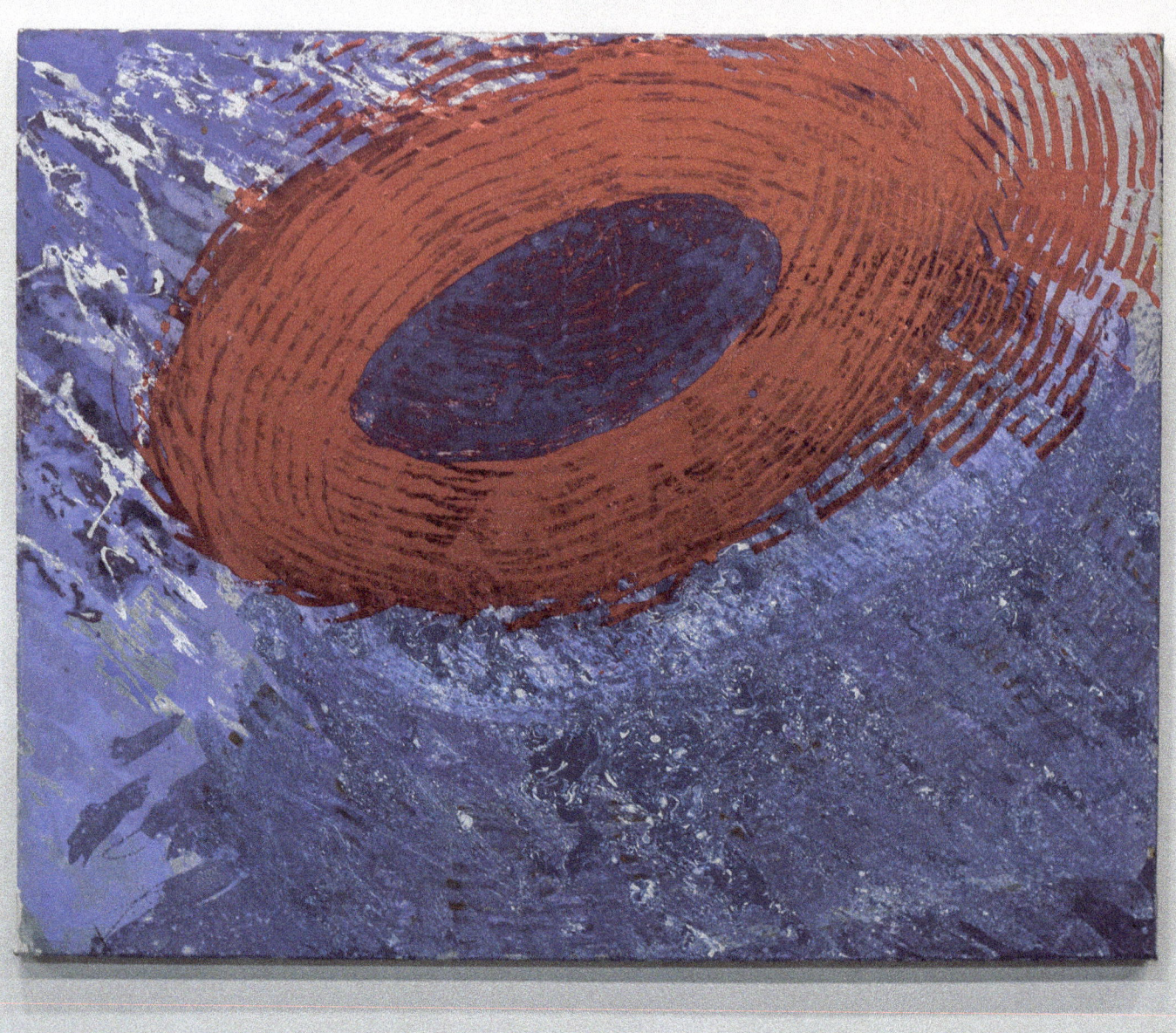

Red Spinner. 2009. Mixed media on canvas, 24 x 30 in.

while spontaneous, is not haphazard. The crumpled folds and furrows of these two reliefs, aided and abetted by singing colors and a sensual S curve in the latter, and the staccato blue-black palette of the former, are at once chromatic and aural. One senses in McGhee's visual tunes, among others, Duke Ellington's gestural sweeps, Charles Mingus's mercurial tempo shifts, Delta blues slurs, and molten African rhythmic riffs.

Other conventions he abandoned were the brush as a means of applying paint and, periodically, a framed canvas as his primary surface. Rather, McGhee has poured, spattered, scrubbed, and mopped, fashioning a DIY inventory of notched, hard-edged implements to spread and flow pigment onto window shades, fiberglass, wallpaper, cardboard, and almost any surface to which paint will adhere. He allows his intuition and the natural viscosities and properties of materials to determine their own pictorial destiny.

For a period, McGhee's utilitarian, paint-mixing sticks became the objets-d'art themselves. The humble, multicolored acrylic- and enamel-encrusted sticks, attached to each other in dazzling structural compositions, are then wall-mounted to maximum effect. *Ring of Fire* (2006), for example, comprised of a crisscrossing assemblage of sticks arranged in a circle, alludes to the unifying symbol often invoked in the artist's vocabulary; *Self Portrait* (2008), a less formal arrangement of sticks, seemingly hurriedly composed, is as gnarly as *Ring* is refined.

Lately, McGhee has come full circle and returned to the human figure. It never entirely vanished from the artist's work but was often so highly symbolized as not to be apparent unless searched for. These recent iterations are acrylic-on-paper studies of the African American female form. They are voluptuous, uncorseted, unashamed, and free from the anorexic strictures of Western notions of beauty. Like all of McGhee's art, their images are shaped at the moment of conception. As muses and prompters of memory, one senses both their physicality and the wonder of their creation. Two of these 2017 images are studies in contrast, utilizing sharply hued backgrounds to highlight the figure-filling forms. *Swimmer* is a study in graceful fluidity with just a dash of blue to establish locale, whereas *Hush* depicts a figure at once authoritarian—note her emphatically pointing finger—and playful.

Like all else that happens in his work/play space, each time McGhee climbs the stairs to his studio overlooking the Detroit River and Belle Isle, he is in search of new ways not to make art as he did the day before. Whether the day's results are abstract, figurative, or somewhere in between, they are sure to embody the cyclic nature of his ever-evolving creative practice. After all, as the artist succinctly observes, "We are visible in all forms of nature."

BILL HARRIS, MARCH 2017

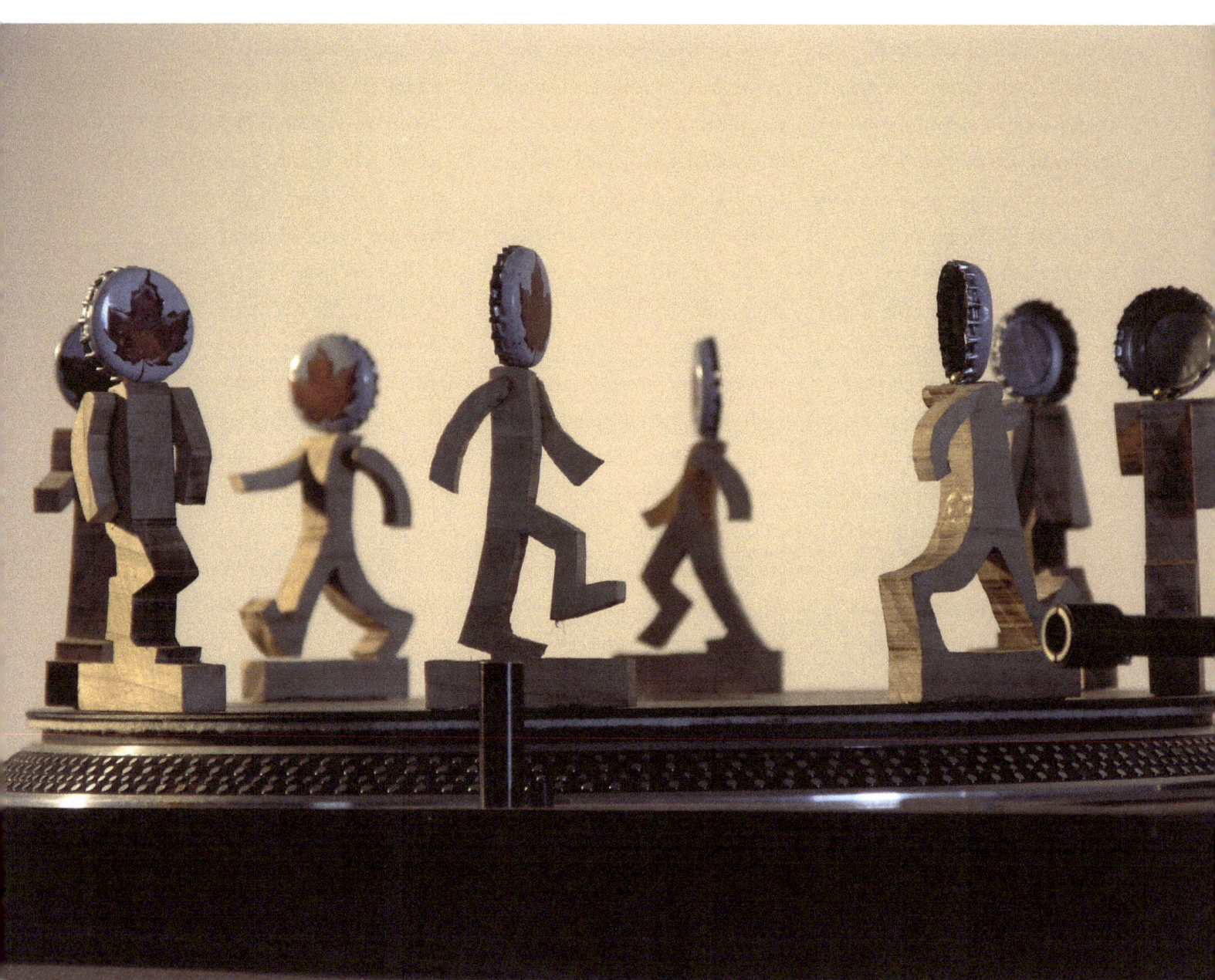

Phi. 2009. Zoetrope (wood, beer bottle caps, strobe light, and turntable).

Born Union, New Jersey, 1957
BFA, Philadelphia College of Art;
MFA, California Institute of the Arts
Lives in Detroit

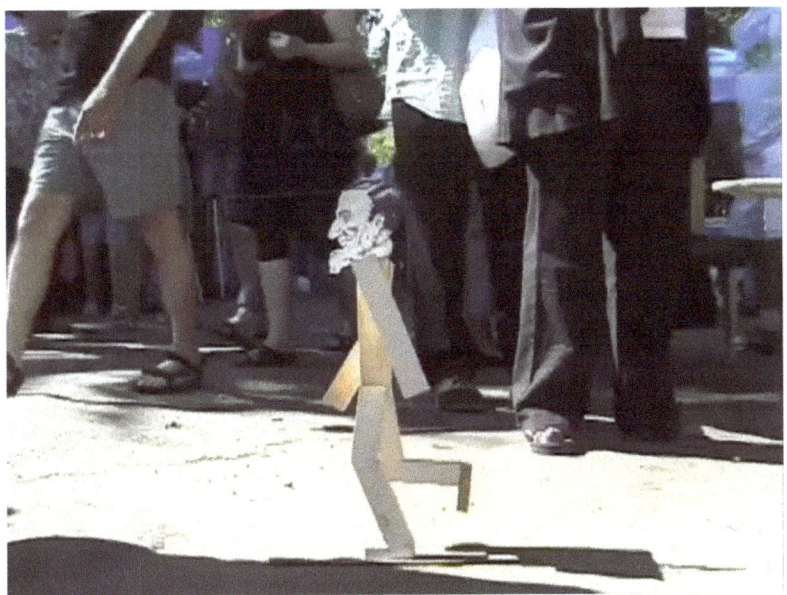

Still from the stop-motion animation *HERE COME 'DA JUDGE.* 2007. 4 min., 2 sec.

To animate is to create the illusion of movement. To bend and release a flip-book and watch the images flicker to life one page at a time is to distill the essence of something that has fascinated Gary Schwartz since childhood. Hand-drawn animation, flip-books, mutoscopes, camera obscuras, zoetropes, and (especially) stop-motion animation: he is endlessly captivated by any nondigital process that can be used to quickly create animated works—and he is never slow to tell you his definition of "quick," which is to "create faster than I can think." Schwartz is a perpetually moving whirlwind of creativity, who edits as he goes, uploads everything to his voluminous YouTube channel, and never revisits old projects.

Schwartz can create so spontaneously because his application of the fundamental building

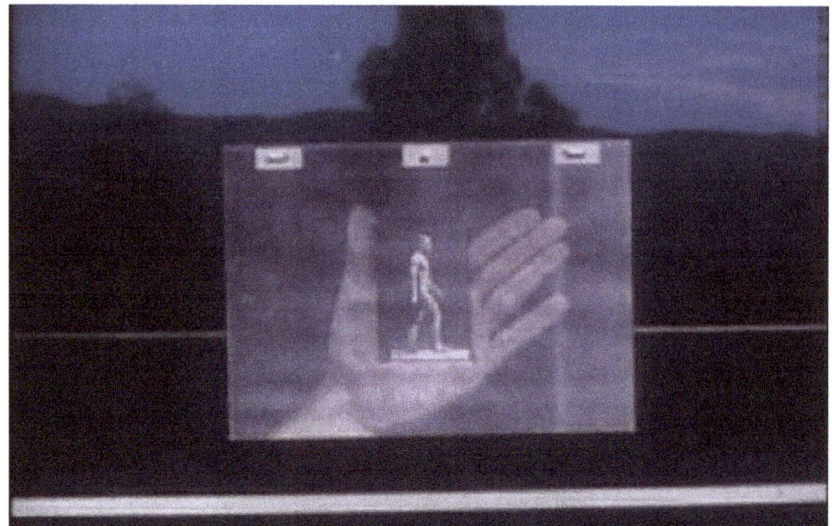

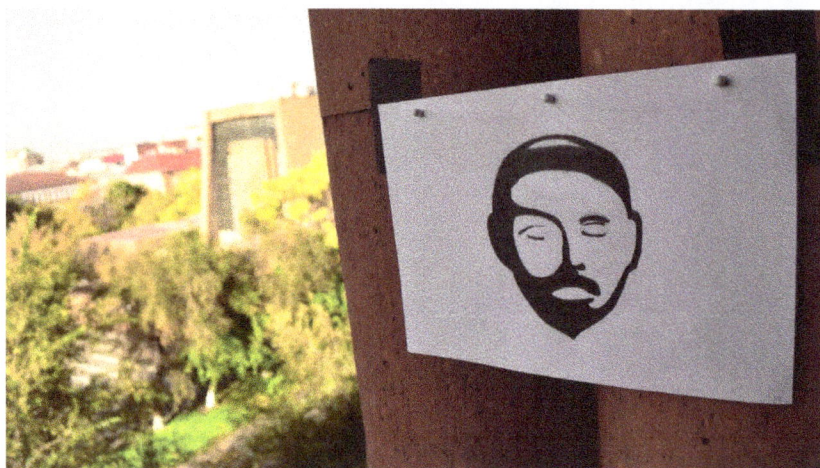

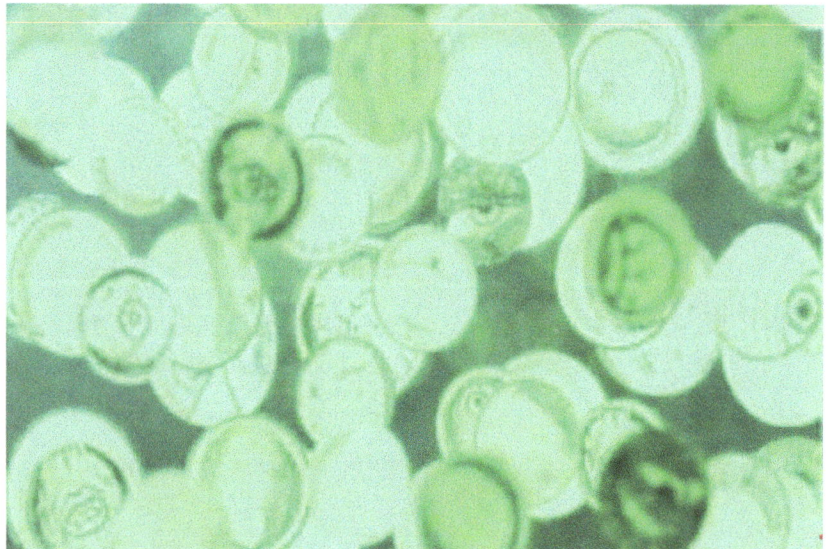

blocks of animation has become habitual. His works often explore a subject by focusing on an iconic figure and having it travel through a terrain representing that subject. For example, the Academy Award–nominated short film ***Animus*** (1982) uses the seminal Eadweard Muybridge stop-motion images of a naked walking man as a device to march relentlessly through the history of animation itself. A representative sequence begins with a clip of Edison's historic kinetoscope recording of a man sneezing, which morphs into a hand-animated version of that clip's final frame, which is then squeezed (in a very Monty Python–esque manner) by the artist's forefinger, before transforming into a handheld movie camera and then a piece of paper, which in turn dissolves, allowing Muybridge's walking man to reemerge pacing the rooftop of the Philadelphia College of Art. A later example is ***HERE COME 'DA JUDGE*** (2007) in which a disorientated Judge Augustus Woodward strikes out from the intersection of Mack and Woodward using his own 1807 plan of Detroit's intricately designed downtown. In turn he visits

(*Top*) Still from the film *Animus*. 1982. 5 min., 3 sec. (*Center*) Still from the stop-motion animation *Exquisite Dilivan*. 2015. 1 min., 36 sec. (*Bottom*) Still from the stop-motion animation *Double, Double, Toil and Trouble*. 2008. 2 min., 5 sec.

Michigan Central Station, Belle Isle, Rosa Parks and Clairmount (on the exact fortieth anniversary of the 1967 uprising that started there), and other Detroit locations, all while mumbling distractedly and incoherently.

There is an autobiographical component to much of Schwartz's animation. The subtext of *Animus* is the story of Schwartz's migration from the east to west coast, and he readily admits that Woodward's confusion in *HERE COME 'DA JUDGE* mirrors his own culture shock at arriving in Detroit after several decades running his own animation company in Hollywood. Schwartz's credits in LA include a (stop-motion) animated introduction to the television special *Donald Duck's 50th Birthday* (1984) and the oft-played Sesame Street short *Alphabet Jungle* (1992). Both are obviously commercial projects but still unmistakably display Schwartz's offbeat sensibility. And if Schwartz was originally disoriented by the move from California, he now considers the transition from Hollywood's ever-present commercialism

to Detroit's low-budget DIY culture to be a liberating experience that has allowed his work to become "sloppier, but far more meaningful."

There is a deeply personal level to Schwartz's continuing interest in walking. As he states in his artist's statement for *Phi*—a zoetrope created for the 2009 show *Walking Distance*—"Walking represents freedom, adventure, exploration, and unknown possibilities . . . . Always moving forward but never getting there. I occasionally lost the ability to walk. I was diagnosed with multiple sclerosis in the midseventies. I continue to explore the inexhaustible question of walking. I haven't got there yet."

Schwartz's collaborations over the years have been diverse and his teaching undoubtedly generous and inspirational. He favors working in locations that are far from the art world mainstream, valuing the open-mindedness and creativity he discovers there. Some examples include the California Prison System and the Detroit School of Art, where he worked with student

animators, singers, and musicians to create works based on lines from Shakespeare (such as the haunting ***Double, Double, Toil and Trouble***, 2008). A particularly rewarding relationship has been with the Tumo Center for Creative Technologies in Armenia. In 2015 he collaborated with students in the cities of Yerevan and Dilijan to create ***Exquisite Dilivan***, a frenetic but fluid meditation on Armenia's metamorphosis from its former status as a member of the Soviet Union into a new national identity. He is currently preparing to return to work on *MISHMASH*, a "mélange of cultural interactions" told through the appearance and sound of the Armenian alphabet. As he enters his seventh decade, Schwartz's lifelong love affair with animation clearly remains undiminished, and his enthusiasm for involving others in his all-inclusive creative process continues to grow.

All of the above mentioned works can be viewed on Schwartz's YouTube channel: ztrawhcsg.

STEVE PANTON, JUNE 2017

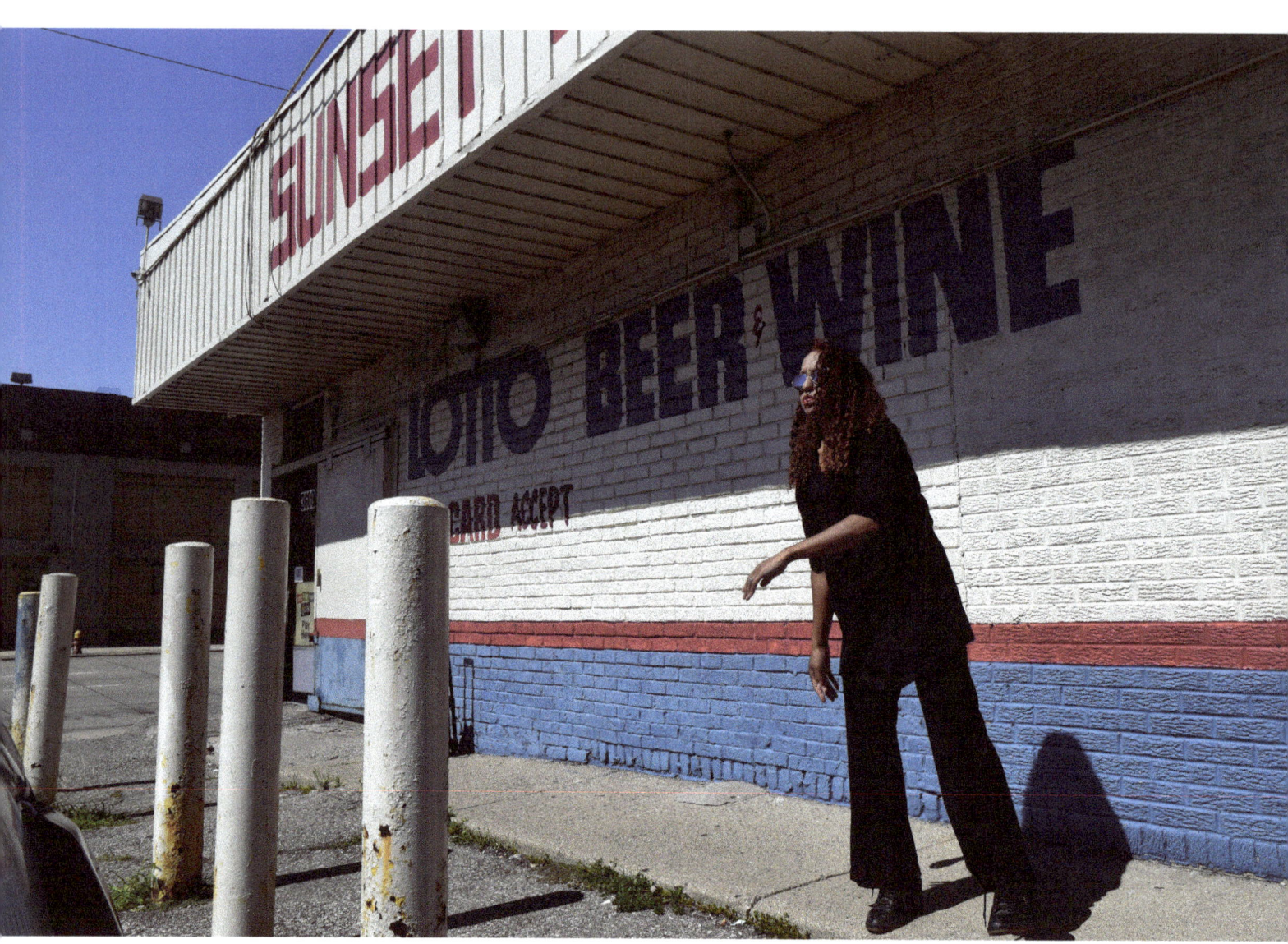

Liquor Store Theatre, vol. 3, no. 3, Untitled 1. 2016.

Born Detroit, 1982
BA, Howard University, Washington, DC;
MA, University of Chicago; PhD, Wayne State University
Lives in Detroit

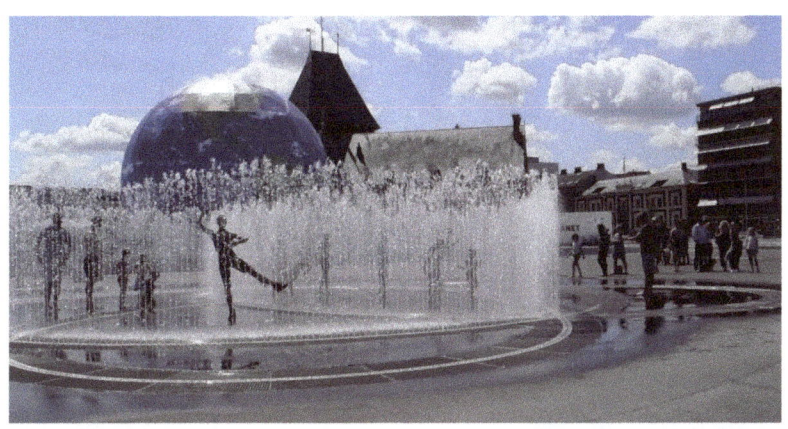

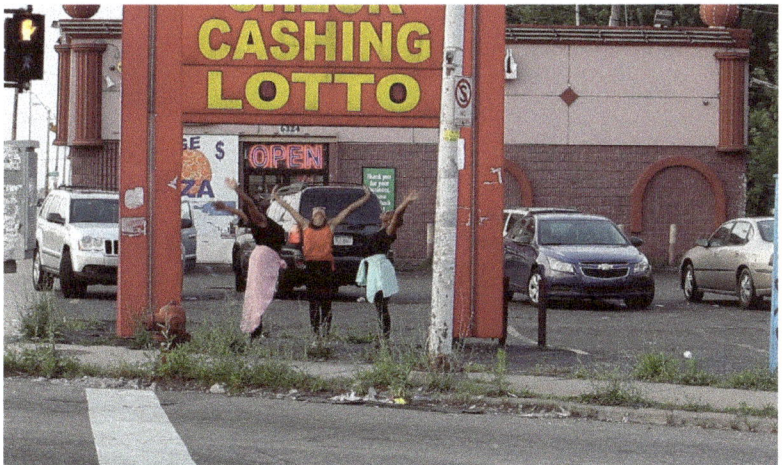

(Top) Havnepladsen Ballet, nr. 7, Untitled 1. 2017. (Bottom) Liquor Store Theatre, vol. 1, no. 3, Untitled 1. 2014.

Art, ever sociable, is always in conversation with something else. One of artist Maya Stovall's primary interlocutors is the city—that ever-shifting concatenation of street, sidewalk, and neighborhood; of people, power, and capital. (This conversation started early; Stovall recalls riding her bike to the Detroit Institute of Arts as a child and developing an "obsession" with the street life she encountered along the way.) For the last four years, she has pursued a related obsession, enacting and documenting an ongoing series of sidewalk performances and ethnographic interviews made near the liquor stores that dot her eastside neighborhood, McDougall-Hunt. Stovall, who trained in classical ballet, holds a master's degree in economics and a PhD in performance studies and cultural anthropology. She approaches the sprawling yet tightly focused **Liquor Store**

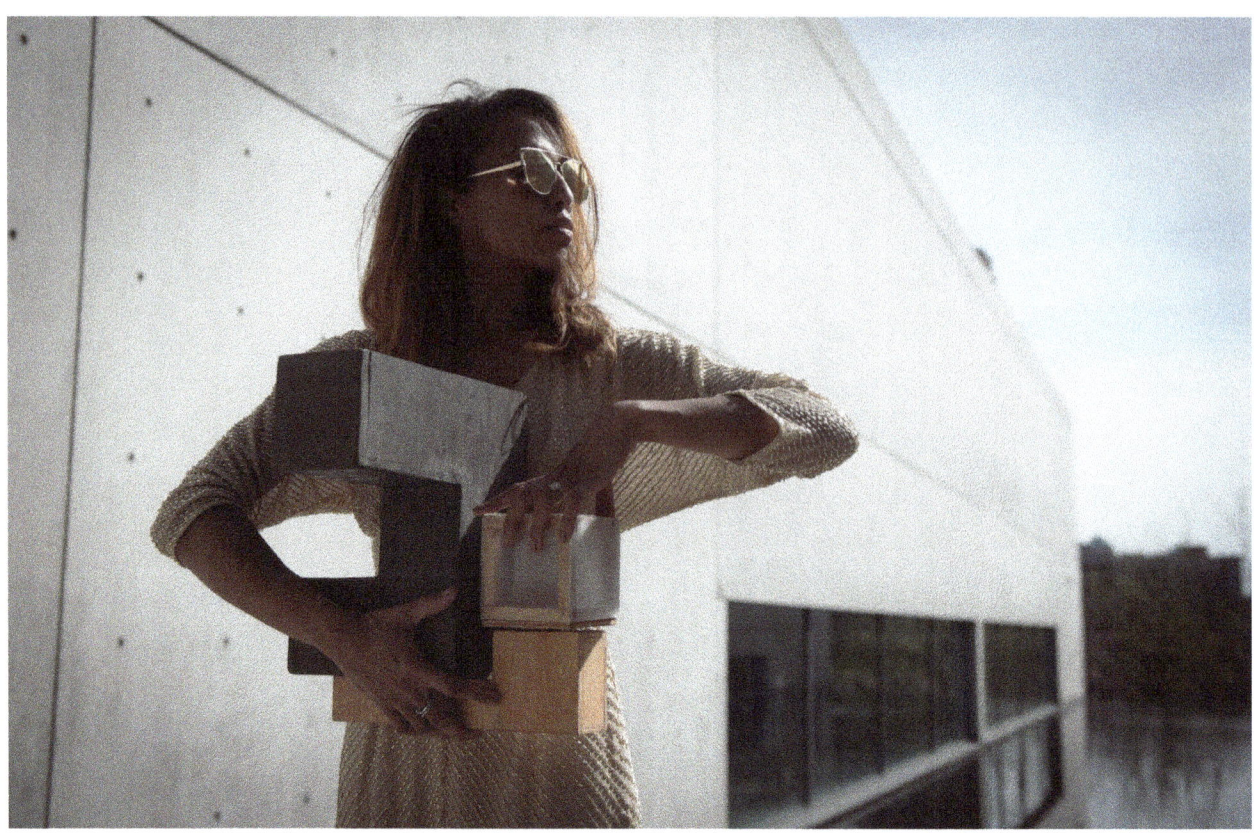

In performance of *Maya Praising Quaint,* April 6–8, 2017, at the Tadao Ando Water Court, Pulitzer Arts Foundation. 2017. Photography by Michael Thomas.

Theatre project as a means to ask what she calls "monumental questions" about human existence via "close, rigorous, devoted, durational looking."

The basics of *Liquor Store Theatre* (2013–present) are as follows: Stovall, as a soloist or with one or two other dancers in tow, shows up, unannounced, outside a local liquor store and begins dancing on the public street or sidewalk. The performances are recorded, usually by Stovall herself or her collaborator, the composer and sculptor Todd "Quaint" Stovall. Inevitably, the dancing

and filming draw interest, and as people wander over to watch, Stovall engages them, asking about their experience of Detroit, their neighborhood, and art. If they are willing, their conversations are recorded and end up in the short videos that Stovall edits and exhibits on her website and in galleries and museums. These are part social documentary and part video dance, their unpolished street-view visuals set to Quaint's pulsing electronic scores.

Watching the videos, one is struck by the banality of the Detroit they represent; this is

neither ruin porn nor the glittering city of the revitalization; it is part of the wide middle ground, the common but undervisualized spaces in which Detroiters go about their everyday business. To be sure, in McDougall-Hunt, the everyday is intricately intertwined with significant socioeconomic distress; Stovall reports the dismal demographics, including a median annual income of $13,000 and an unemployment rate of 40 percent. Under such conditions, as elsewhere in the city, liquor stores flourish. There are, in fact, eight in McDougall-Hunt's 0.39 square miles, providing, as Stovall notes, not only their namesake product, but also household goods, electronics, and, significantly, a space where residents can see and connect with friends and neighbors.

Stovall thinks of *Liquor Store Theatre* as a "backstage view" of one Detroit neighborhood. By using her work to amplify the voices of her neighbors, whom she has summoned with her surprising, surreal street dance, she privileges the underprivileged, moves the marginal to the center, and presents a close-up look at Detroiters who, in turn, present some of the complexities of real life in Detroit. (They muse variously about the past, present, and future; about transformation, development, and gentrification; and about their individual places in this mix.)

It is not possible to plan to attend a *Liquor Store Theatre* performance; like Stovall's earlier Detroit dances, performed in urban gardens, they are intended for the people who happen upon them. But Stovall does perform under more traditional circumstances as well, and two recent pieces help crystallize some of the formal and conceptual underpinnings of her work. Her penchant for serialism and minimalism,

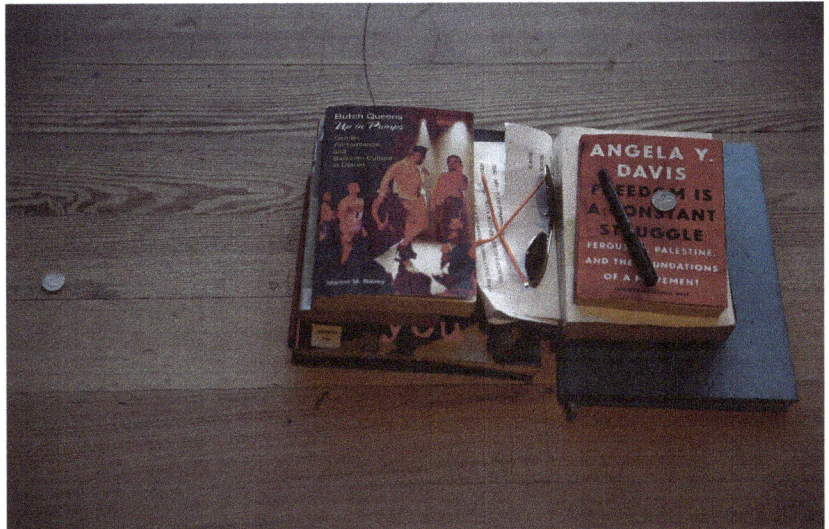

Literature, as part of the performance of *Maya Stovall: MANIFESTO*, May 17, 2017, at the Whitney Museum of American Art. 2017. Photo © Paula Court.

for instance, is laid bare in **Maya Praising Quaint** (2017), a simple, obsessive dance staged at the Pulitzer Arts Foundation in St. Louis that found her standing, holding one of Quaint's interactive sculptures, and, for 360 minutes over the course of a weekend, using her hand to repeatedly rotate a piece of it. **MANIFESTO** (also 2017), performed at the Whitney Museum in New York, was a series of ten tableaux that included chance-based readings of various theoretical texts that have informed *Liquor Store Theatre*, daylighting the feminist, queer, and Marxist currents that swell beneath it.

Stovall's work in *Liquor Store Theatre* has been widely seen (not least through its inclusion

in the 2017 Whitney Biennial) and Stovall, starting from her center, is taking the opportunity to "envelop Detroit in a global conversation" and to do what she does locally elsewhere. Currently, she is in Aarhus, Denmark, where she is daily enacting her **Havnepladsen Ballet** (2017). She's dancing in a fountain in a public square, recording the performances, and interviewing people who stop by, getting the street-level skinny about life in Aarhus, Denmark, and the EU. The context is different, but the impulse is the same: to dance, to inhabit a place, to start a conversation—to "think," as the artist puts it, "in multiple ways at once."

MATTHEW PIPER, JULY 2017

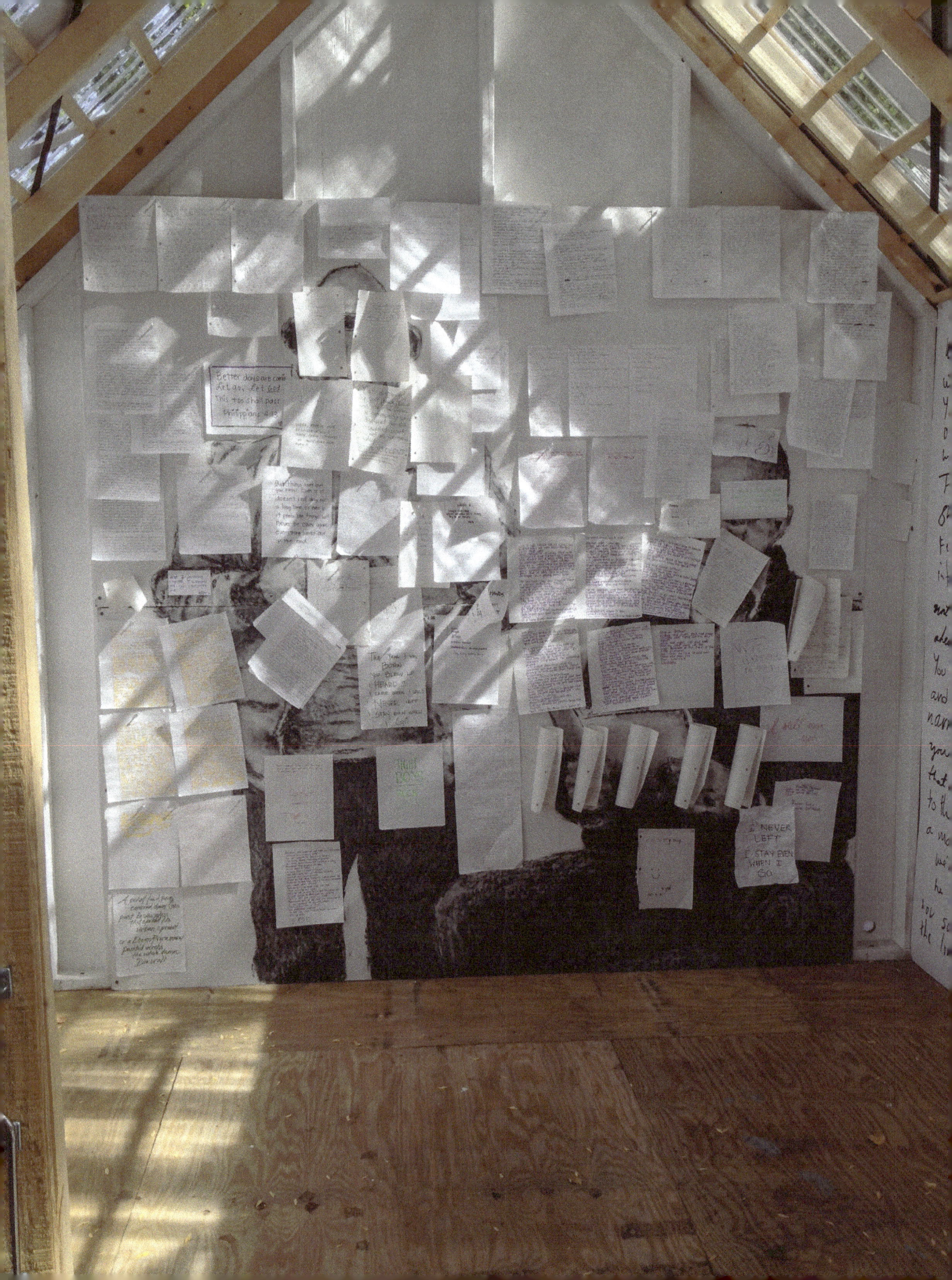

Born Kansas City, Missouri, 1981
BFA, Kansas City Art Institute; MFA, Cranbrook Academy of Art
Lives in Detroit

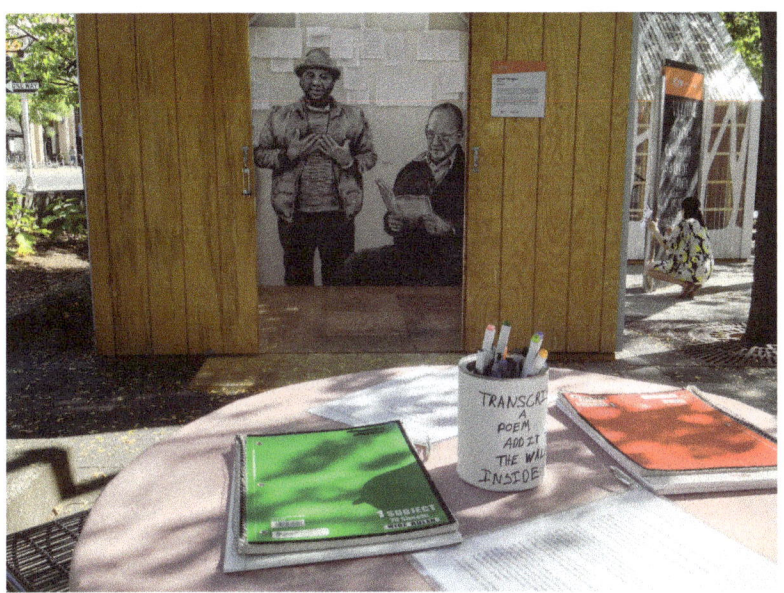

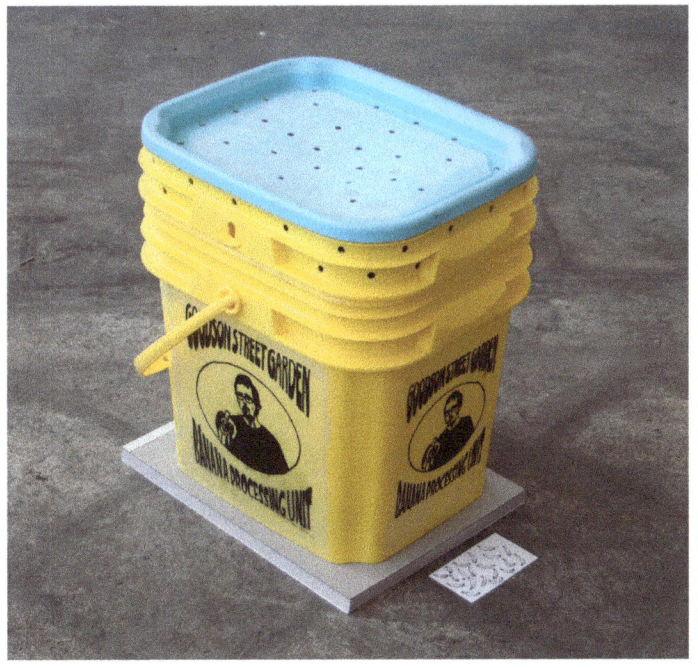

Andrew Thompson considers art to be his "life-organizing principle." It is, for example, how he researches topics that interest him, how he collaborates with people he likes, how he remains untroubled by the question of what to do with surplus funds, and even how he investigates traumatic events from his past. Thompson believes there is no inherent meaning in life, and hence we must all create meaning for ourselves and those around

(Top) Five Years Ago . . . . 2016. Social sculpture: Ink, backlit film, charcoal, paper, poetry from David Blair and Philip Levine, and participation, 10 x 10 x 10 ft.

(Bottom) The Goodson Street Garden Banana Processing Unit. 2014. Plastic, newsprint, red wigglers, banana peels, participation, 18 x 14 x 12 in.

(Opposite) Five Years Ago . . . . 2016. Social sculpture: Ink, backlit film, charcoal, paper, poetry from David Blair and Philip Levine, and participation, 10 x 10 x 10 ft.

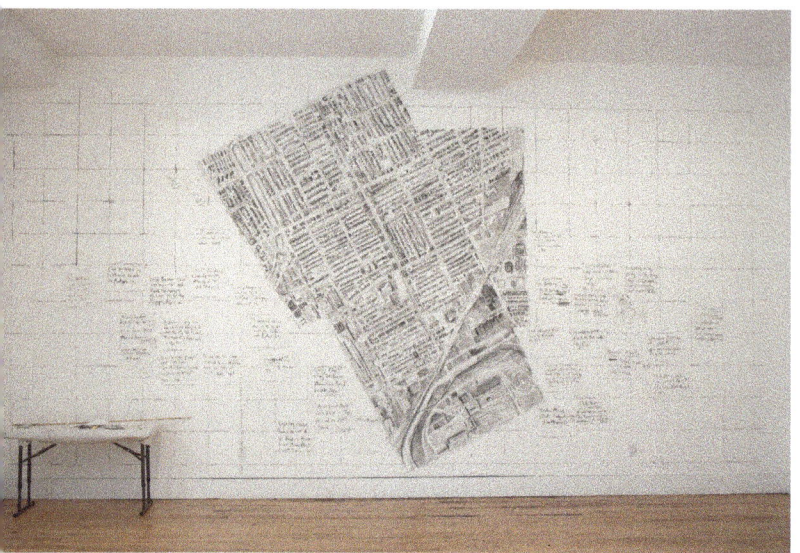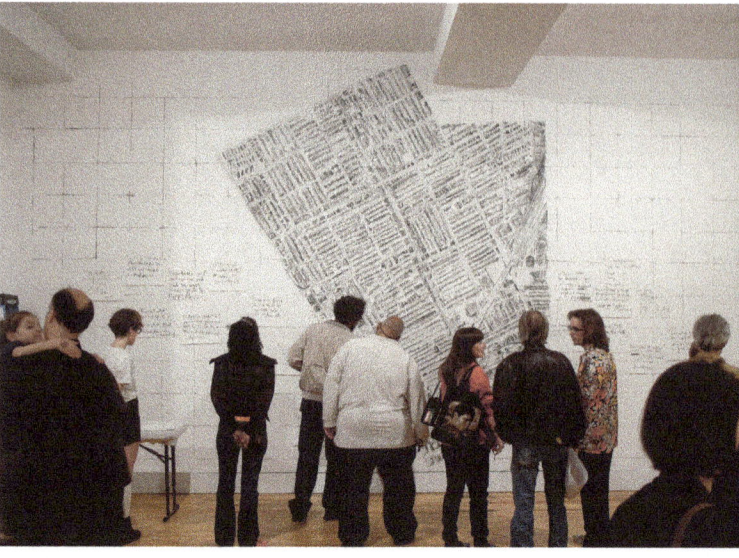
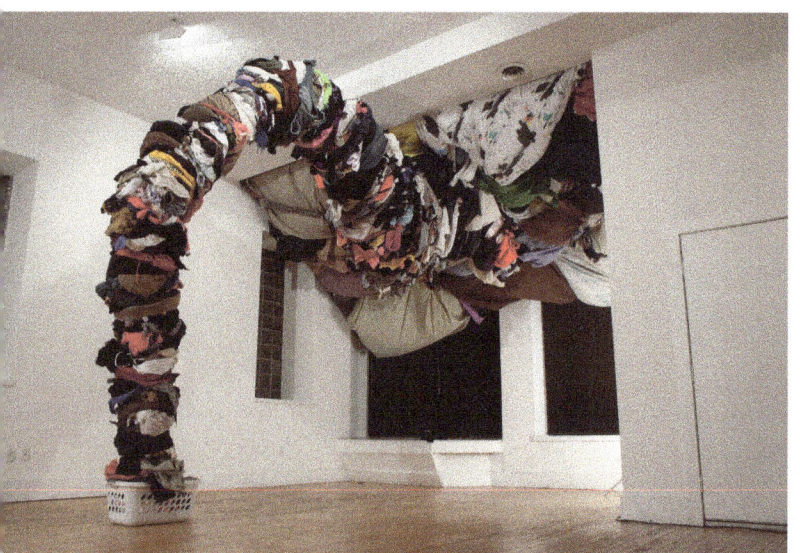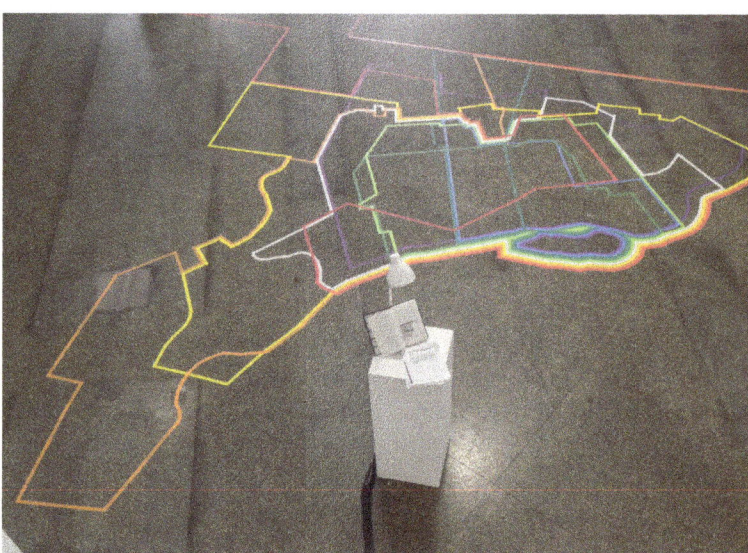

(Top left and right) Redact Hamtramck. 2012. Charcoal, paper, participation, and video documentation, 14 x 22 x 2 ft. *(Bottom left) Clothes Pit: Since You're Gone.* 2011. Used clothing, laundry basket, wood, 14 x 18 x 20 ft. *(Bottom right) Representing Congress: Detroit's Belle Isle District 1893–2013.* 2016. Masking tape, lamp, the book *Rat F**ked* by David Daley, images from Kenneth C. Martis, 5 x 40 x 40 ft.

us. It is a philosophy that propels him along a creative path of his own design, free from the careerist moves often considered essential in the game of being an artist.

Thompson typically prefers to work with recycled materials. He is conscious that art should

first of all do no harm, and that by repurposing landfill-bound material his work already creates value. ***Everyone Says Hi*** (2015), for example, was an ice-cave-like installation in a corner storefront constructed from surplus mail. The title references a favorite

song of Thompson's by David Bowie, one line of which goes, "I'd like to get a letter." It is a supremely sentimental tune that is in tension with the actual origin of the envelopes, which as Thompson puts it, are "almost exclusively from bank and credit

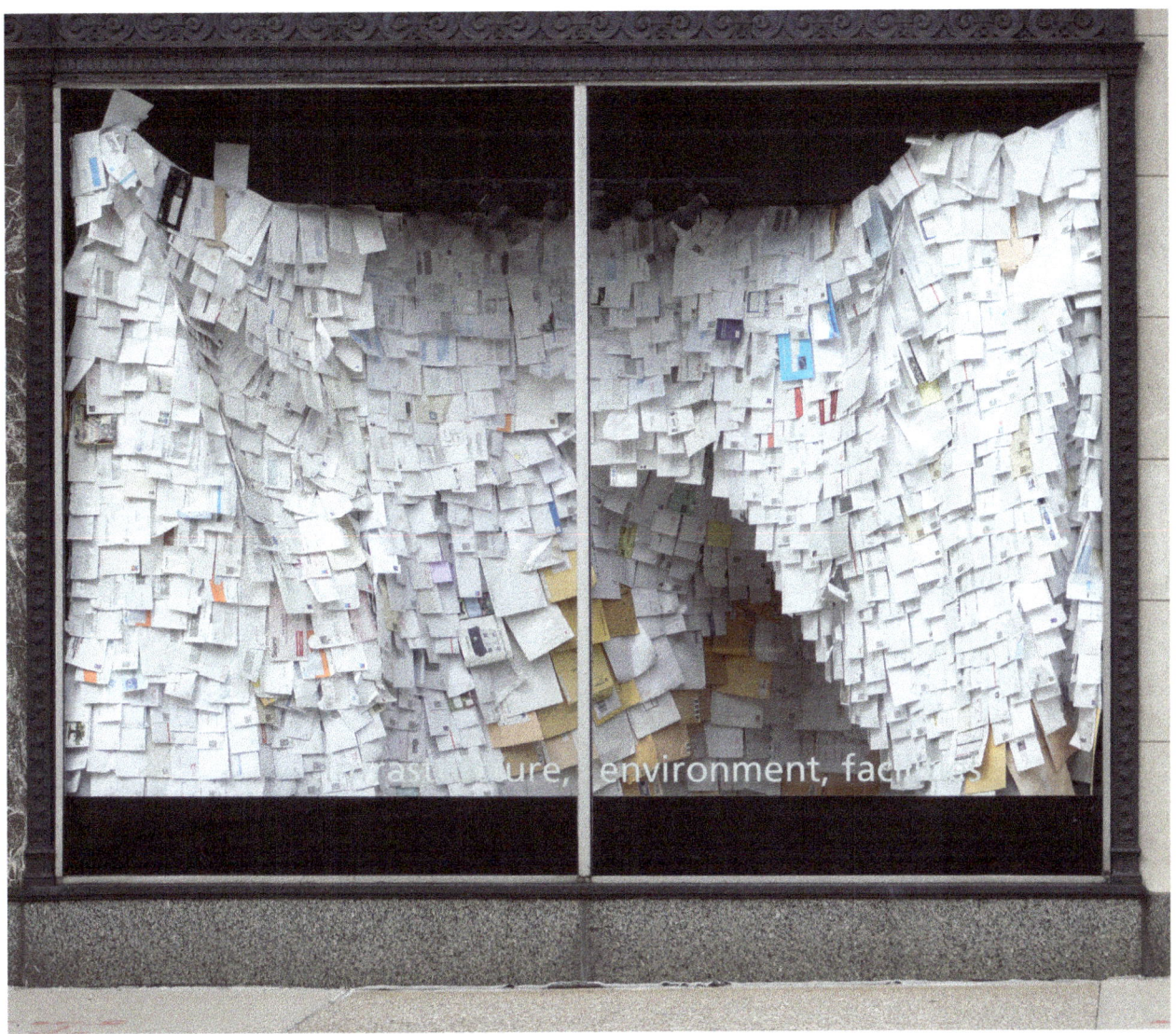

Everyone Says Hi. 2015. Used envelopes and fabric, 9 x 14 x 14 ft.

card statements, junk mail, and debt settlement offers sent to my house," adding that "person-to-person correspondence from loved ones are rare, but they're in there" and that "the piece is a conflation of my desires, a wish list of wanting to have meaningful, intimate interactions but instead being overwhelmed by, and embedded within, a culture of consumerism and credit. I want more than I give; I spend more than I have. All the creditors say 'hi.'" Like much of Thompson's work, it has elements of both comedy and tragedy.

There is an educational and discursive element to much of Thompson's art. In 2016, he was inspired by an investigation of contemporary gerrymandering to explore how the congressional boundaries surrounding his Eastern Market home have evolved over time. The resulting work, ***Representing Congress: Detroit's Belle Isle District 1893–2013,*** used colored painter's tape to construct the historic boundaries on the floor of a large temporary gallery space. The piece is simultaneously a criticism of the

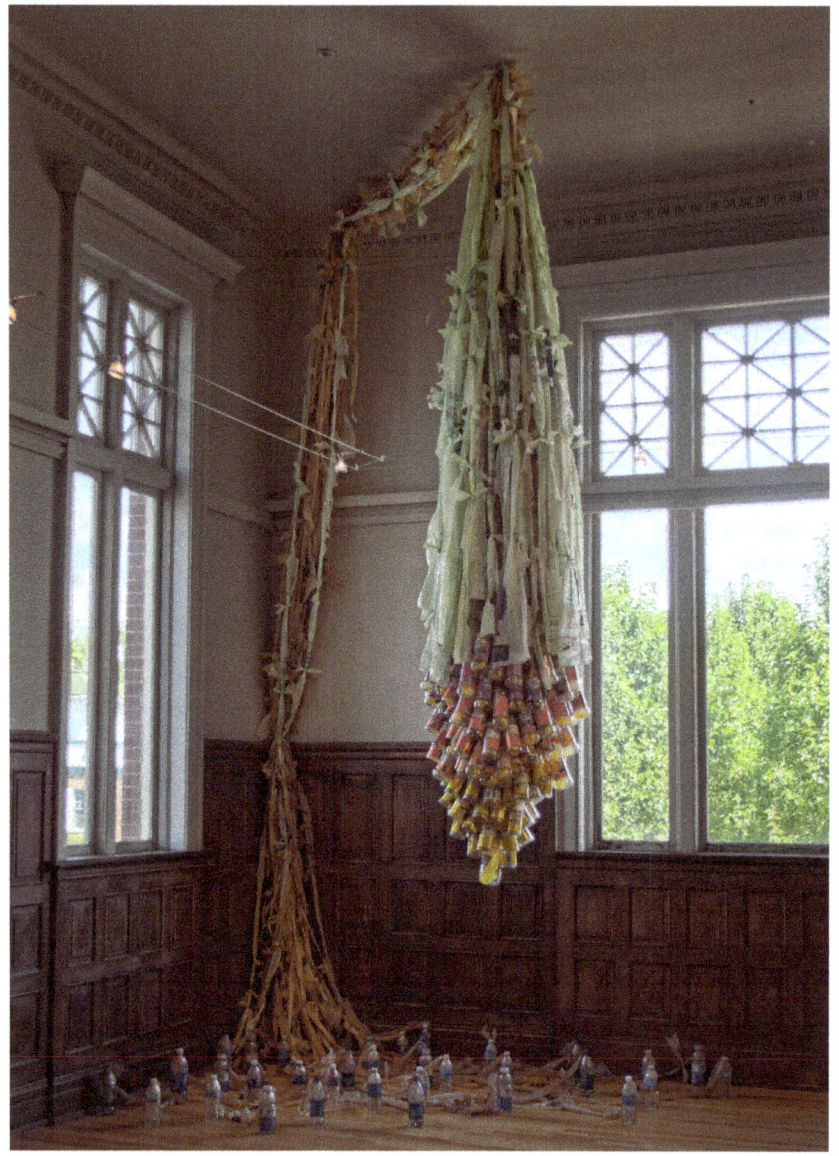

state of politics, a meditation on the fragile nature of contemporary American democracy, and a reflection on the etymology of the word "draw"—what does it mean to "draw" an electoral boundary in a time when they are determined by voter pattern modeling and optimization algorithms, and what does it mean for an artist to reclaim the action of drawing?

Thompson often invites others to contribute to the making of his art. For example, *Clothes Pit: Since You're Gone* (2011) used clothes donated by friends to construct a fourteen-foot-high swirling "tornado" emerging from a clothes basket on the gallery floor; *Redact Hamtramck* (2012) was a large-scale charcoal drawing / stop-motion animation that showed how an aerial view of the eponymous city evolved from 1949 to 2012, and which acted as a framework to collect the memories of gallery visitors; and *Five Years Ago . . .* (2016), in which recent

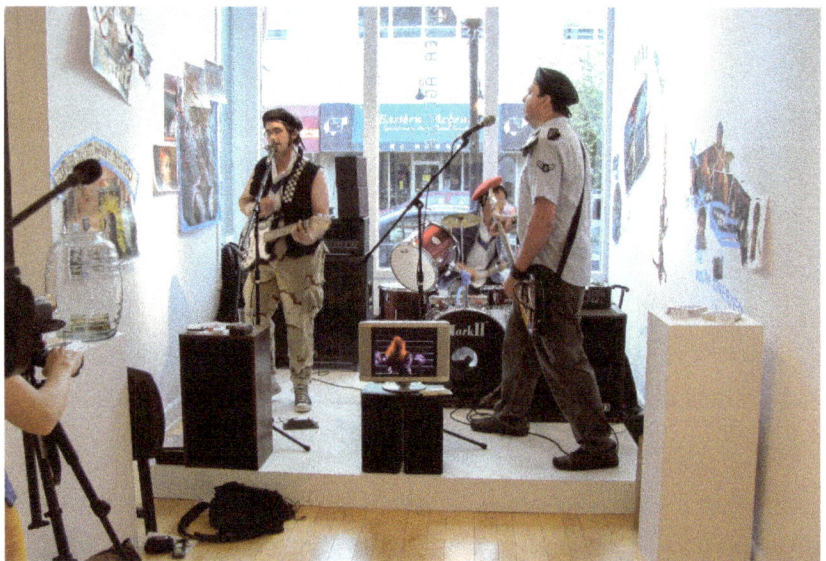

(Top) Untitled (Anton Art Center). 2012. Used grocery bags, used water bottles, water from the gallery, 16 x 8 x 8 ft.

(Bottom) The He-Bops (Play Cyndi Lauper in the Style of the Clash). 2008. Live band, stage, wall collages, video, 8 x 8 x 8 ft. Photography by Jack Summers.

arrivals to the city transcribed poems from two iconic Detroit writers—"Detroit (While I Was Away)" by David Blair, whose untimely death in 2011 was a major shock to the city's creative community, and "What Work Is" by Phillip Levine, who became America's poet laureate that same year—in a powerful metaphor for the continuous evolution but fundamental resilience of Detroit's cultural memory.

Thompson's art is rarely confrontational, but often exhibits a deadpan subversive quality that works to deflate the cultural pretensions or rule set of a given situation. For example, *Untitled (Anton Art Center)* (2012) showed Thompson circumventing a gallery rule that limited artwork height to avoid interference with the lighting, and *The He-Bops (Play Cyndi Lauper in the Style of the Clash)* (2008) saw him expressing his (totally sincere) admiration for Lauper while gently undermining the seriousness of the gallery setting and "The Only Band That Matters." *The Goodson Street Garden Banana Processing Unit* (2014) was Thompson's contribution to a group show celebrating the humble banana, and encouraged visitors to deposit their banana peels into a composting pot for later reuse in the artist's garden. Its unpretentious nature, and casual inclusion of elements of recycling and participation, make it a prime example of the apparently chaotic, but actually remarkably coherent, work of this prolific artist.

STEVE PANTON, JULY 2017

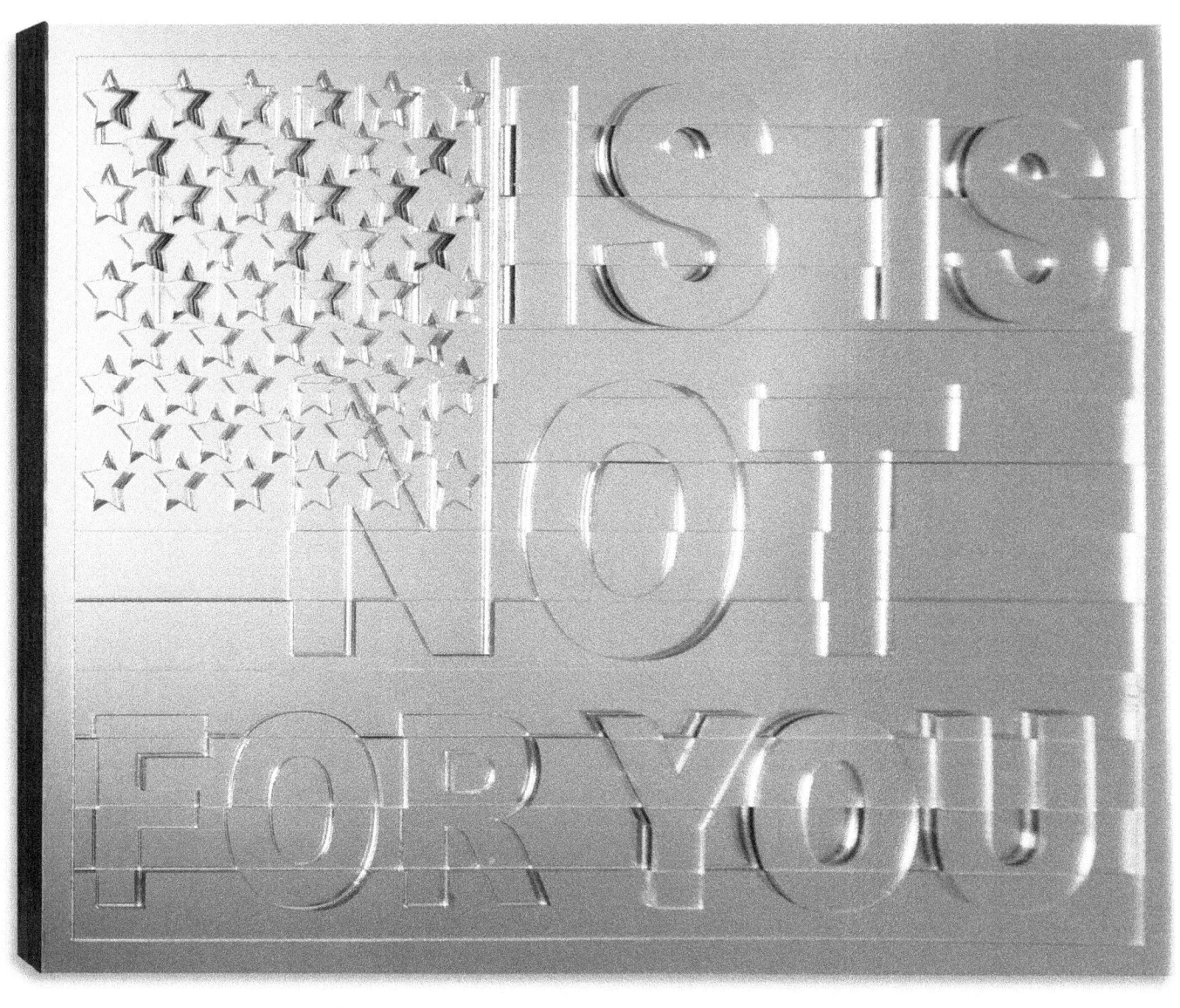

Ain't No Future in Your Front. 2017. Wood and mirrored acrylic, 26 x 38 x 1 1/4 in.

Born Detroit, 1982
BS, Eastern Michigan University; MFA, Cranbrook Academy of Art
Lives in Detroit

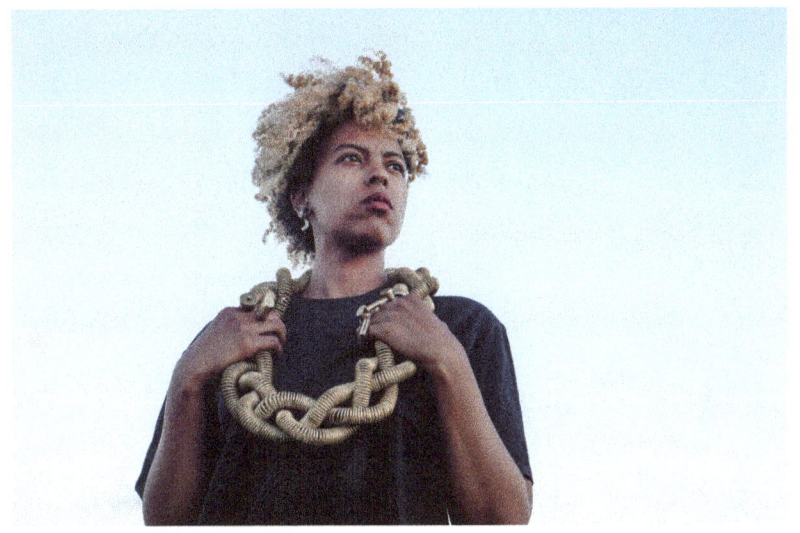

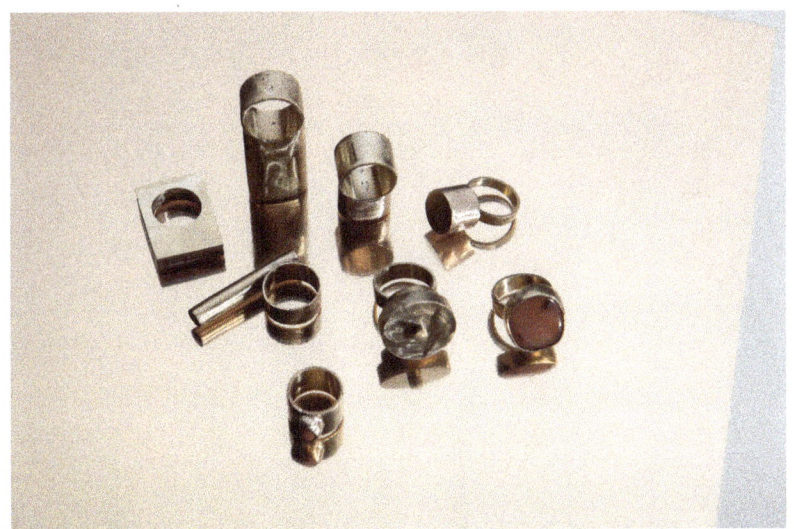

(Top) *I'm Tryin to Be Hopeful but I See What You Doin.* 2015.
(*Bottom*) *Full Circle.* 2015. Brass rings, dimensions variable.

Tiff Massey is an artist whose explanations for her work often defy your overeducated readings. The recurring motifs of head-wearables and hair, for example, are not something the artist relates to Carrie Mae Weems, but rather Massey's wide-ranging experiences of Detroit. After a few of these negated readings, you learn to keep inferences to yourself, rather than risk being corrected.

Massey wears many of her own pieces. Her Cranbrook Academy training as a metal-smith includes the craft of a fine jeweler. While out at Detroit galleries and in her signature videos for her 2015 Kresge Arts in Detroit fellowship and the Society of North American Goldsmiths, Massey can be seen wearing a large **brass ring** on her right hand. The ring looks a bit like an architectural model

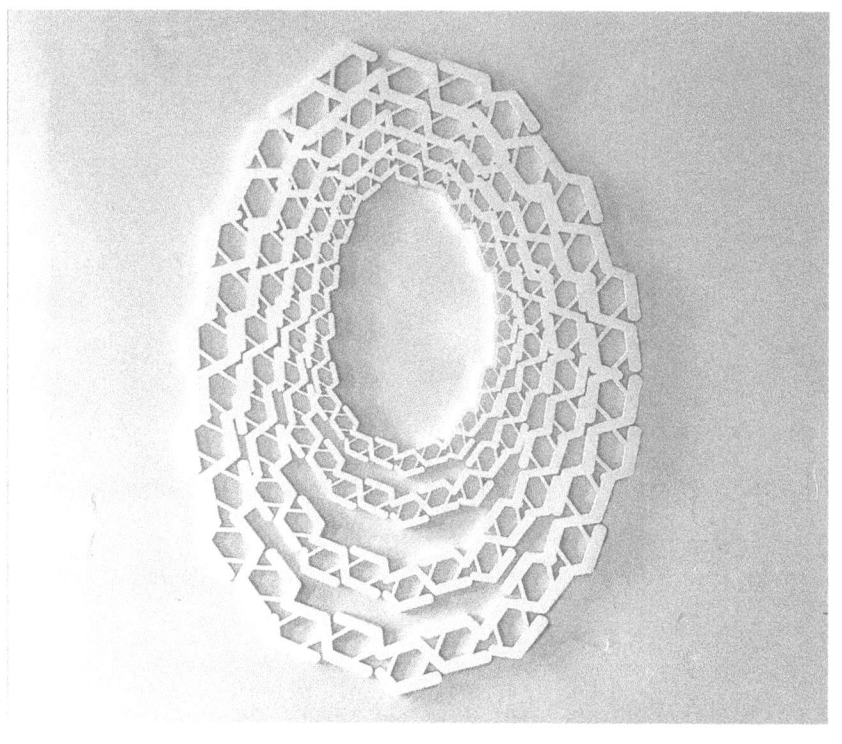

of a skyscraper. The Joe Louis fist and the Renaissance Center skyline—two metonyms for the city of Detroit—now dialogue with each other in my mind

This is the effect of Massey's work. Scales jump, materials that are heavy and cold become liquid and abstract—bodies, sculptures, words, and adornment shift in sequence and significance. For instance—is a large woven piece more of a sculpture, or is it large jewelry, or clothing? This is the case for *Mashoi Pathway I Part II* (2017). The answer changes as one puts the piece on. Massey gestures you toward a mirror. A large swath of precision-cut leather is draped over your shoulders. The artifact exists somewhere between lace and body armor. You are surprised by the physical weightiness. In the reflection, the extent of patterning and the broad fit impart a formality. You square your shoulders.

All of these effects are calibrated by the artist. As Massey says of the weight of her metal

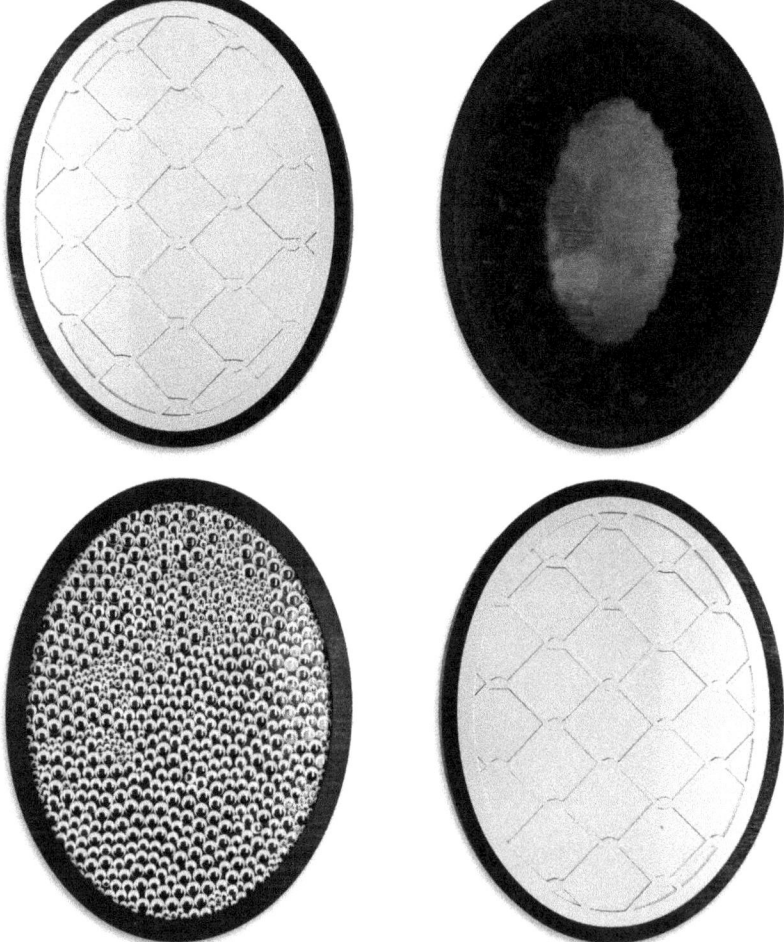

(Top) Mashoi Pathway I Part II. 2017. Wood, 43 1/2 x 31 in.
(*Bottom*) Four Mirrors from the *B(l)ack Then They Didn't Want Me Now I'm Hot They All On Me* series. 2016. Various media and dimensions.

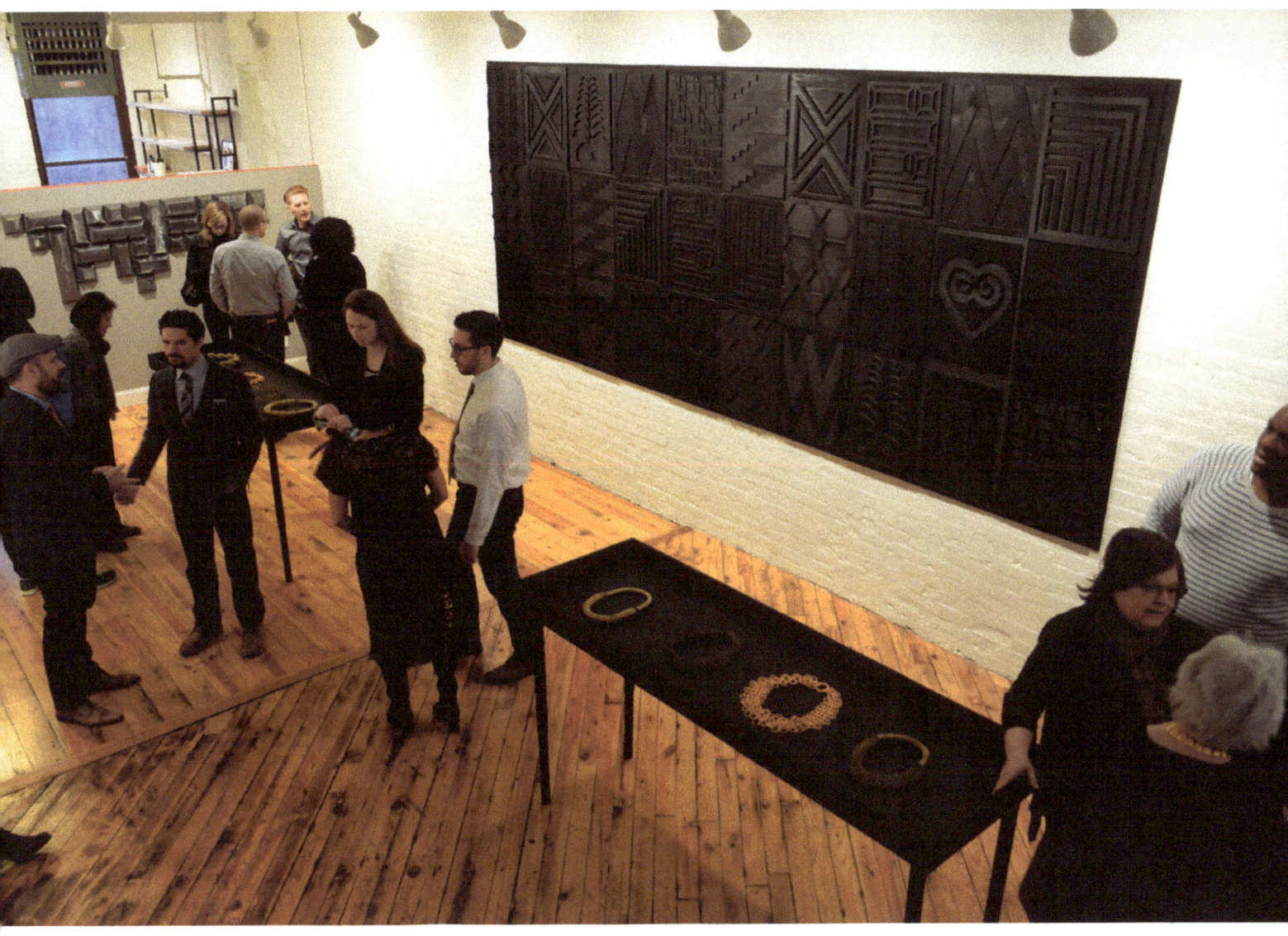

Noir Quilt Code 2 (installation view). 2015. Wood, 180 x 72 in (variable).

objects and wearable pieces, "I want you to feel me." Like her work, this statement vacillates from the physical to the colloquial use, implying empathy or agreement (see Anthony Hamilton's "Do You Feel Me?" or YB Keem's "You Feel Me, N*gga?"). From physical material to the interpersonal, the work modulates between these two modes of "feels." Whether planning a performance and weaving costumes, crafting **bracelets**, or designing a **public sculpture**, this interplay is a repeated operation in the artist's practice, especially around embodiment and the gaze.

Her piece **Ain't No Future in Your Front** (2017) consists of a mirrored face sculpted in relief with the thirteen stripes and stars of the American flag. Placed amid the stars and stripes is also raised text in all capital letters reading "THIS IS NOT FOR YOU." One could trace the lineage of this artwork to Jasper Johns and Glenn Ligon, but, like much of Massey's work, it can also be read as an amalgamation of everyday urban space—an American flag, a

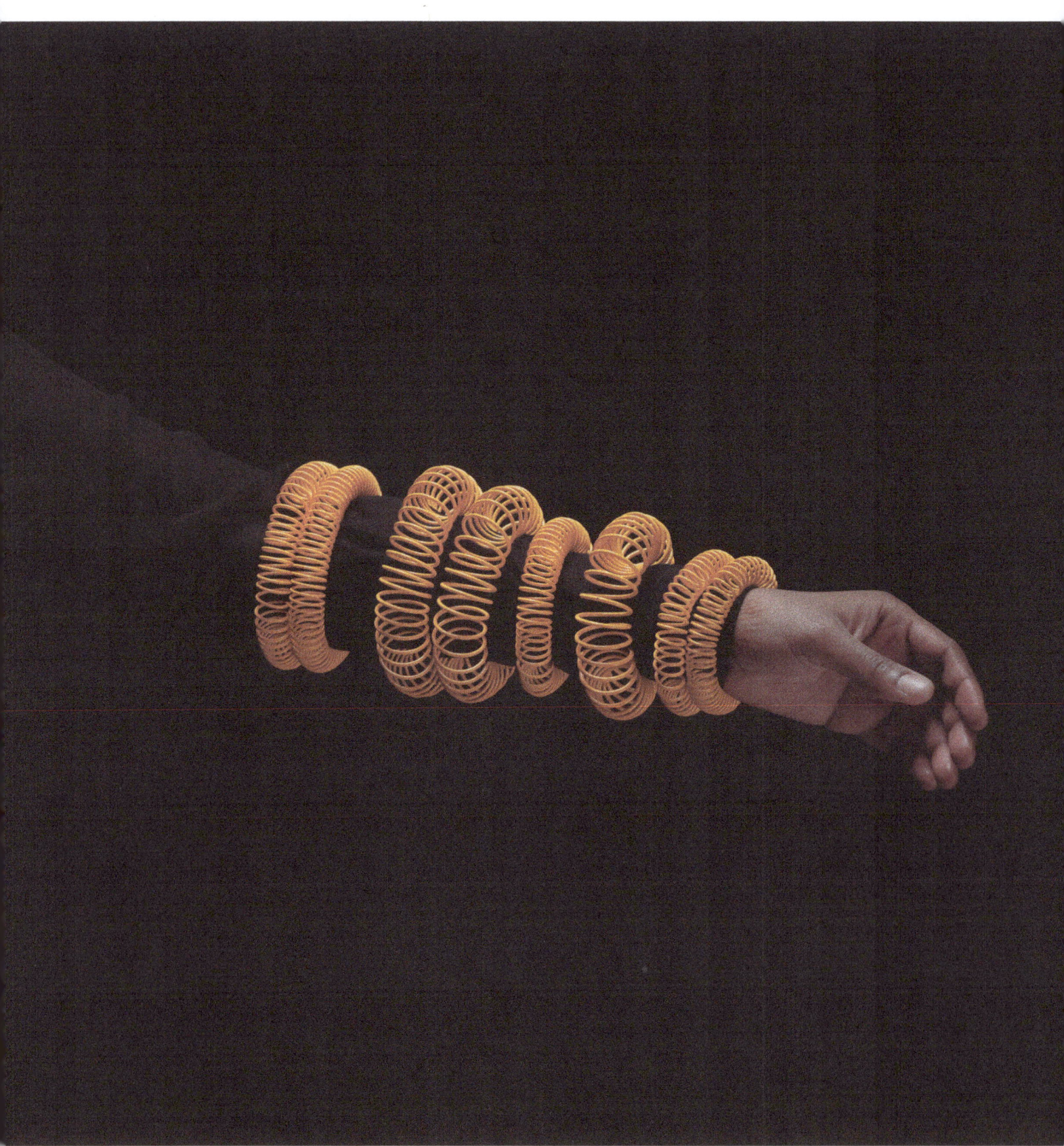

Coils. 2014. Powder-coated brass bracelets, various dimensions.

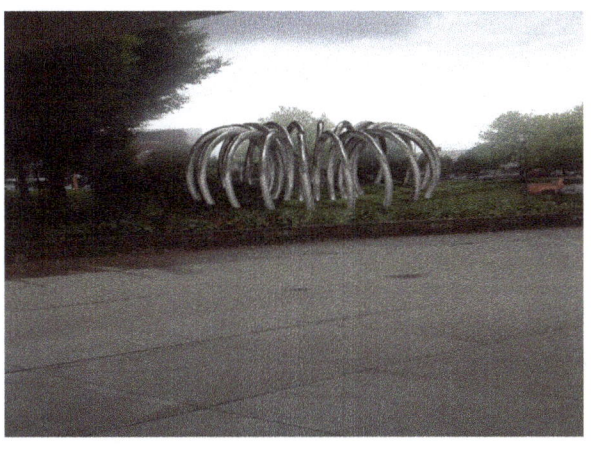 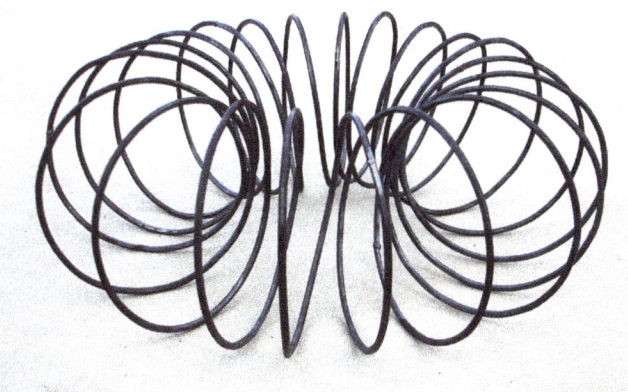

(Left) SPRING rendering. 2017. *(Right) SPRING Prototype I.* 2017. Steel, 39 x 39 x 14 in.

mirror of the scale that could be encountered in a restaurant bathroom, text that could be a street sign or block lettered in the spirit of NO PARKING.

The confluence of the flag and text in the mirror of *Ain't No Future in Your Front* is two-fold. One imagines a subject of the sort that WEB DuBois elucidated more than a century ago—the Black American as a person negated by American forms of citizenship and participation. The American flag is NOT FOR YOU if you are this subject, encountering this artwork and reflected in it. Alternatively, a viewer who regards the American flag as a neutral symbol of citizenship, one who recognizes the flag as symbol without being negated by it, still encounters the same message. "THIS IS NOT FOR YOU." Seeing one's own reflection and the sculpted pattern of a banal flag, one is rejected by the artwork. This artwork is NOT FOR YOU. The piece is then a negative, or double, of itself.

Massey's work objectifies the double consciousness that DuBois unpacked in *The Philadelphia Negro* and Frantz Fanon explicated for a postcolonial world. Many of Massey's works appear twice, changed in material or surface treatment. The seriality performs as a reflection or a negative. Massey's titles are often highly coded and specific, becoming almost small performances of wordplay, in addition to how a piece may directly engage text in the art object.

Massey was educated and trained as a scientist before entering art school and learning the craft of metalwork. Don't sleep on her. She's currently working on a bracelet so large that it makes a public space you can walk through and a 1980s Cadillac that generates its own filmscript. In her own words, this is "finally some shit for us."

V. MITCH MCEWEN, AUGUST 2017

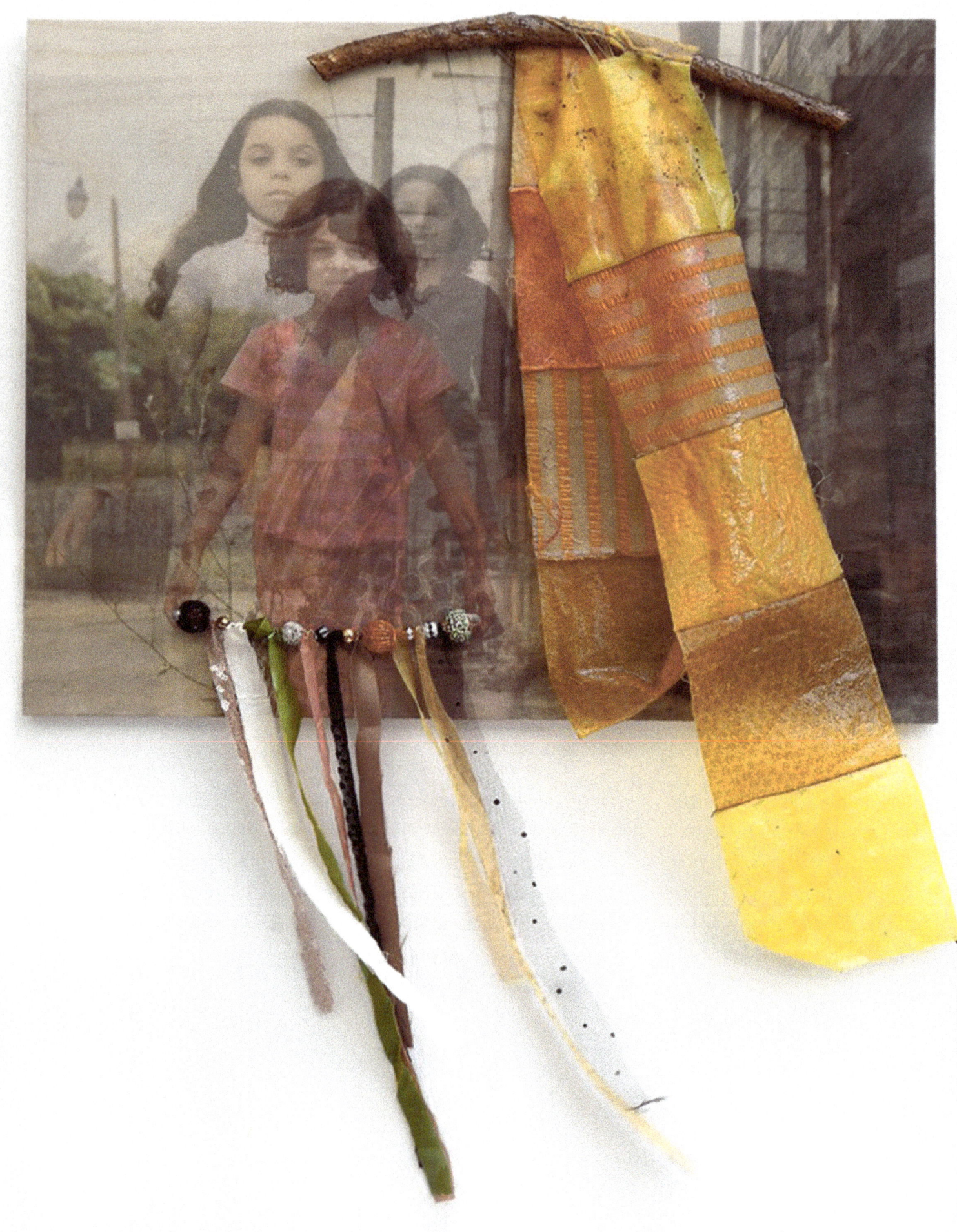

Born Paramaribo, Suriname, 1975
BFA, Cooper Union, New York; MFA, University of Michigan
Lives in Detroit

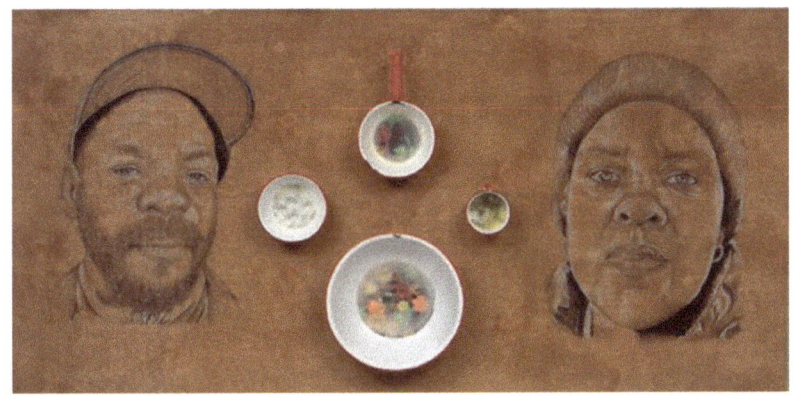

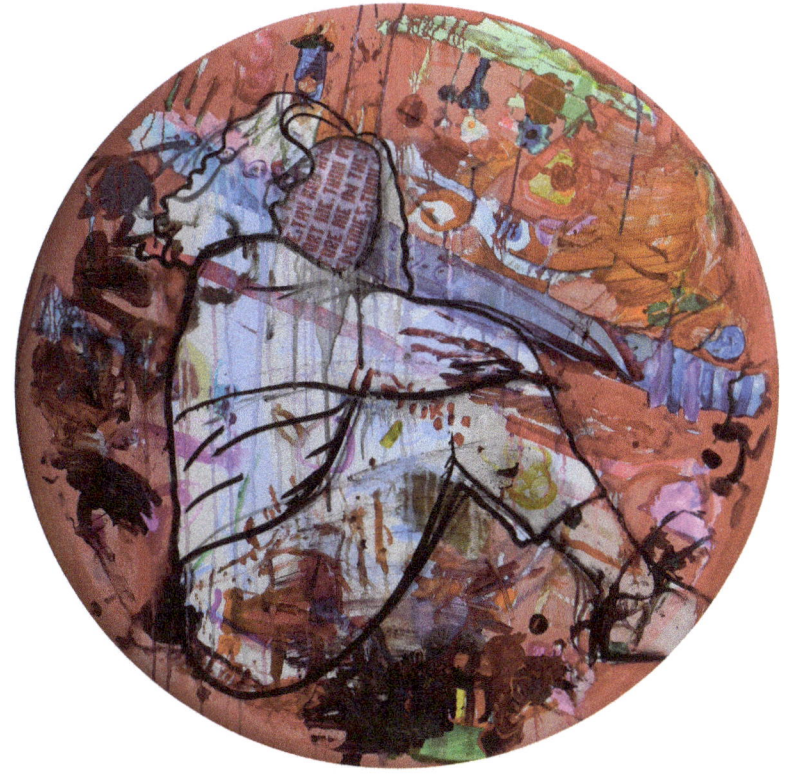

In her recent practice, Detroit artist Yvette Rock presents a series of self-imposed challenges while vigorously engaging with ideas about media and methodology to tell her visual stories. Her processes seem open to these questions: How does one construct a body of work? Where does it begin? Is it a series of investigations or a more concrete endeavor? Is it a thematic undertaking or an accumulation of disparate art-making over time? Rock's approach encompasses all possibilities. Newly created and found materials have made their way onto her studio worktable alongside oil, acrylic, gouache, watercolor, charcoal, graphite,

(Top) Plague of Poverty. 2012. Mixed media on wood, 72 x 36 in.
(Bottom) Battle for Life. 2017. Mixed media, 36 inches in diameter.
(Opposite) Community Conversation with Tenuous Equilibrium #3. 2016. Mixed media on wood, 20 x 30 in.

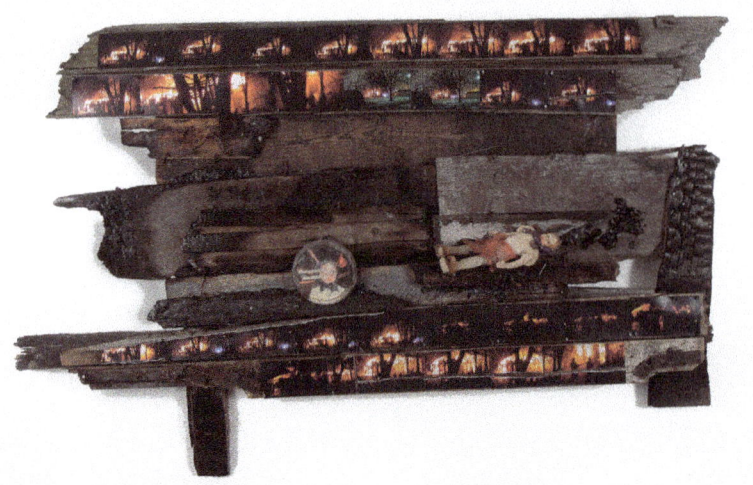

Plague of Arson and Fire, Study 1. 2012. Mixed media assemblage, 72 x 36 in.

Conté crayon, turpentine, damar varnish, linseed oil, printmaking tools and inks, pastels, gesso, medium, and on and on. Over time Rock has sown a rich inventory of resources from which to venture.

Thematically, she has developed a series of works based on the many issues facing the urban landscape seen and unseen, recognized but neglected. In the assemblage **Plague of Poverty** (2012), Rock, a formidable storyteller, sets the stage, building a case for immediate communication between her subjects and the viewer. In preparation for this work, Rock interviewed people living in homeless shelters, listening to their stories and drawing their portraits. The combination of the portraits, beautifully drawn on wood, with the placement of ordinary household objects such as cups, bowls, and plates, establishes an environment. Here the process of expression and documentation creates a sense of immediacy. Rock's intent to present conversations for the viewer is intensified through these chronicles. Reading like a newspaper headline, the artist's conversation moves to the related **Plague of Arson and Fire** (2012) constructions. Assembled from charred planks of wood from destroyed homes, children's toys, and photographs of fires, these remain a startling footprint of urban disaster.

The process of combining several diverse methods such as drawing, assemblage, weaving, and found objects within individual works builds and expands Rock's narrative. In the series *Community Conversations* (2016), the artist has chosen to blend, connect, and combine traditional art materials with created materials not usually regarded or associated with the art process. These include patterned fabric cut into strips and treated with resin, giving the appearance and feel of waxed paper. Wood, plastic, and board have replaced paper as a surface for drawing. Birch printing blocks have become the ground for collage, with photography providing a figurative reference. Rock uses the cloth strips as small banners in the work **Community Conversation with Tenuous Equilibrium #3** (2016). These works accommodate small, handwoven elements such as beads, ribbons, and sequins with black-and-white photography. This seemingly haphazard quality of much of Rock's three-dimensional work defines an important aspect of her approach to art-making. The element of time is addressed as well, as her imbedded stories unfold and the viewer takes into account the use of a range of media. Chronicling the conversation in this way demonstrates the

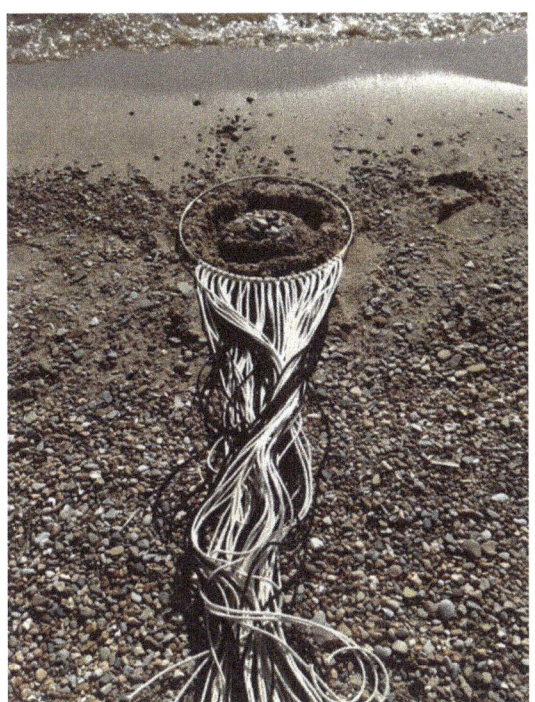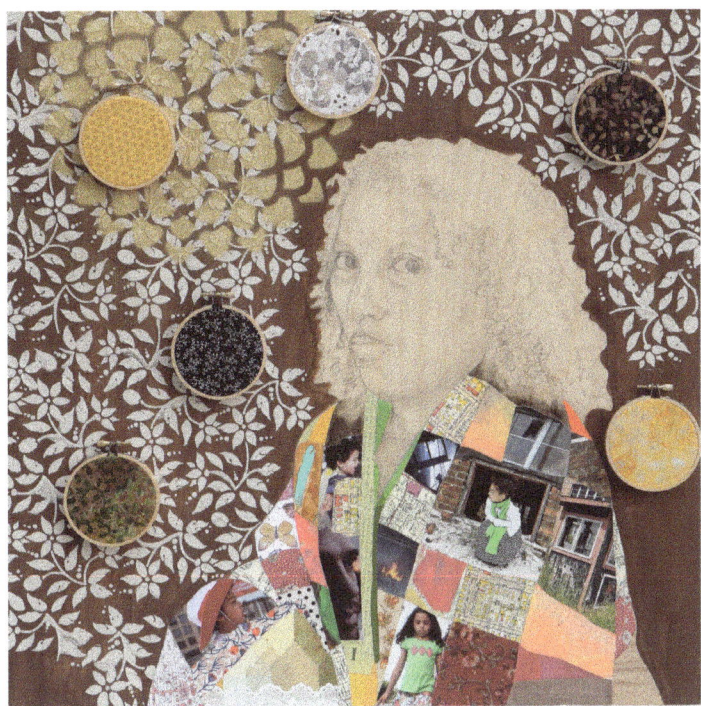

(Left) One. 2017. Mixed media laid over sand and pebbles. *(Right) Self-Portrait.* 2016. Mixed media collage on wood, 24 x 24 in.

artist's willingness to present new paths of understanding while deepening the search for clarity.

Rock creates images that project transparency rather than volume in **Self-Portrait** (2016) and other portraits on wood in one of her current series. The artist maintains tension between forms by employing a neutral palette with the asymmetrical placement of colorful circular elements. Several works in the portrait grouping are on circular wood panels upon which the artist has combined collage and drawing. On other inkless printmaking blocks appear carved patterns, portions of

Detroit city maps and stencils of floral surfaces, found papers, and objects. They are notations for expansion, laying groundwork for the environmental and installation works to come.

The circle is a preferred form within this artist's range, as seen in new paintings like **Battle for Life** (2017). The use of transparency and overlays in these figurative paintings by Rock are joyous and lyrical, potent with color markings. The circular canvases enhance the compositions for her figurative ideas. They are freely rendered, imbued with brilliant, vibrant brushstrokes, yet reminiscent of the classical tondo format.

Within her practice, Rock seeks creative solutions in a myriad of investigations about community and art-making. As she seeks balance within the process, she expands with new conversations as seen in her current circular ground works, including **One** (2017). Working directly into the earth, the artist explores environmental and installation methods by drawing forms into the ground at varying levels, placing stones as markers. This conceptual approach is exemplary of her visionary and ongoing acceptance of new challenges.

SHIRLEY WOODSON, AUGUST 2017

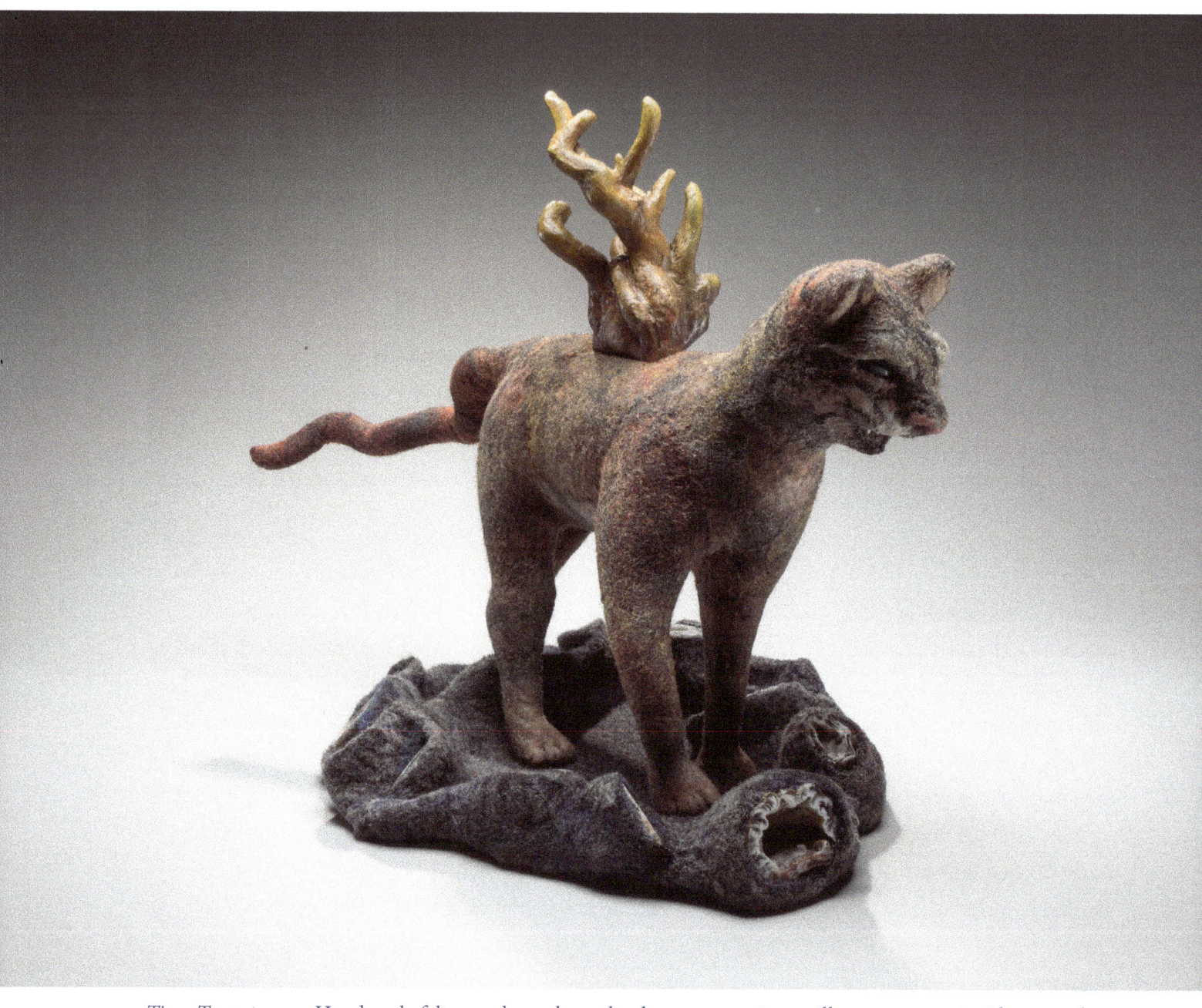

Tiger Teapot. 2013. Handmade felt, wood, geodes, cabochons, porcupine quills, 12 x 19 x 10 in. Photography by Tim Thayer.

Born Brooklyn, New York, 1947
BS, Wayne State University; MFA, Cranbrook Academy of Art
Lives in Pleasant Ridge, Michigan

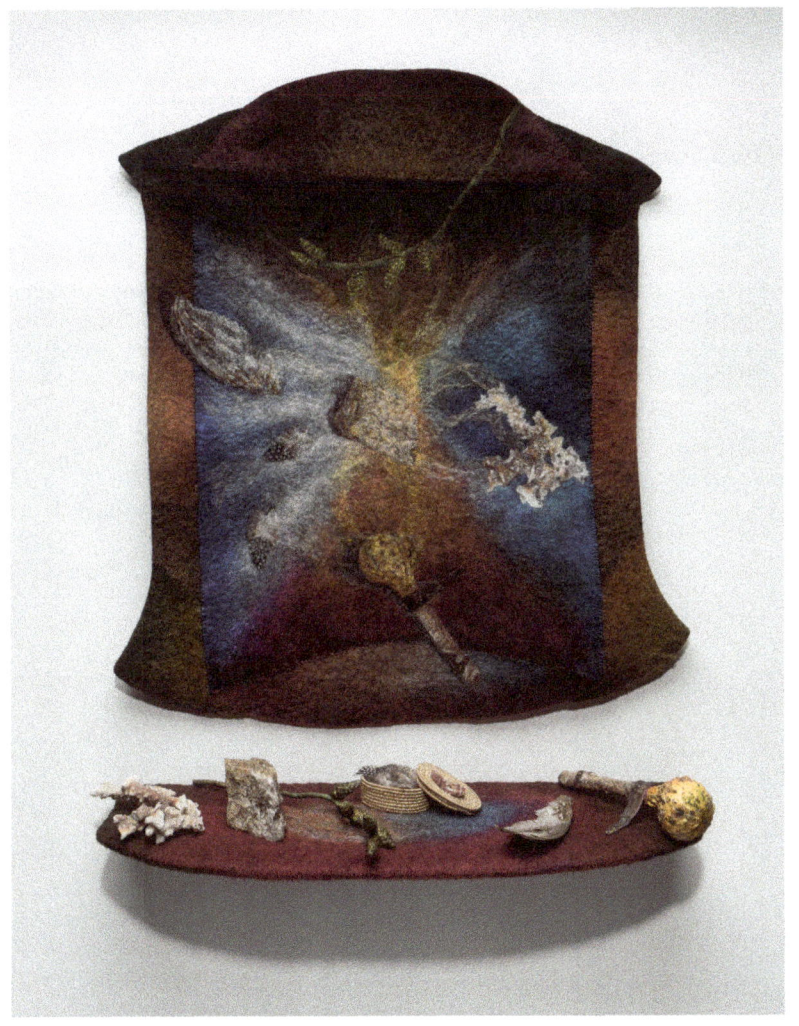

Threshold #3. 2016. Handmade felt, basketry, hand stitching, crystal, feathers, coral, gourd, pine branch, and birch bark, 38 x 28 x 8 in. Photography by Tim Thayer.

In all its darkness, playfulness, mystery, and grotesquerie, the work of Susan Aaron-Taylor embodies a search for wholeness through the embrace of contradictions and dichotomies. Over the last five decades, she has explored dualities through bodies of work that mine the realms of dreams and alchemy, sources that also served the fifteenth-century artist Hieronymus Bosch in his famous *Garden of Earthly Delights*. Both draw on these and other symbolic systems to produce a spiritual cosmogony both terrifying and compelling, imaginative and surreal. But unlike Bosch's painted allegory of humanity's fall from grace, Aaron-Taylor's mixed-media sculptures, constructed of materials such as handmade felt, wood, shells, stones, bones, and beads, are more a search for grace. That search dives into the self and its

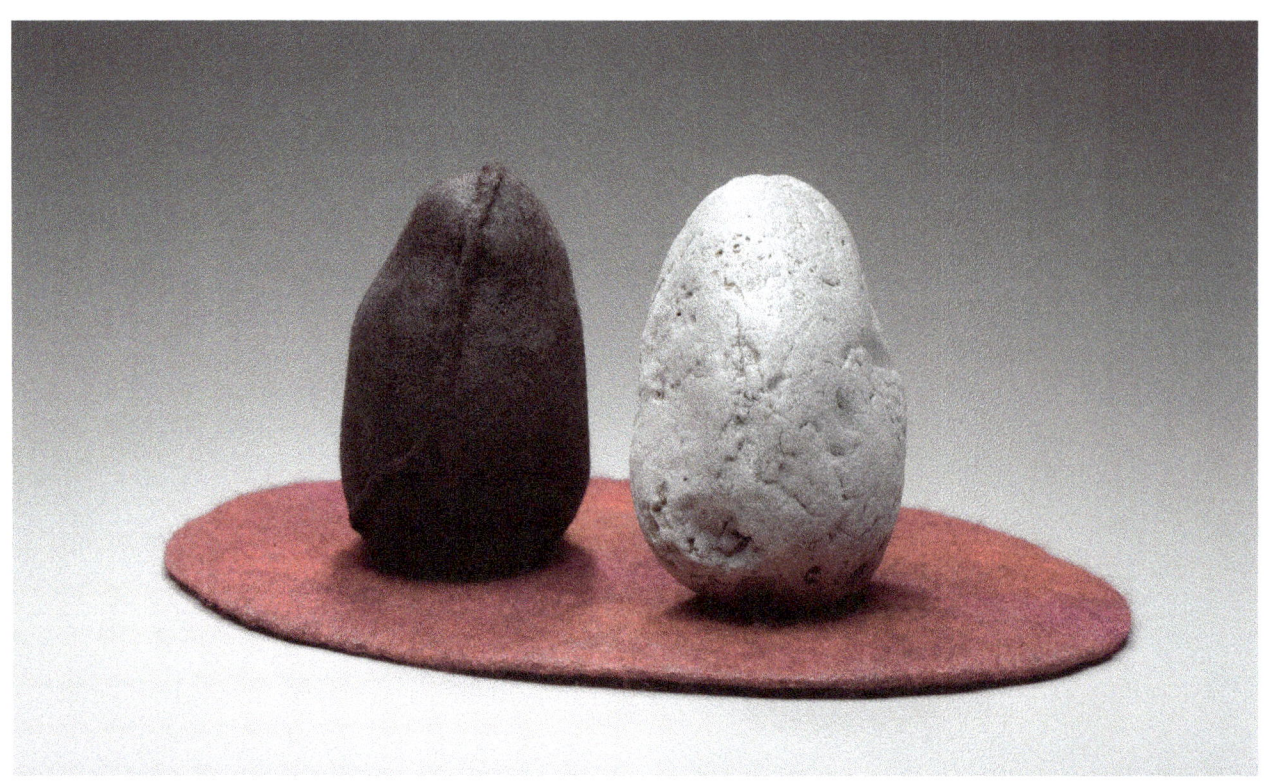

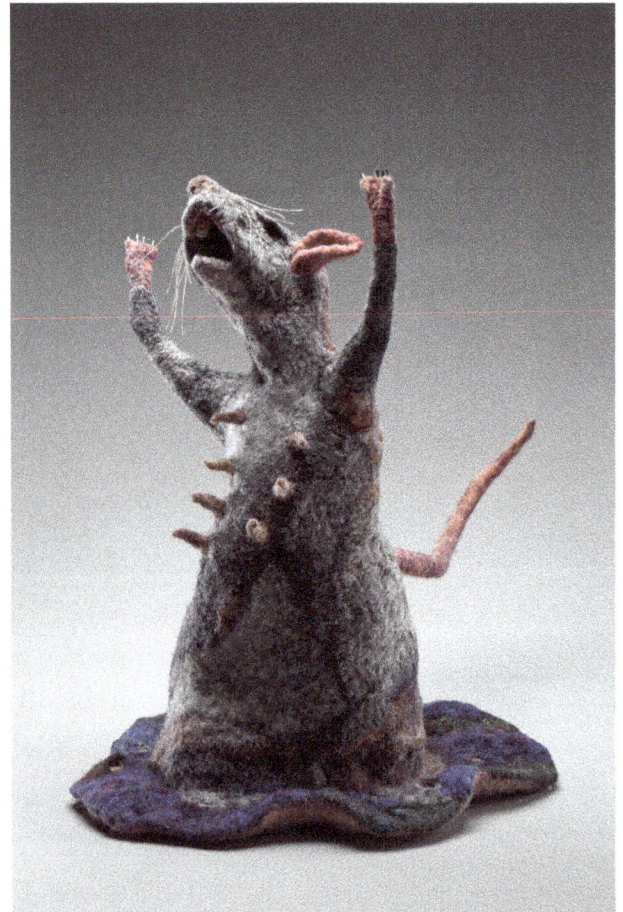

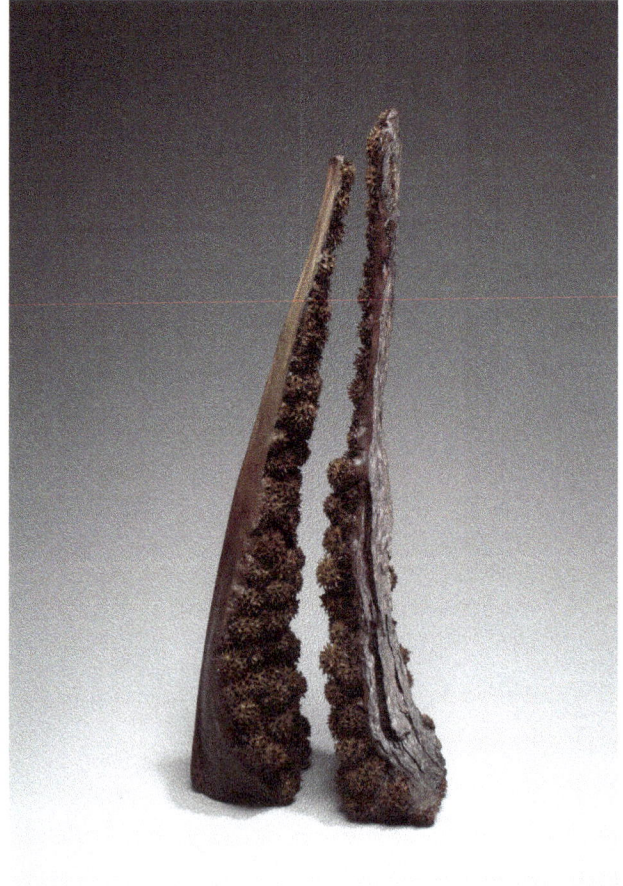

(Top) Polarity. 2006. Rocks and handmade felt, 7 x 17 x 12 in. Photography by Tim Thayer. (*Left*) *Water Rat.* 2011. Handmade felt, stones, and stitching, 16 x 11 x 18 in. Photography by Tim Thayer. (*Right*) *Soul Shard #18.* 2004. Bark, tree pods, and encaustic, 17 x 10 x 9 in. Photography by Tim Thayer.

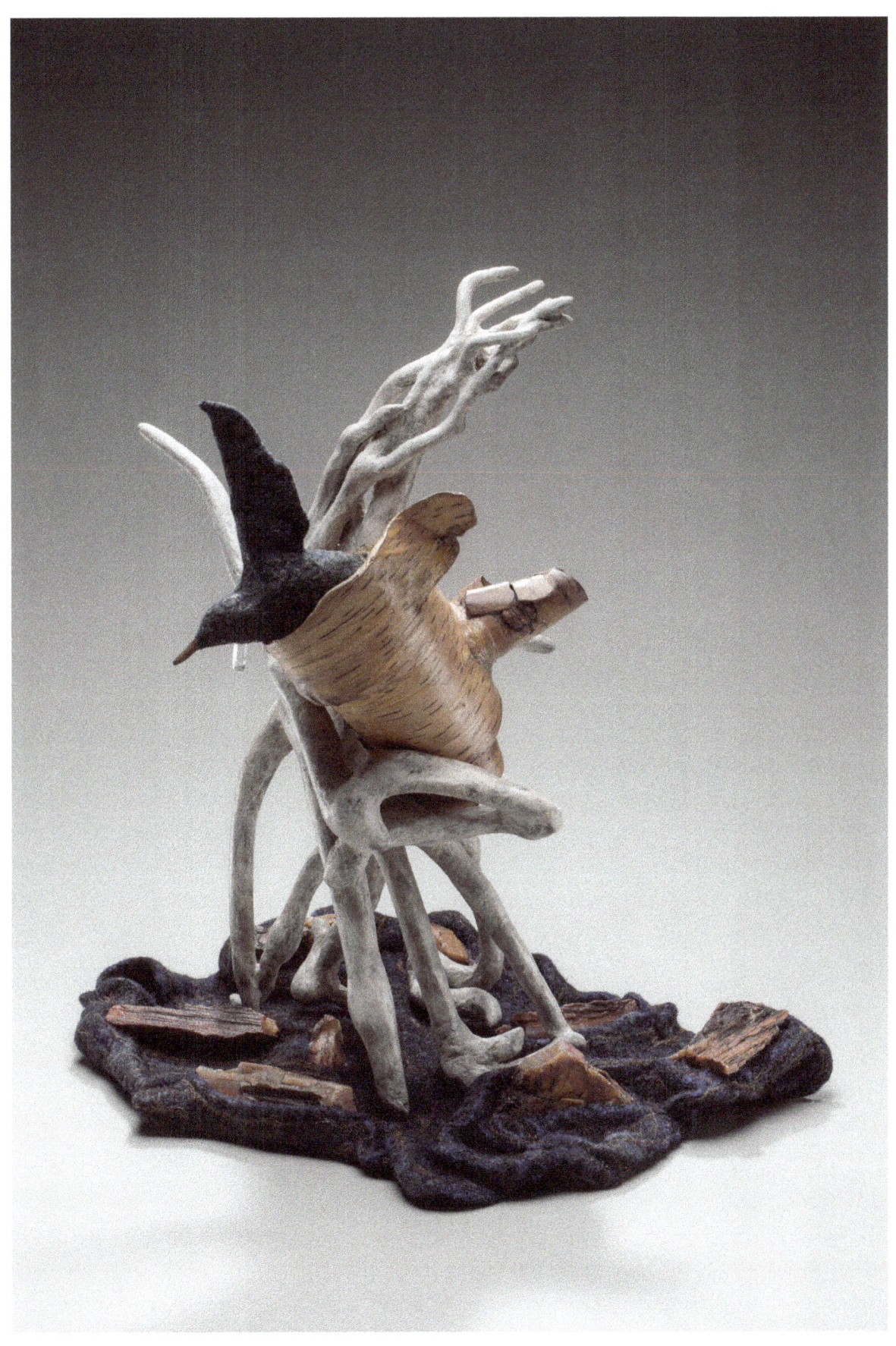

Starling Teapot. 2014. Roots, birch bark, handmade felt, petrified wood, raw flax, kōzo, quartz crystal, 14 x 12 x 13 in. Photography by Tim Thayer.

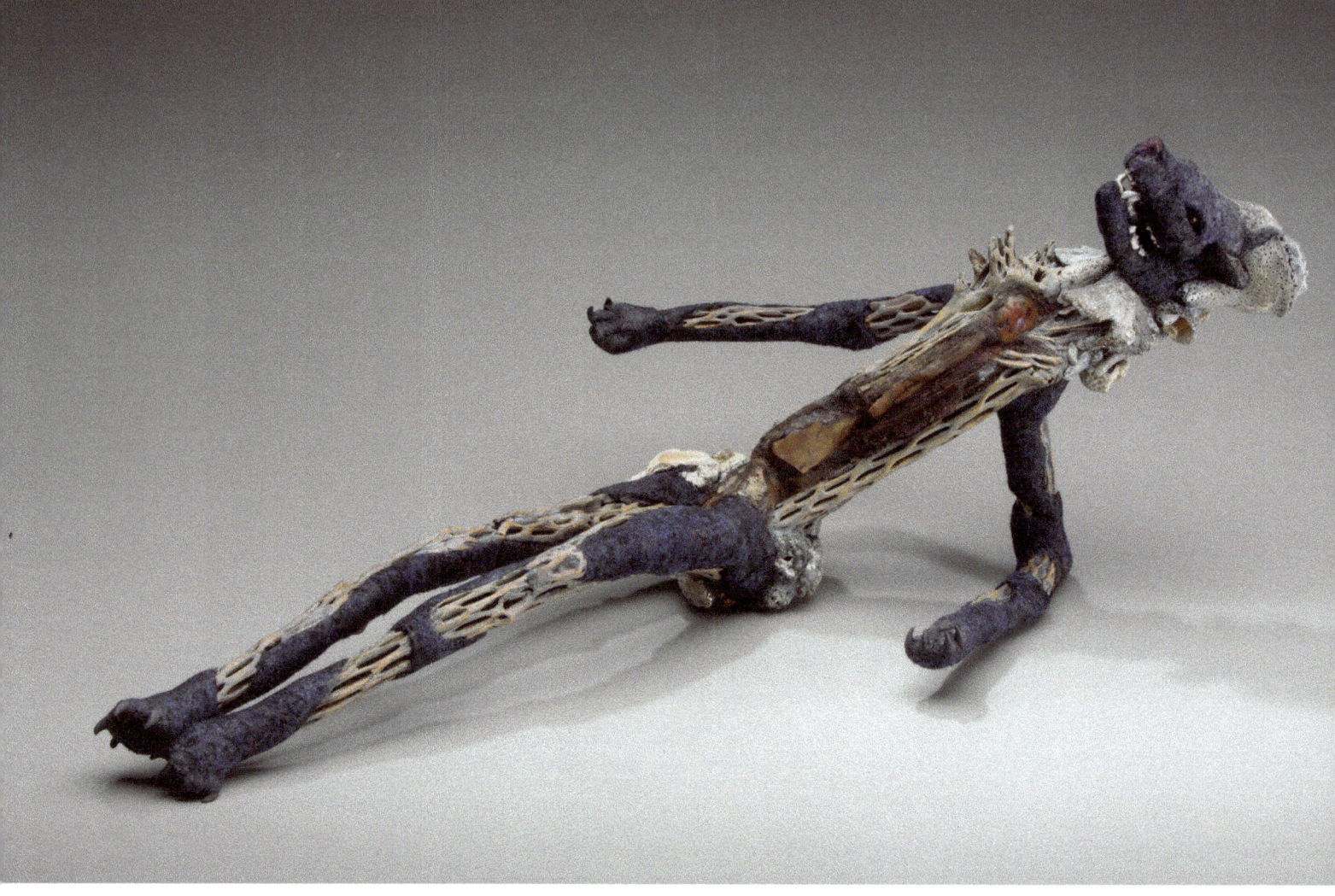

Guide. 2015. Cholla cactus, shells, handmade felt, petrified wood, animal skull, agate, and banded iron, 12 x 29 x 14 in. Photography by Tim Thayer.

myriad incongruities, a self which does not so much learn to travel from dark to light on its lifelong journey as to incorporate both in the cycle of existence.

Drawing on various transcendental practices and Jungian psychology, from Jung's theory of archetypes and the collective unconscious to the world of shamanism, Aaron-Taylor's work engages with the ineffable concept of duality as expressed within the individual, the self and the natural world, and spirit and matter. In **Polarity** (2006), for example, from her *Dreamscape* series, Aaron-Taylor juxtaposes two simple forms that echo one another in shape. One is hard, white natural stone while the other is covered by soft, dark, handmade felt with a visible seam. They sit on a red felt pad, like a pool of energy evocative of blood, and convey in their solemn pairing the unity and division within the psyche or between the inner and outer world, with the need for protection from the latter conveyed by the tightly drawn felt covering, like a second skin. In the *Soul Shard* series, **Soul Shard #18** (2004), made of bark, tree pods, and encaustic, shows two tall, slender forms confronting each other more directly, each smooth on the outside while burly and prickly on the inside, yet soaring upward together in curving harmony. Fittingly, her work has appeared on the cover of *Jung Magazine*.

Using dream symbolism that is sometimes poignant,

sometimes humorous, Aaron-Taylor often conveys complex emotional states through animals. In **Water Rat** (2011), from the *Dream Game* series, a rodent-like creature throws up its arms, lifts its tail, and even seems to point its teats, in gestures of supplication, complaint, or frustration, like an overtaxed mother.

Aaron-Taylor's most recent body of work, *Journeying*, followed the death of her own mother. Using handmade felt to create two-dimensional altar cloths behind three-dimensional altars, they serve as visual elegies to death, departure, and transformation. In **Threshold #3** (2016), the sculptural objects on the altar are reproduced in a kind of transcendent space on the vertically hung altar cloth, evoking an uncanny sense of real versus unreal, material versus immaterial. The felt altar cloth pulls us simultaneously into interior and exterior space while the work as a whole suggests both visible and invisible worlds.

For the same series, Aaron-Taylor produced the semireclining, wolf-like figure **Guide** (2015), a title that evokes the animal spirit guides of shamanism. In shamanism, the world's oldest healing tradition, animal spirit guides or totems can deliver messages, help with a difficult transition, accompany you on your life's journey while reminding you of your strengths, or represent your inner fears. Thus they can help, protect, educate, heal, and inspire. Both ferocious and supplicating, *Guide*'s interior seems exposed on its exterior in another pose of supplication, this time with its heart visible, transparently willing to take on all slings and arrows in the service of its mission.

Aaron-Taylor also uses animals in playfully metaphorical ways. Her *Teapot* series, for example, embodies some of her most lyrical works, including the elegant **Tiger Teapot** (2013) and the astonishing **Starling Teapot** (2014). Both vessels retain the requisite hollow chambers along with spouts, handles, and removable lids, but they are more suited to serving tea in a magical wonderland than in your kitchen, offering the unadulterated joy of children's fantasy tea parties via connection to a strange and beautiful natural world.

DORA APEL, AUGUST 2017

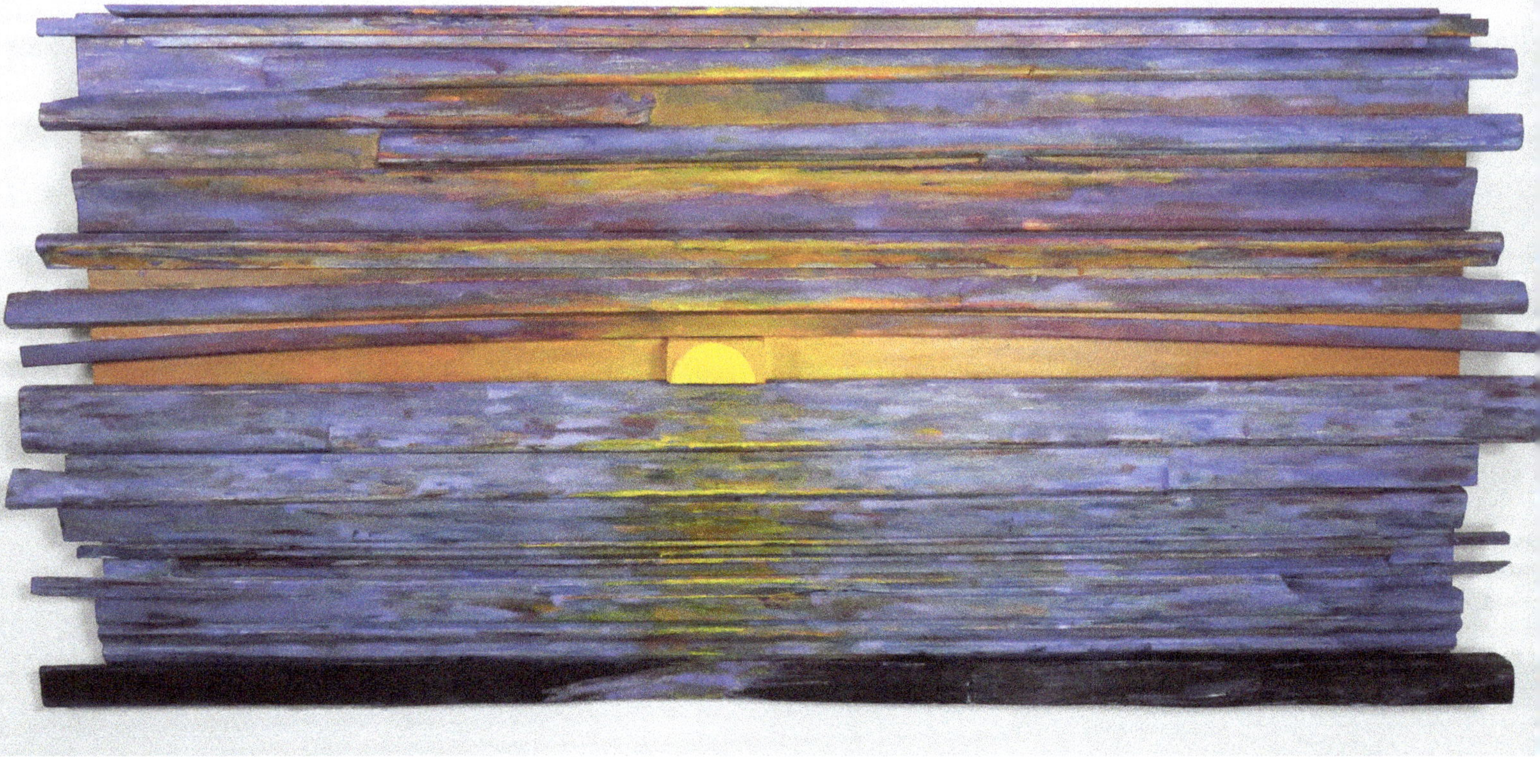

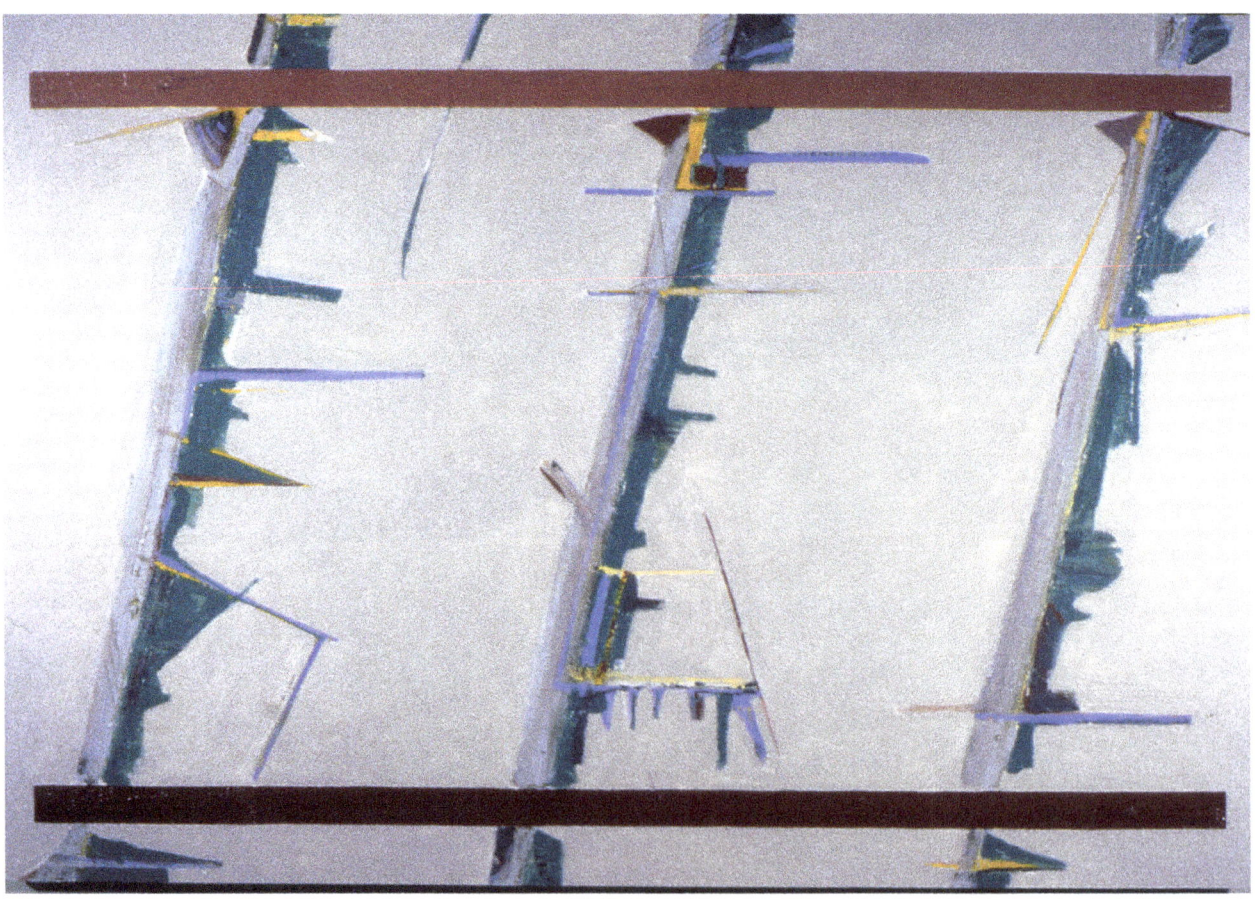

(Top) As the World Turns. 2015. Oil on wood, 24 x 53 in. (*Bottom*) Contrary Motions. 1978–79. Oil on canvas, 60 x 84 in.

Born Detroit, 1945
BFA, MFA, Wayne State University
Lives in Detroit

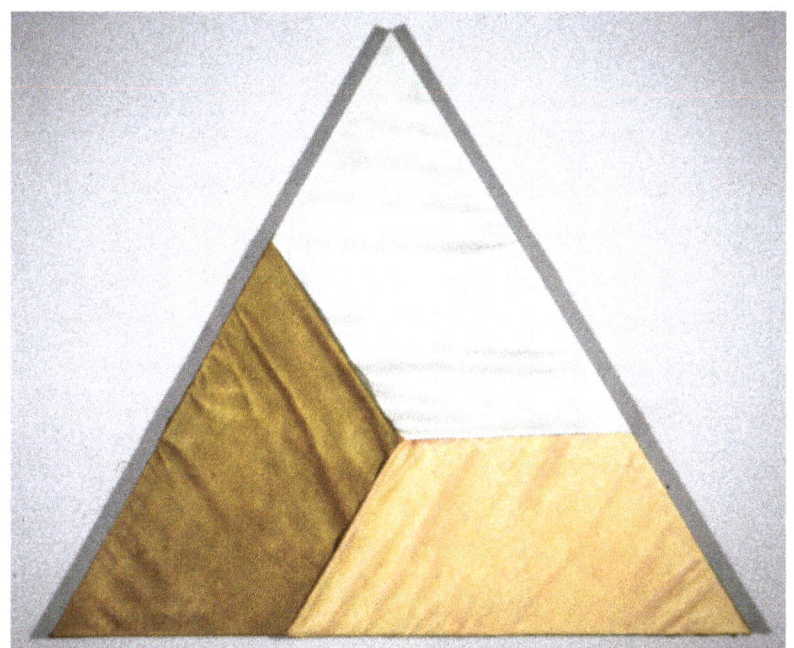

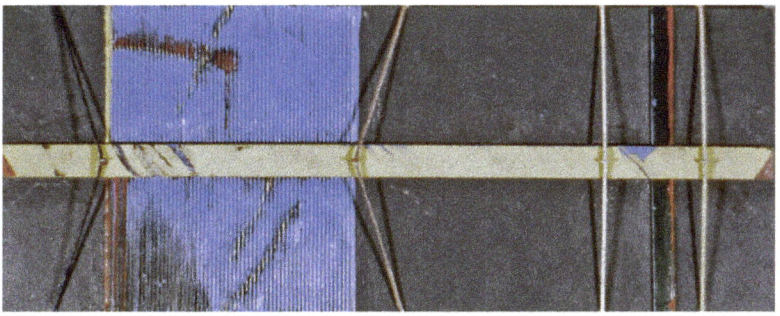

(Top) Autumn. 1995. Oil, canvas, wood, 33 x 38 in. *(Bottom)*
Detroit 2. 1979–80. Wood, cardboard, canvas, rope, oil, 26 x 66 in.

What is an artist's practice but a universe unto itself? A total environment, with the artist at the center, in which a vast but finite set of ingredients—think experiences, materials, impulses, and predilections—cohere, by means both mysterious and prosaic, into related forms that evolve over time. It's an apt metaphor for the work of Gary Eleinko, a lifelong Detroiter who came of age as a painter during the bricolage days of the Cass Corridor movement (where any cast-off thing could become art) and who remarks with frank wonder that, "Everything in the world is made up of ninety-eight natural elements. There's nothing else. Ninety-eight ingredients make up everything we know."

Scientific knowledge is one of the many distinct elements that come together to form Eleinko's ever-evolving universe. Others

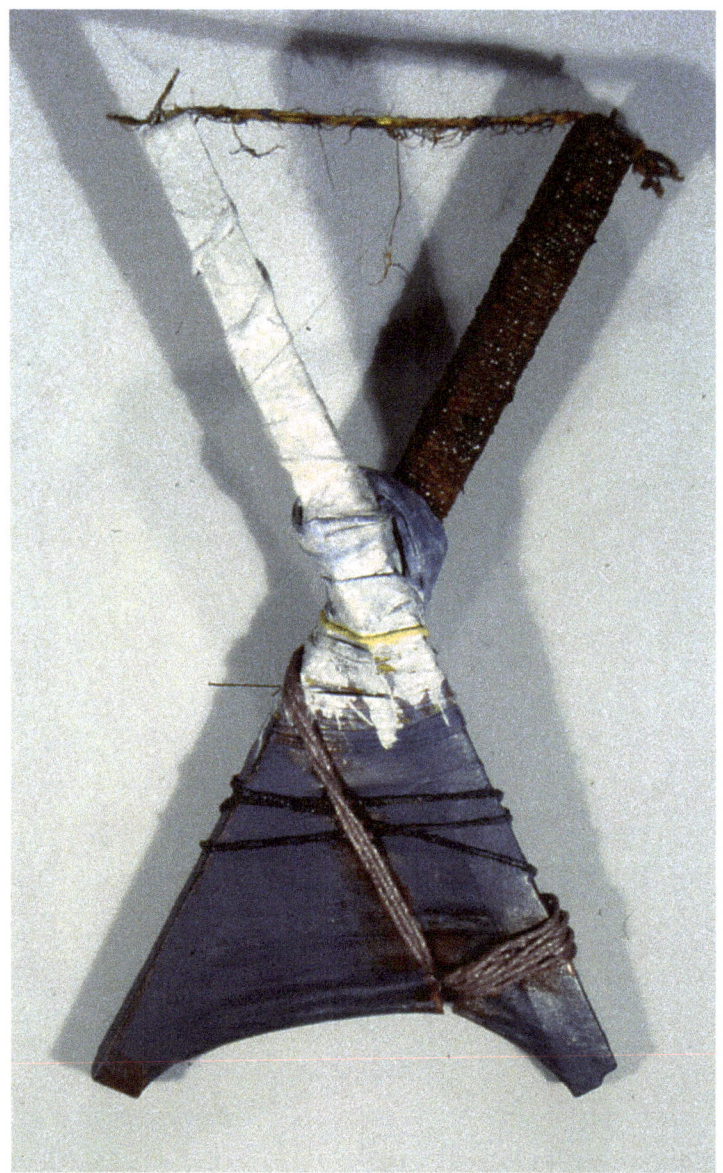

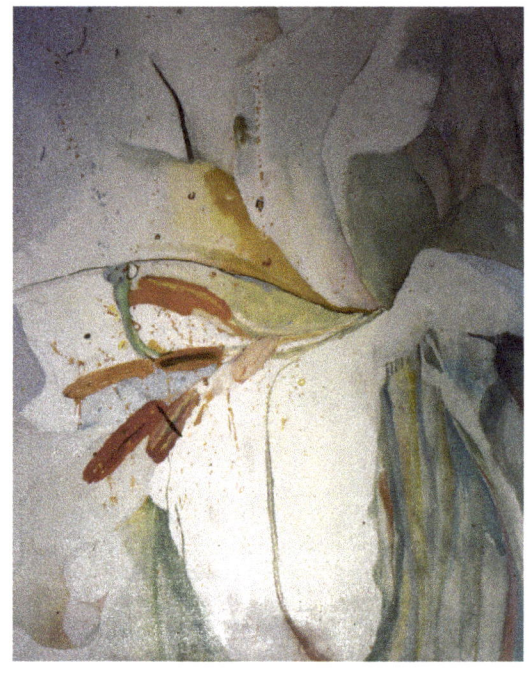

(Left) Held Fast. 1985–86. Canvas, wood, cloth, rope, 28 x 16 in.

(Right) White Lily #2. 1973. Oil on canvas, 48 x 36 in.

include a fascination with the natural world (particularly plant life and natural disasters), a tendency toward certain shapes (bars, lines, Xs, and triangles proliferate), and a consummate craftsman's concern with construction and form. In an age of increasing interdisciplinary promiscuity, Eleinko is a monogamous maker. He labors daily in the full-to-brimming Corktown studio he has occupied since 1988 over canvas, paper, wood, and found objects—arranging, considering, painting, and building. As a painter, he is part of an influential movement of artists who reconceived the painting in sculptural terms, as a constructed object—who remembered, for instance, that canvas is a malleable material, confined to the familiar shapes of square and rectangle only by stretcher bars and convention.

To break the rules, though, you have to first learn them, and Eleinko started his career conventionally enough, painting flowers on regular rectangular canvases. His accomplished early work, inspired by Georgia

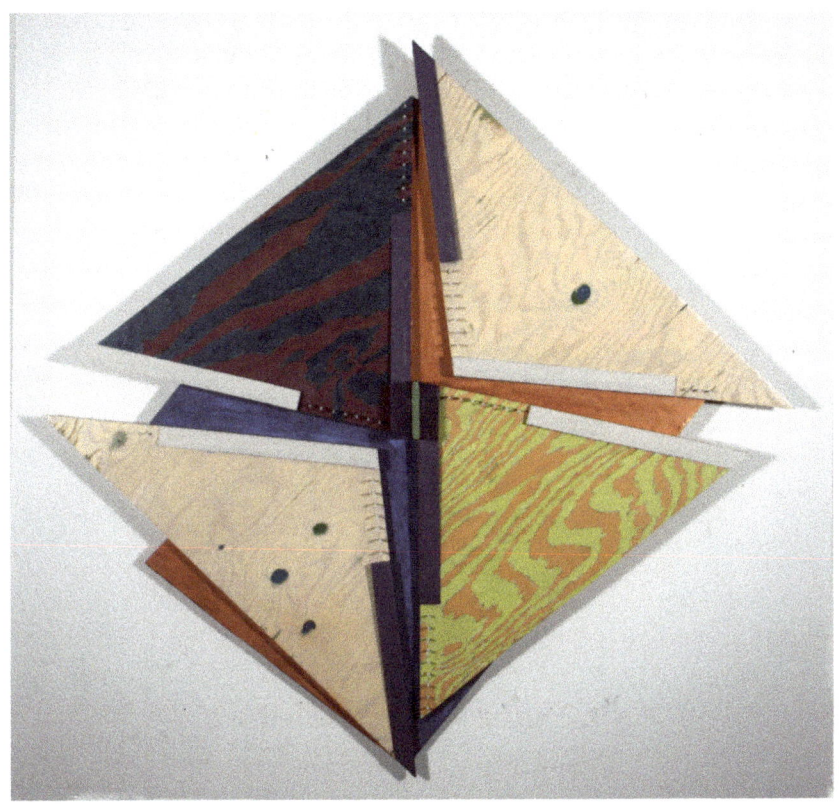

Desert Fault. 2007–8. Wood, nails, oil, polyurethane, 47 x 48 in.

O'Keeffe, revels in sensitive, close-up botanical studies like **White Lily #2** (1973) that are rendered in soft, absorbing textures and subtly graded hues.

These were followed by a series of abstract works, a shift that Eleinko says was expedited when he purchased two albums by the up-and-coming avant-garde composer Philip Glass, whose early experiments in music as perpetual motion machine made a profound impression. **Contrary Motions** (1978–79) was Eleinko's first translation of Glass's vocabulary to his own language of abstract painting

and heralded a new body of postminimalist works on paper and canvas that are dominated by strong horizontal bars and intersecting diagonal lines but imbued by the artist's fine, painterly gestures: a world of shifting subjectivity within an objective, geometric framework.

The idea of enclosure, of the tension between what is held within and hidden from without, became a dominant theme in Eleinko's dimensional paintings of the 1980s. In the late seventies, reviewing a collection of his work as installed in a gallery at the Fisher Building, he says he began

to imagine all the bars and lines coming out from the paintings' surfaces, taking up actual space, and so went to work on combines like **Detroit 2** (1979–80), which is executed on canvas but which includes wood, cardboard, and rope affixed to its flat surface. The entirely dimensional work that followed, typified by pieces like **Held Fast** (1985–86), in which Eleinko manipulated and combined painted canvas, rope, and sundry other materials in ways that emphasized restraint, binding, and wrapping, have a distinctly pent-up affect; they're abstract formal

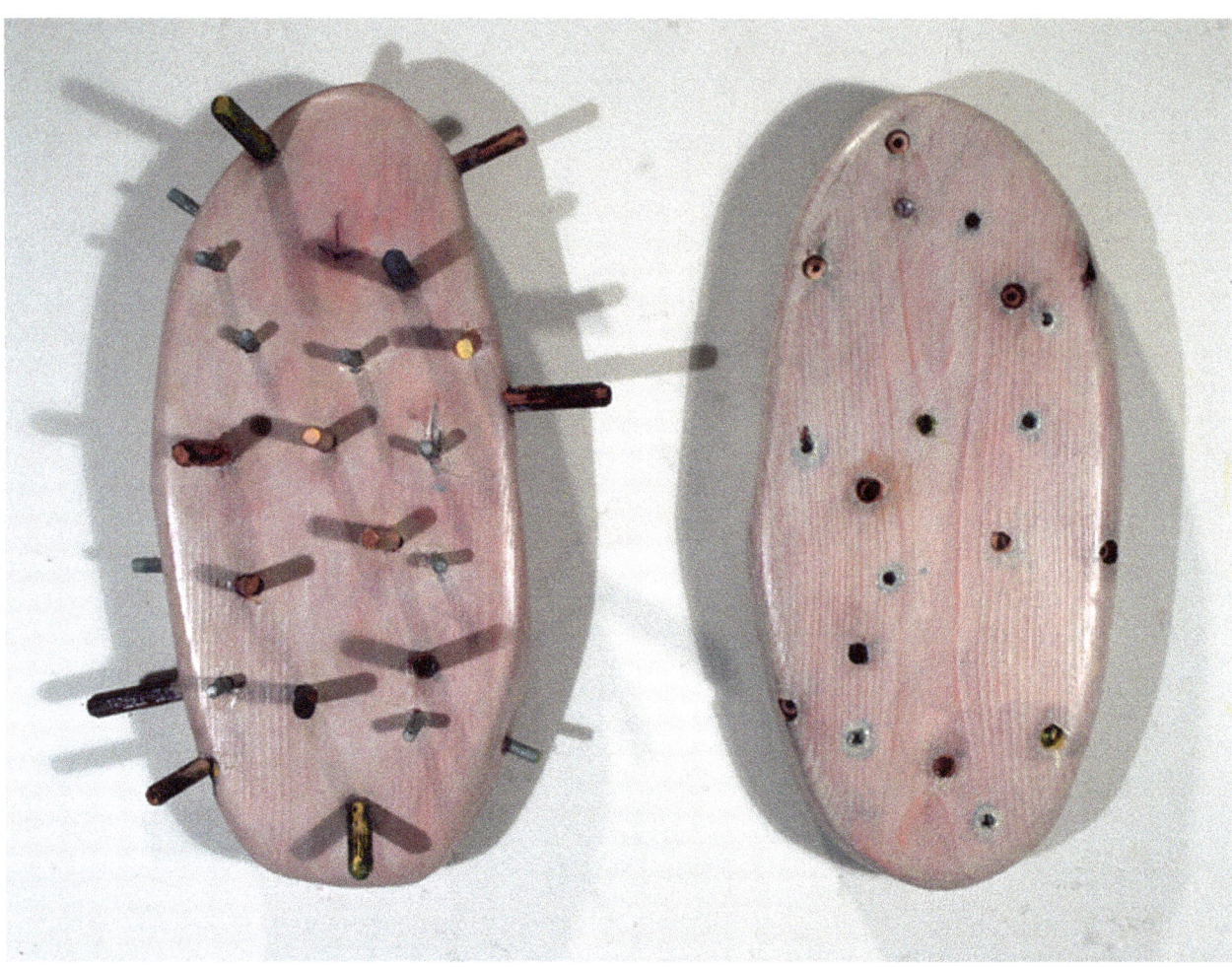

Two Souls. 2009. Oil on wood, 14 1/2 x 19 in.

experiments with vaguely unsettling pyschosexual implications, summed up by a friend of the artist's who referred to this body of work as "organic bondage."

The organic component is a significant one; the natural world has remained a recurrent touchstone for Eleinko even as his modes and methods have shifted over time. In the nineties, for instance, he created simple, meditative, shaped canvases like ***Autumn*** (1995)

that were inspired by the seasons. Later, he made ***Waterfall*** (2006), a showstopping assemblage of painted hose fragments that cascades six and a half feet from top to bottom, as well as ***Desert Fault*** (2007–8), a lively dimensional painting inspired by tectonic stress.

Whereas Eleinko's oeuvre from the seventies through the nineties can be formally divided with relative neatness into distinct periods, this recent work

defies such categorization. These days, he says, he's making what he wants to make and allowing himself to follow tangents and atypical impulses. The resulting work includes a series of small constructions inspired by each of those ninety-eight elements, as well as compelling dimensional one-offs like ***Two Souls*** (2009), inspired by the scarring effects of his Catholic upbringing, ***Curvy Composition*** (2011), a compact homage to

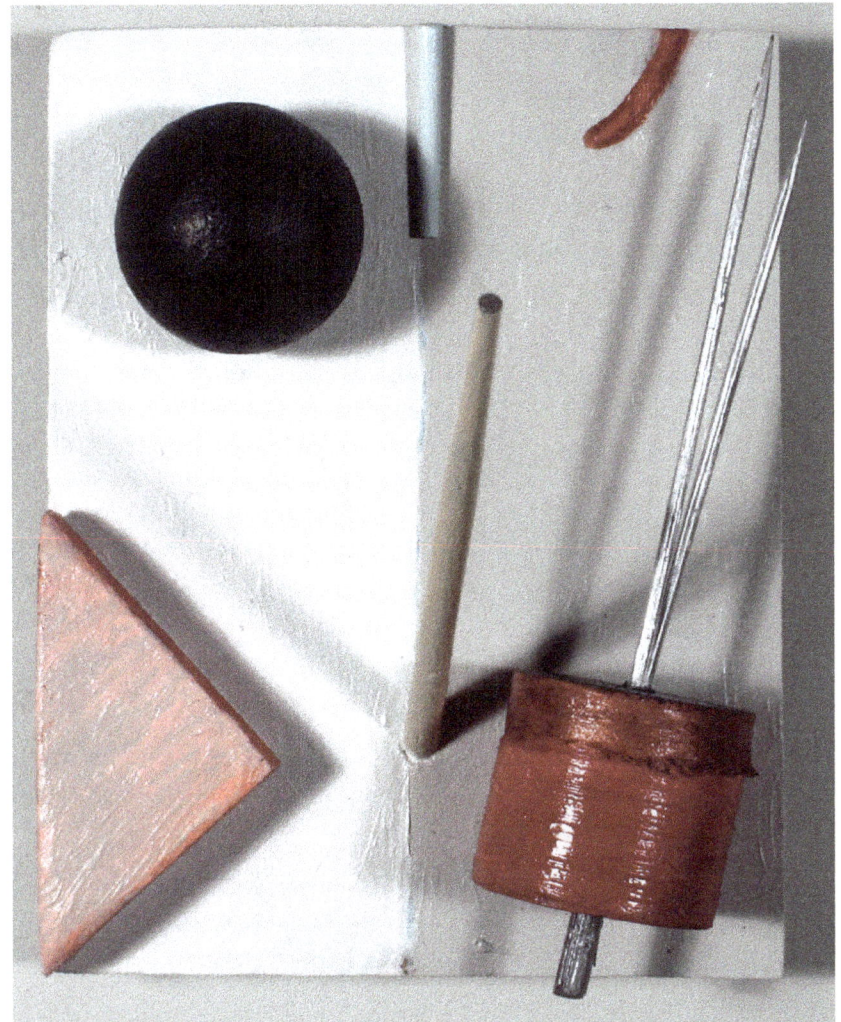
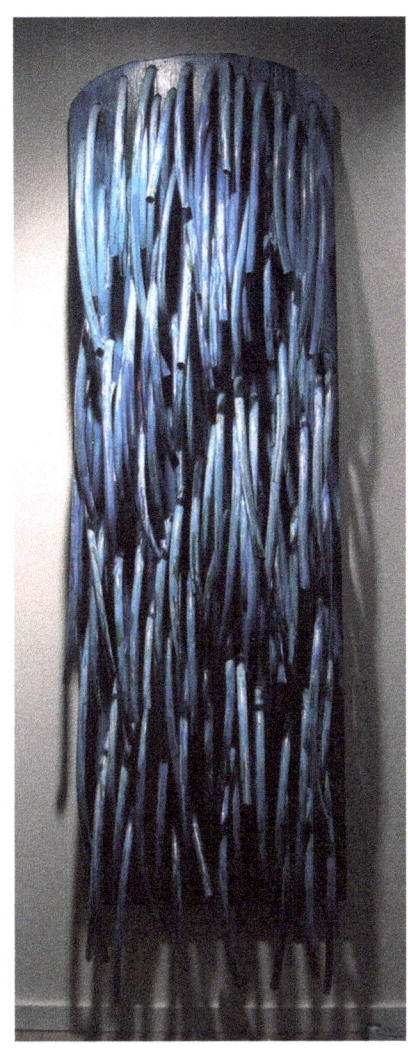

(Left) Curvy Composition. 2011. Oil on wood, 8 x 7 x 6 in. *(Right) Waterfall.* 2006. Wood, garden hoses, oil, polyurethane, 80 x 26 in.

Russian constructivism, and *As the World Turns* (2015), a sunset painting that successfully sheds the trappings of kitsch (even as its title winks at the challenge). Eleinko's forms, in other words, have come unbound—and look, the universe is expanding.

MATTHEW PIPER, SEPTEMBER 2017

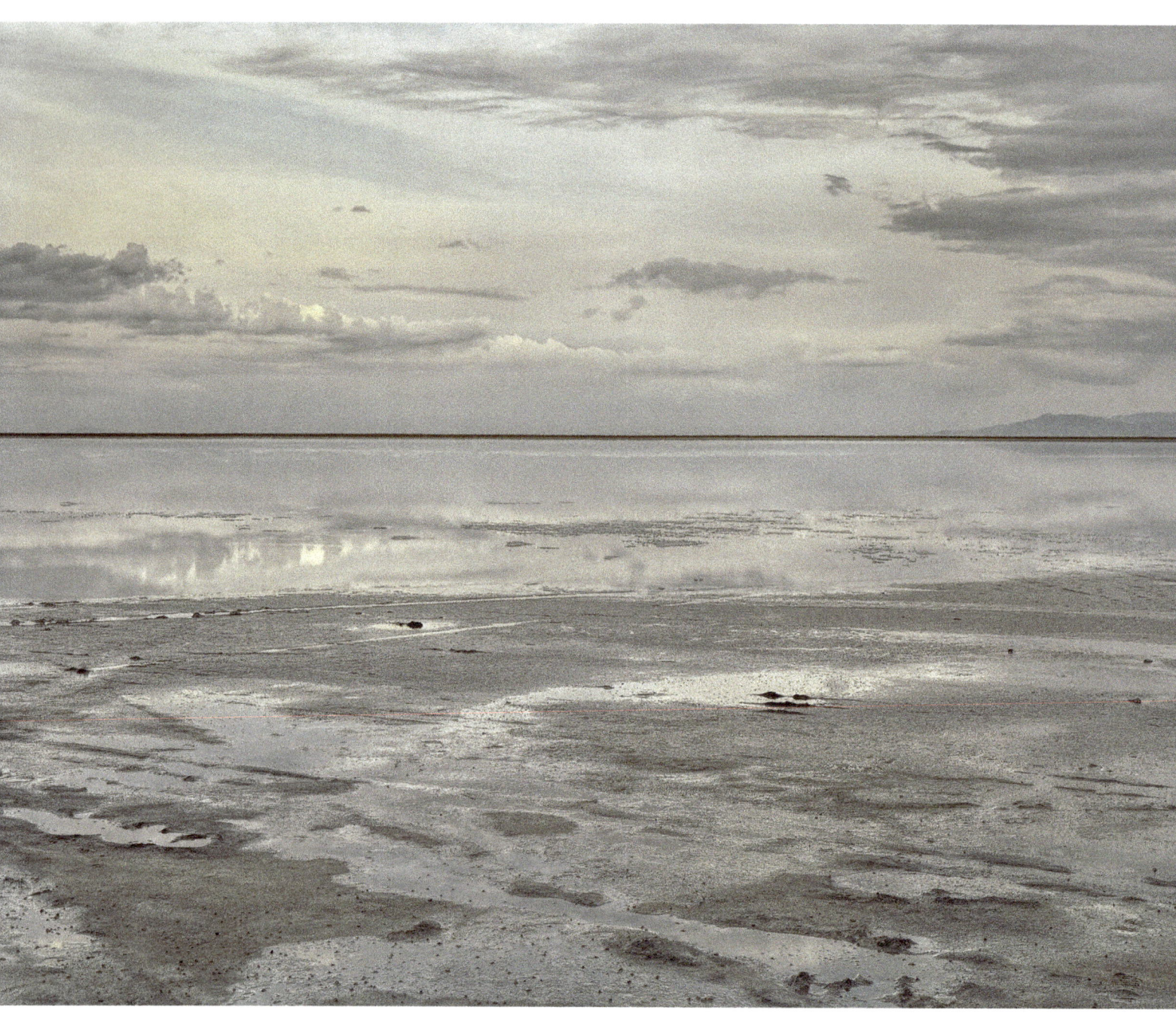

Bonneville Salt Flats, Tooele County, Utah. 2006. Archival pigment print, 44 x 52 in.

79 // CARLA ANDERSON

Born Philadelphia, Pennsylvania, 1943
BFA, College for Creative Studies; MFA, Cranbrook Academy of Art
Lives in Royal Oak, Michigan

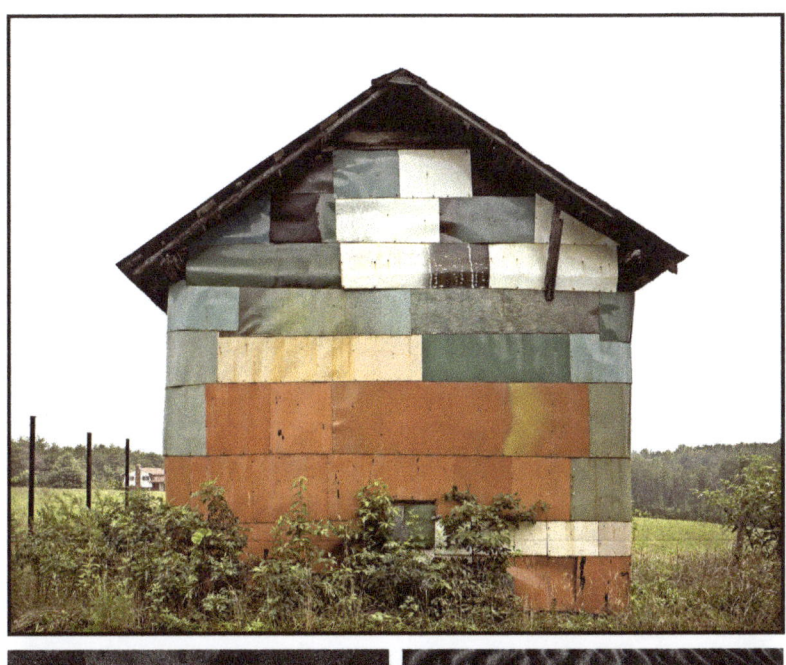

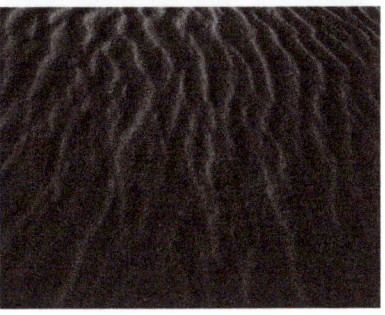

(Top) State Highway 704, Stokes County, North Carolina. 1997.
Lambda print, 11 x 14 1/8 in.
(Bottom) State Highway 321, San Juan County, New Mexico, 2014
(left) and *Stukkshes, Iceland,* 2012 (right). Archival pigment prints,
17 ½ x 45 in. overall.

Striding smack into the dusty but revered genre of land and sea photography a few decades ago, Carla Anderson began her determined, protracted pursuit to record wondrous sites "seen with fresh eyes." Undaunted by the preponderance of land- and seascape vistas produced by nineteenth-century masters like William Henry Jackson, Gustave Le Gray, and Timothy O'Sullivan, she vowed to chronicle overfamiliar scenes "in a way that made them unfamiliar." Thus began Anderson's quest to evolve a vision uniquely her own, little realizing at the time that the distinctive aesthetic she sought would not materialize until 2006.

Her sensibility, which she describes as a melding of "being rooted to the earth and letting go into light and color," yields singular images that are "minute rather than an overview."

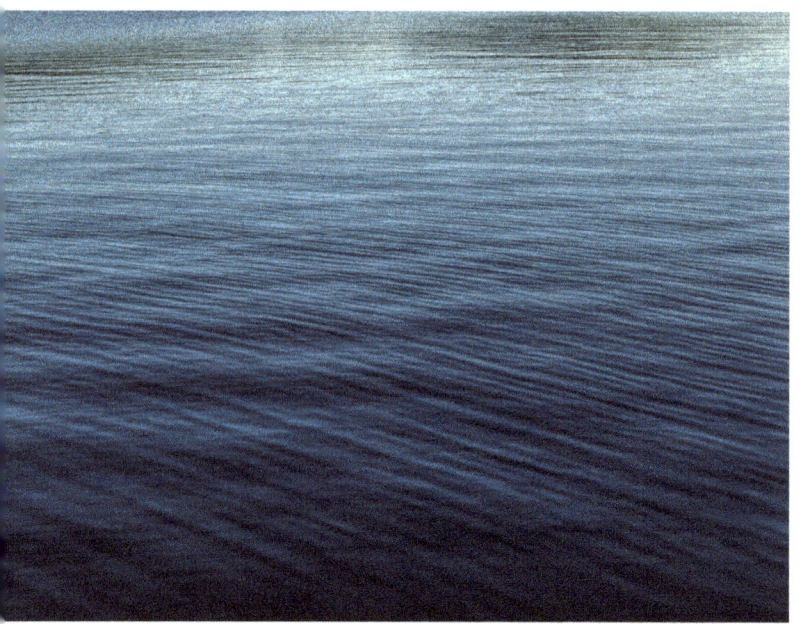

(Left) Lake Superior #2, Marquette County, Michigan. 2017. Archival pigment print, 30 x 40 in. (*Right*) *West Fjords 4, Iceland.* 2016. Archival pigment print, 44 x 51 in.

To discover such views, she has consistently and methodically maintained a peripatetic pace of weeks-long treks to both national and international locales that, most notably of late, have led her thrice to Iceland.

Long before such inspiring sojourns abroad, Anderson studied with Bill Rauhauser (1918–2017), celebrated Detroit street photographer and long-time teacher at the College for Creative Studies. Subsequently, she too focused on black-and-white vernacular photography through the 1970s, featuring houses in downriver Detroit and a series of neighborhood doorways. Multiple viewing and shooting

excursions down South followed, precipitated in part by William Agee and Walker Evans's 1941 *Let Us Now Praise Famous Men*. In her series, Anderson aimed to document the imminent loss of the distinctive buildings, sites, and ethos of the South, as well as to capture the palpable effect of gauzy southern light. In the early nineties, she switched to color, in part to fix images as vividly on film as in her memory, producing such photos as **State High-way 704, Stokes County, North Carolina** (1997), one of a series of starkly frontal views of semiderelict, photogenic structures (here, a patchwork quilt comes to mind) bathed in an aura of silvery light.

In the course of subsequent expeditions to the American Southwest to confront the much-recorded, hallowed terrain of the romantic sublime (skyscraping mountains, plunging valleys, and the brinkmanship of a cliff's edge vantage point), Anderson determined to "look downward and avoid the horizon line," in part to camouflage where she was standing and what direction she might be looking. For her, the eureka photograph, taken as usual with a large-format camera mounted on a tripod, is **Bonneville Salt Flats, Tooele County, Utah** of 2006. Here, the gray-brown sweep of flats, water, mud, and sky coheres as a singular, blended chromatic

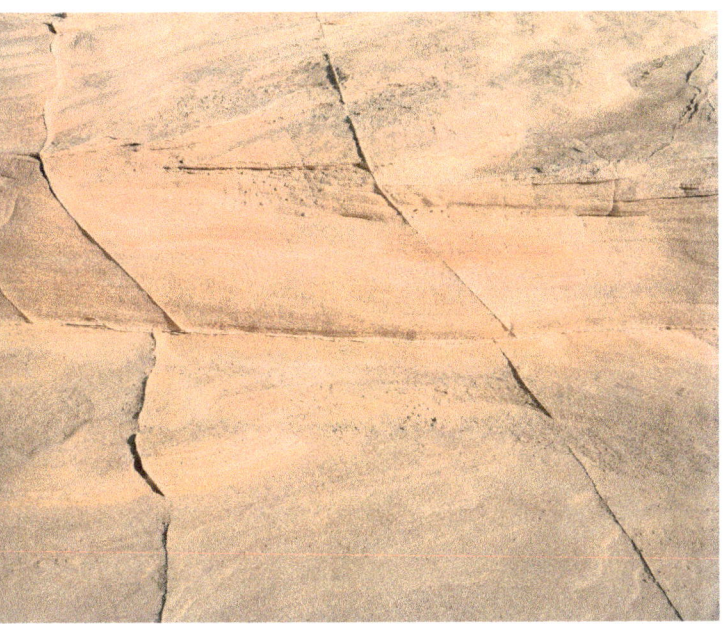 

(Left) Valley of Fire, Nevada. 2014. Archival pigment print, 30 x 40 in. *(Right) Lake Huron, Alpena, Michigan.* 2017. Archival pigment print, 30 x 40 in.

entity in which a partly cloudy sky is reflected in the water below and the palest and thinnest-of-thin horizon lines reinforces the shallow spatial field.

In *Valley of Fire, Nevada* (2014) a grid of red sandstone squares that skews diagonally across the surface may read both as horizontal ground plain and cliff face, emphatically shunning a horizon and suspending, rather than grounding, the spectator in a color field of ruddy red. A similar effect occurs in *West Fjords 4, Iceland* (2016), where the cloudy overcast transforms reflective water into a gray monochrome. Its larger-than-usual scale, at forty-four by fifty-two inches, overwhelms the spectator in a tonalist haze. Anderson's occasional interest in augmenting the impact of individual pictures is also apparent in a series of diptychs in which images from different shoots and different countries may be joined together to suggest a global consonance between divergent sites, as in *State Highway 321, San Juan County, New Mexico* (2014, left) and *Stukkshes, Iceland* (2012, right), linked as they are by darkling hues and tactile textures of sand and rock.

A culmination of sorts occurs in a recent group of brimming, edge-to-edge glimpses of Lakes Huron and Superior from 2017: *Lake Huron, Alpena, Michigan* and *Lake Superior #2, Marquette County, Michigan*. Now photographing digitally, Anderson distills the rhythmic motion of these boundary-free, ceaselessly undulating depths of burnished blue. Neither mirror-calm nor churning and tempestuous, their weight and tacit power is nevertheless sensed and felt. Glints of light and sparkling reflections skip across the restless surfaces that, seemingly free of human interference or presence, roll on and on.

DENNIS ALAN NAWROCKI, SEPTEMBER 2017

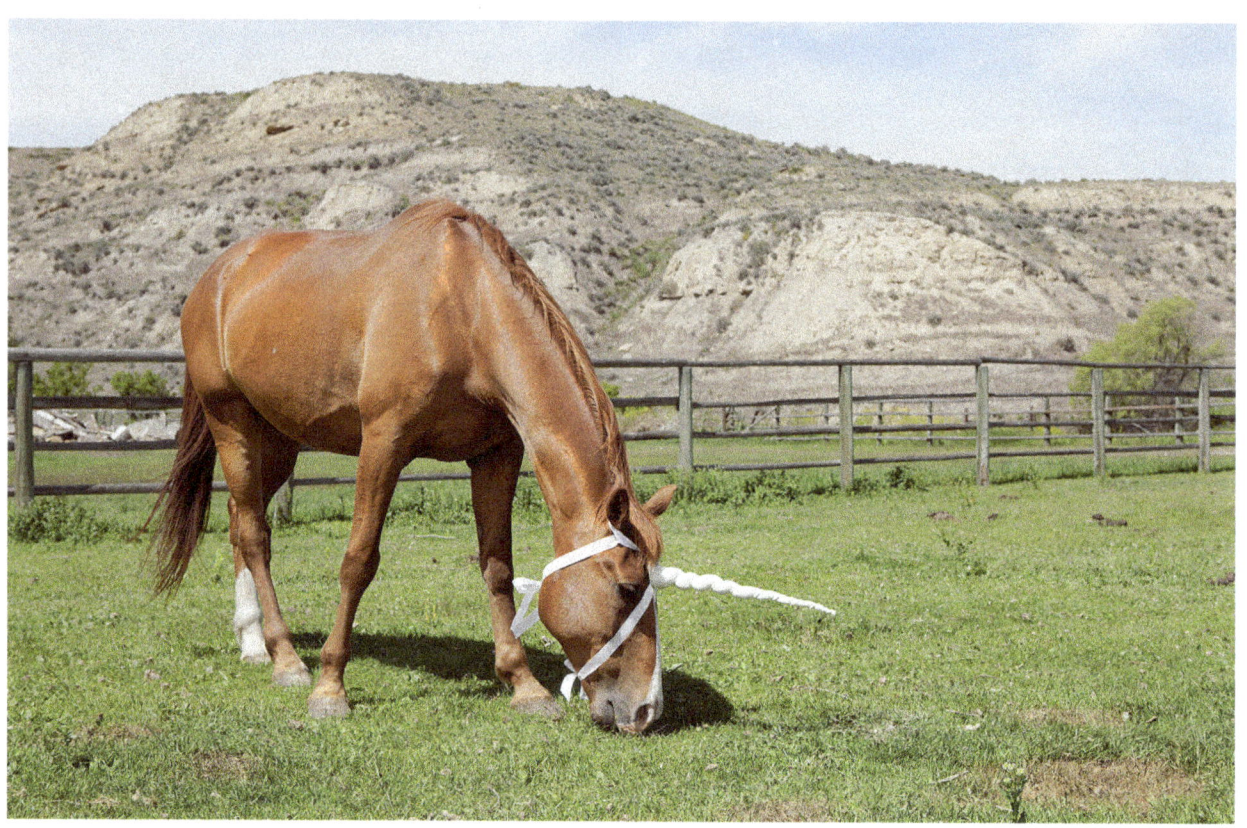

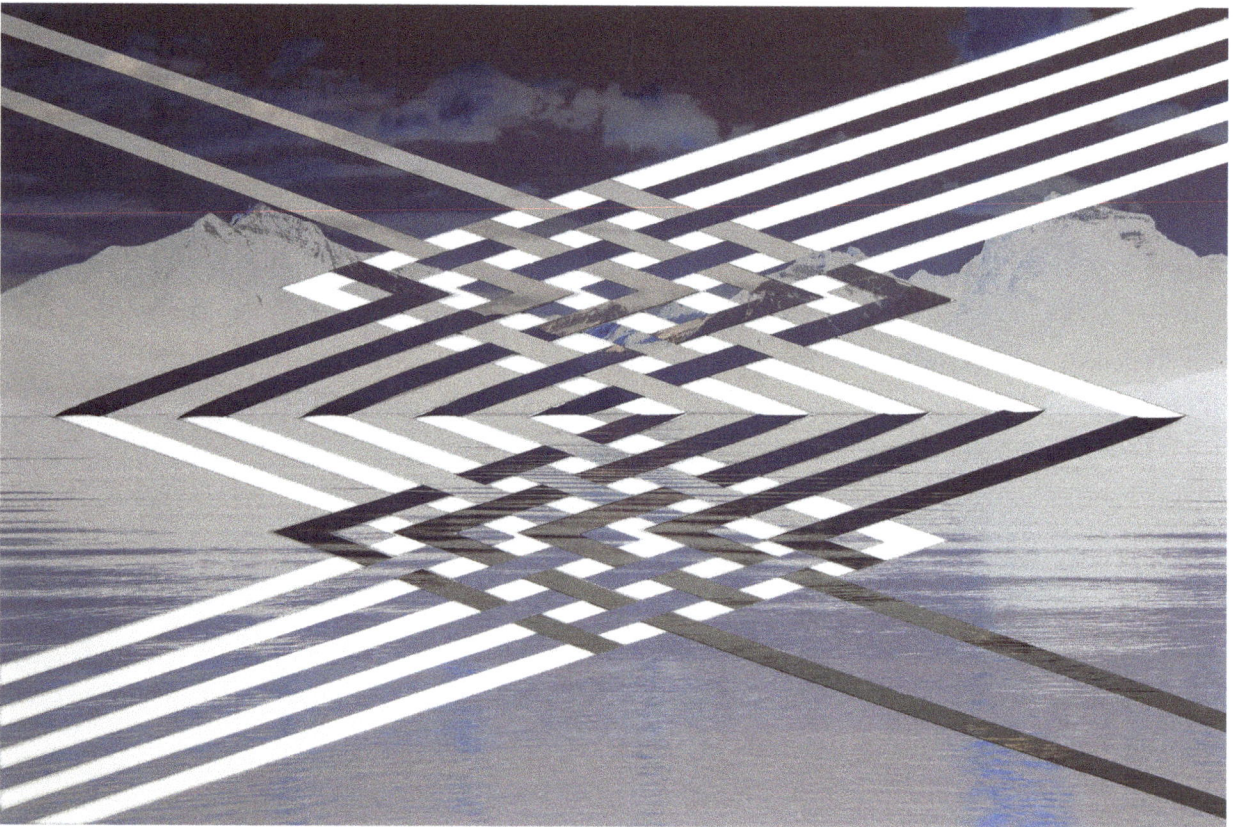

(Top) Virgin Land, Wyoming (Blue Eyes in the Pasture). 2012. Archival digital print, 25 x 35 in. (*Bottom*) *As Above, So Below (Lake McDonald #1)* front. 2015. Cut and folded double-sided archival print, 13 x 19 in.

Born Huntsville, Alabama, 1976
BA, Vassar College, New York; MFA, Rhode Island School of Design
Lives in Detroit

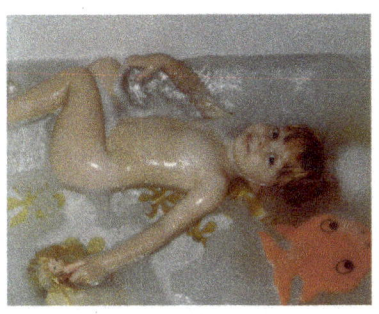 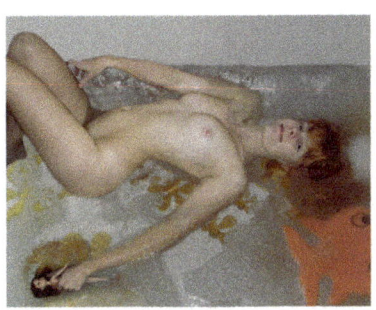

Millee lying on her back 1979, 2006. 2006. Archival digital prints,
3 1/2 x 4 in each.

A photograph is a powerful object—it carries the assumption of truth like no form of image-making ever has. Like the bards of old, it confirms our truth by telling and retelling our stories. Like the ancient myths those bards repeated, photographs carry hidden messages that draw difficult, paradoxical truths out of our shadows.

The photographic work of Millee Tibbs examines the dark reflection of such fairy tale tropes as girlish innocence, wild land-scape, and unicorns. Identity, memory, and place are, in Tibbs's images, composed not of real truths or events but of images that stand in for, and claim to be evident of, those truths and events that define our worldview. Tibbs's work argues that the images we turn to for nostalgia, ground-ing, and beauty index times and places that, in fact, never truly

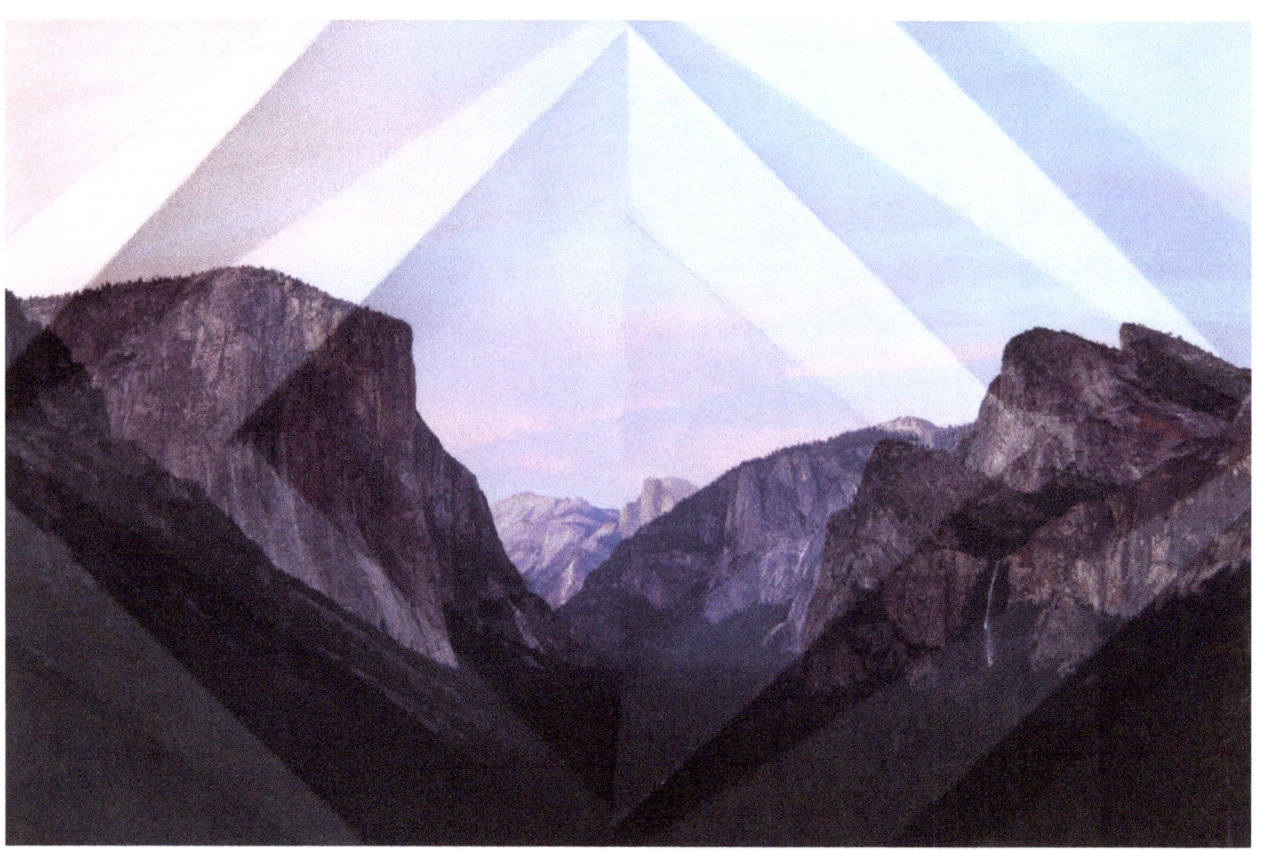

Mountains and Valleys (Yosemite #1). 2013. Archival digital print, 40 x 26 in.

existed—or at least, not as we, aided by the breadcrumb trail of documentary images, recall them.

Tibbs recalls the young adult onset of her discomfort at being in front of the camera as presaging an awareness of the photograph's uncanny trickster power and a growing curiosity to harness it. In *This Is a Picture of Me*, a body of work made in 2006, she staged a collection of photographs of herself in early childhood with her adult body. These tart, compact diptychs are identical down to the smallest detail except for the age of their subject. Child and grownup Tibbs float in a bathtub, talk on the phone, and embody various touchstones of personal history in arresting, flashbulb lighting. They spring open a Pandora's box of uncomfortable questions and truths—about the photograph's uncanny state of fabricated reality, the absurdity of their title's claim (What is a picture? Who is "me"?), and the way our identity becomes more complicated, and difficult to look at, as we move through life.

Every photographic exploration of Tibbs's has a similarly dark, humorous, unflinchingly raw paradox as its kernel. In the body of work *Virgin Land*, Tibbs unpacks her childhood obsession with unicorns alongside the mythical creature's descent through Western culture from a grand, deeply holy icon to the kitschy ground of Trapper Keeper covers and little girls' treasure shelves. The undeniable phallic symbolism of the unicorn is an awkward truth—yet it is, somehow, as Tibbs puts it, "A phallus that feminizes." Its power has come into the hands of young people as a projection of latent sexual desire. Tibbs's placement of makeshift "unicorns" into iconic, drippingly sentimental Western landscapes reveals a similar paradox to that of the unicorn—the strange way in which we, aided by images, tend to gender and empower landscape. Our most iconic American landmarks—the vast mountain ranges, deserts, and prairies found in the western states—have come to illustrate American exceptionalism, manifest destiny, and the promise of unbridled freedom that is problematically foundational to American identity. Like the unicorn, these symbolic flashpoints in the landscape are quite masculine. Like the unicorn as well, they are cocooned in curiously feminine descriptors. The word in which the indices of the unicorn and the western landscape dovetail is "virgin." The virgin woman, solely capable

of luring the unicorn from his forest lair, is essential to the unicorn's myth. "Virgin" land, or land untampered with by human settlement, follows and is followed by every image we associate with the American West.

Images that provoke a sentimental response are a special interest of Tibbs's—even she is not immune to their seductive pull. Her recent work makes a sharp break from the frankly conceptual, "smart-assed" (her words) photographs she's been known for hitherto. A new group of images, titled *Mountains and Valleys*, examines the essence of the visual sublime—famous mountainous landscapes from the American West. These images are the beloved childhood photographs of our culture—they index the ideals of beauty, space, and power that can take on a deceptive "innocence" the same

way our small, personal pictures do. The ease with which she manipulates the physical surface of a photograph into elegant folds, then photographs the folded photograph, incorporating illusionistic shadows and delicate stratifications of cracks that straddle the creases, echoes the easy manipulation of emotional response wrung by photographers of manifest destiny. As Tibbs's ideas take on more visually communicative forms, her process becomes more physical. Her new work is developed in the darkroom using traditional, analog techniques to twist familiar landscapes into undulating, geometric forms that do not allow the eye to rest. Giving the eye no place for rest is Tibbs's forte. It's a good thing—our eyes need wakening.

CLARA DEGALAN, OCTOBER 2017

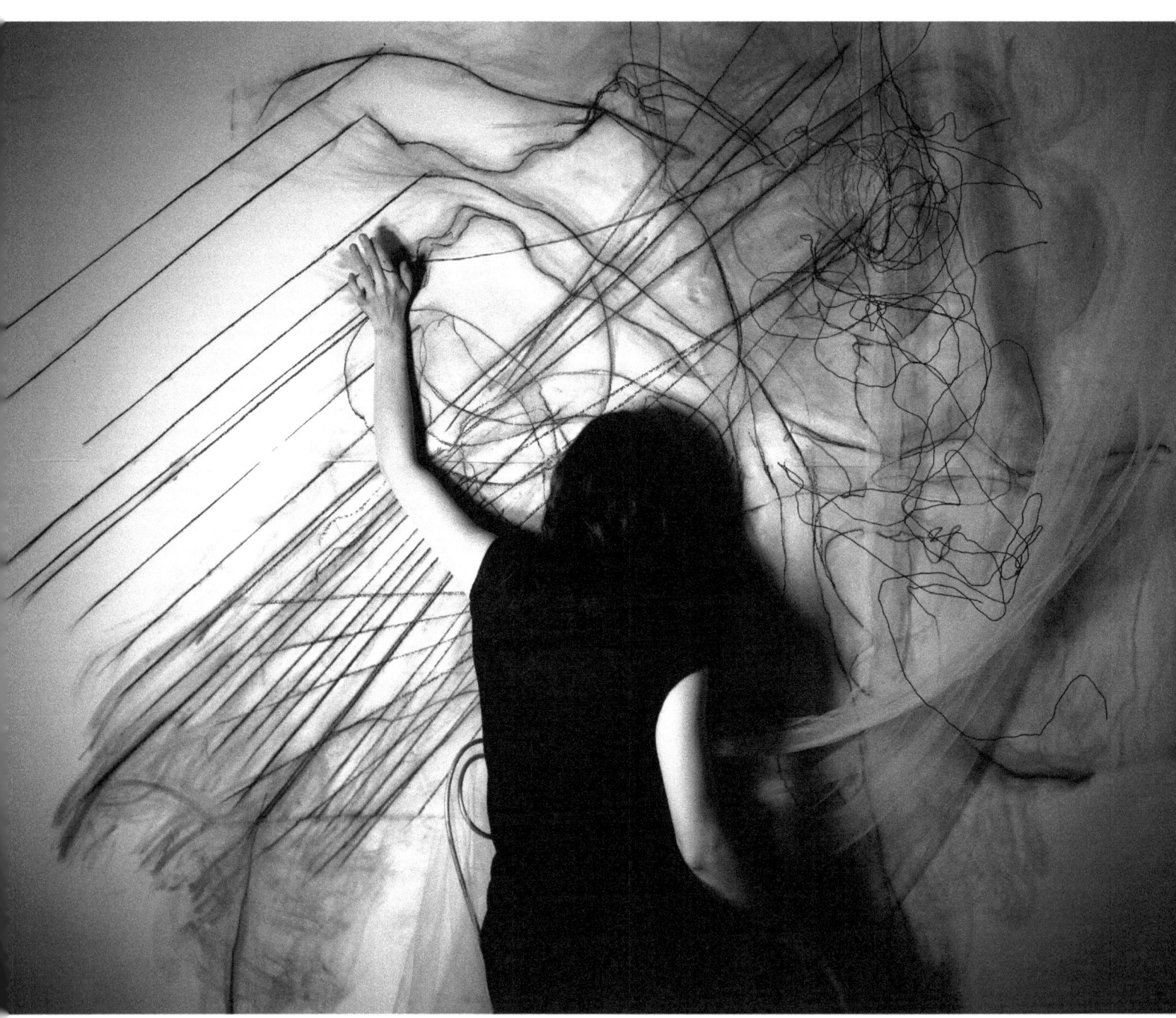

Labyrinth. 2010. Archival inkjet print, 30 x 24 in.

Born Detroit, 1981
BA, Lawrence University, Wisconsin;
MFA, Cranbrook Academy of Art
Lives in Hamtramck, Michigan

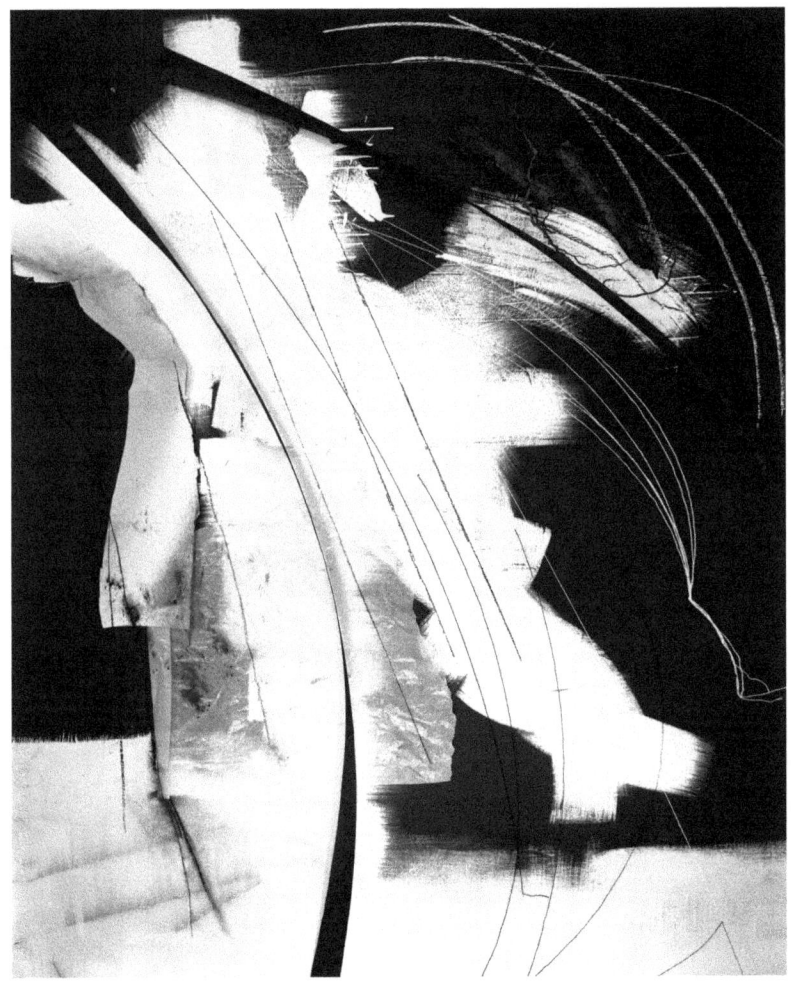

Anchor. 2015. Archival inkjet print, 40 x 50 in.

Lauren Semivan's enigmatic, tour de force black-and-white photographs—no color, no digital—are shot with an early twentieth-century, large-format, tripod-mounted camera. The realization of her mystifying tableaux entails sheets of film, reams of negatives, and even the use of a home darkroom. Semivan's retardataire, hands-on practice is akin to other recent throwbacks that captivate millennials and boomers alike, including old-fashioned acoustic instruments, vinyl, and flip phones.

Semivan's images are, however, quintessentially contemporary inventions. Despite the cumbersome, antique equipment, her interdisciplinary mosaics of abstraction, process and performative procedures, staged (or set-up) scenes, and her pictorial perception of the oft-thrumming tensions between conscious and

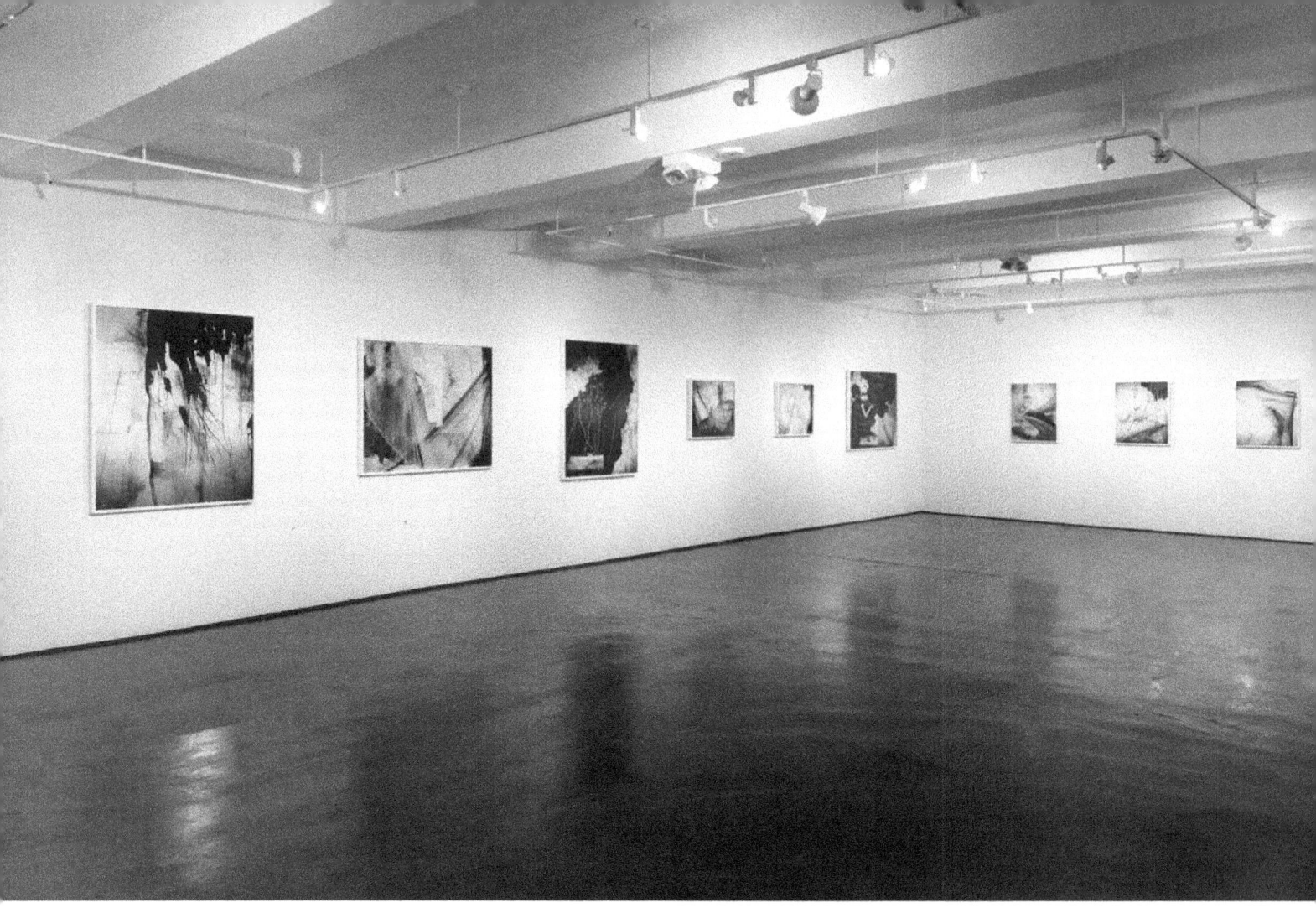

Pitch, partial view of exhibition at Benrubi Gallery, New York. 2017.

subconscious states of mind, yield psychodramas at once rational and irrational. Her artist statements, albeit tinged with surrealist overtones, reiterate the unease aroused by her photographs: "The images often contain something of the everyday to ground them, juxtaposed with something extraordinary or out of the world to set them free from the realm of the everyday. I use my own body within the work to anchor the images within a place of dreams and personal emotions."

Decidedly not the lingo of a straight or "decisive moment" photographer. Her teachers at Wisconsin's Lawrence University, Julie Lindemann and John Shimon, plus critic Lyle Rexer (*The Edge of Vision: The Rise of Abstraction in Photography*, 2009), were particularly influential on the evolution of Semivan's sensibility.

Like many artists, Semivan works in series, aggregates of thirty or more images born of hours improvising in a modest, ten-by-twelve-foot studio:

painting and repainting wallboard; moving domestic furnishings in and out; stringing string, wire, and thread; festooning fabric; wielding charcoal and chalk; and choreographing the occasional walk-ons into her mise-en-scènes. Recent bodies of work, often under construction for two or three years, include *Pitch* (2015–17), *Observatory* (2010–14/15), and *Pataphysics* (2004–06).

Even a partial installation view of ***Pitch*** (2017) illustrates the

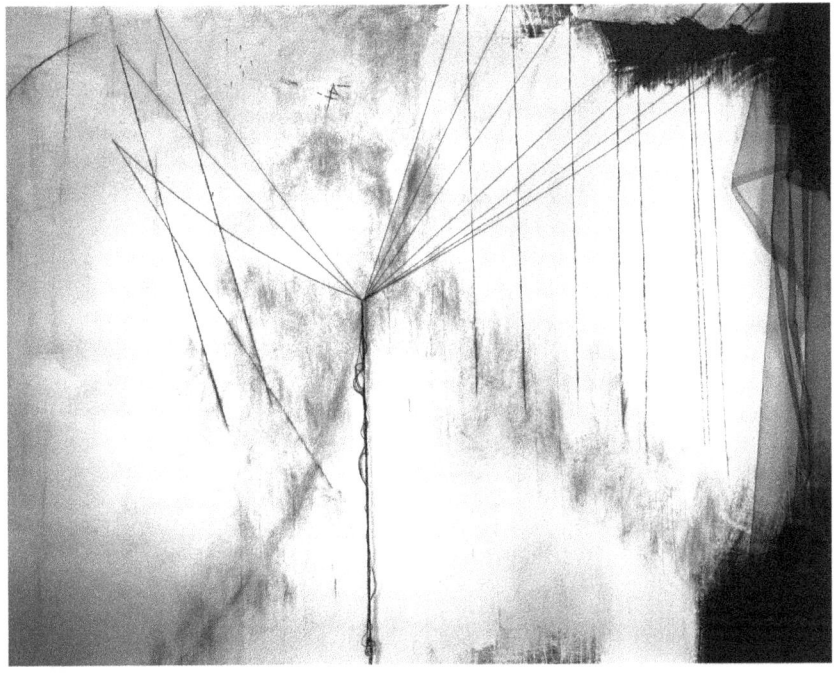

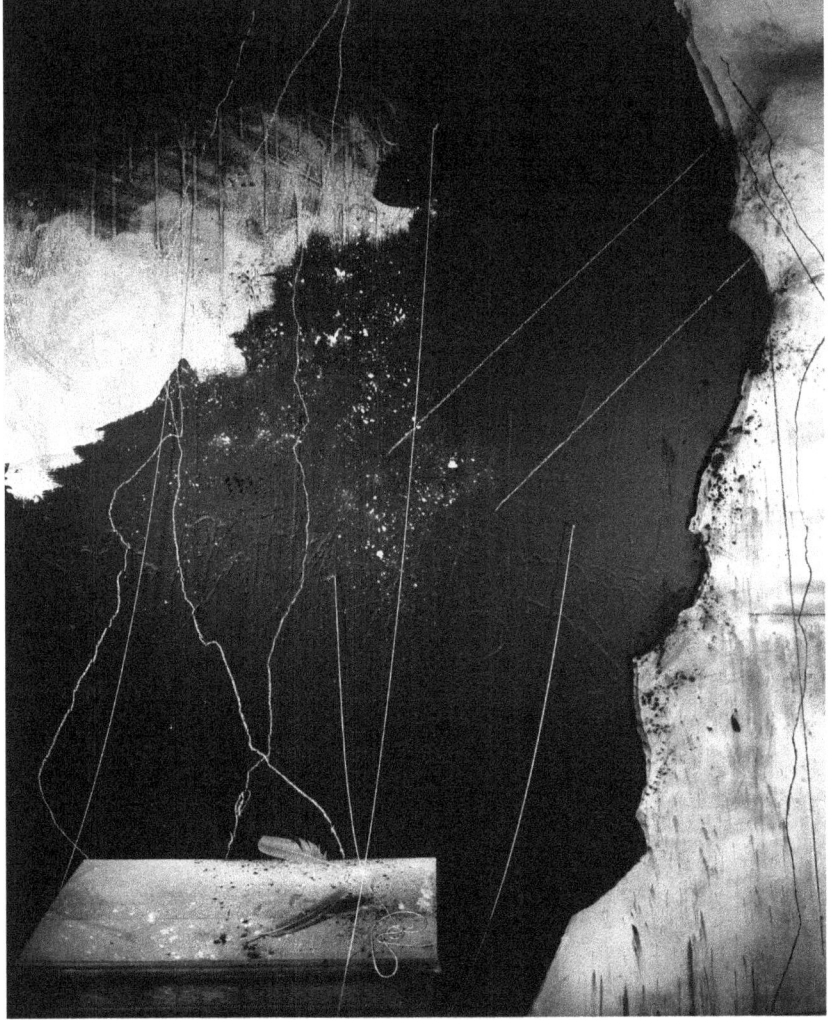

varied sizes, vertical and horizontal orientations, and visual impact of her multipart, black-and-white ensembles. Two vignettes from the series, **Anchor** and **Seven Sisters**, both 2015, conjure up contrasting states of mind. The centripetal composition of the former, anchored within rectilinear parameters, is stabilized as well by its arching, concentric curves of paint, ribbons, and chalk. The taut, linear structure of *Seven Sisters*, indexing the now-demolished smokestacks that once ranged along the Detroit River, is spare and spacious, its entire left side invitingly offering wide-open, boundary-free vistas. Alternately, **Flour, Chalk, Feathers**, also 2017, sucks one into a rather bleakly somber milieu replete with wispy feathers and dark, random splotches of paint on a small, battered table isolated against a gaping, pitch-black background.

Conversely, *Observatory* is laden with likenesses of Semivan, visible in partial and often obscured views, whose

(Top) Seven Sisters. 2015. Archival inkjet print, 24 x 30 in.
(Bottom) Flour, Chalk, Feathers. 2017. Archival inkjet print, 40 x 50 in.

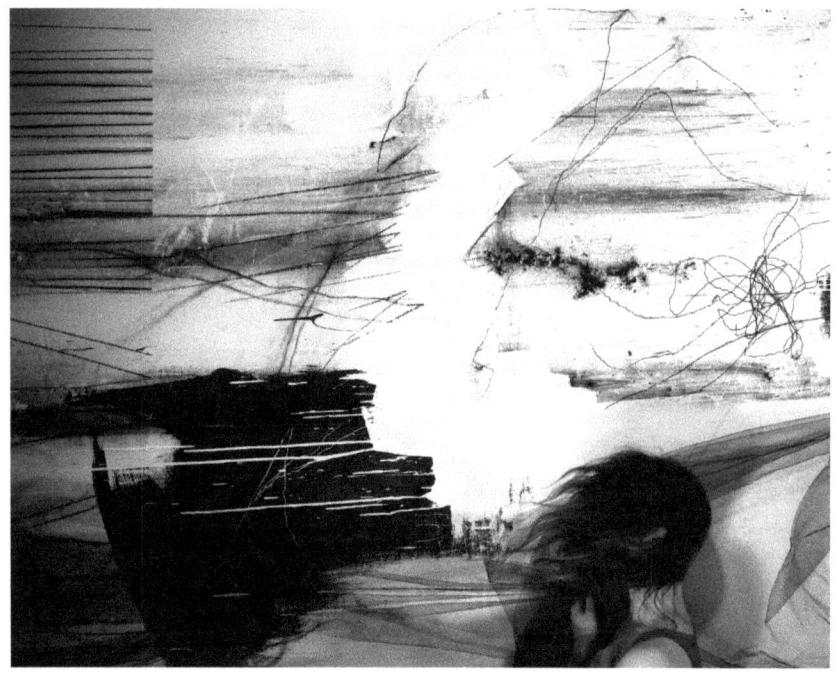

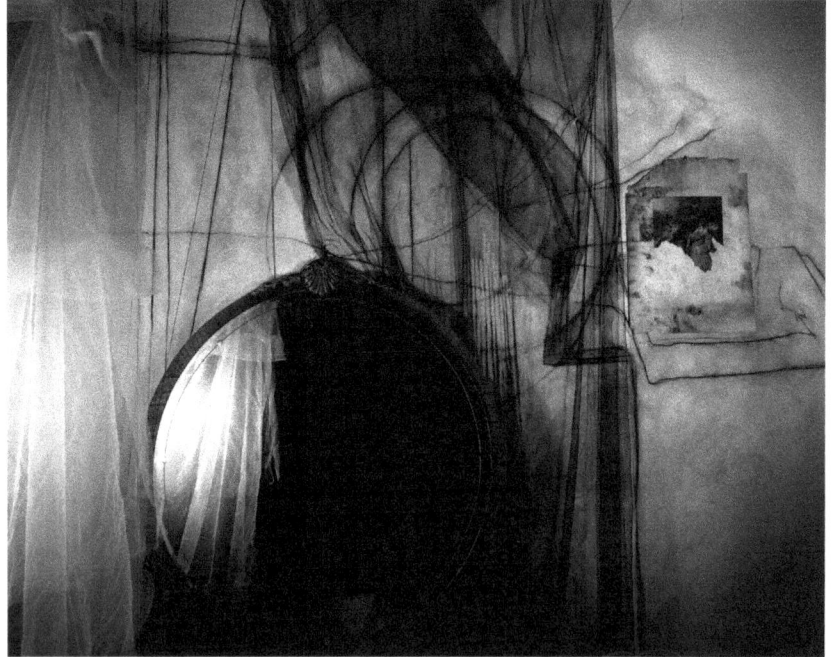

(Top) Wind 2. 2012. Archival inkjet print, 50 x 40 in. *(Bottom)* Mirror. 2010. Archival inkjet print, 30 x 24 in.

poses and gestures that signal the volatile emotional solos being enacted. Tellingly, Semivan is present in both the first and last illustrations of the book, in effect bracketing the existential dilemmas of her dramatis persona. In **Drawn** (2015), for example, shot in front of a motley background of fabric, tulle, and paint, her hand reaches in from the right to stretch and "draw" multiple strands of string suspended in space. In **Wind 2** (2012), her immovable, defiant head at bottom right withstands a gust of wind from behind that not only whips her hair across her face, but simultaneously propels in a parallel direction the horizontal threads, lines, and rivulets of paint above her. And, as if reasserting control in **Labyrinth** (2010), her half-length figure, with back turned to the viewer, raises her arm to free herself from the web of threads and wires swirling about.

Mirror (2010), another episode from *Observatory*, while minus a human presence, is dominated by the yawning, black void of a circular looking glass. Save for the reflection of a glowing, white drift of tulle, only one other dim shape is visible within the black ring. Semivan's vintage

appearance, per the artist, "grounds" and personalizes her dream-like narratives. In gallery installations, the gallerist usually sequences the images, but in the 2017 publication of *Observatory* as a picture book, Semivan laid out the chronology of forty-four pictures herself. Fully half of them include the artist in nuanced

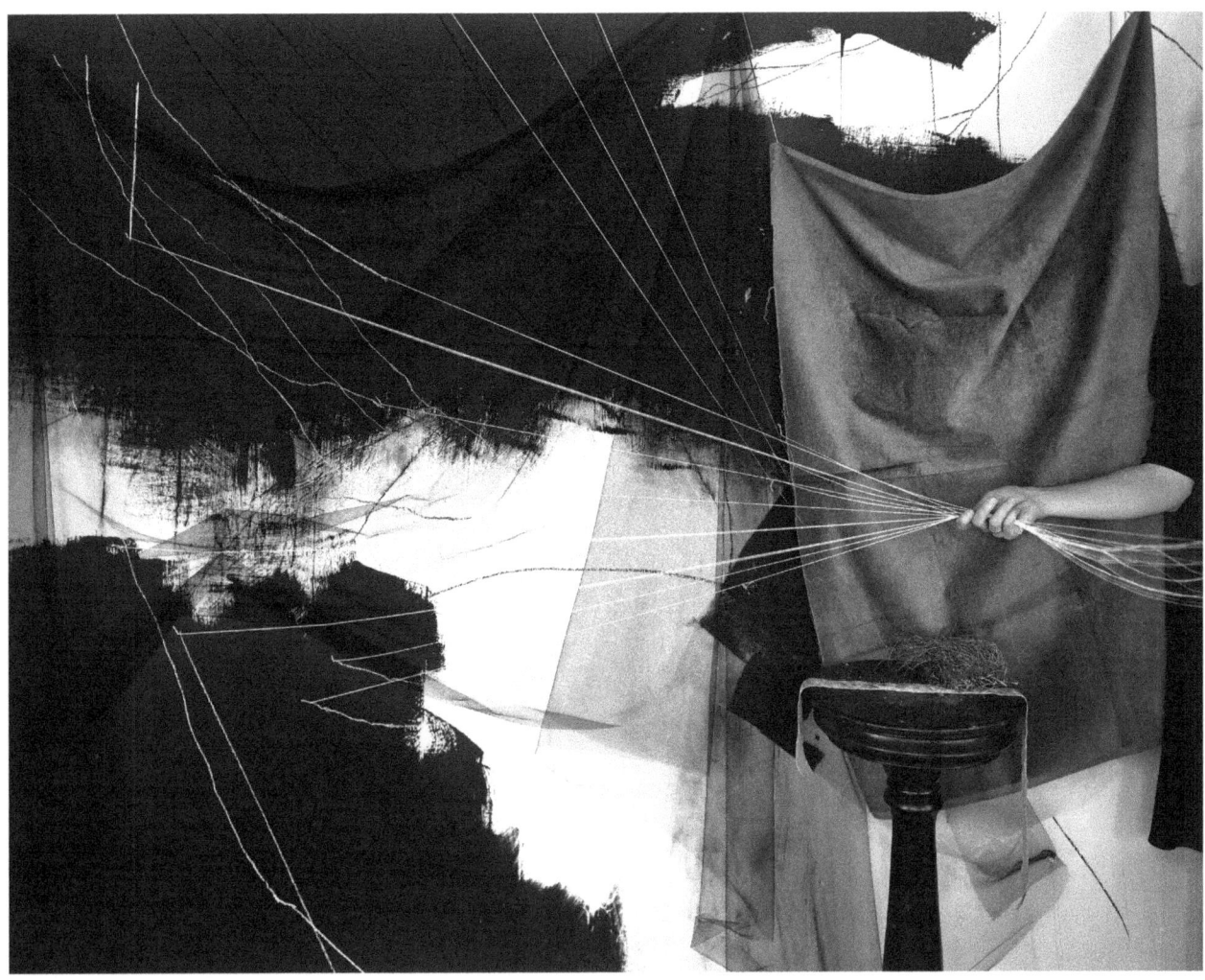

Drawn. 2015. Archival inkjet print, 24 x 30 in.

camera is glimpsed there, lurking. It—and the photographer—are the elemental agents that perpetrate the shifting scenes and fluctuating moods of these cryptic scenarios. Who, after all, can resist Semivan's avowal to fathom the inner recesses of the human vessel: "I consider photography to be both a tool for escape, and an instrument for self-knowledge: a door into the dark." There, in darkness and solitude, eye-opening epiphanies, dramas, enigmas, and more await.

DENNIS ALAN NAWROCKI, OCTOBER 2017

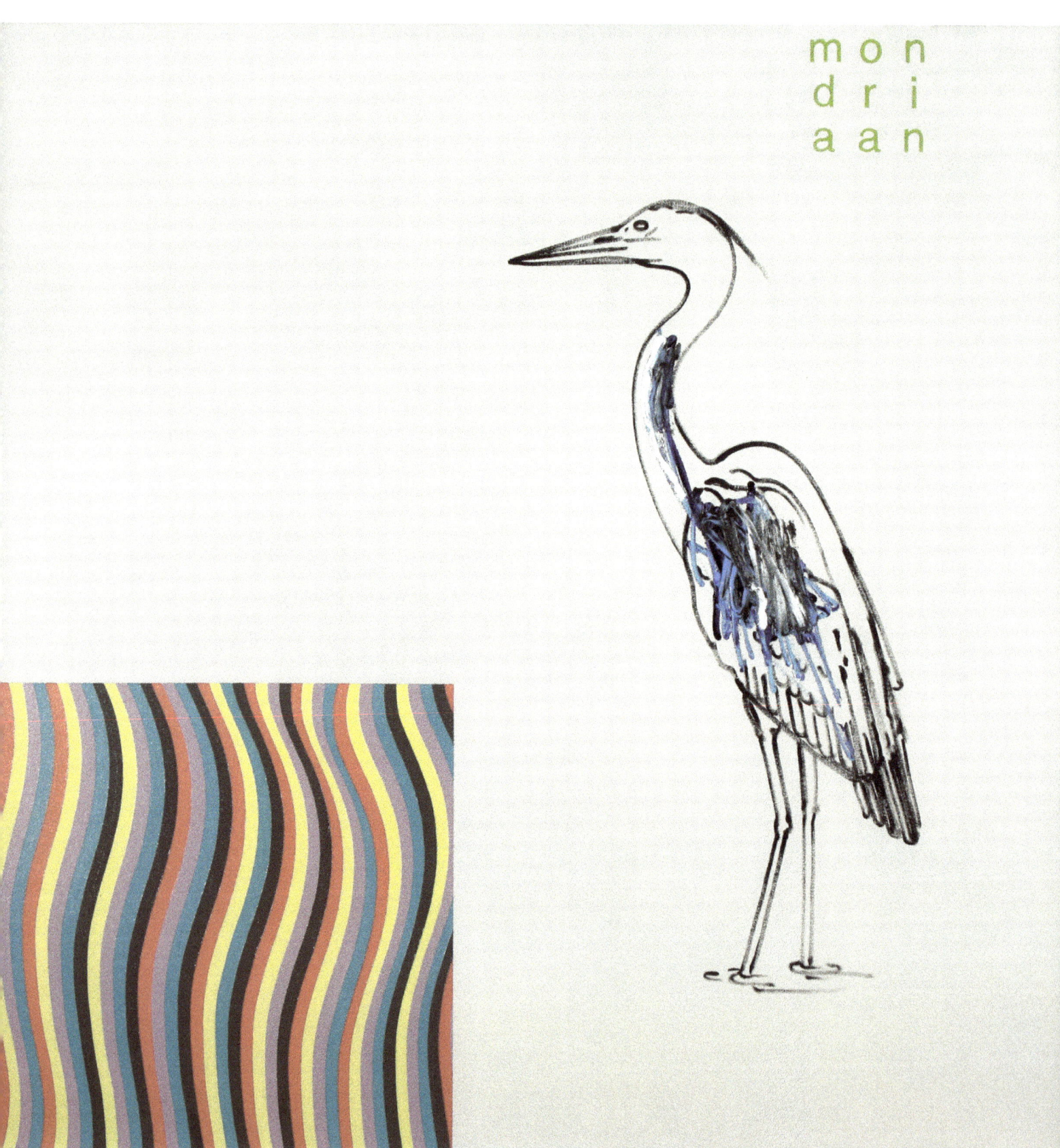

mon
dri
a an

Heron. 2009. Oil on canvas, 48 x 48 in.

Born 1951, Ann Arbor, Michigan
BA, Calvin College, Michigan; MFA, Wayne State University
Lives in Grosse Pointe Farms, Michigan

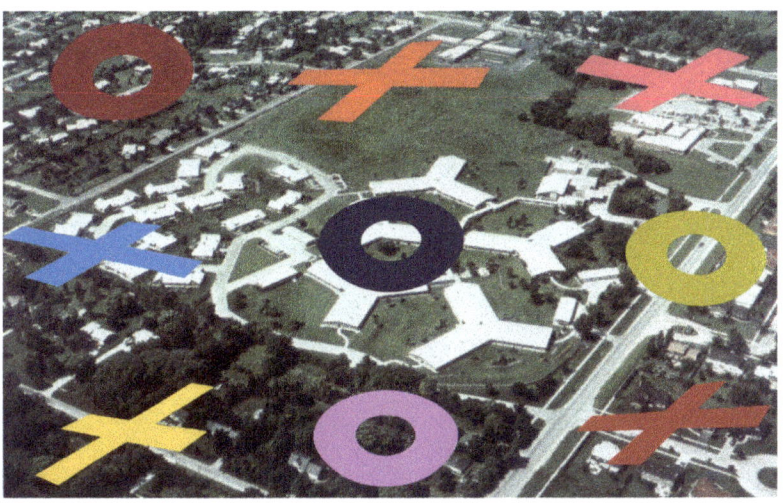

Comparing Theories. 2003. Digital print, oil paint, canvas on wood panel, 28 x 44 in.

What do an oscillating fan and a Josef Albers "square" have in common? Nothing. Nothing at all. They aren't even in the same category of things. A fan is a fan, a practical object in the world. An Albers square, by contrast, is a study in color and shape. It's an abstract work of art that has no obvious purpose.

So why did Timothy van Laar make a painting (**Fan**, 2009) that consists precisely of one fan and one Albers square? Van Laar, who is currently the Chair of Fine Arts at the College for Creative Studies was, for thirty-two years, a professor of art at the University of Illinois at Urbana-Champaign. He's also published three books on art. Van Laar has been thinking about and making art for more than forty years. Surely, then, he put these two strange items together in one painting for some reason.

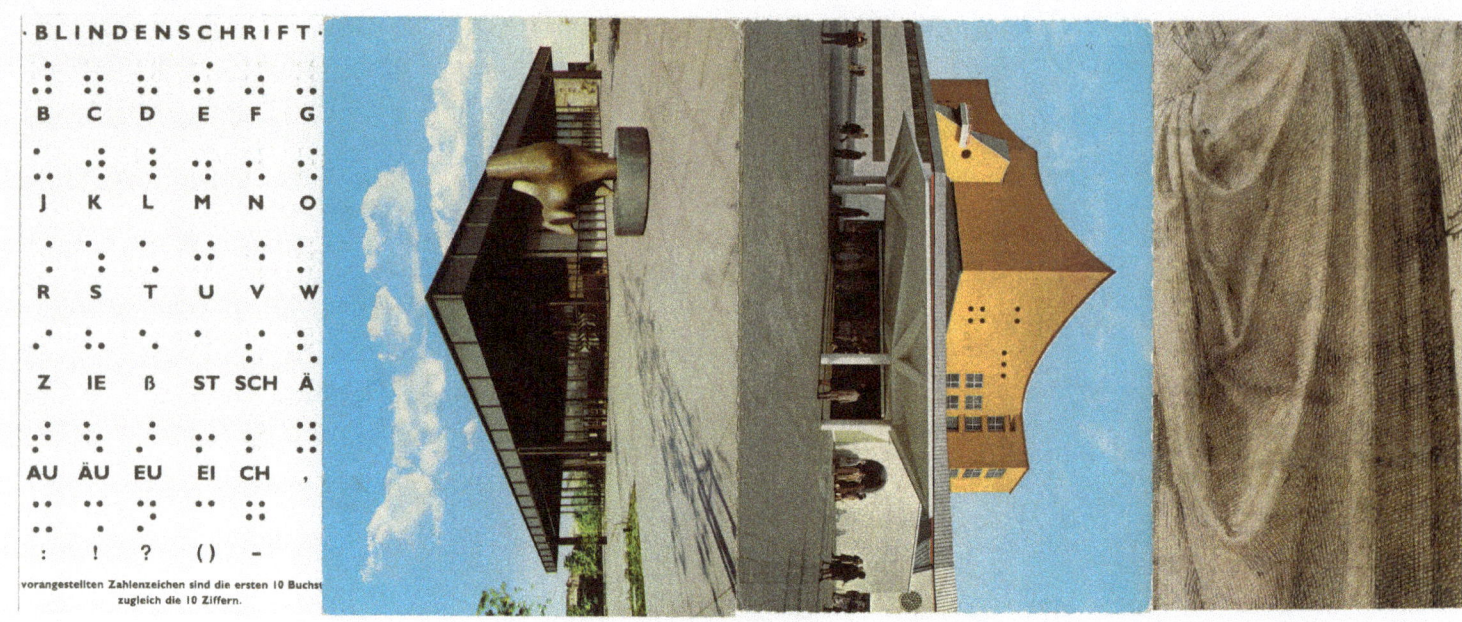

Berlin 1. 2002. Collage, 5 3/4 x 13 3/4 in.

The first step in figuring out this conundrum is to look at a lot of other pictures by Timothy van Laar. What you learn in doing so is that van Laar is a fan of visual puzzles, enigmas, irony, and puns. Some of his paintings are, as he himself admits, basically dumb jokes. He once painted a canvas (**Heron**, 2009) that contains a bunch of colored wavy lines in one corner, the name "Mondrian" in another, and a tall bird (presumably the heron), in the center. The joke is that Mondrian, a painter of straight lines and hard geometry, hated curves and birds. So, van Laar painted a "tribute" to Mondrian that is replete with curves and birds even down to the typology of Mondrian's name, which is a bunch of curvy letters.

Van Laar has also created hundreds of collages composed of picture postcards from all over the world. Generally, he takes three or four postcards and places them side by side in a frame, lengthwise. Looking at the postcards in their new setting, you begin to notice similarities in certain shapes, colors, structural elements, and designs that speak to one another across the cards. One such work, **Berlin 1** (2012), consists of a braille postcard, two modernist buildings in Berlin, and a statue of someone wearing a robe. The first thing you notice is that the "holes" of the braille look just like the holes in one of the modernist buildings. As you look closer, you begin to see tons of subtle variations on the themes of curves and angles throughout all four of the postcards.

Or take **Comparing Theories** from 2003. Van Laar has taken an utterly banal postcard showing an anonymous suburban

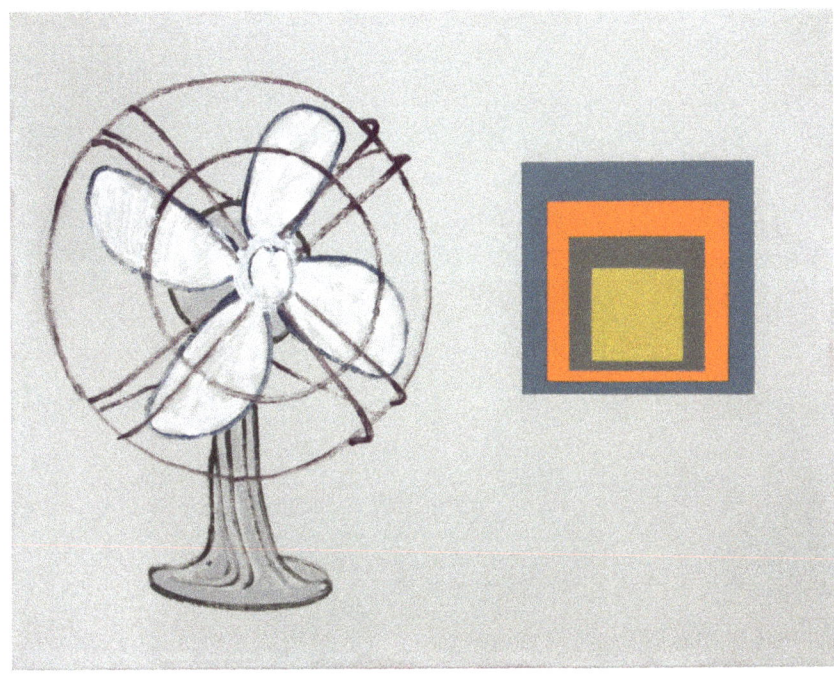

Fan. 2009. Oil on canvas, 16 x 20 in.

landscape. He transferred the image from the card onto a canvas and then painted large Xs and Os in bright colors over the image. The gods have been playing a giant game of tic-tac-toe. But as you look closer, you realize that the landscape itself was already a game of tic-tac-toe, since many of the buildings and streets, seen from above, form the shapes of letters. Are we looking at a system of secret signs or just the dumb accidents of urban design?

Coming back to *Fan*, we can now understand better what van Laar is up to. He starts with an enticing witticism—the funny and absurd juxtaposition of a mundane object (fan) and a bit of "high art" (Albers square). Then the mind and the eye begin to dig deeper. Gradually, interesting relationships are discovered. First, the number four: four squares of color in the Albers square, four blades to the fan. Next: motion. Fans whirl around and the blades take on different visual forms as they move. But the Albers square moves too. Albers created his squares to be visually dynamic, with colors vibrating and pulsating against one another. So here's another, deeper, van Laar joke. When we first started to look, we thought of the fan as the more "real"

object. But now, it is the Albers square that moves and lives.

Deep questions about art and representation filter out from what began as a visual gimmick. The more van Laar paintings one looks at, the more one becomes convinced that there are relationships to be found between all things. That's to say, in van Laar's painterly universe, there is always some way to connect one thing to another thing, via structure, or meaning, or sign, or association. These connections are, in a sense, the means by which things communicate with one another and thereby with us as well.

MORGAN MEIS, NOVEMBER 2017

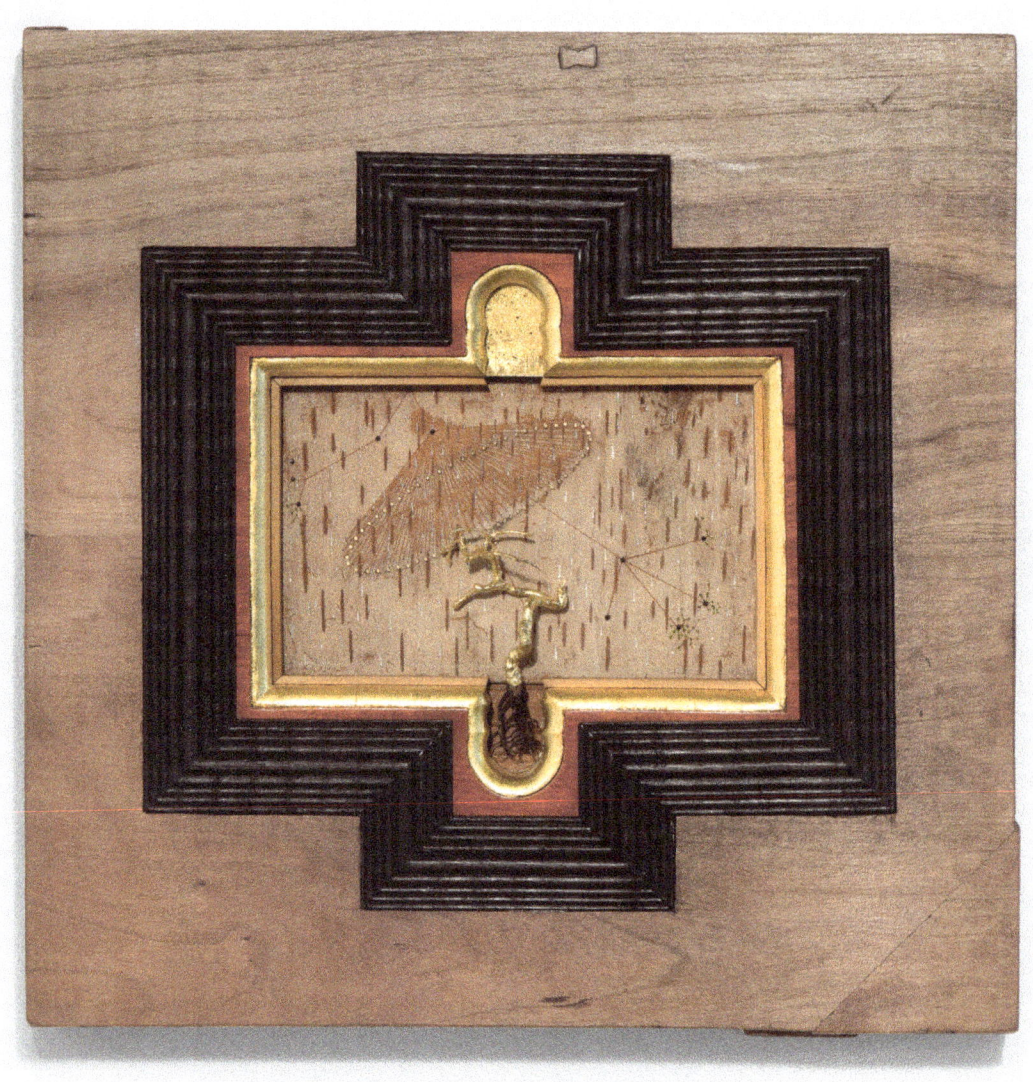

Crown. 2017. Wood, birch bark, gold leaf, bonsai tree, 12.5 x 12.5 x 2 in. Photography by PD Rearick.

83 // SHARON QUE

Born Sharon Queriograssa, Detroit, 1960
BFA, University of Michigan; Associate's (Manufacturing
Engineering), Macomb Community College
Lives in Ann Arbor, Michigan

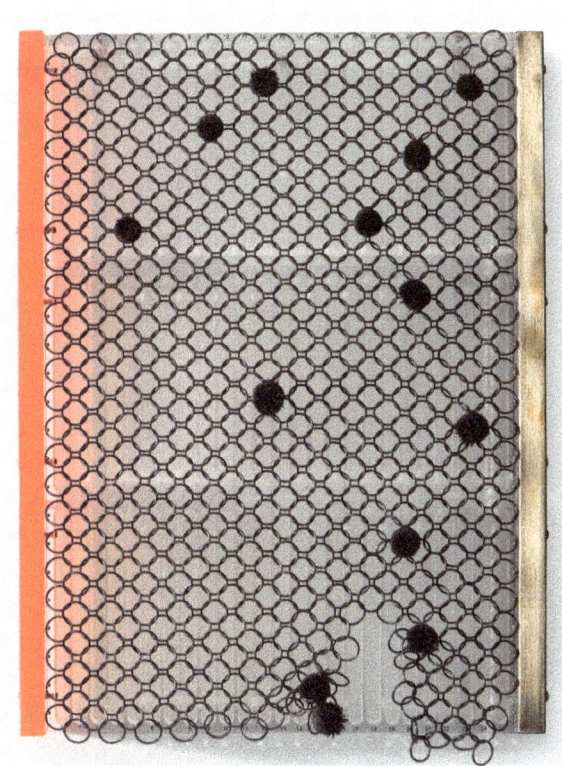

Night's Silent Veil. 2017. chain mail, brass, magnetite, plexiglass, 20 x 14 x 3 in. Photography by PD Rearick.

Works of art communicate in myriad ways: some shout, some whisper, some never shut up. Sharon Que's constructions seem only to cast meaningful glances, encouraging, cajoling, even daring the viewer to suss out what lies behind them.

These elegant, often playful works seem familiar, as if one had seen them somewhere before. They exude whiffs of history and utility, of alchemy and manufacturing, of harmonies and dissonances. Their references range from surrealist juxtapositions to *trompe l'oeil* to craft traditions. Que experiments with scale, materials, and varying levels of abstraction to create works that are meditations on objects and systems from the microscopic to the cosmic.

Que has been making objects for more than thirty years. She credits her awakening as an artist as a consequence of her eye-opening travels to Italy, Greece, and Turkey in the mid-1980s. Bucking family tradition by going to art school instead of becoming an engineer, she nevertheless earned her journeyman's card in a skilled trade, as a wood model maker at General Motors. This exacting craft not only honed her woodworking skills but also gave her the financial independence to set up a studio. Remarkably consistent even from her earliest days in the studio, her approach to her work is centered in the complementary choices of natural and mechanical forms that, when combined, blur the distinction between them. Her painstaking craftsmanship is evident in the high degree of finish in all of her constructions, as well as in her insistence on process as an important part of making. Few of the elements of her works are found objects. Instead, objects with interesting shapes, such as the multiple seed pods in *Adrift* (2017) are cast into another material; the exploration of the intricacies of the shape through the casting process is integral to the work.

Que calls herself a "material person," in that she responds to and is excited by substances and their properties. She discovered

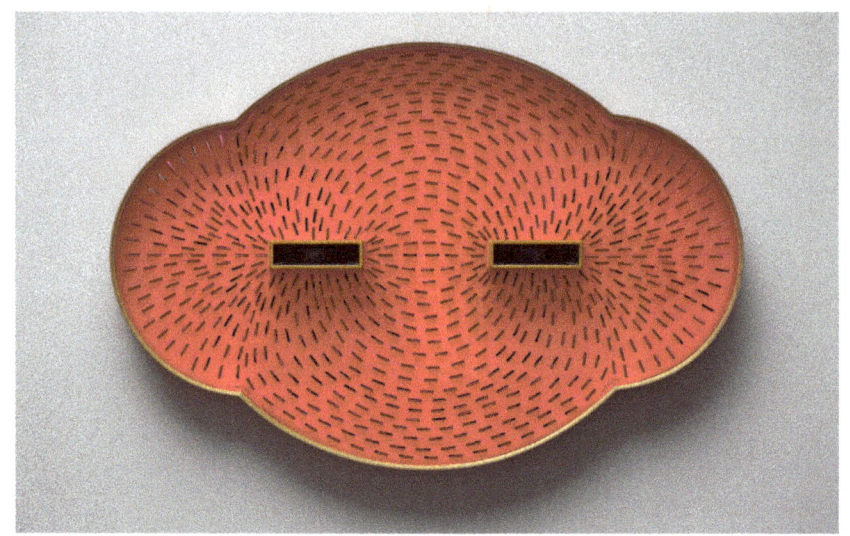

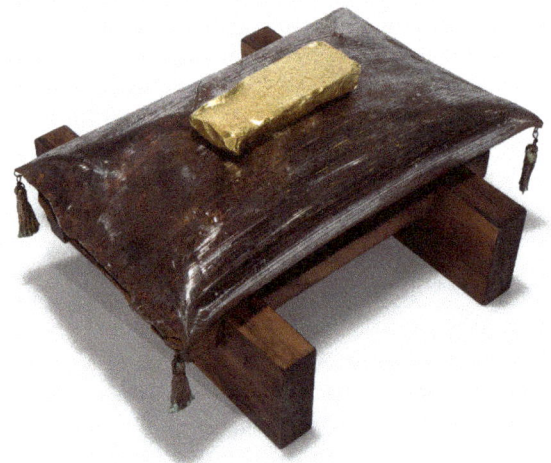

(Top) Dear Mr. Fantasy. 2014. Pink plexiglass, wood, gold leaf, 16 1/2 x 24 1/2 x 2 in. Photography by Eric Wheeler. *(Bottom) The 12th of Never.* 2017. Steel, gold leaf, wood, 12 x 22 x 18 1/2 in. Photography by PD Rearick.

magnetite (ferrous-ferric oxide), a mineral that is one of the most magnetic substances in nature, while at the Lake Michigan shore and realized the potential of its grainy, black, sand-like particles as a natural way to create patterns. An image of the polarized regularity of the magnetic field appears in many works, such

as *Dear Mr. Fantasy* (2014), but the use of magnetite in small spheres that cling to the surface of *Night's Silent Veil* (2017) allows her to use the magnetic field as a manipulated found object analogous to the night sky. Birch bark, with its strong linear pattern, is a natural substance that she often pairs with a man-made element;

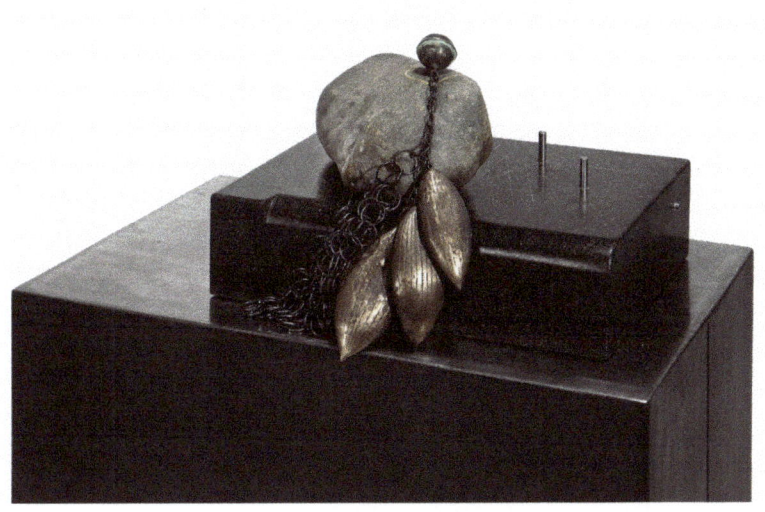

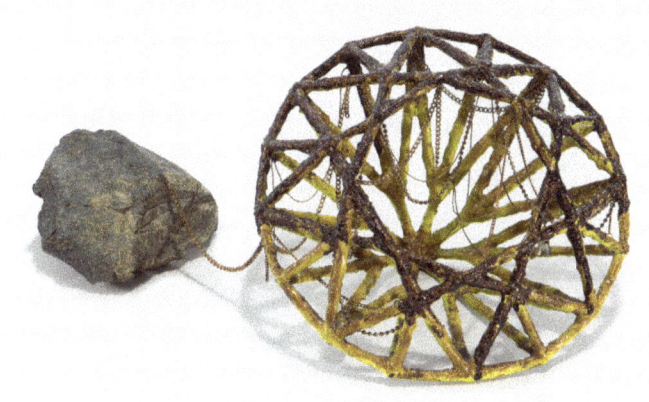

(Top) Adrift. 2017. Stone, cast bronze, steel, 7 x 12 x 12 in. Photography by PD Rearick. *(Bottom) Dark Fireworks.* 2016. Bamboo, paint, chain, stone, 6 x 8 x 6 in. Photography by PD Rearick.

in works such as ***Crown*** (2017), the piece of bark is overlaid by a printed data visualization diagram that resembles the form of a Japanese umbrella. The addition of a gilded bonsai tree and a sixteenth-century Dutch-style picture frame creates a remarkably exotic mélange of east and west that emphasizes pattern to create image.

Que's deft combinations of physical elements often lead viewers to overlook the subtle emotional undercurrent of her work. Often the mood seems to be melancholy, evoked by dark coloration, a sense of being anchored or bound, or a suggestion of emotional ambivalence. ***Dark Fireworks*** (2016) is one of many works that feature

an object chained to a stone, here the outline of the facets of a classic diamond. The titular fireworks might suggest the flashing of light from the facets, but this diamond is made of more pedestrian bamboo, perhaps a rueful suggestion that it is not "forever." ***The 12th of Never*** (2017), inspired by a recent trip to the Alhambra, is a visual pun that shows her sly humor. A found piece of steel that suggests the shape of a pillow sits on a polished wood support, decorated with cast steel "tassels" and balancing a gold-leafed bar. "The 12th of Never," a popular song from the mid-1950s, refers to an occurrence so far in the future that it will never happen: a love that never dies, a pillow that never softens, even under the weight of gold bullion.

Her intimate constructions are reminiscent of the work of artists like Joseph Cornell, a collector of ordinary objects that had personal, often ambiguous significance. Transcending a simple literal reading, Que's works explore the mysterious links between what we know and what we feel.

MARYANN WILKINSON, NOVEMBER 2017

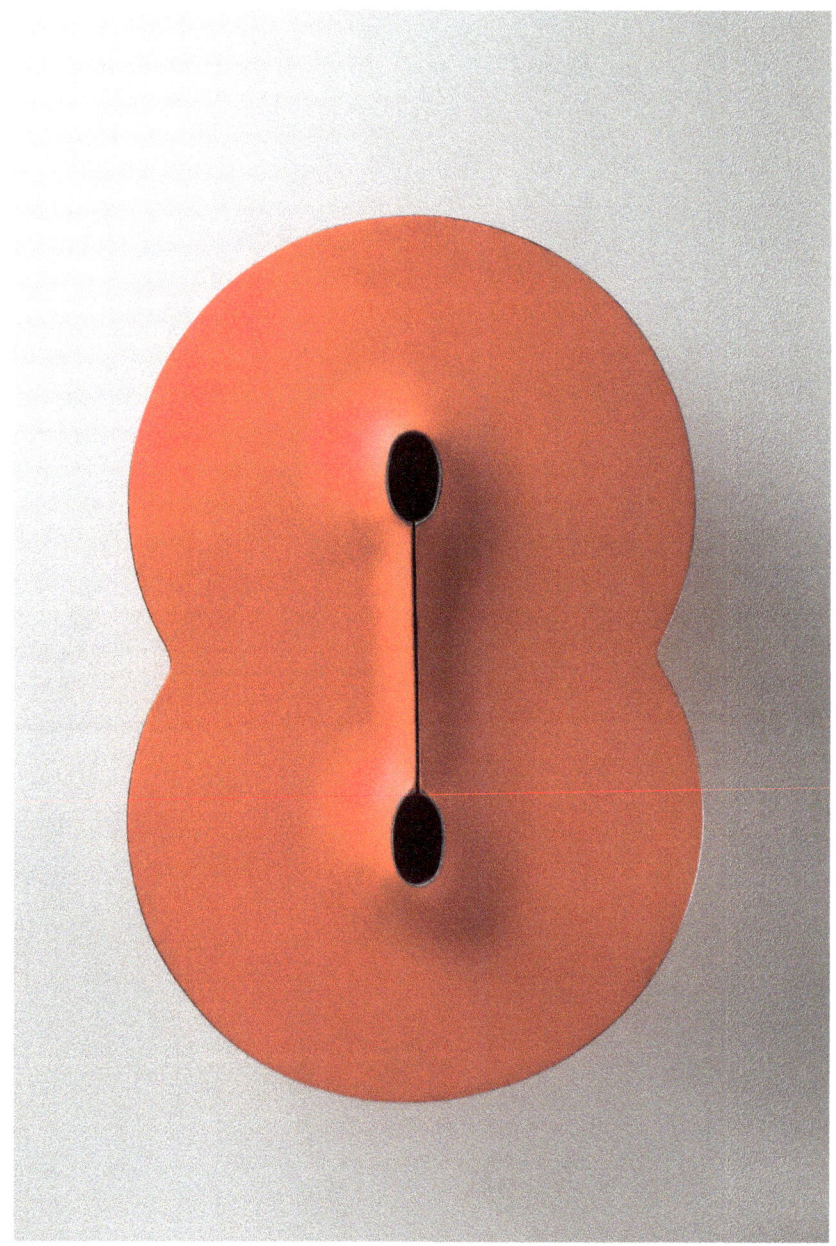

Red Bindu. 2016. Fabricated steel, 32 x 18 x 10 in. Photography by Tim Thayer.

84 // TOM PHARDEL

Born Detroit, 1950
BFA, Eastern Michigan University; MFA, University of Michigan
Lives in Ann Arbor, Michigan

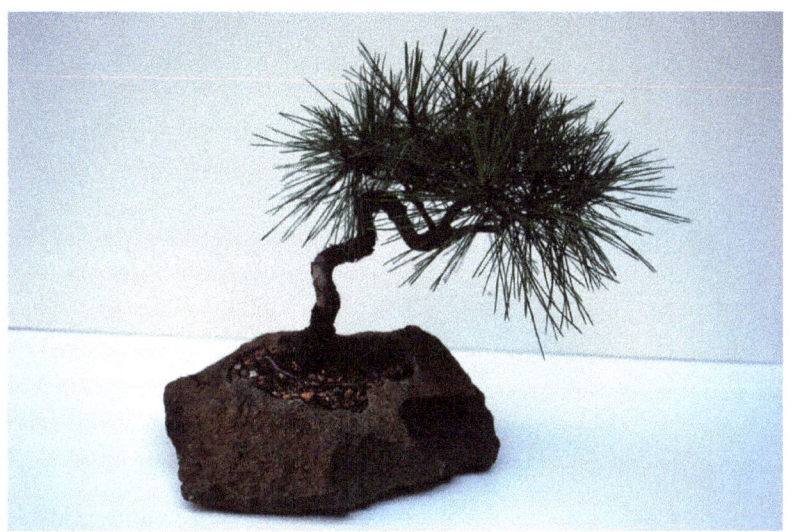

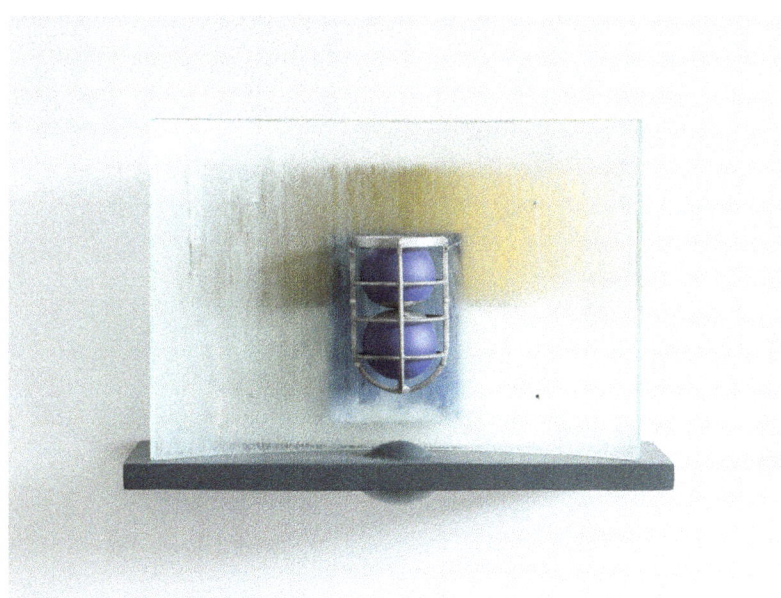

(Top) Bonsai tree. *(Bottom) Blue on Blue—The Couple.* 2016. Steel, glass, wood, 16 ½ x 24 x 9 ½ in. Photography by Tim Thayer.

Tom Phardel—sculptor, ceramist, and curator; beekeeper and bonsai enthusiast—has long played a critical role in the Detroit art community as both an artist and a supporter of other artists, and of course of the ceramic tradition. Serving as (much beloved) teacher and chair of ceramics at the College for Creative Studies for thirty years, he has inspired successive generations of students while pursuing his own artistic path, a path that has led him to a body of work notable for its sense of mystery, spirituality, and devoted connection to the natural world.

Phardel's curiosity about the magic of ritual, paired with a strong respect for spiritual practices, has been prominent in his mind and art ever since childhood, when his fascination with the intricate, mysterious ceremonies of the Catholic Church left an indelible mark

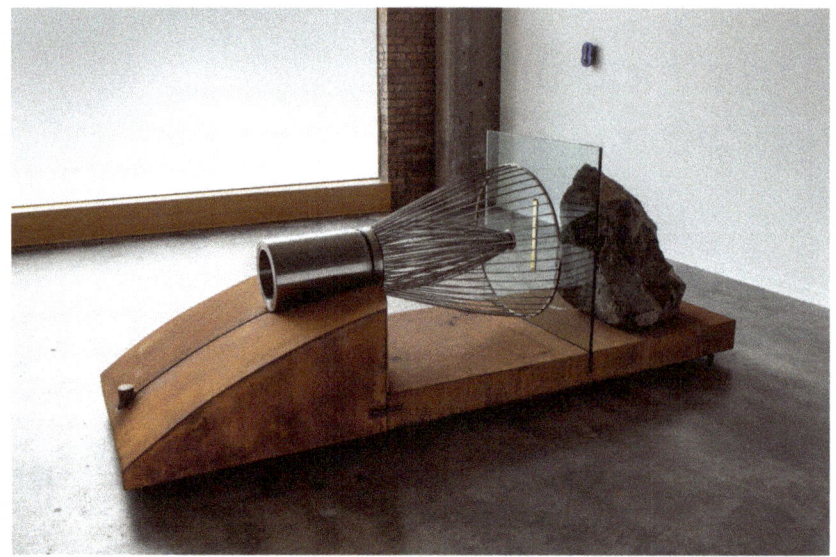

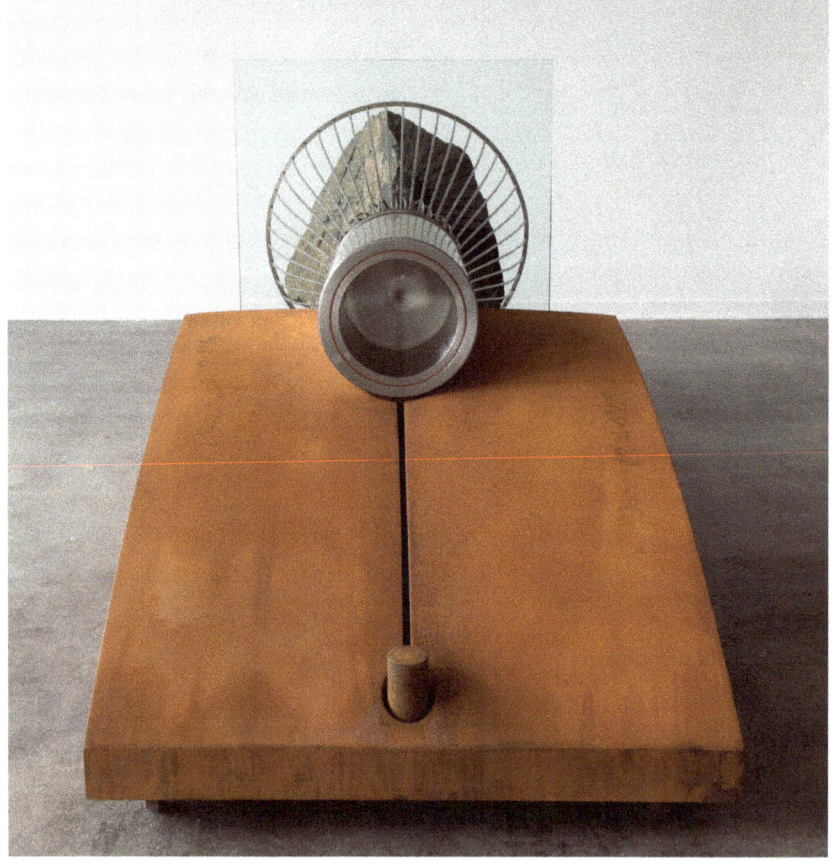

(Top) Tea Whisk and Boulder. 2016. Steel, glass, and gold leaf, 4 x 10 ft. Photography by Tim Thayer.

(Bottom) Tea Whisk and Boulder (detail). 2016. Steel, glass, and gold leaf, 4 x 10 ft. Photography by Tim Thayer.

on him. Inspiration from trips to far-flung countries such as Japan and India remain evident in his work many years later, including his fascination with **bonsai trees**.

Although he has been sculpting bonsai for around twenty-five years, Phardel is adamant that he is only a beginner. He is an attentive caretaker of a small yet captivating forest of bonsai (over thirty trees), many in their own handmade containers, and each one with a distinct personality. Phardel sees the meticulous pruning and shaping of the trees as consonant with his art practice, although he does admit it takes an added knowledge of horticulture to be successful. Many of his trees made their public debut in a 2014 exhibit at Detroit café and exhibition space Trinosophes.

Phardel is consistently busy, wanting to stay active and maintain his creative vigor. He is intent on rethinking and expanding his visual vocabulary in order to effectively convey his ideas and feelings about the connectivity between art and nature, and between human beings and the lessons proffered by the natural world. Working both within his previous wheelhouse as well as venturing outside his comfort zone, his objects embody

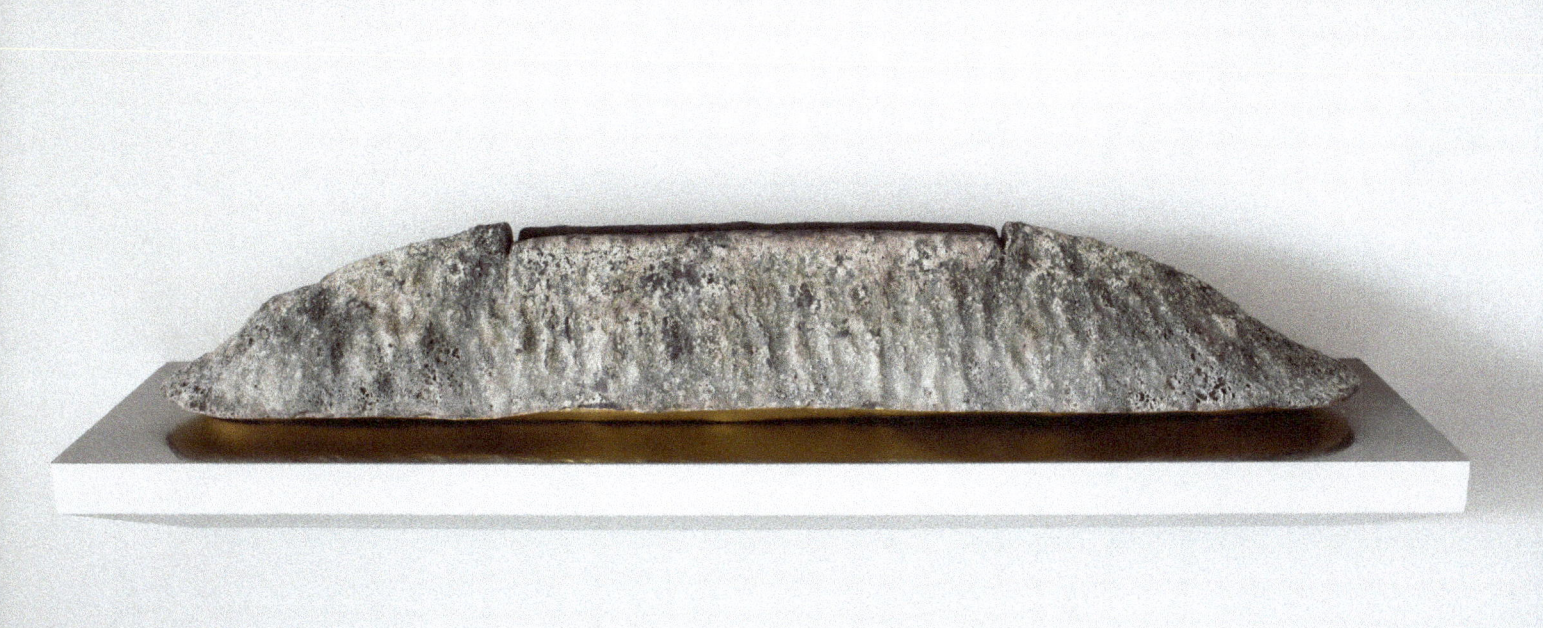

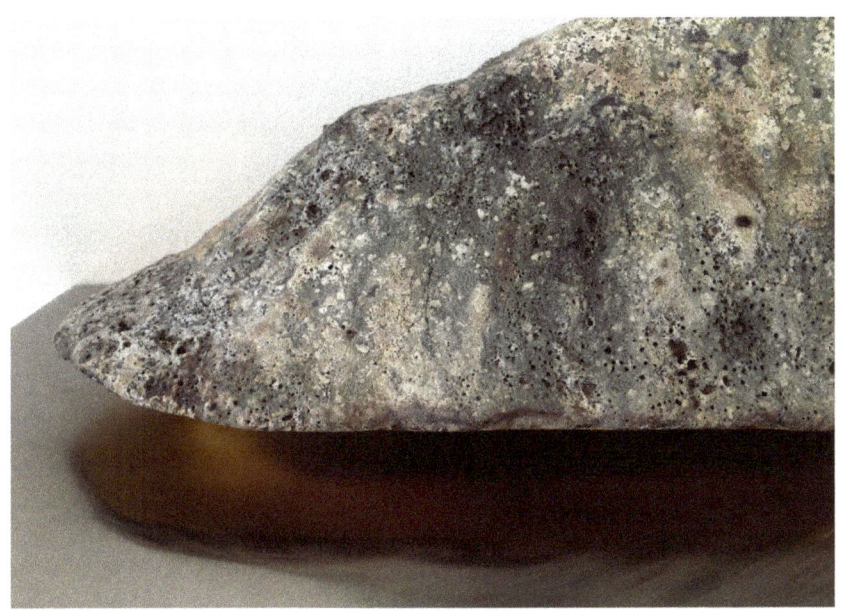

(Top) Levitating Mountain. 2016. Ceramic and gold leaf, 6 x 36 x 6 in. Photography by Tim Thayer.

(Left) Levitating Mountain (detail). 2016. Ceramic and gold leaf, 6 x 36 x 6 in. 2016. Photography by Tim Thayer.

strength, precision, and mystery. He also revisits and rethinks relationships between forms (circles, swelling curves, rectangles), materials (steel, clay), and space.

Tea Whisk and Boulder (2016) stands at the heart of his most recent work, a meditation on nature versus science. The whisk is a sleek proxy for the modernized world. Resembling an antenna or a space-age listening device, it converses with the boulder (excavated by the artist) through a plate of glass. A slender elliptical opening in the glass is rimmed in gold, suggesting that any dialogue passing through is highly valuable. Phardel waxes philosophical about the boulder: "I wanted to convey the idea that it [the rock] can teach us something. We think that we know everything but maybe we don't."

As if floating serenely above a thin sheet of brushed stainless steel, the rough-hewn *Levitating Mountain* (2016) reveals a rich gold-leaf underside reflected on the mirrored surface. The labor-intensive creation of the petite mountain required multiple firings, which slowly built up the geologic history of the form with each trip to the kiln. *The Space Between* (2016) also features an undercut bottom and an exterior rich with texture, but the form itself is entirely different.

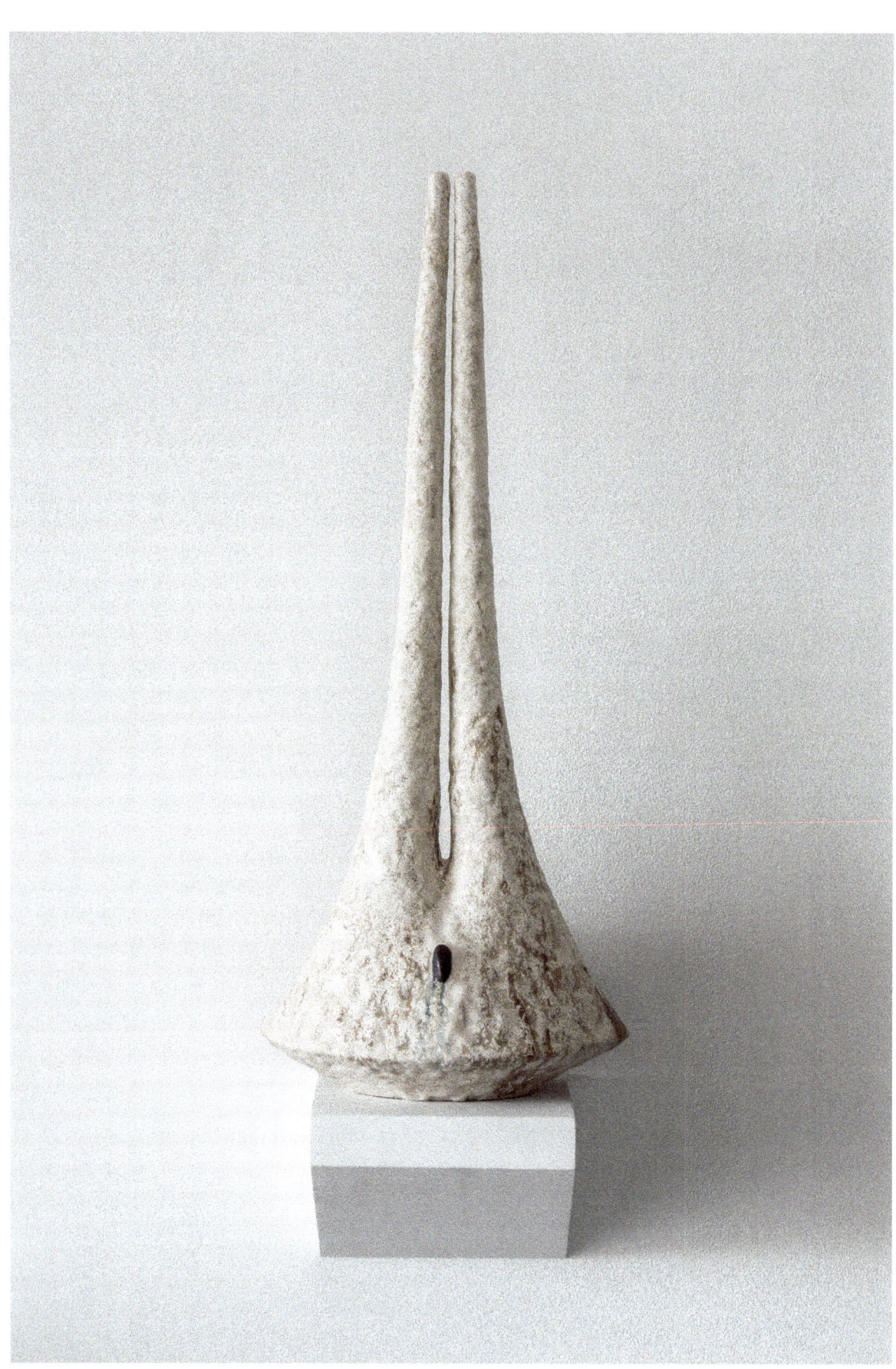

The Space Between. 2016. Ceramic, 28 x 12 x 9 in. Photography by Tim Thayer.

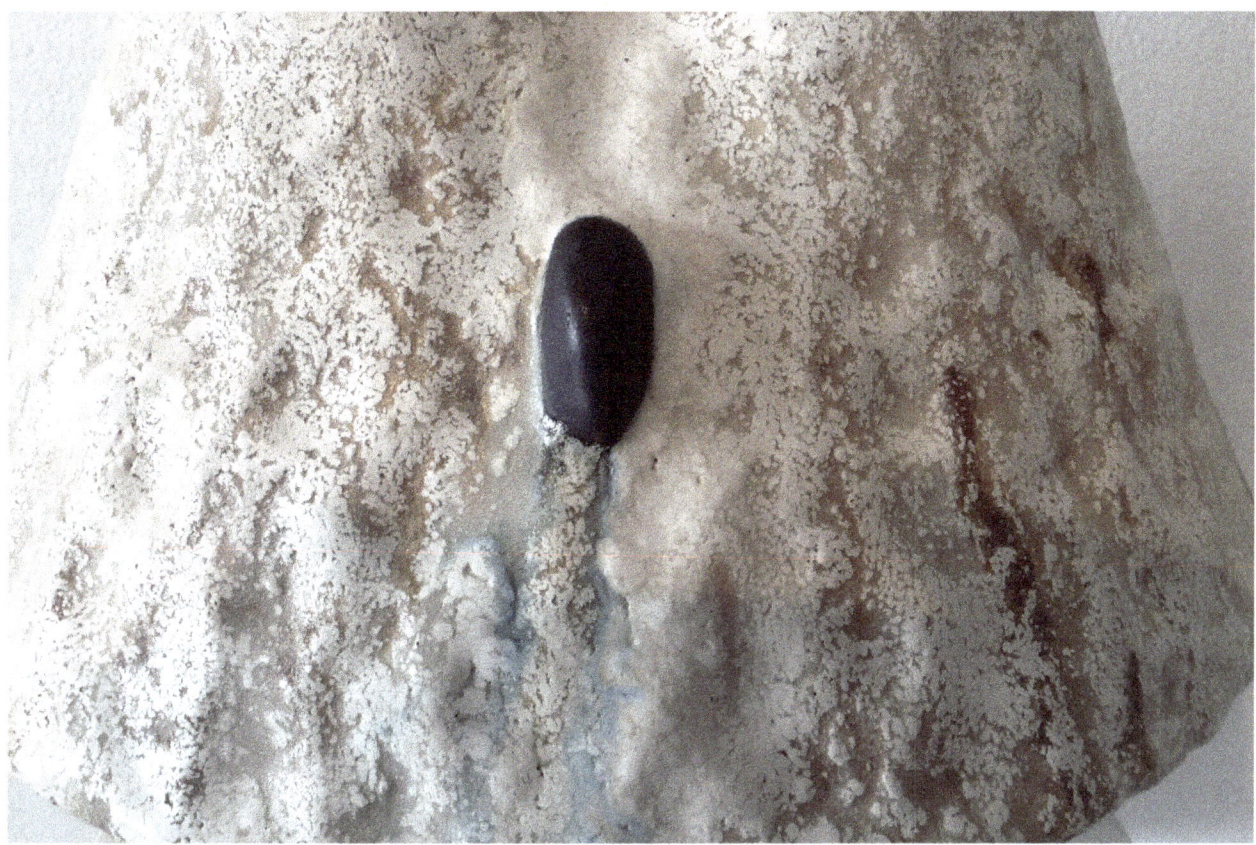

The Space Between (detail). 2016. Ceramic, 28 x 12 x 9 in. Photography by Tim Thayer.

Two long, slim, tube-like extrusions gracefully separate from the base, leaving an exquisite, impossibly thin slice of powerful negative space betwixt the duo.

In a departure from the earth tones of his previous work, Phardel has introduced blue and red, two vivid primary colors specifically selected for their importance in various global religions. In **Red Bindu** (2016), a wall-mounted relief, two circles merge to suggest a shape not unlike a cell undergoing mitosis, an expansion that represents the pure potential in everyone. The

two-lobed aperture in the middle of the form evokes a darkened, "unseeable" inner space, redolent of mystery and intrigue. The fabricated steel of *Red Bindu* boasts a brilliant saturated surface consisting of over thirty coats of paint painstakingly sanded down between layers. **Blue on Blue—The Couple** (2016), meanwhile, features two blue spheres in a cage stacked one on top of the other. The place where they make contact is a cool burnished silver. The curved, acid-etched opaque glass rectangle lends the work a sense of obscure, time-worn mystery.

One of the artist's main ambitions is to transport his audience to a contemplative, entranced state. "I want to make work that you want to be with, as well as look at," Phardel explains. Though his cryptic, mixed-media structures may sometimes feel intangible—as if the answer from the oracle is enticingly just beyond reach—as always, the aura of his imagery and the generosity of his spirit carry the day.

HEATHER EARNLEY, OCTOBER 2017

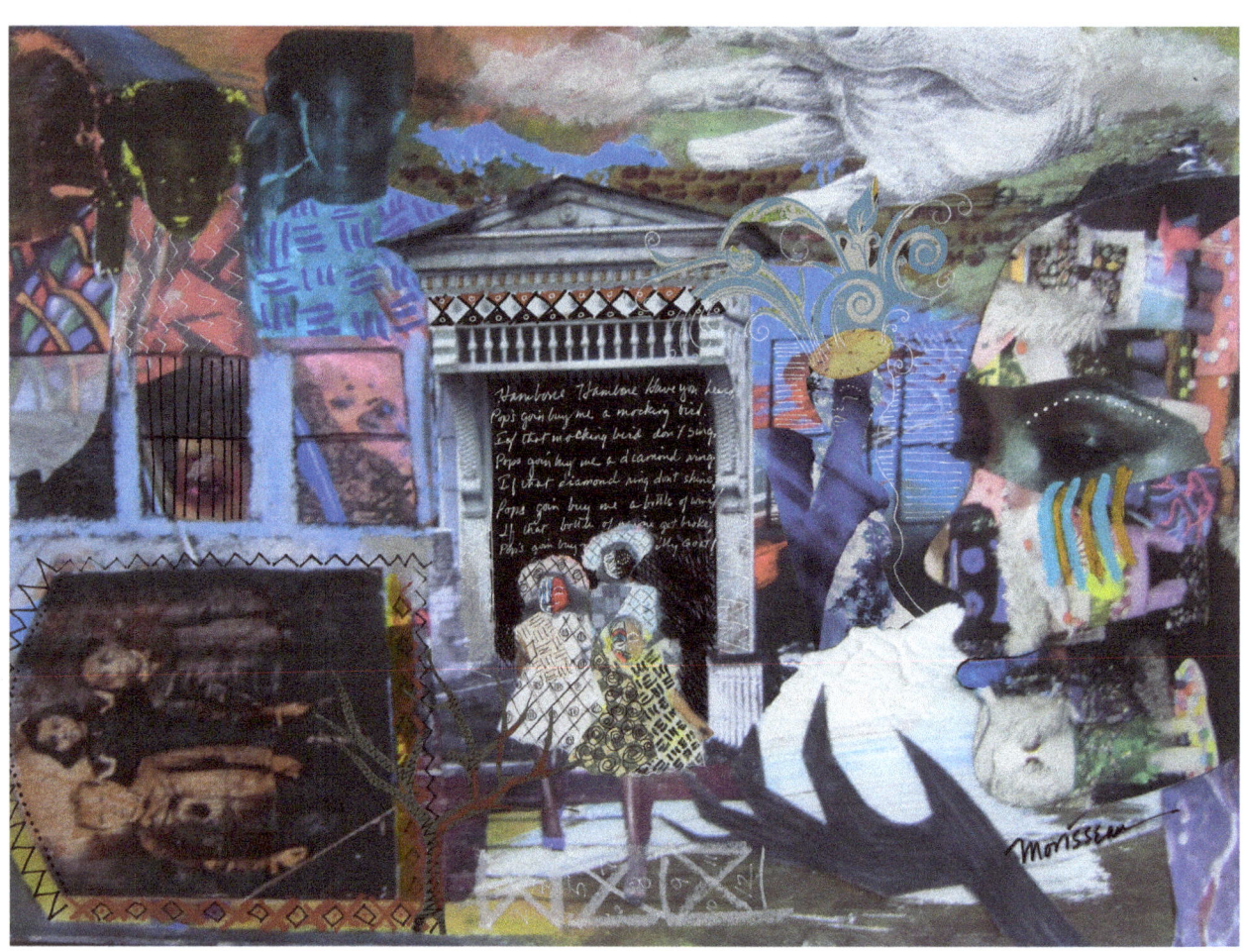

Generations. 2012. collage on paper, 16 x 20 in.

Born Detroit
BS, Central State University, Ohio
Lives in Detroit

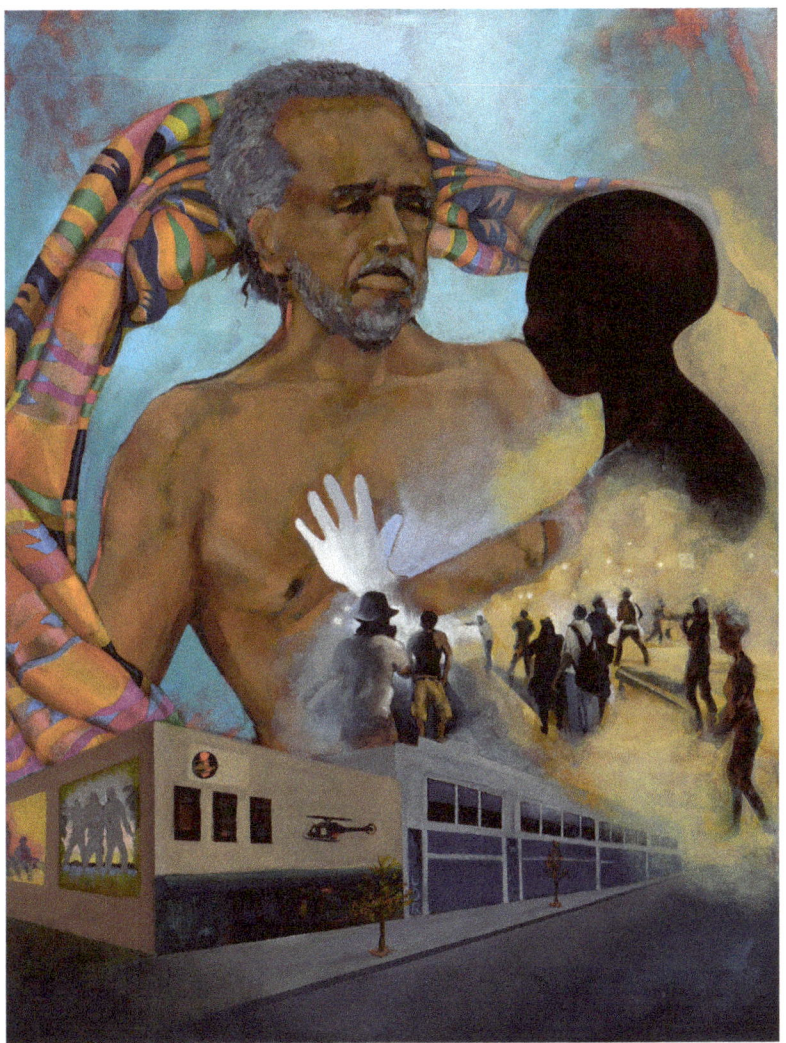

Legacy. 2015. Oil on canvas, 40 x 50 in.

Consider the art of Carole Morisseau as a bridge—as an expansive structure made of color, composition, and story that is intended to join differing generations, cultures, ethnicities, and classes.

Morisseau makes art, she says, as an expression of her soul, but accepts that approach to be nonparadigmatic. On a universal level, she sees the role of an artist as one of sharing: of ideas, a story, an aesthetic experience. Hence, the bridge analogy; one has to be willing to step on it and cross to the other side to see, to understand, and to learn. As she puts it, "There is always something to learn, something to experience, and, therefore, always something to express."

The inspiration to create art grows from her personal experience and often originates from a basic fascination with color or

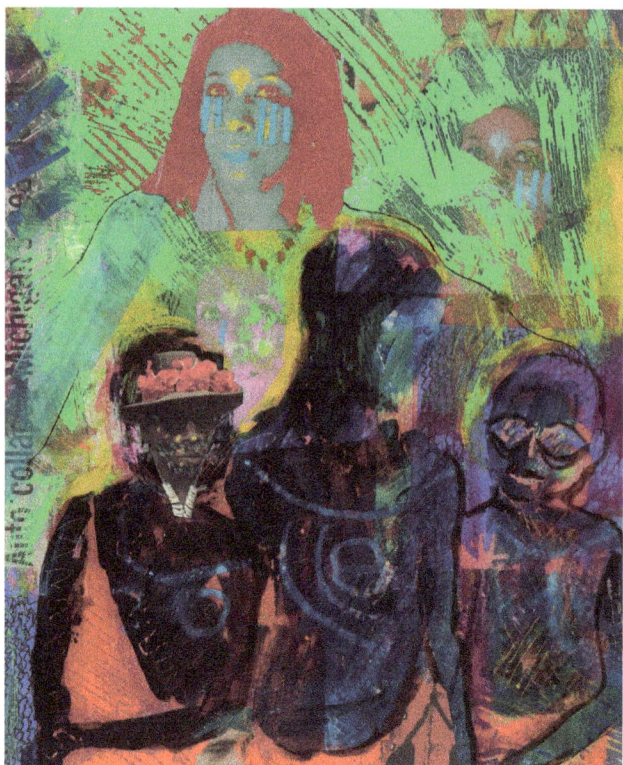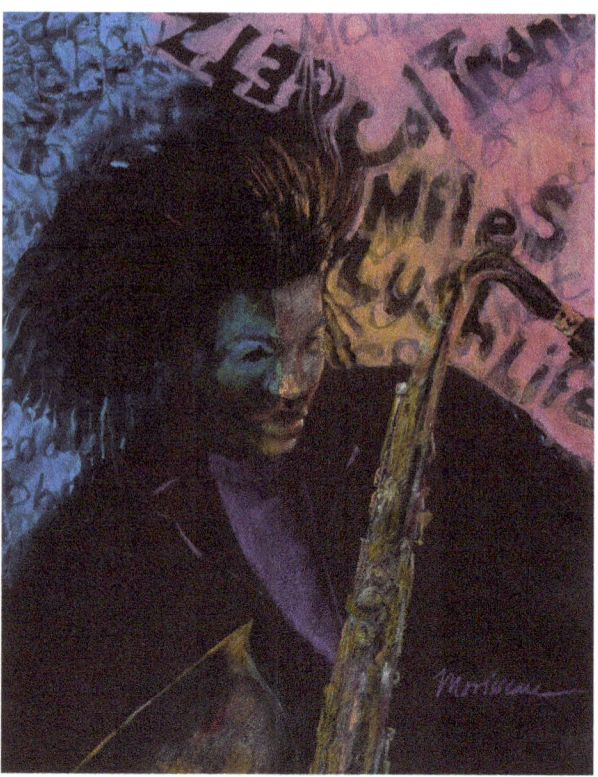

(Left) Track of My Tears. 2012. Mixed media on paper, 14 x 16 in. (*Right*) *The Musician.* 2008. Mixed media on paper, 18 x 24 in.

form. From there, she believes that her role is to convey the personal experience in a meaningful and visually engaging way. Color and composition are crucial. While most of her art is figurative, her exploration of color-form potency occasionally results in abstraction. The effect can be seen in **Hummingbird 5831** (2012), where the palette shifts, drawing the viewer from the sharp and bright upper left to the subtle pastel tones at the lower right, as if intimating the darting flight of a hummingbird. Even in her quick figure studies, she remains mindful of the composition: "I like to choreograph the viewer's eye—what is the first thing that you see and how does it make the eye travel?"

Fascination with color underpins *Conversations with Color*, a recent series that depicts celebrities, but in a noncommercialized fashion. Rather, Morisseau attempts to convey in it the complexity of lives spent on the pedestal of publicity. The frequent juxtaposition of colors in the portraits, as if to contrast both the glamour and darkness present within one entity, makes them symbolic of the allure and peril of that way of life (see *Prince*, 2016, and **Whitney**, 2017).

Morisseau's variety of inspirations is reflected in her flexible choice of medium. She feels just as comfortable using charcoal, graphite, ink, Conté crayon, or pencil as she does working in elaborate collages. (See **Generations** or **Track of My Tears**, both 2012.) She also works with oils (*Legacy*, 2015), acrylics (*Pueblo Woman*, 2007), tempera, and combinations of the above (**The Musician**, 2008).

A lifelong Detroiter, Morisseau pays homage to her native city with landscapes that sometimes emphasize its beauty (*Belle Isle Conservatory*, 2015);

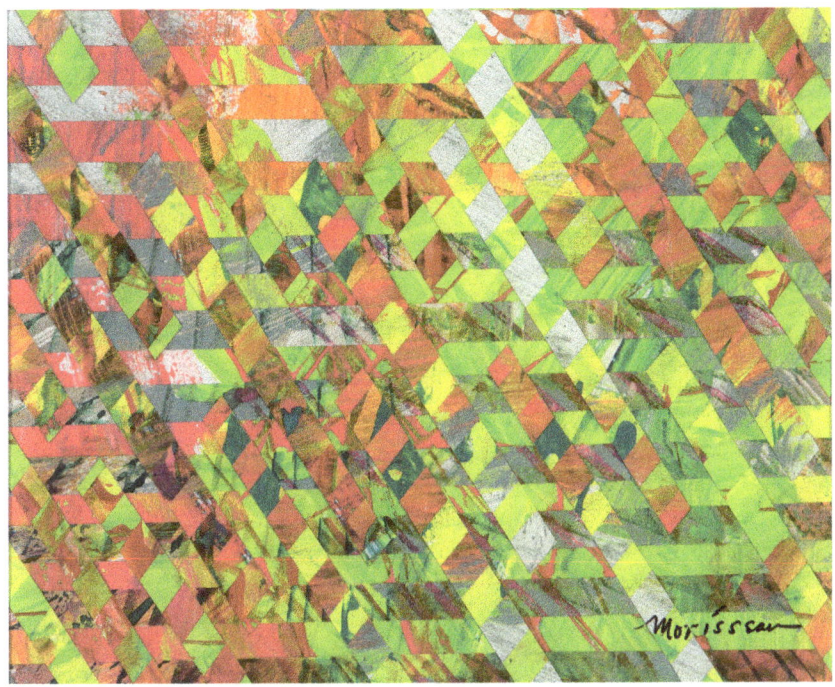

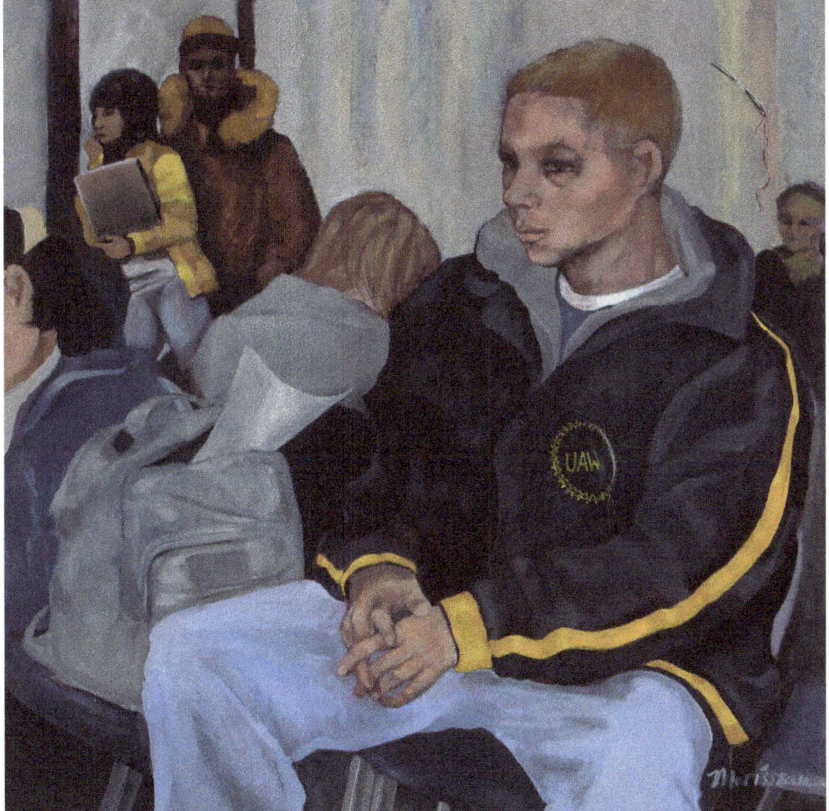

(Top) *Hummingbird 5831.* 2012. Collage on paper, 10 x 12 in.
(Bottom) *The Wait.* 2008. Oil on canvas, 36 x 36 in.

in other instances they express concern with the deterioration of the urban landscape (*Home in Detroit,* 2015). The human form, however, dominates her imagery, with faces serving as particular inspiration. She dignifies people by making them the vehicles of her stories, stories in which narrative inconclusiveness is an integral part of the work's interpretative potential.

She enjoys working in series. One of them, *Unemployment,* directly gives voice to those affected by the recession. ***The Wait*** (2008) features a young man in the center of the composition, sitting with flat affect and hands crossed on his lap, while surrounded by others who also wait listlessly. But this is no doctor's office; the detail on the subject's jacket—the UAW logo—matters, situating the scene in the fraught context of labor and economic upheaval. Thus, social concerns emerge as a prominent feature of Morisseau's art.

Without imposing interpretations, Morisseau hints at what matters to her and why it should also matter to the viewer. A now-retired teacher of Detroit Public Schools and Cass Technical High School, she believes that passing

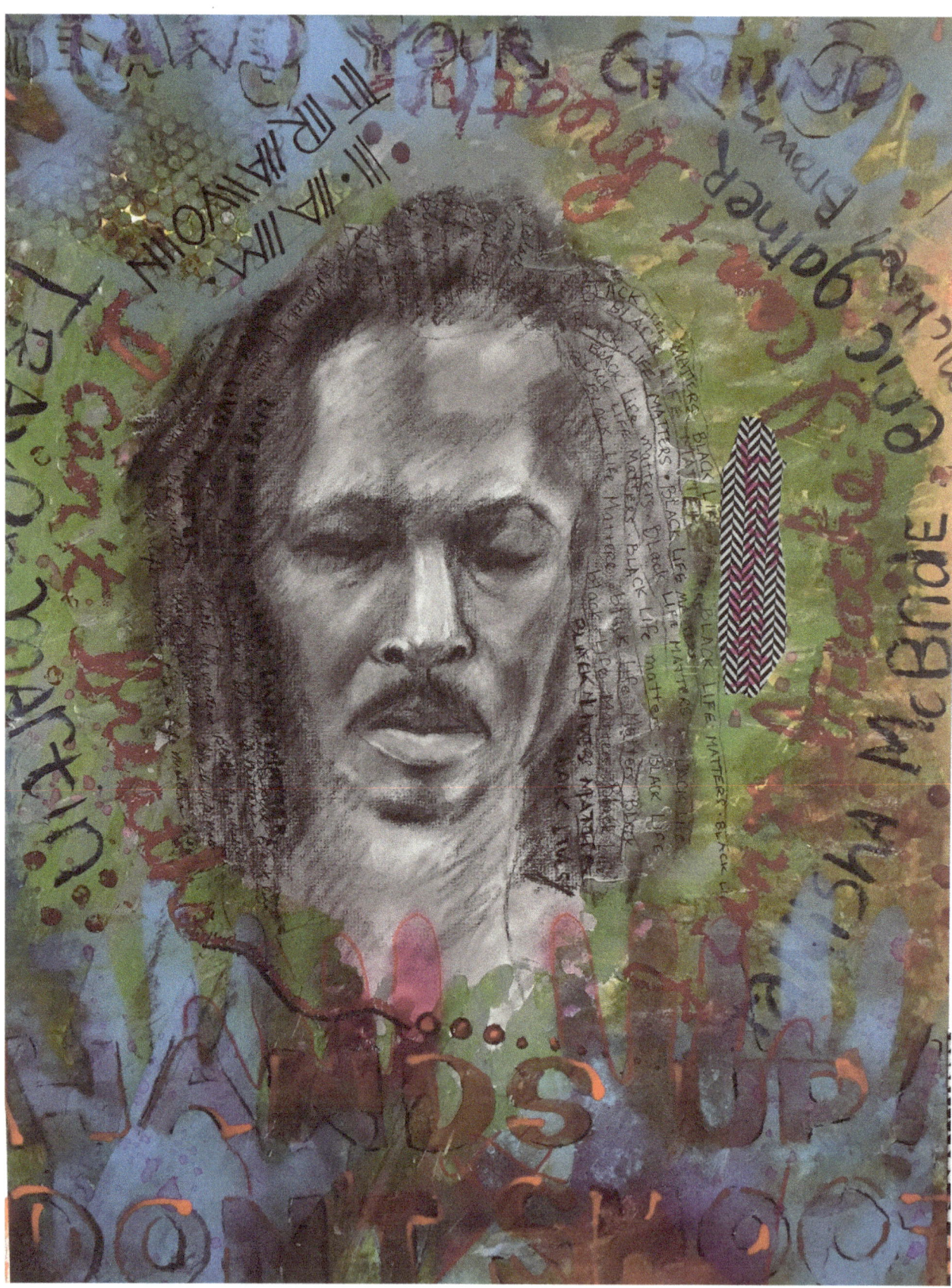

I Can't Breathe. 2015. Mixed media on paper, 18 x 24 in.

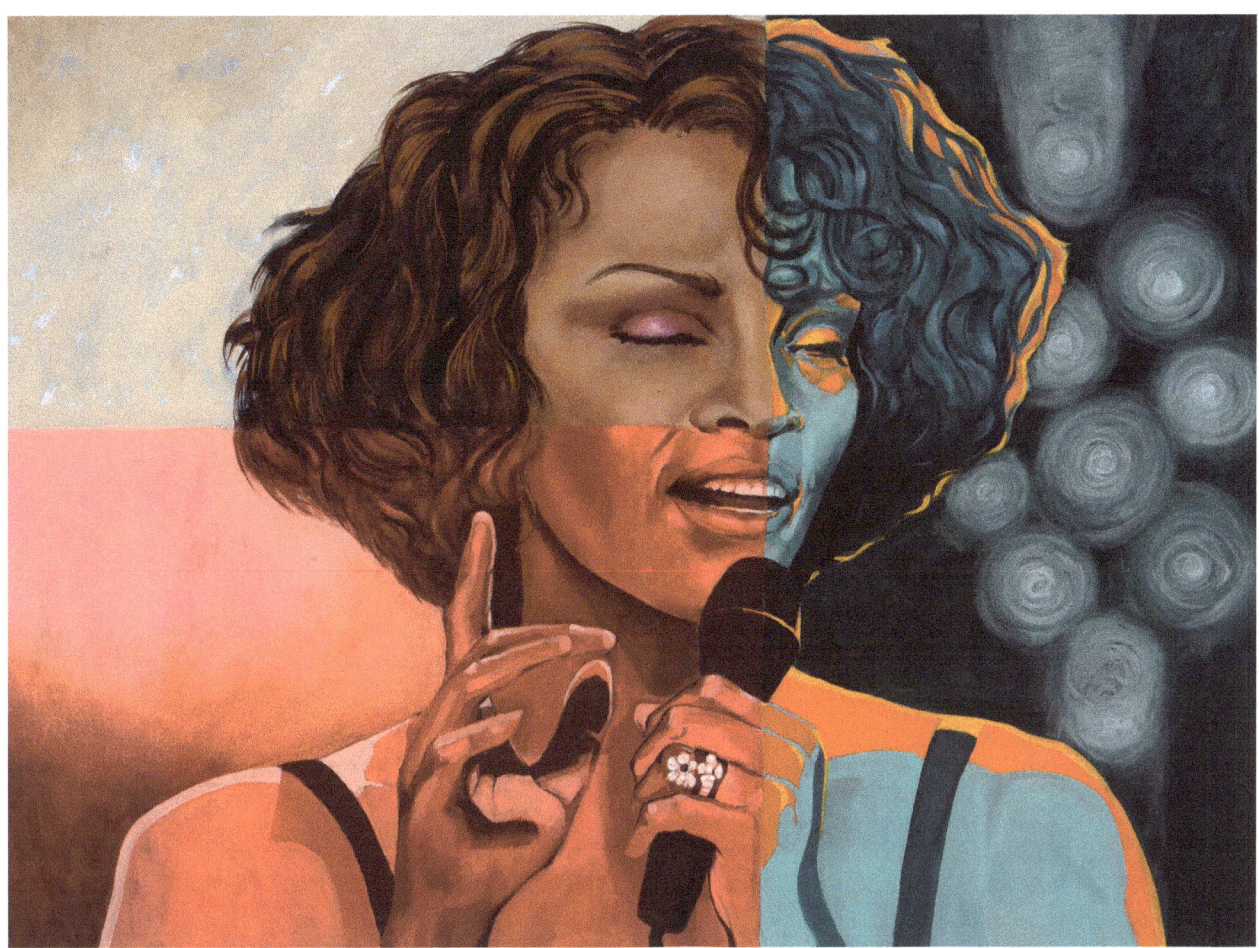

Whitney. 2017. Oil on canvas, 36 x 48 in.

on wisdom, values, and knowledge is her responsibility and
hopes that her art compels the
viewers to feel that obligation as
well. An example of that atti-
tude is revealed in **Legacy** (2015),
where human relationships,

intergenerational bonds, and the
importance of the individual as
an essential part of the communal
fabric come to the fore. In **I Can't
Breathe** (2015), the allusion to
the death of Eric Garner echoes
the dramatic plea of many: Let

us breathe. Those images confirm
yet another of Morisseau's strong
convictions, that "Art is a sign
of the times in its own way."

XAVIER TALVELA SWIECKI, SEPTEMBER
2017

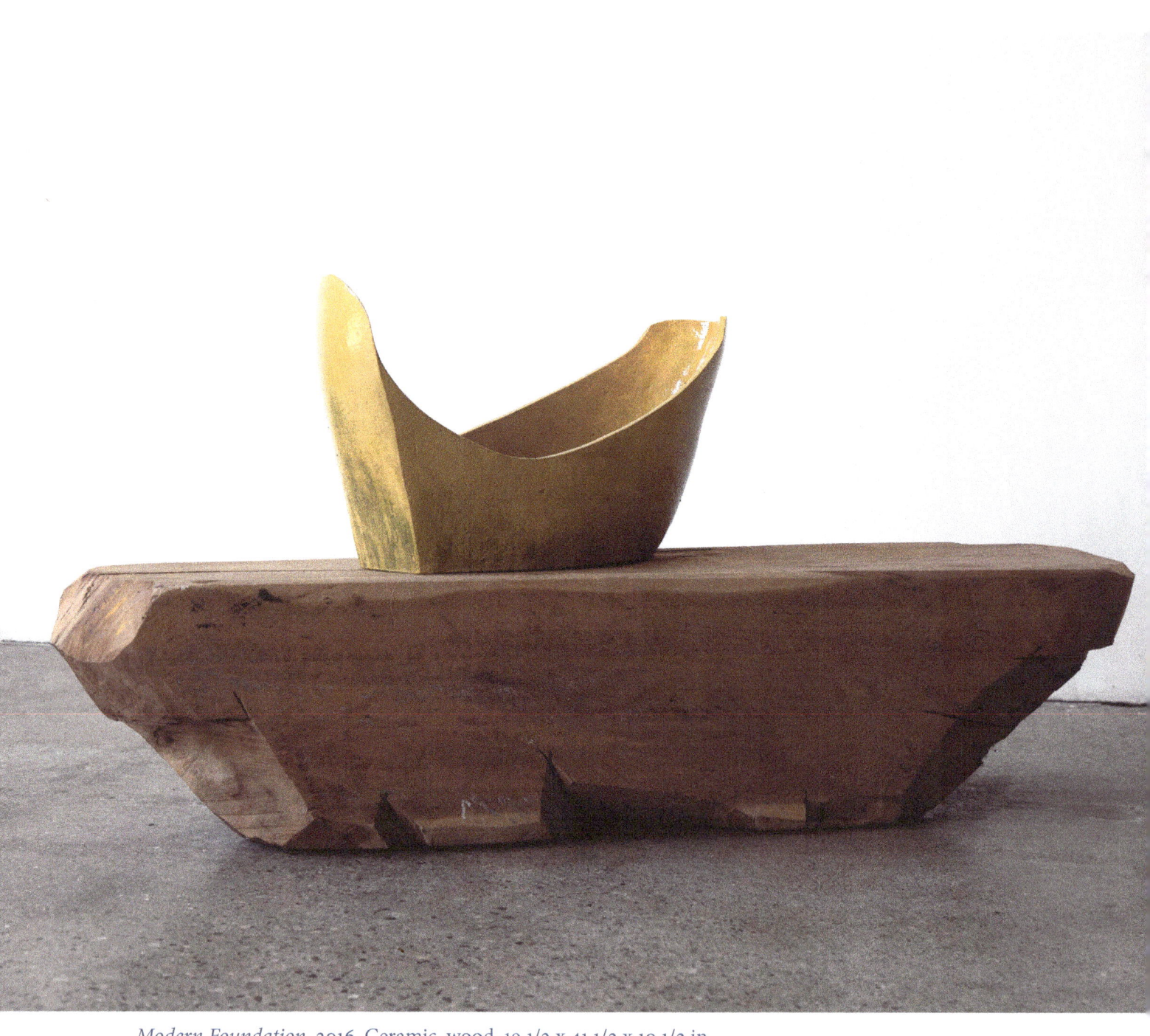

Modern Foundation. 2016. Ceramic, wood, 19 1/2 x 41 1/2 x 10 1/2 in.

86 // LAITH KARMO

Born Royal Oak, Michigan, 1980
BFA, College for Creative Studies; MFA, Cranbrook Academy of Art
Lives in Bloomfield Hills, Michigan

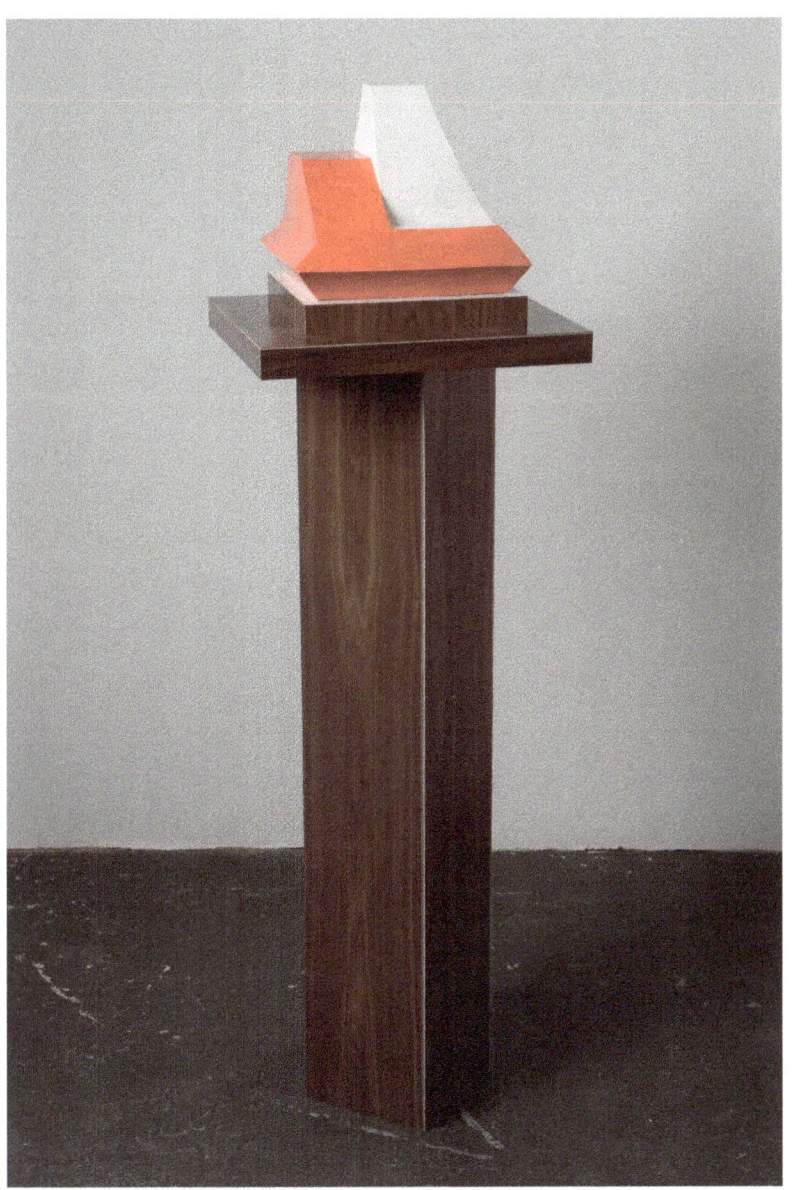

Towers of Svaneti. 2008. Ceramic, veneer, 66 x 18 x 18 in.

Unpacking the practice of ceramist Laith Karmo is perhaps best expedited by focusing on the polar goals of his aesthetic evolution over the last decade and a half. First up are the brash, jazzy, chromatically shiny abstract sculptures presented in his first solo show in 2008, and then, post-2009, the gradual embrace over the next several years of the proverbial, evergreen forms (pots, bowls, ewers) and muted tonalities of his "objects of utility and contemplation."

A key example of the former, from Karmo's first one-person outing, is ***Towers of Svaneti*** (2008). This sleek, sharp-edged, architectonic form, glazed ultra-red and snow white, fairly dazzles the eye. Resting atop a tall, look-at-me pedestal veneered with faux-wood Formica, its shaft angled diagonally to avoid the usual static vertical support,

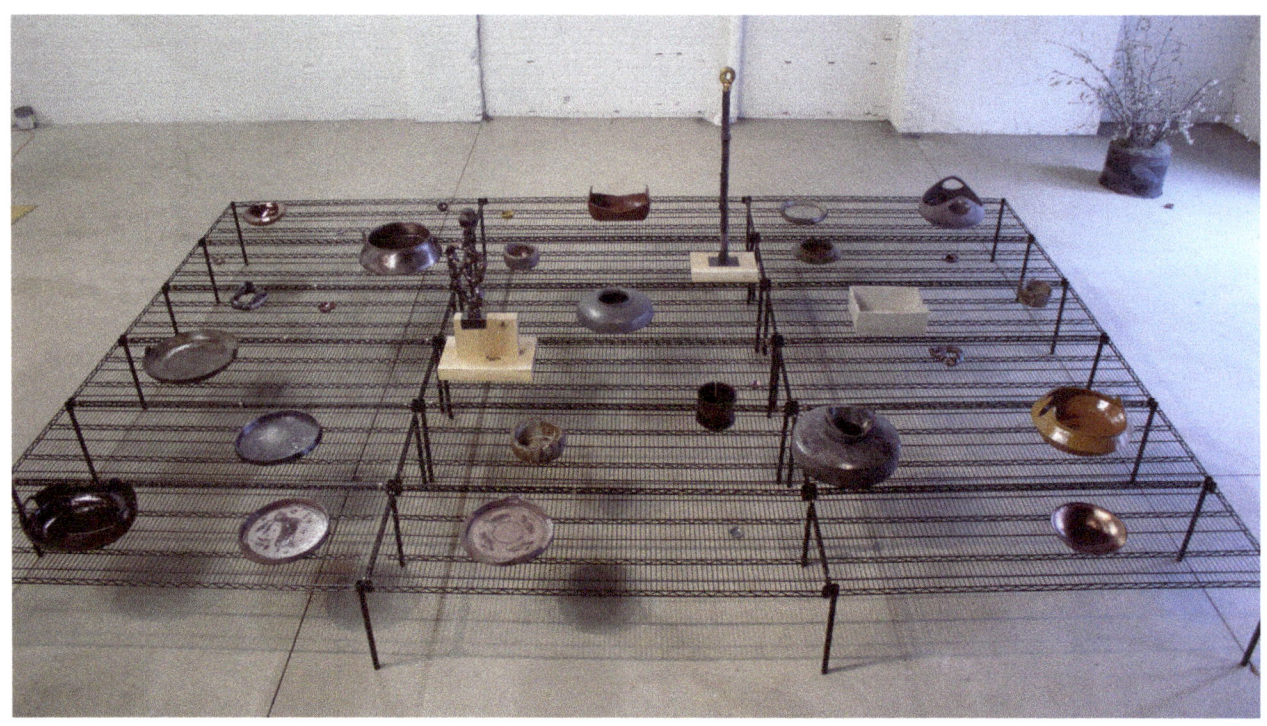

Cultivating Civility (installation at Museum of Contemporary Art Detroit). 2013. Ceramic, wire shelving, oak, 5 x 18 x 12 in.

this compound of eccentric shape and quirky pedestal trumpets, per Karmo, the "new." As well, Karmo's artist statement boasts that "contemporary design and architectural trends" inspired this inaugural display. *Svaneti*, along with other works from the show, including *Faith in Bling* and *Old Age / Young Blood*, were billed as "The Newest Work of Laith Karmo," as if currency were the Holy Grail.

Seven years later, Karmo's sharp left aesthetic swerve inspired **Modern Foundation**

(2016). Here, a ravishing, yellow-gold vessel floats on a capacious pedestal hewn from raw wood by Karmo himself. The title alerts us to the shapely, boat-like form of a midcentury creamer, or even a banal, jumbo-size gravy boat. Elegantly glamorized by its golden luster, this precious, one-of-a-kind pouring utensil holds sway over the low-slung, roughly carved mount. As an ensemble, it exists at a decided remove from the high-flying pedestals and flashy bling of 2008's "newest works"; *Foundation*, and pieces

like it, feel grounded, while allowing the beatified object (quasi receptacle / quasi objet d'art) to glow softly on a broad perch.

Yet commonalities between old (relatively) and recent Karmos persist: the proclivity for uncommon shapes, whether abstract or vessel derived; the congenial interlocking of object and support; and the push-pull of the ongoing, inherited tussle between fine art and craft over the last seventy-five years (think Peter Voulkos and John Glick, for starters).

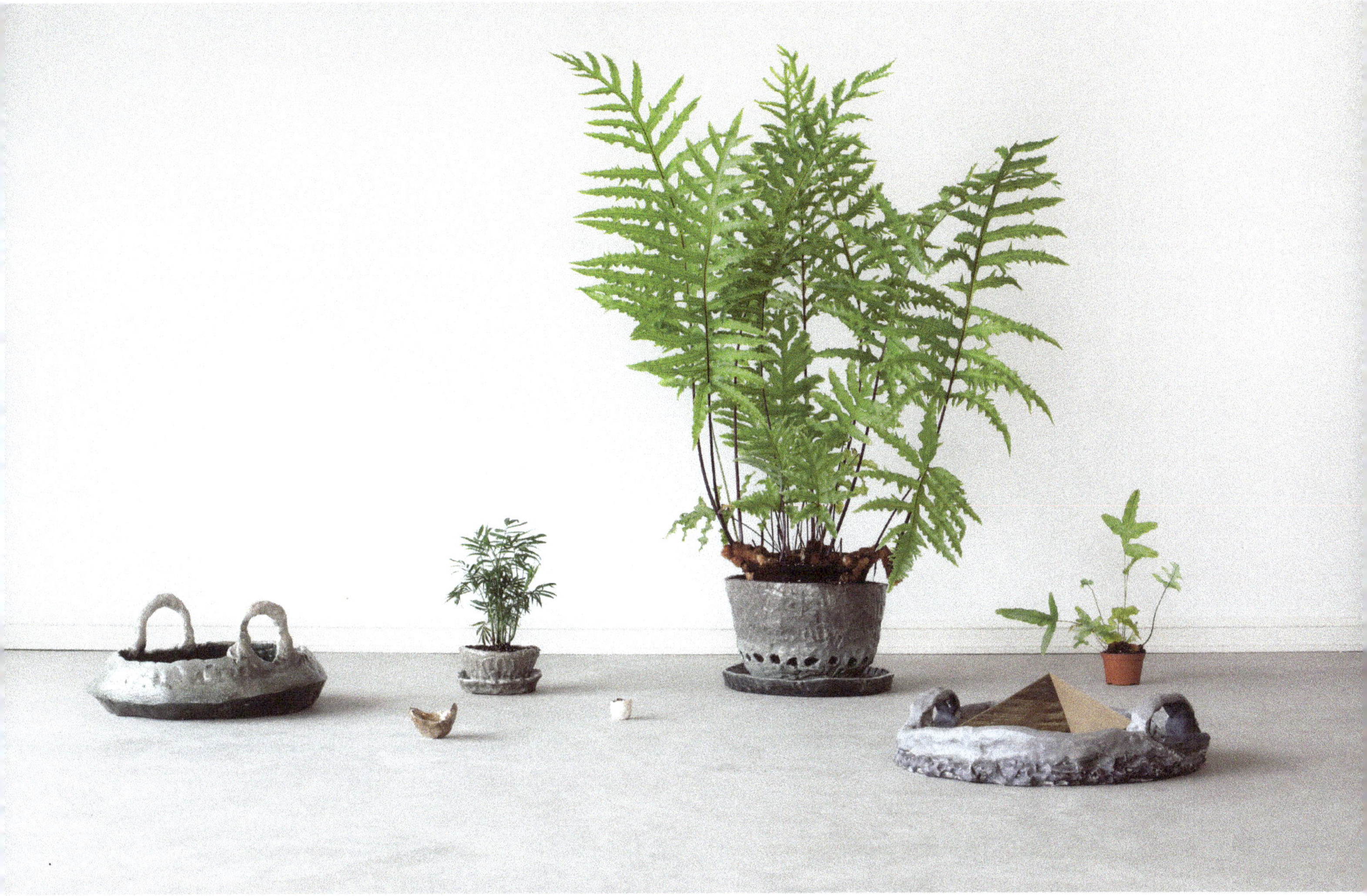

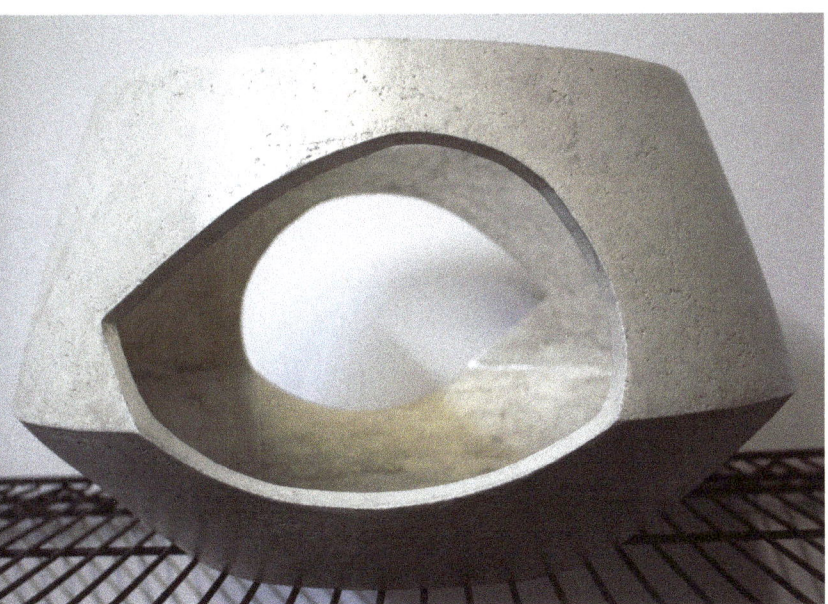

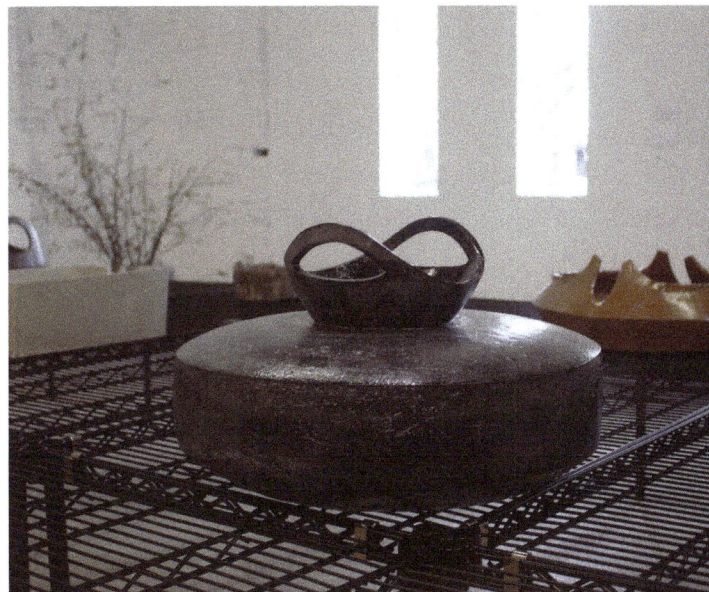

(Top) Cultivating Civility. 2009. Ceramic, plants, dimensions variable. *(Left) Halcyon Native.* 2014. Ceramic, 12 x 16 x 16 in. *(Right) Pangaea.* 2013. Ceramic, 12 x 22 x 22 in.

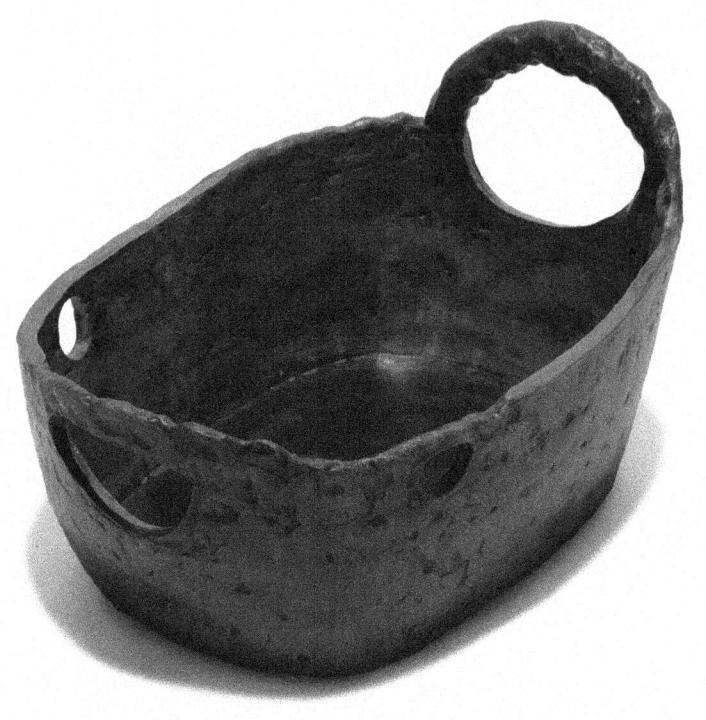

Bath. 2011. Ceramic, 16 x 16 x 22 in.

The harbingers of *Modern Foundation* debuted in 2009 and accelerated therefrom. The first embodiment, titled **Cultivating Civility**, unveiled a cluster of utilitarian containers in battleship gray hues. As staged by the artist, cache pot and planter are garnished with several varieties of ferns, among the oldest flora on the planet, to underscore his turn to the elemental forms of this core cluster of vessels. Converging interests prompted this redirection: a renewed interest in the quotidian forms that had originally lured him, as an undergrad,

to clay as a medium; impactful as well was the confluence of marriage, a young family, and a dawning appreciation of artifacts intrinsic to age-old communal/global gatherings and the "spirituality of people who made them." Hence, platters, bowls, planters, teapots, ewers, crocks, and gathering baskets, along with a tot-size **Bath** [tub] (2011) and miniature **Canoe** (2013), began to spill from the studio, the bounty of his vision of a harmonious commonweal.

By 2013, in a spacious installation also entitled **Cultivating**

Civility, Karmo's timeless yet idiosyncratic inventory of ceramic wares was laid out across a black grid of knee-high, see-through steel shelving (a communal platform). Replete with a wiry Giacometti-like figure (the artist?) titled *Dark Craft* and a four-foot-tall *Solstice Staff*, as a symbol of authority, a field of trays, bowls, plates, and platters spread airily across the gallery, an earthly counterpart to sun, moon, stars, and planetary bodies on high. A recurring detail, among the bowls in particular, is the prevalent eye-like opening that both animates and implies anthropomorphic associations, especially since eye-to-eye contact is basic to shared human interactions and transactions. Indeed, in many of his objects, the ocular opening serves as both looker and ergonomic handle, as in ***Pangaea***. Here the "eye-bowl,"

elevated on a plump, round ceramic cushion, like a crown on a pillow (that in turn rests on a shelf), attests to its centrality in Karmo's cosmology. Occasionally, and stunningly, the amplified, all-seeing eye looms so broadly, as in ***Halcyon Native*** (2014) that the function of bowl as bowl is all but denied.

Instead, the magnified eye trains its gaze on each and every observer, as if to foster civil behavior and civility in general—sharing, conversing, touching, and embracing. Prescient and timely, to say the least.

DENNIS ALAN NAWROCKI, DECEMBER 2017

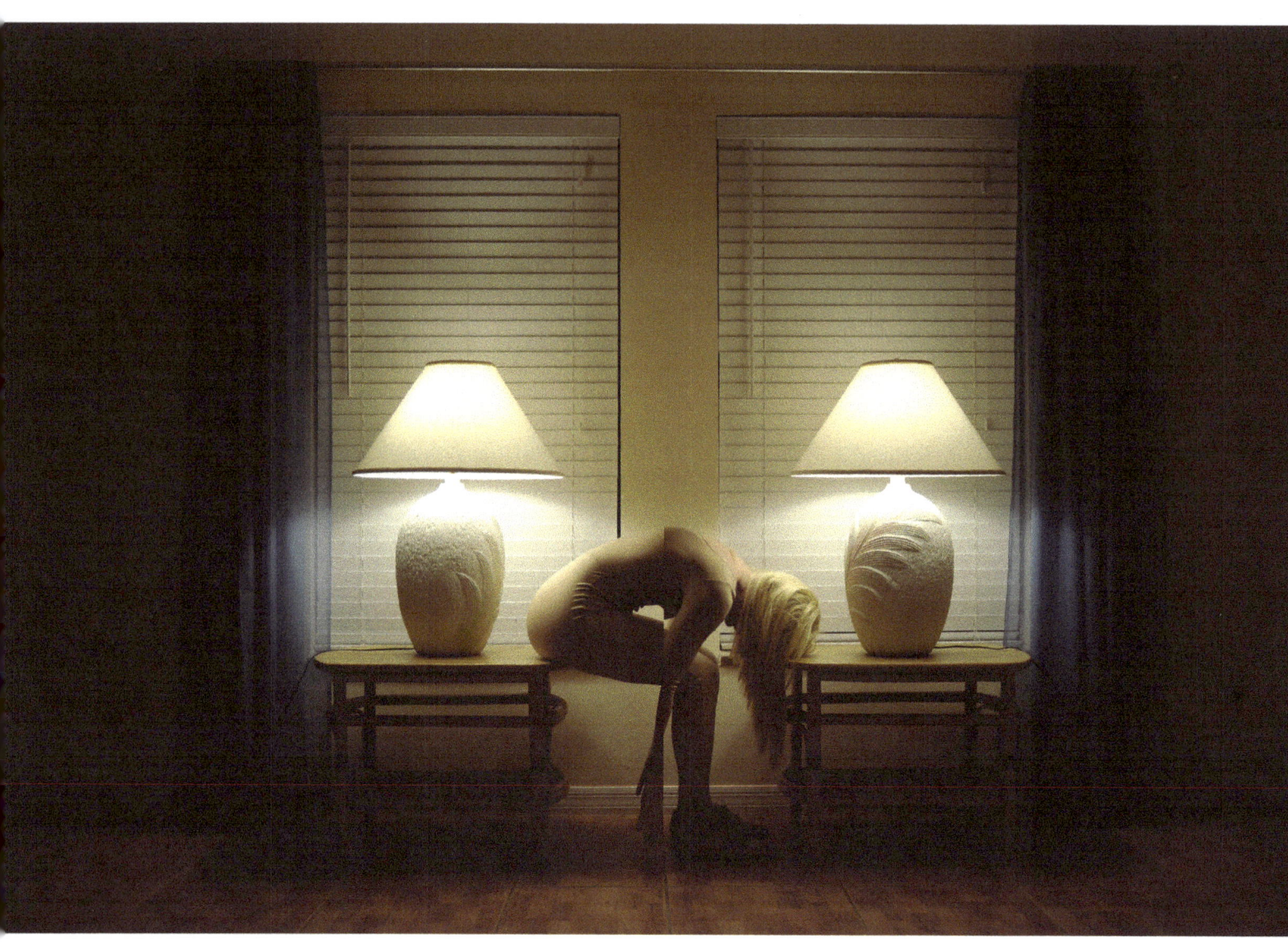

Evening Fragments. 2014. Color photograph, 30 x 37 in.

Born Detroit, 1975
BFA, College for Creative Studies
Lives in Detroit

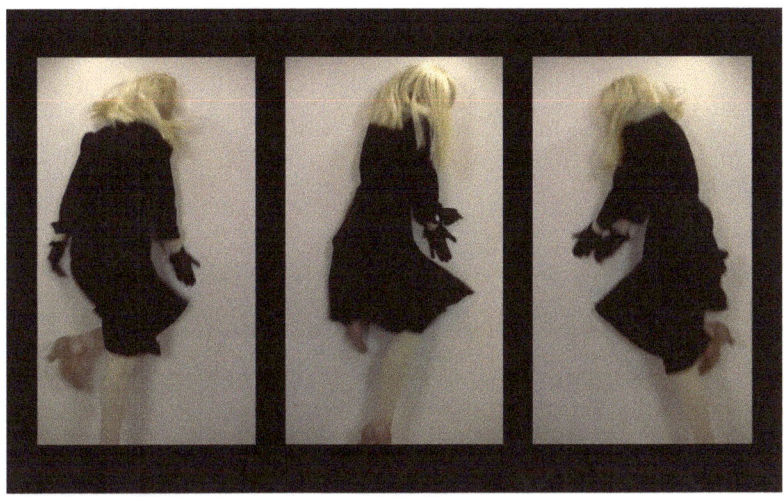

Hitting the Wall. 2015. Video, 10-minute loop.

It makes sense that Nicola Kuperus was onstage at the Detroit Institute of Arts recently, running her big yellow vacuum up and down a strip of beige carpet. And that a few minutes later, her face obscured by a long, black wig, she started to *play* the vacuum, using an effects pedal to modulate and amplify its heavy roar. And that a few minutes after that, she pulled out a tall, pink vase and began to fill it, maniacally, with fake plants, while on a screen above her, another Kuperus appeared, dressed up and gesticulating like a cross between a magician, Laurie Anderson, and some faceless horror movie creep, and that *that* Kuperus had the same vase, which she began to *slap* with her white-gloved hand, asking it, over and over again, "Ya like that?"

It makes sense. After all, at the base of **The Perfect Accent**

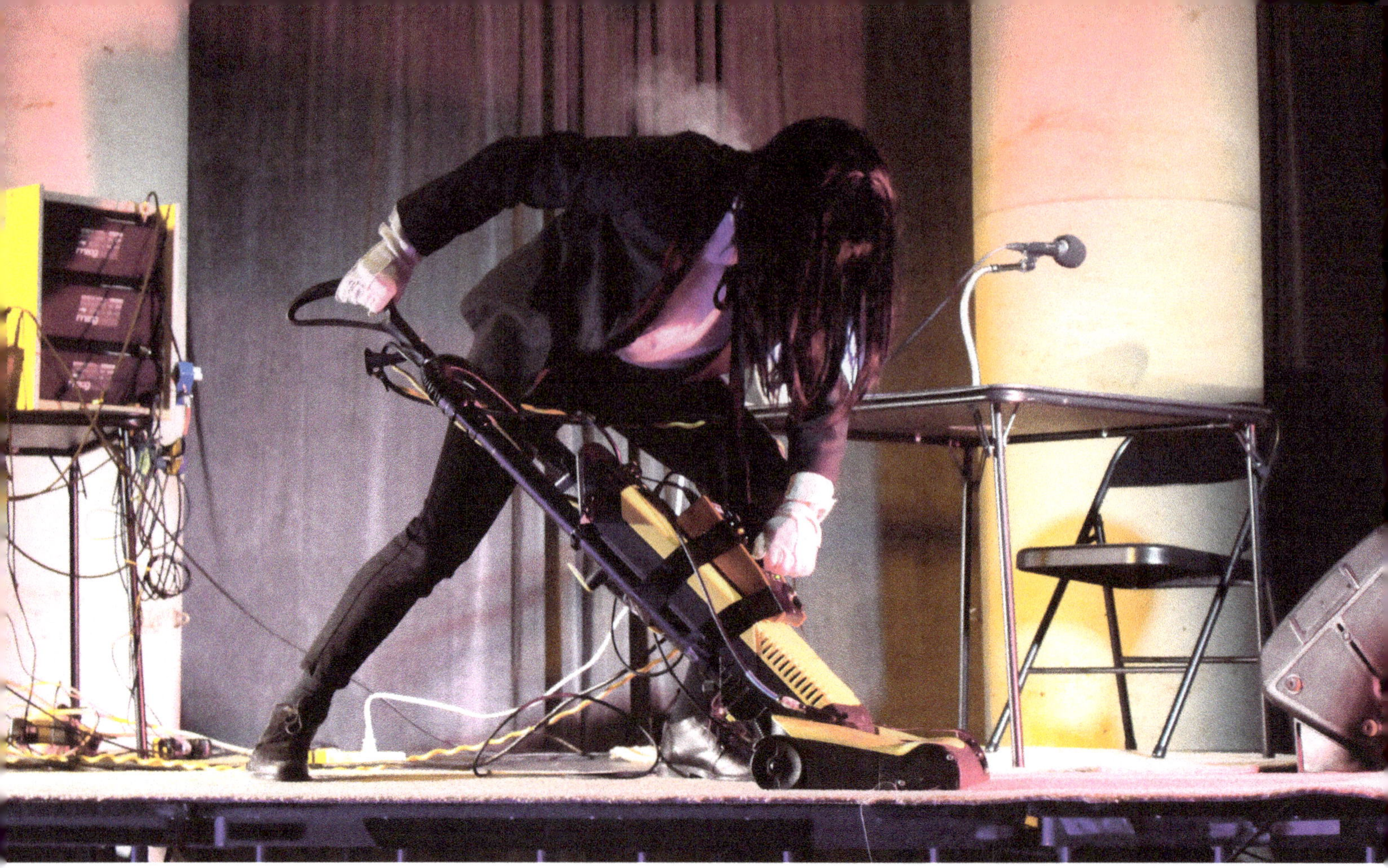

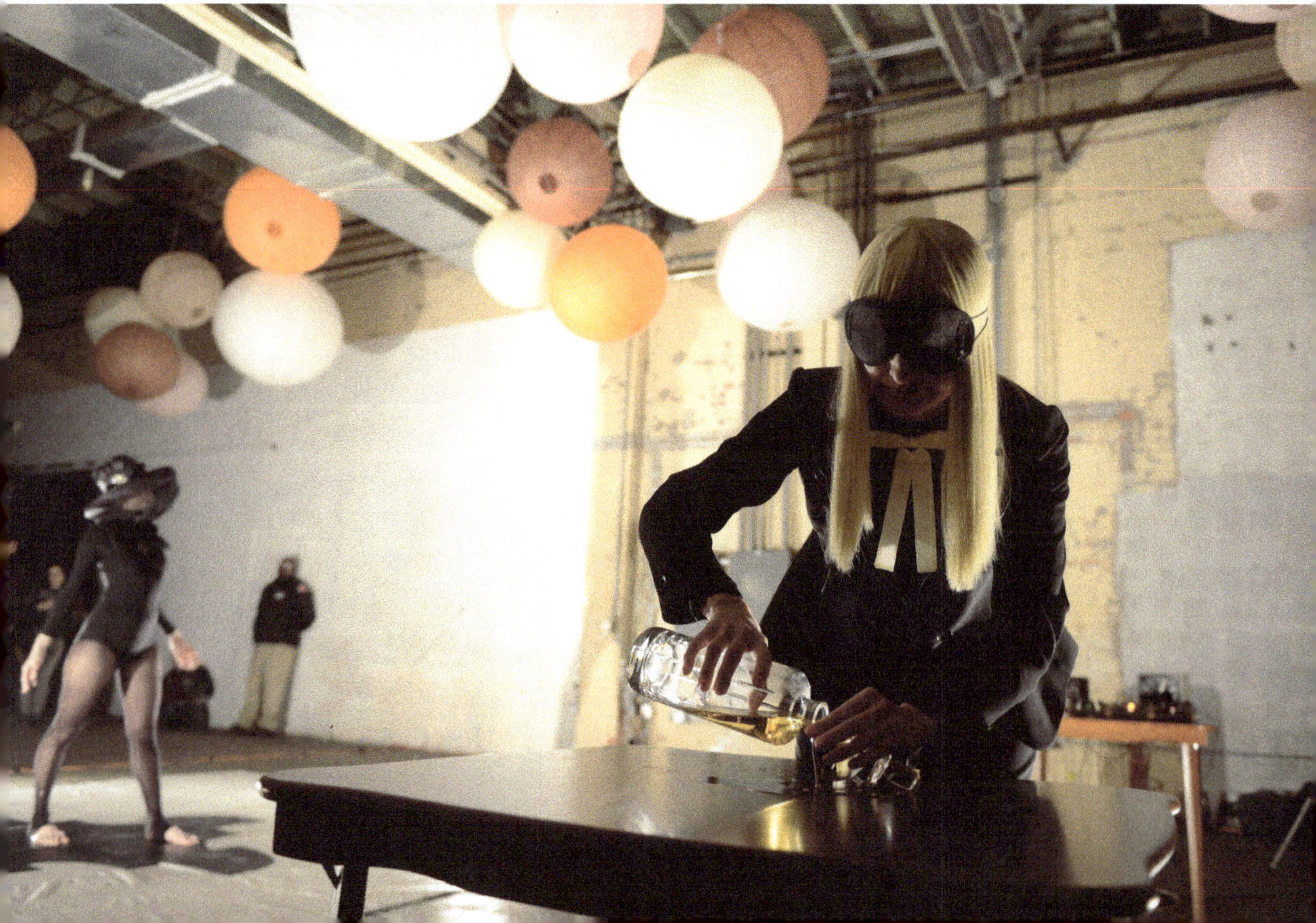

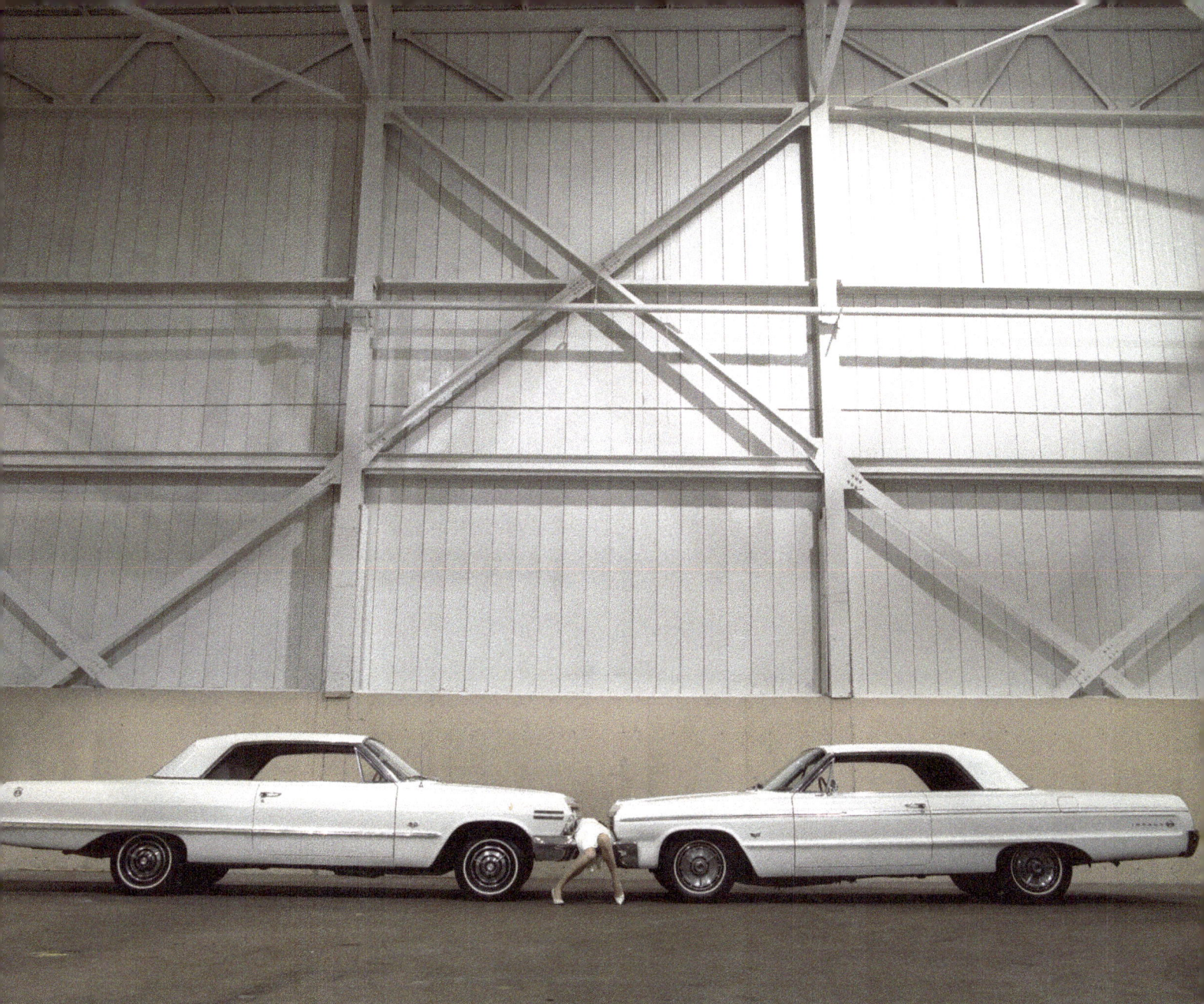

(Top) Impala. 2010. Pigment print, 30 x 37 in.

(Opposite, top) The Perfect Accent Piece (performance as Kuperus/Miller). 2017. 30 minutes. Photography by WSU Art Galleries.

(Opposite, bottom) Women Dancing with the Spirits: No. 1 (performance with Biba Bell). 2015. 20 minutes. Photography by Riva Sayagh.

Piece (2017), a collaborative performance with Adam Lee Miller, lies a grab bag of familiar obsessions and tendencies that Kuperus carries with her from a prolific, twenty-year career in art and music—obsessions we've seen before, in different forms.

Here, for instance, is her fascination with the faceless, objectified body and its obverse,

the curiously humanized object. Headless women proliferated in Kuperus's most widely known body of work, her "*classic car*" series of 2000–2010, for which she photographed the bodies of slender, elegantly dressed women in, on, and around luxurious, behemoth automobiles. A curiously cool, antiseptic answer to pin-up

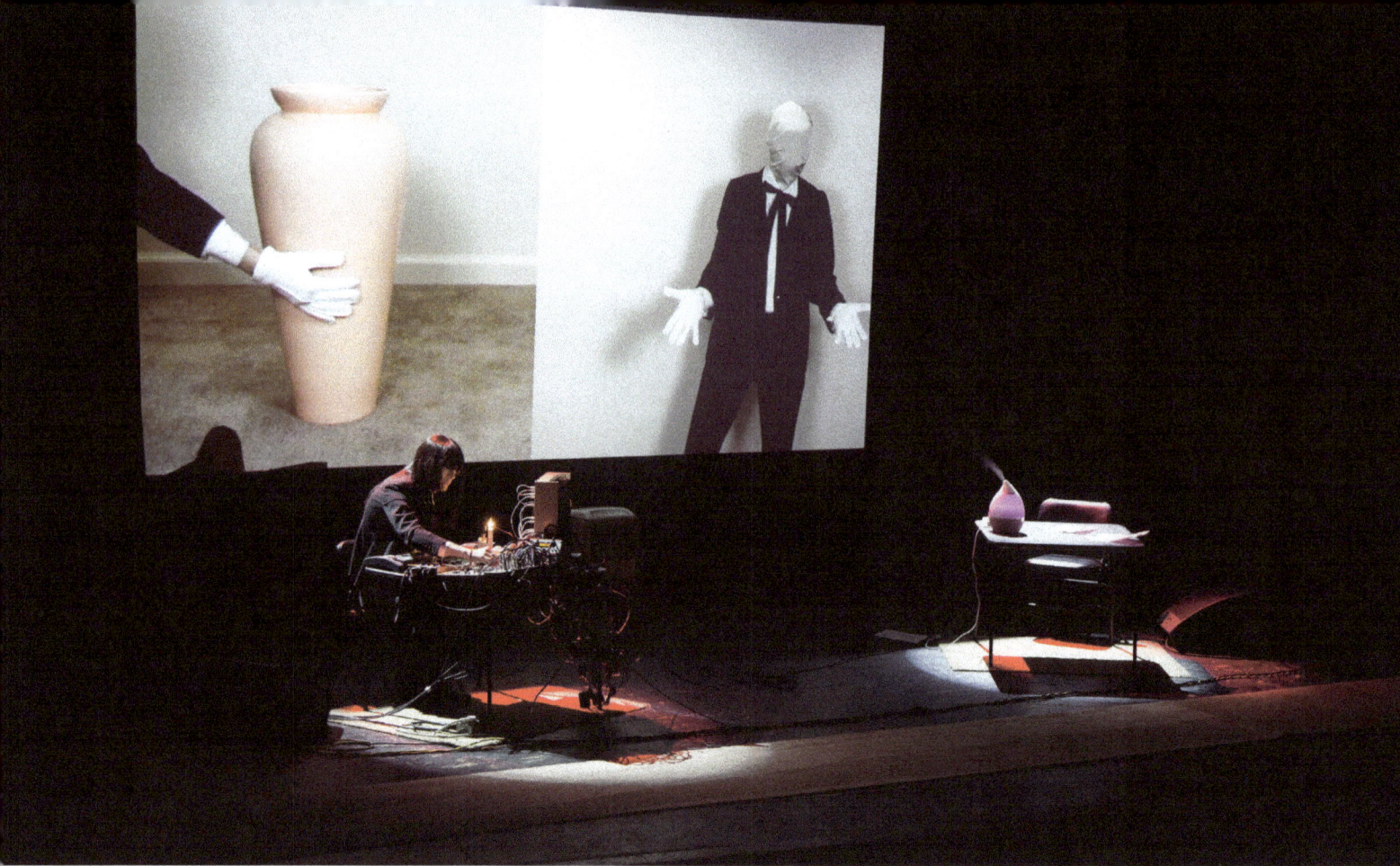

The Perfect Accent Piece (performance as Kuperus/Miller). 2017. 30 minutes. Photography by Danielle Campbell.

girls and hot rods, this series invites a feminist reading that Kuperus herself deflects—for her, the literal *object*-ification of these bodies isn't about some pathological tendency toward depersonhood, but simple form. "I was trying to take the body," she says, "and make it just as sculptural as the cars."

And yet, Kuperus's work is too fetishistic, too psychosexually fraught, to ever *just* be about form. Here too, after all, is her almost alien hyperawareness of the weirdness and pathology embedded in everyday life—or, to put it another

way, of the ubiquity and banality of perversion. As the front person of ADULT., the electro band she formed with Miller in the late 1990s, Kuperus became known for her monotone delivery of lyrics like, "Do you like my handbag? It's filled with lots of money. / I want to spend my money on entertainment." To listen to ADULT. records, especially the early ones, is to encounter Kuperus as android: almost human yet insistently other, observing and reminding us how profoundly strange our desires and habits are, how untidy our emotions.

The Perfect Accent Piece elaborates on these established themes (and sundry others), but it also represents a notable emergent tendency in Kuperus's practice: the use of the artist's own body. In a variety of recent photographs, videos, and performances, Kuperus has started to literally embody her ideas in time and space, a shift that has opened up compelling new opportunities for the evolution of her creative vision.

Consider one of the first series for which she served as both photographer *and* subject, *Attempting Camouflage* (2014), in which

Kuperus, wearing a blonde wig and costumed to mimic her domestic surroundings, is nevertheless an insistent object that does a terrible job blending in. The effect can be at once beautiful, funny, disquieting, and a little heartbreaking, as in *Evening Fragments* (2014), where her body rests, awkwardly and unmistakably, between two end tables.

Hitting the Wall (2015) is a three-channel video in which the artist—again bewigged in blonde but this time wearing a black trench coat and black gloves—is seen from behind as she repeatedly falls or flings her body against a wall. The images evoke a disturbing scenario of futility or heedless self-harm, but through careful looping and editing, the dull *thuds* made by her triplicated body as it collides with the wall become something else: a sharp, shifting, engagingly rhythmic composition.

Her interest in testing physical limits took a still more visceral form in Kuperus's first performance work, a collaboration with dance artist Biba Bell called ***Women Dancing with the Spirits: No. 1*** (2015). Staged at the Museum of Contemporary Art Detroit, *Women Dancing . . .* found a blindfolded Kuperus taking regular, timed breaks from creating a driving electronic composition to serve tequila shots to Bell, whose dancing, not surprisingly, grew less precise, more fluid and disoriented as the performance wore on.

For Kuperus, whose photographs and videos are meticulously composed, chance and unpredictability are key forces that drive her, increasingly, toward performance. Toward embodiment. In her vigorous embrace of this new pursuit, which she describes as both "liberating" and "kind of terrifying," she has begun to shatter her immaculate surfaces, revealing the depths—vivid, riotous, uncomfortable, and absurd—that have long churned beneath them.

MATTHEW PIPER, DECEMBER 2017

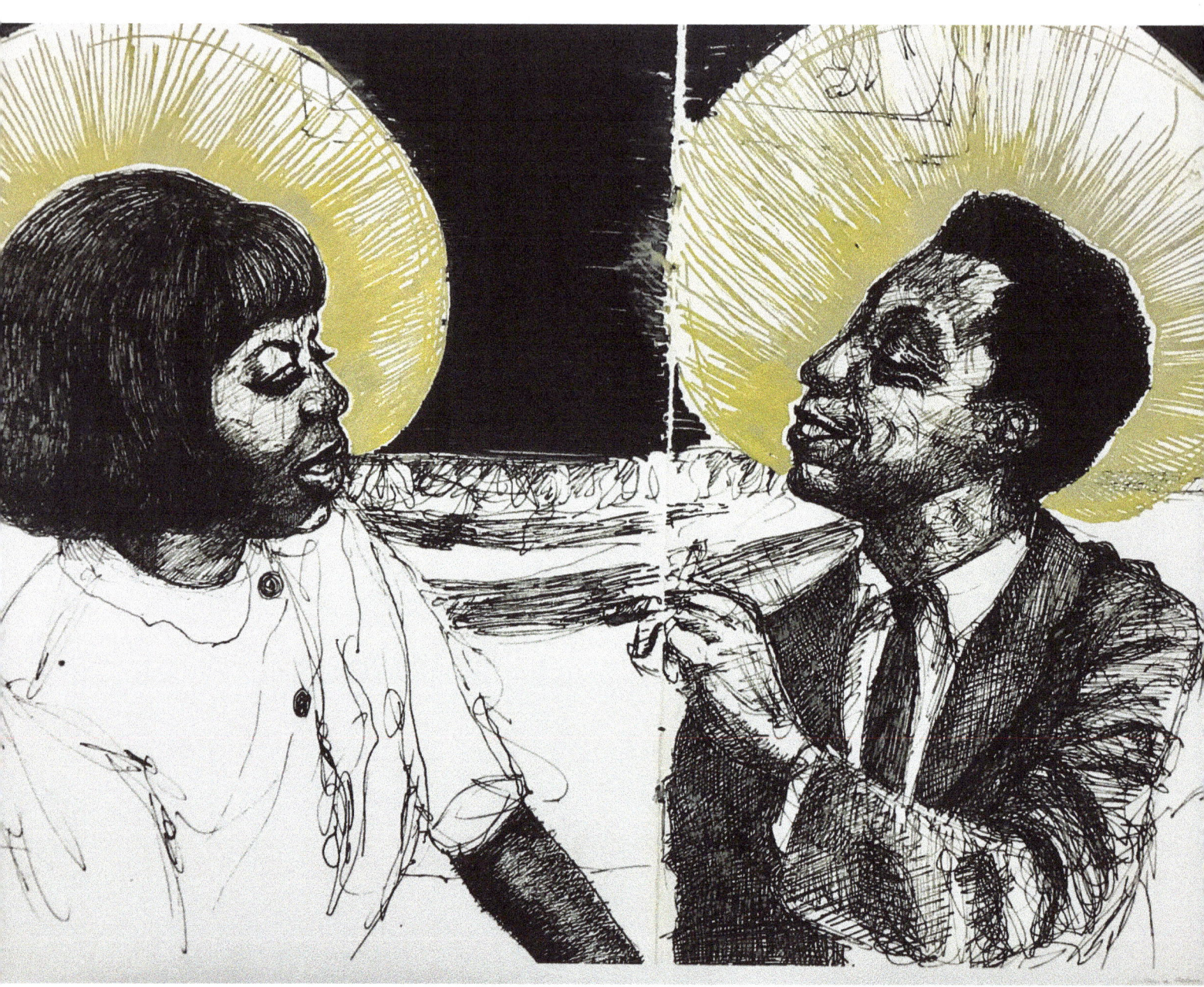

Saints and Sinners. 2017. Ink on paper, 22 x 30 in. Photography by Nichole M. Christian.

Born Detroit, 1967
BFA, College for Creative Studies
Lives in Detroit

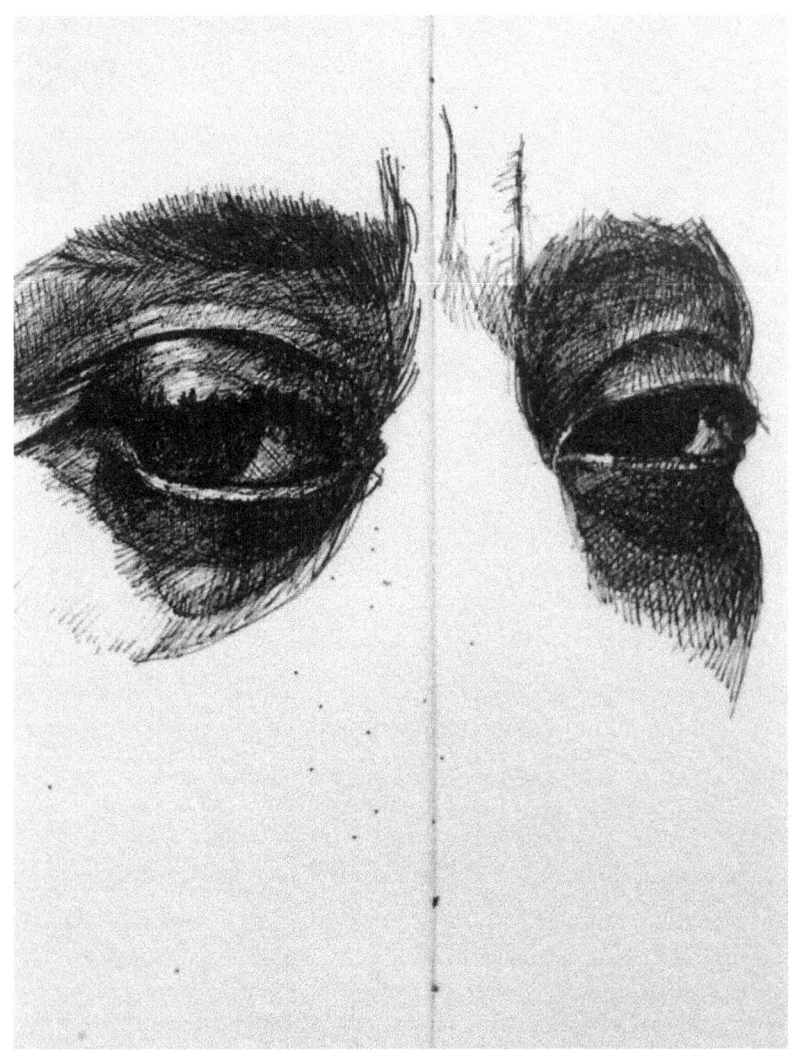

A Witness. 2017. Ink on paper, 11 x 15 in. Photography by Nichole M. Christian.

Every artist has an origin story—a tale of becoming.

Some artists remember, as Sabrina Nelson does, "like it was yesterday." In fact, Nelson's moment dates back to the fourth grade—around Valentine's Day. "The teacher had asked us to draw a heart. So I did and this boy said, 'You didn't draw that; girls can't draw.'" Nelson chuckles, recalling how swiftly she schooled the boy ("I was like, 'Yes, I can.'") But the humor in her voice and lightness in her eyes fade as she explains the moment's imprint. "He really gave me my feminist wings and my artist wings. I've been drawing ever since."

All these years later, Nelson's art is far more textured, socially inspired, and multidimensional. She is a lover of work that ignites conversation, of muses who defy easy understanding, and she

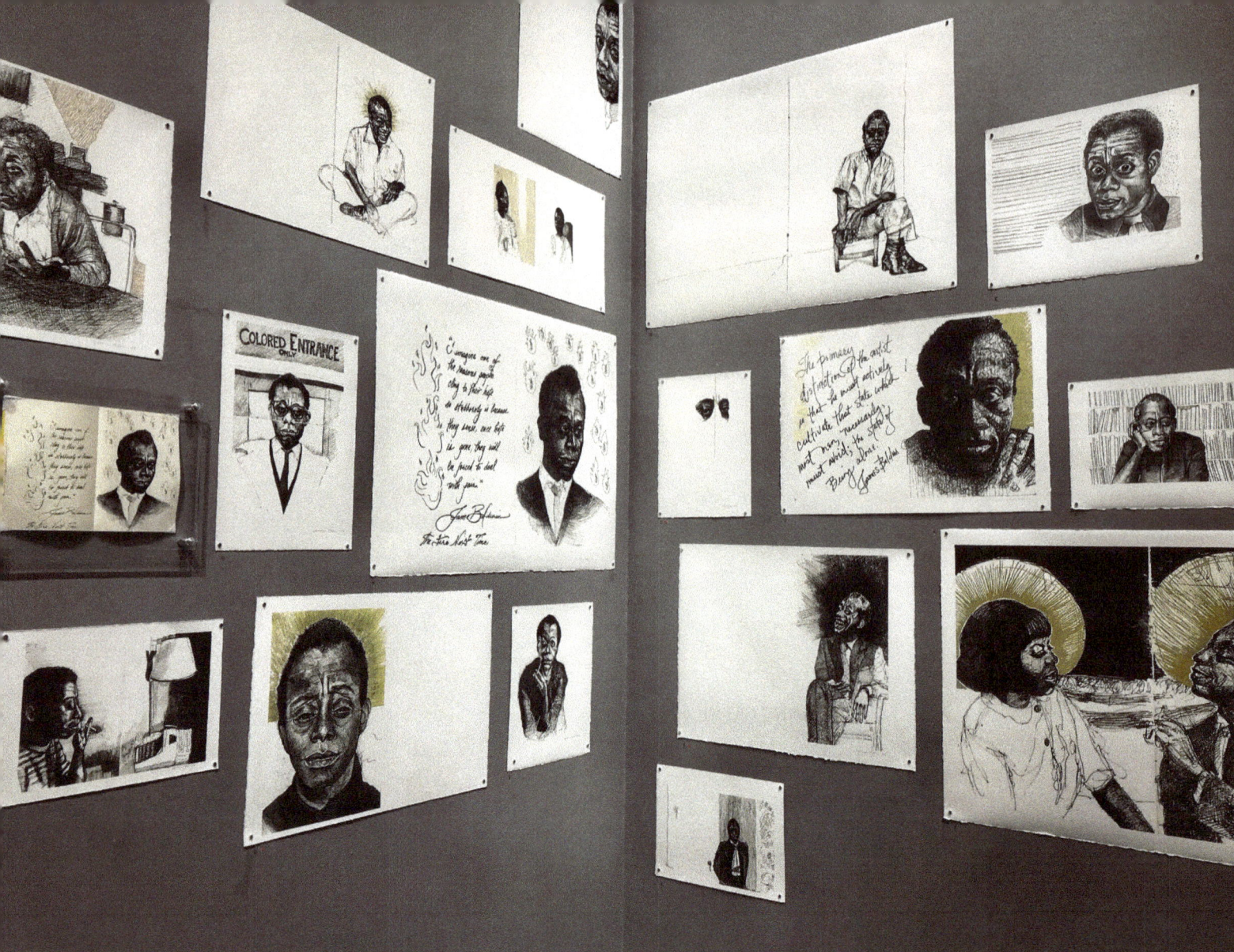

Baldwin & Me (installation view). 2017. Photography by Nichole M. Christian.

is a proud maker of imperfect figurative drawings and paintings that intentionally call viewers closer. "I can draw with exactness, do a portrait that looks so real," she says, "that it's just the exercise of drawing the realness. But I don't want my work to be that. I want it to be imperfect because perfection is a lie."

To Nelson, who also teaches drawing at the Detroit Institute of Arts, "the *gesture* of drawing has more to say. It's about who's drawing versus what, or who, they're drawing. It's harder too because you have to let go of all the things you've been taught and just feel your way through."

Nelson explores this idea to its extreme in ***Baldwin & Me*** (2017), a series of intimate ink-and-paper sketches of the iconic author James Baldwin.

Rather than simply capture Baldwin's well-known features, the gap in this teeth, Nelson opted for a mix of heavy, spare, partial, and even slightly exaggerated "essence" drawings. The collection was a focal point of the College for Creative Studies' group show, *Evidence of Things Not Seen*, works—including pieces by her son, Yale-trained artist Mario Moore—that explore

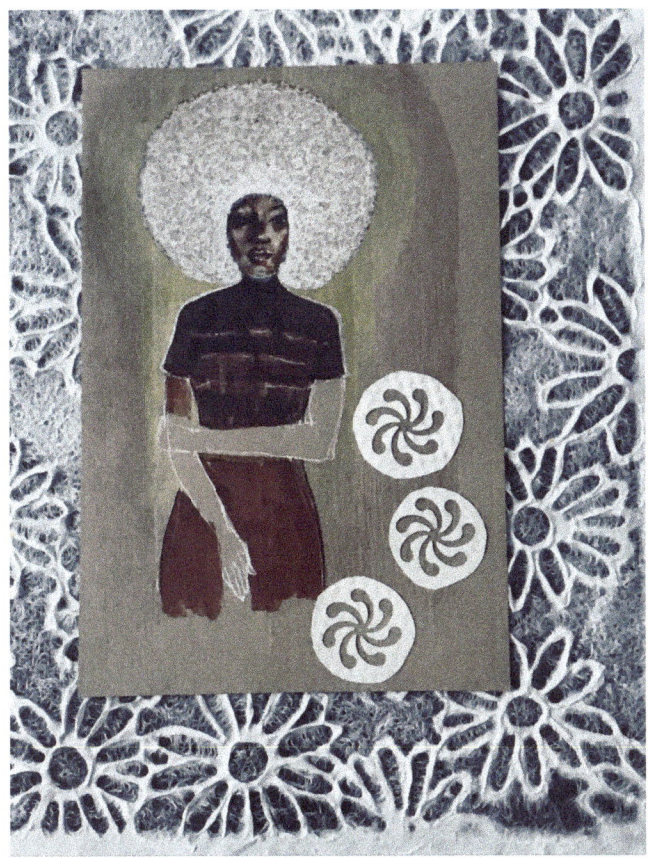

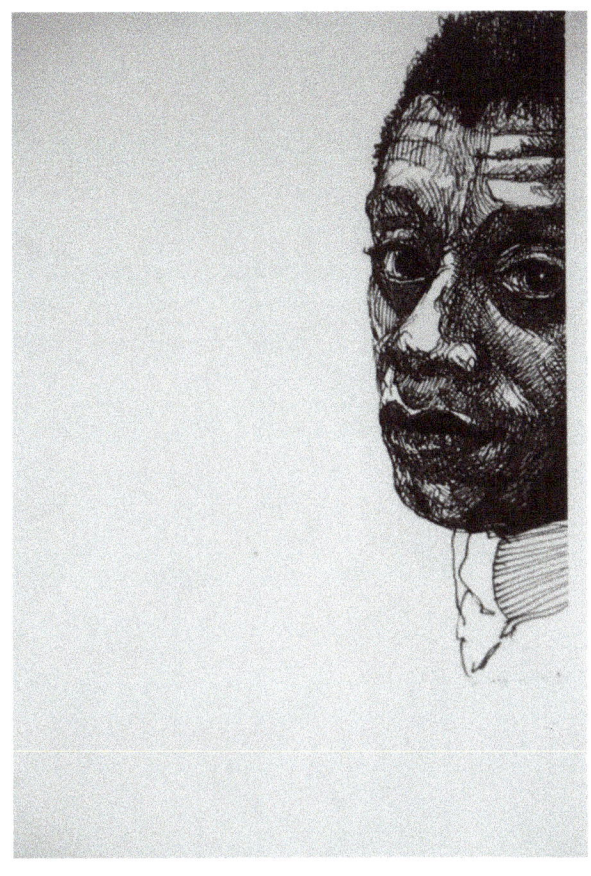

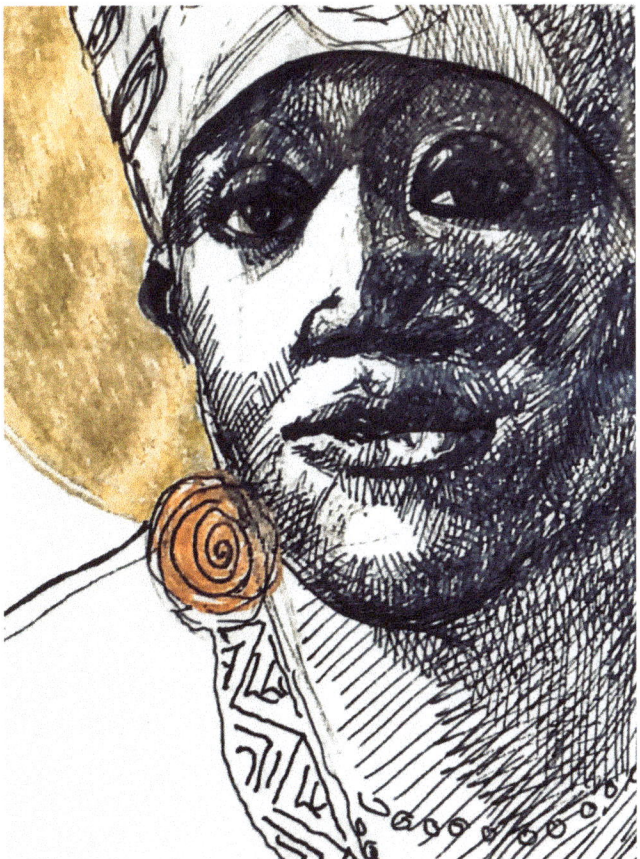

(Top left) *Lawdy Lil Mama after Barkley L. Hendricks.* 2016. Mixed media, 30 x 40 in. Photography by Nichole M. Christian.

(Top right) *Nobody Knows My Name.* 2017. Ink on paper, 11 x 15 in. Photography by Nichole M. Christian.

(Bottom) *Charity Hicks Water Warrior, #wagelove.* 2016. Ink on paper, 24 x 36 in. Photography by Nichole M. Christian.

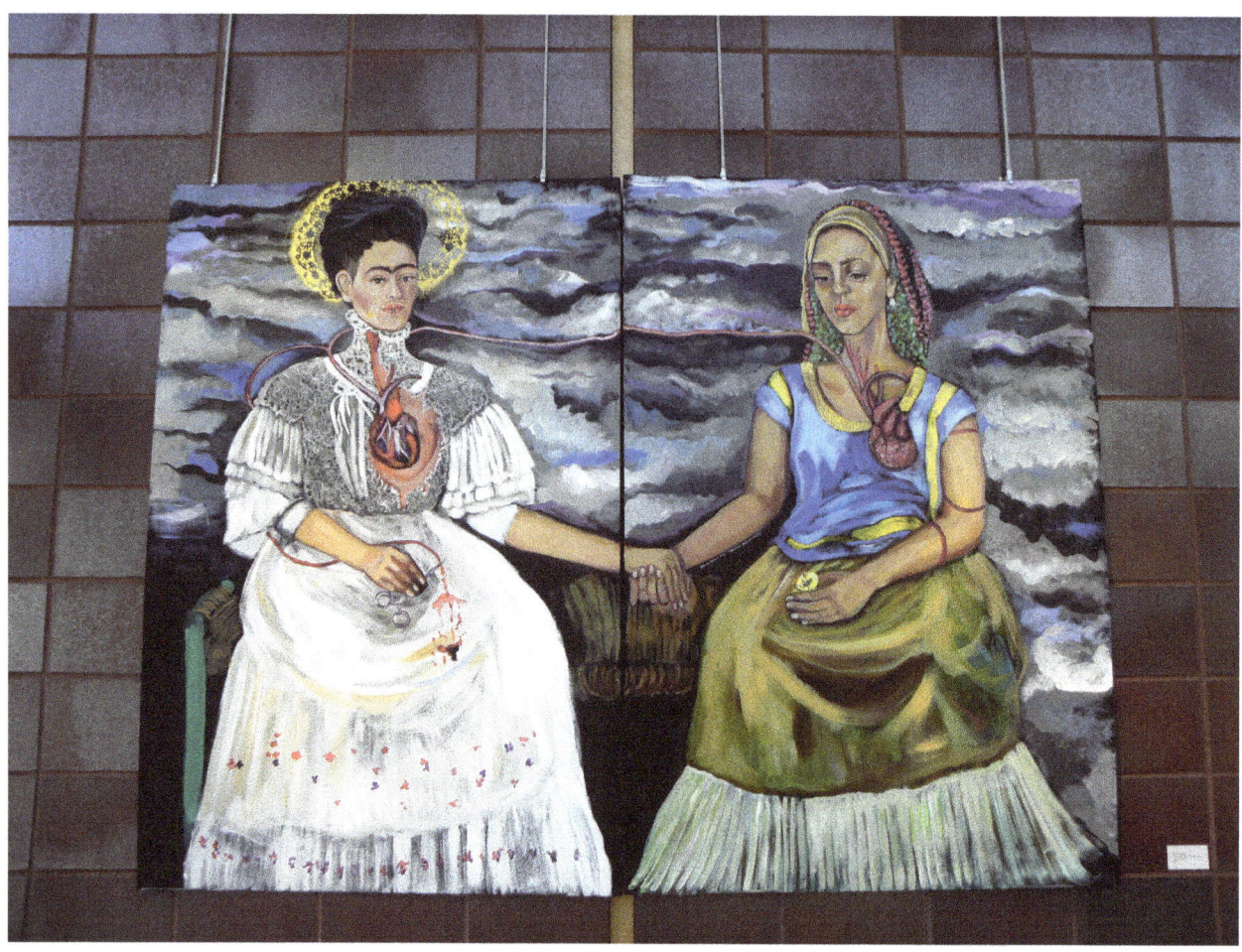

Me & Frida, Whole Heart / Her Hurt. 2015. Acrylic on board, 30 x 40 in (each panel). Photography by Heather Earnley.

interconnected realms of black life. (CCS is also where Nelson works. She's recruited for CCS for nearly twenty-five years.)

It's easy to imagine the author and the artist sitting and swapping laughs, but Baldwin became a muse only by accident. Nelson happened to be accompanying friends to the James Baldwin Conference in Paris, when suddenly she was asked to submit sketches. Nelson quickly "baptized" herself in his image and his words. "Anybody can draw James Baldwin and people have," she says. "This was about finding James Baldwin in me. I could hear him, his sassiness, his love of life and of a good laugh and his blackness; the essence of who he was and how he lived, that's what I wanted the work to show."

Nelson's reverence for Baldwin is second only to that of Frida Kahlo. The Mexican painter is the subject of one of her signature works, *Me & Frida, Whole Heart / Her Hurt* (2015), an acrylic on board that juxtaposes vibrant colors with a subtle and bloody commentary on Kahlo's infamous heartbreak. The piece is a testament to one of Nelson's secret wishes. "I like to think that I am the spirit of her child that she left behind," she says, referring to a miscarriage Kahlo suffered in 1932 at Henry Ford Hospital. "I was born at Henry Ford."

What Nelson sees in Kahlo—an unyielding spirit of freedom and fiery femininity—partly explains why she has mostly trained her pen, pencils, and paintbrushes on women. "For so long, I hadn't done drawings of men because I thought so many others had given them life. I am always drawn more to the underdog. For me, usually that's women." With ***Charity Hicks Water Warrior, #wagelove*** (2016), Nelson felt compelled to celebrate the life of Charity Hicks, the woman whose protest against water shut-offs in Detroit drew the attention of the United Nations and earned her the moniker "The People's Warrior." A mixed-media piece titled ***Lawdy Lil Mama after Barkley L. Hendricks*** (also 2016) pays simultaneous tribute to the strength of black women, in general, and to the late postmodern painter Barkley L. Hendricks, in particular.

A woman is also at the heart of Nelson's next big project, illustrating poet Jessica Care Moore's new book-length tribute to Sandra Bland, a twenty-eight-year-old black woman who was found hanged in a Texas jail. "Women can't ever see ourselves enough. Especially now."

As passionate as Nelson is about the social relevance of the subjects she takes on, there is another hidden, more personal element embedded in every creation. Some call it drive. She calls it her *Detroitness*. "This is who I am. This is my line. I'm always making. I *never* stop."

NICHOLE M. CHRISTIAN, DECEMBER 2017

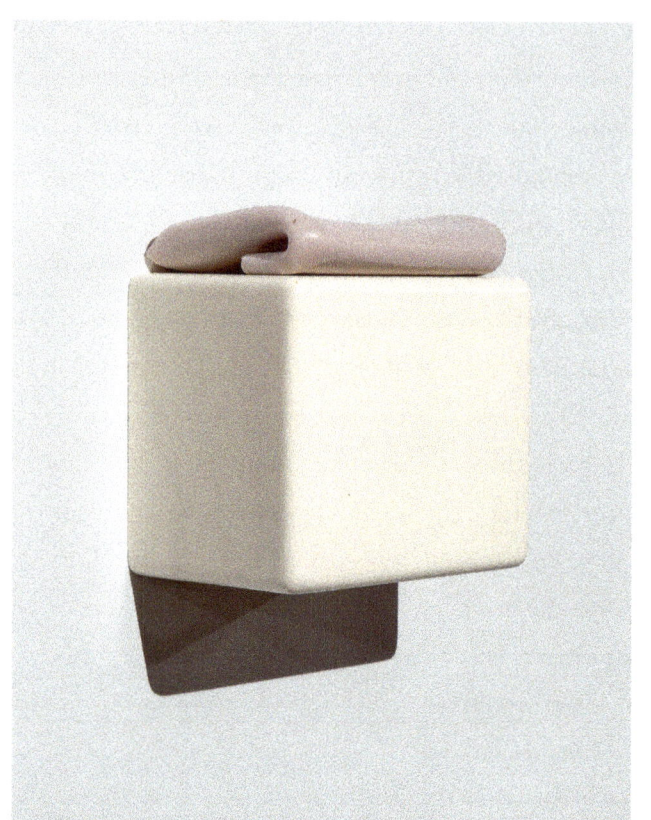
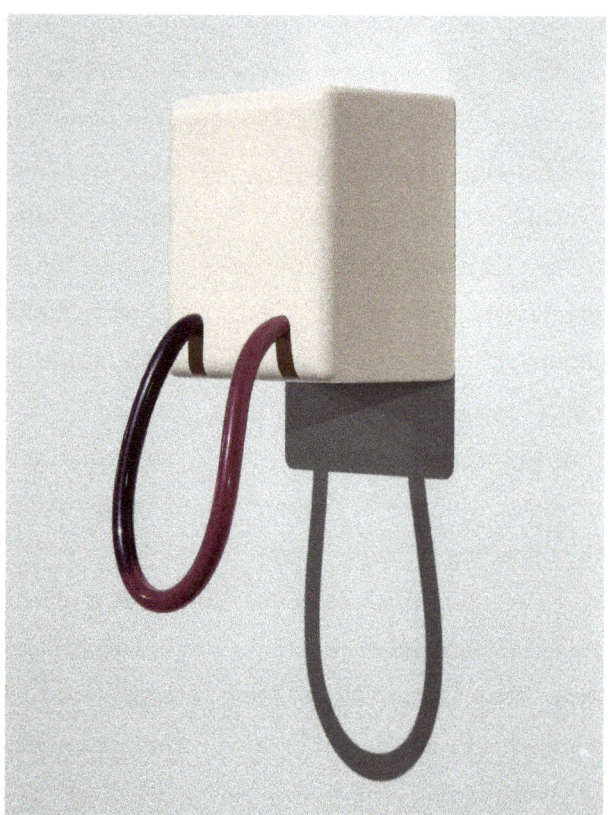
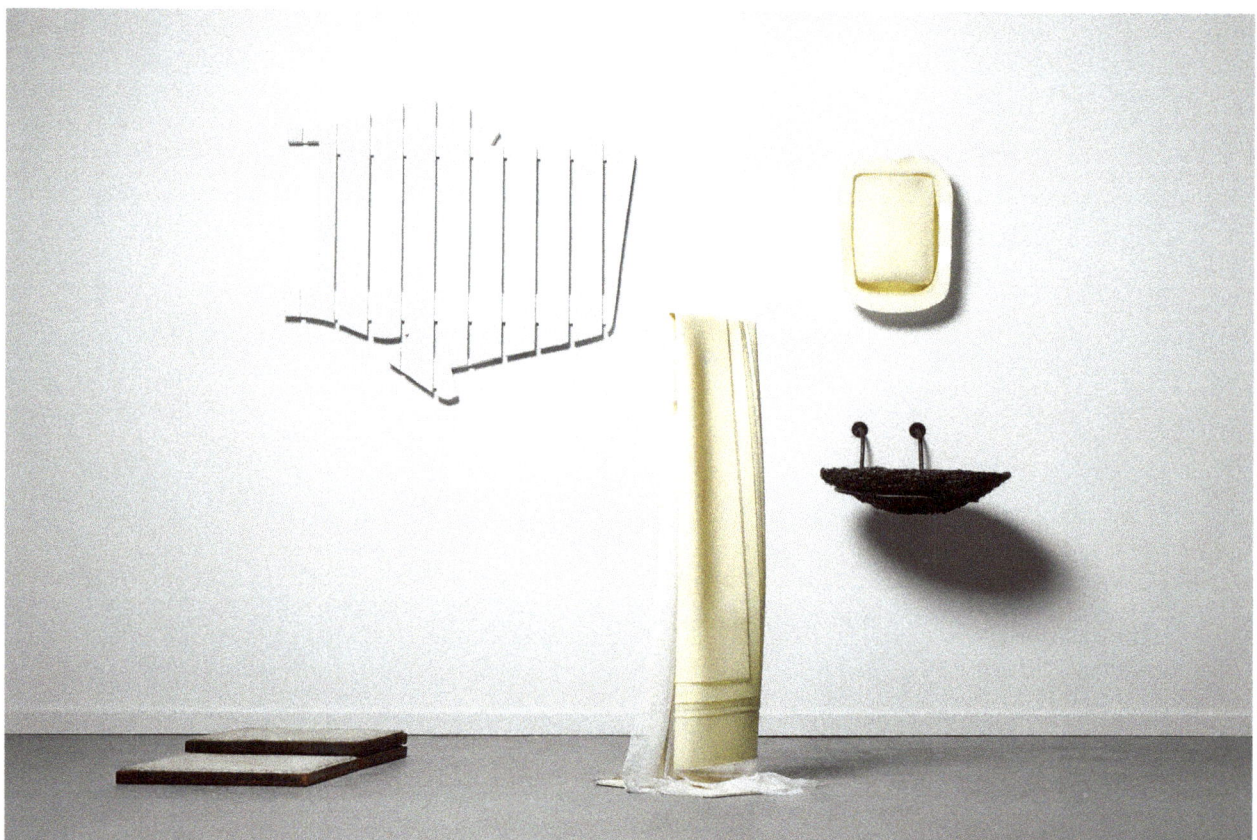

(Top left) Betty. 2017. Pigmented silicone, fiber board, paint, 11 x 10 3/4 x 7 in. Photography by PD Rearick. *(Top right) Stella.* 2017. Pigmented silicone, fiber board, paint, 15 1/2 x 7 1/2 x 9 1/4 in. Photography by PD Rearick. (*Bottom*) *Morning Routine.* 2016. Steel, wood, silicone, netting, concrete, dimensions variable. Photography by Micaela Ruiz.

Born New York, New York, 1985
BA, Carleton College; MFA, Cranbrook Academy of Art
Lives in Detroit

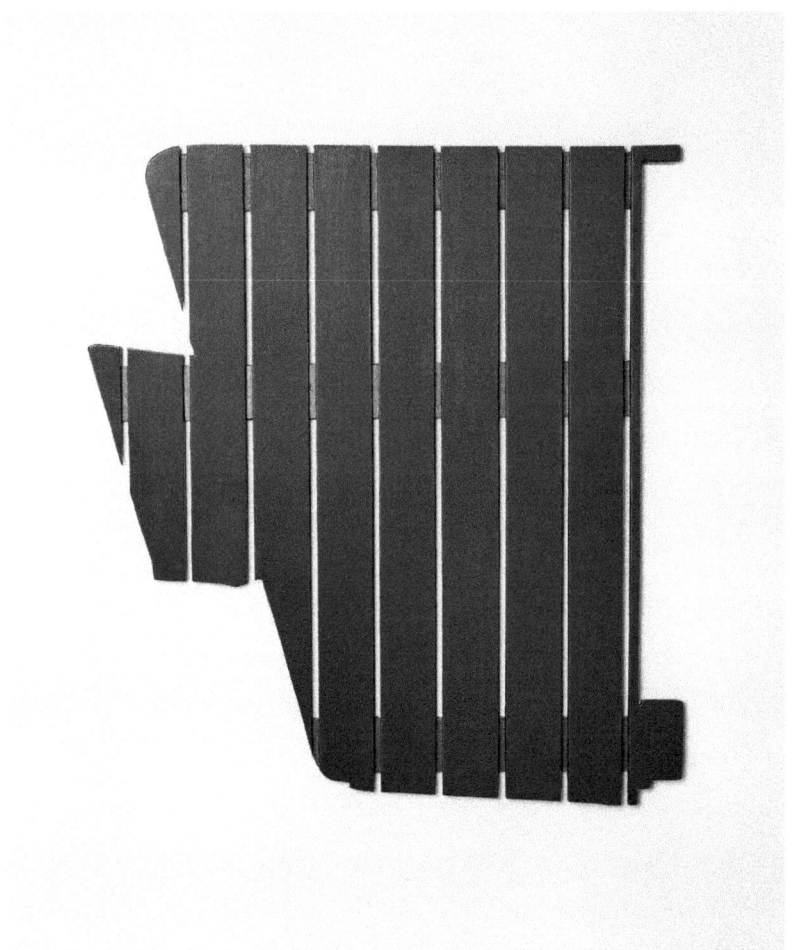

Detroit Excerpt No. 2. 2016. Wood, house paint, 36 x 43 x 1 1/2 in.
Photography by Micaela Ruiz.

Sophie Eisner is not from Detroit and does not put on airs about it. As a young artist who moved to the area in 2013 and to the Motor City in 2015, she thinks it's important to do a lot of listening. Eisner travels extensively, having just recently returned, for instance, from Mongolia. Wherever she goes and whatever she makes there, she brings elements from her childhood home in New York City with her. One of the notable qualities of Eisner's practice is her ability to take a familiar object in a familiar place, such as the pink tiles in the bathroom of her studio, and use materials, such as pigmented silicone, to think about the object from a different perspective. By presenting this same object with different materials and shape, Eisner invites the viewer to recall that they have seen this object

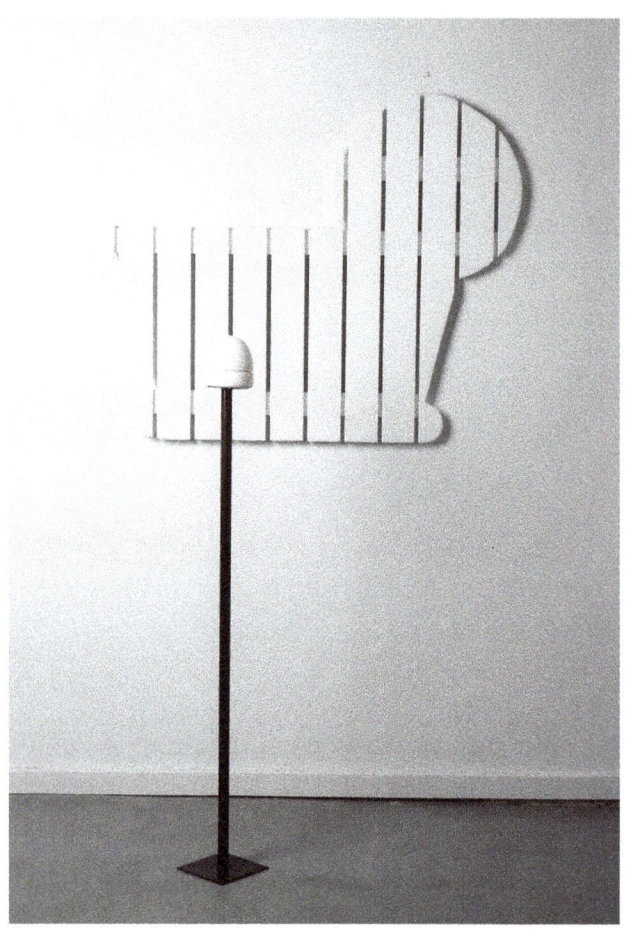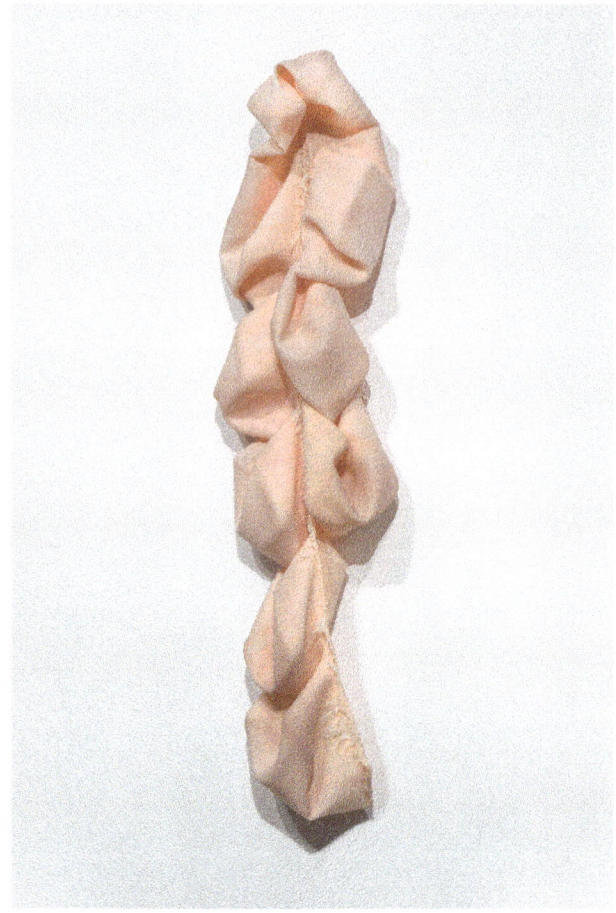

(Left) Placeholder. 2016. Wood, house paint, steel, cast plastic, 40 x 36 x 43 in. Photography by Micaela Ruiz. *(Right) Soft and Heavy* (vignette 2). 2017. Pigmented silicone, 65 x 13 x 10 in. Photography by PD Rearick.

somewhere before and to wonder where. Eisner's work gives viewers a fuzzy feeling of familiarity.

Consider *Morning Routine* (2016), a sculpture-installation comprised of five elements made out of materials ranging from silicone to steel to wood and house paint. It evokes the experience of stepping into a bathroom, looking in the mirror, washing, and grabbing a towel. However, all of the materials normally seen in these situations—porcelain, tile, metal,

glass, cotton—have been replaced with others: steel, wood, silicone, and netting. A steel "sink" or a silicone "mirror" are not the most common materials for a bathroom. Stepping from the conventional into the unconventional—note in particular the two-step threshold that invites entry to the room—allows Eisner to take the ordinary and magnify its importance in our daily lives.

While most of what Eisner represents in *Morning Routine*

are objects of daily life, there is one component that stands out from the others. It looks a bit like a painted fence and is mounted on the wall of the installation. Eisner has made other versions of this element and explains that it is inspired by the silhouettes of business signs in Detroit. (This one in particular also evokes the white picket fence of idealized American life.) Other versions of this piece include *Detroit Excerpt No. 2* (2016) and *Placeholder* (2016). *Detroit Excerpt No. 2* is intended to be exhibited on its own. In Eisner's studio, several of these silhouettes line the wall above her desk.

Business signs are visual cues that many people walk by every day without necessarily noticing their presence. But in Detroit, the art of sign-making has been a major part of the city's culture for decades: from Henry the Hatter on Broadway Street to Mr. Fish on Vernor Highway. By drawing attention to these shapes, Eisner magnifies an element of urban life that is sometimes taken for granted. *Placeholder* features what could be a lamp in front of one of these silhouettes, almost as if Eisner is bringing to light this special part of Detroit's culture.

Shining light on the ordinary and changing how one might normally see is what Eisner does naturally. With *Soft and Heavy* (vignette 2) (2017), Eisner takes a familiar pink tile color seen in many bathrooms and kitchens from the 1950s and 1960s and applies it to what nearly looks like an oversized strand of DNA. (Many people have an ingrained memory of a place with that color inside of it, in what one might call a home's genetic history.) There are elements of this pink hue in *Betty* (2017), a tan-colored box with what appears to be a gently folded tongue on top. If Betty is a portrait, then her tongue is twisted, which indicates a lack a speech. *Stella* (2017), a similar

piece, has another tongue-like contour sticking out of another tan box. Both pieces suggest the idea of the tongue not being used for language but instead for play: curling the tongue, sticking the tongue out, but not talking. As Eisner is new to Detroit and has mentioned that she wants to do a lot of listening, these sculptures almost emulate her desire to play with materials, as well as to see, taste, and hear the city. Perhaps *Stella* and *Betty* are subtle self-portraits, evocations of what Eisner desires to be, and to listen for, while becoming a new and evolving member of Detroit's art community.

ALLEGRA ROSENBAUM, DECEMBER 2017

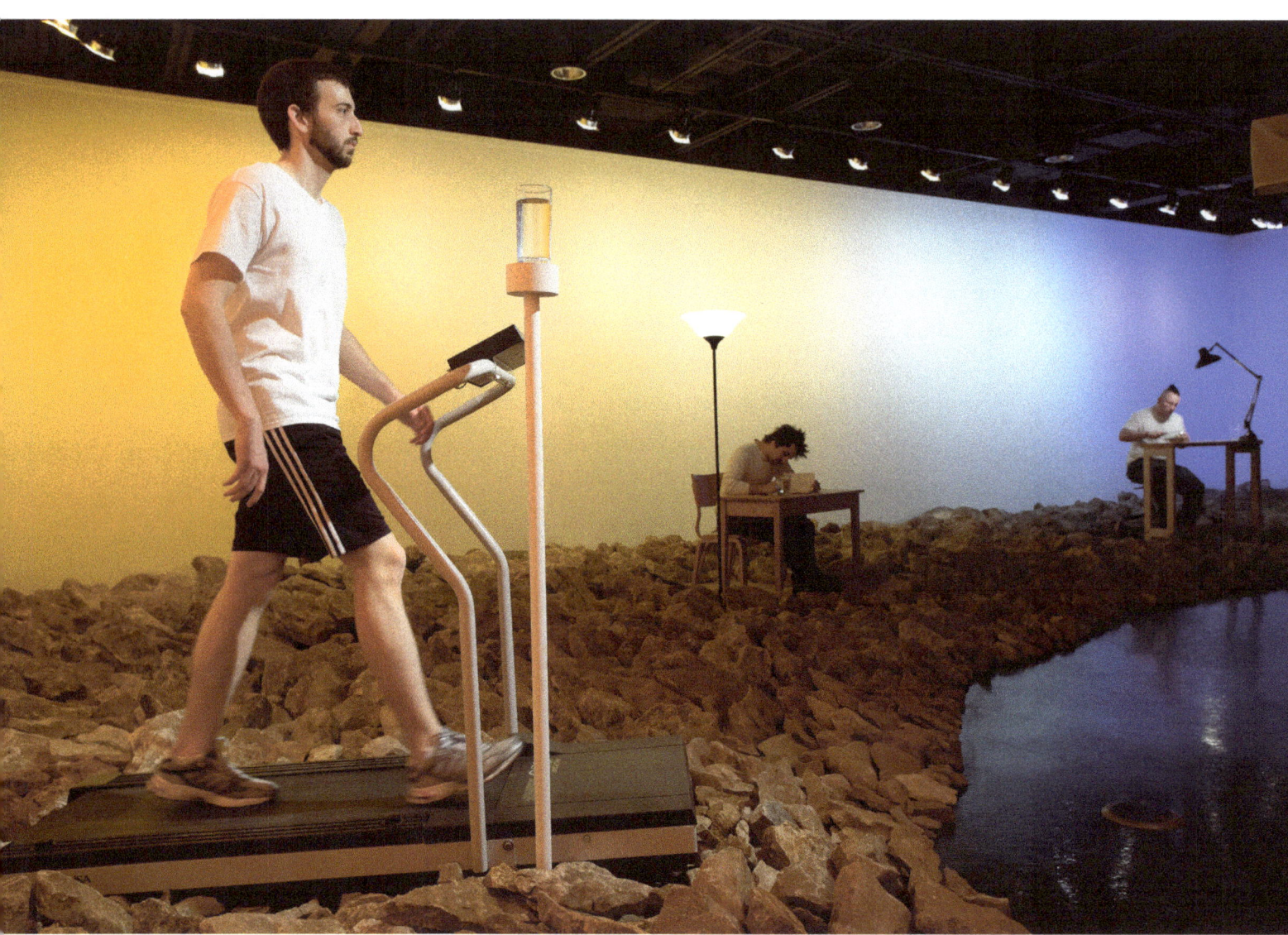

In Our Time (Art and Design Gallery, University of Kansas, Lawrence, KS). 2014. Found local limestone, Masonite, framing, chalk speakers, contact microphones, treadmill, hand-fabricated sterling silver egg, hand-fabricated maple work bench, playing cards, journal, colored lighting gels, furniture, glass cups, other furniture. Photography by Aaron Paden.

90 // ELI GOLD

Born Ithaca, New York, 1987
BS, Skidmore College; MFA, University of Kansas
Lives in Detroit

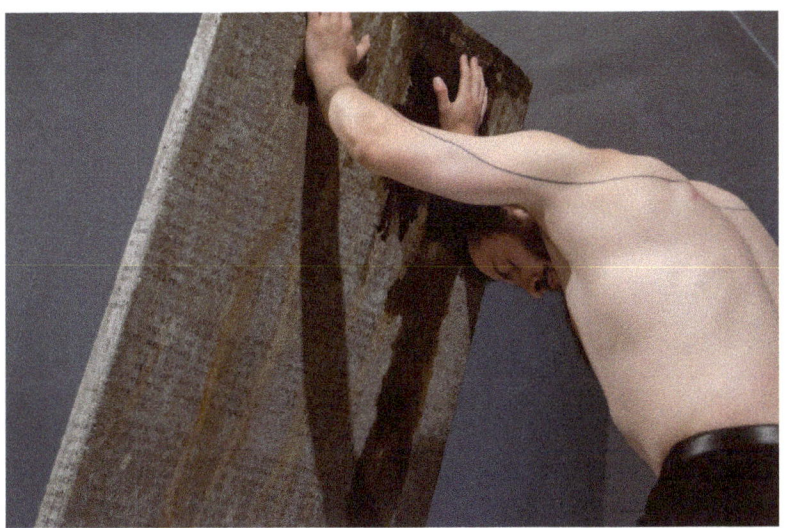

Braced (Defibrillator Gallery, Rapid Pulse Performance Art Festival, Chicago, IL). 2016. Performance, fabricated cement slab, white cloth, used motor oil. Photography by Holly Arsenault.

Eli Gold's conceptual performances explore the value of labor in art by using the artist's own body as medium, material, and live-tested instrument. To consider art as a form of labor places emphasis on measures of time and physical effort, and on the demonstration of the processes by which a work of art is made. In addition, Gold's work exposes how gestures of doing are inextricably intertwined with gestures of feeling, as his practice foregrounds how institutions such as art galleries regulate human behavior. The conceptual approach to performance art in Gold's work also makes intellectual labor significant, as an *a priori* plan prefigures each task-based event—whose execution is an ultimately perfunctory affair.

Gold was trained in metalsmithing and jewelry at the University of Kansas, Lawrence,

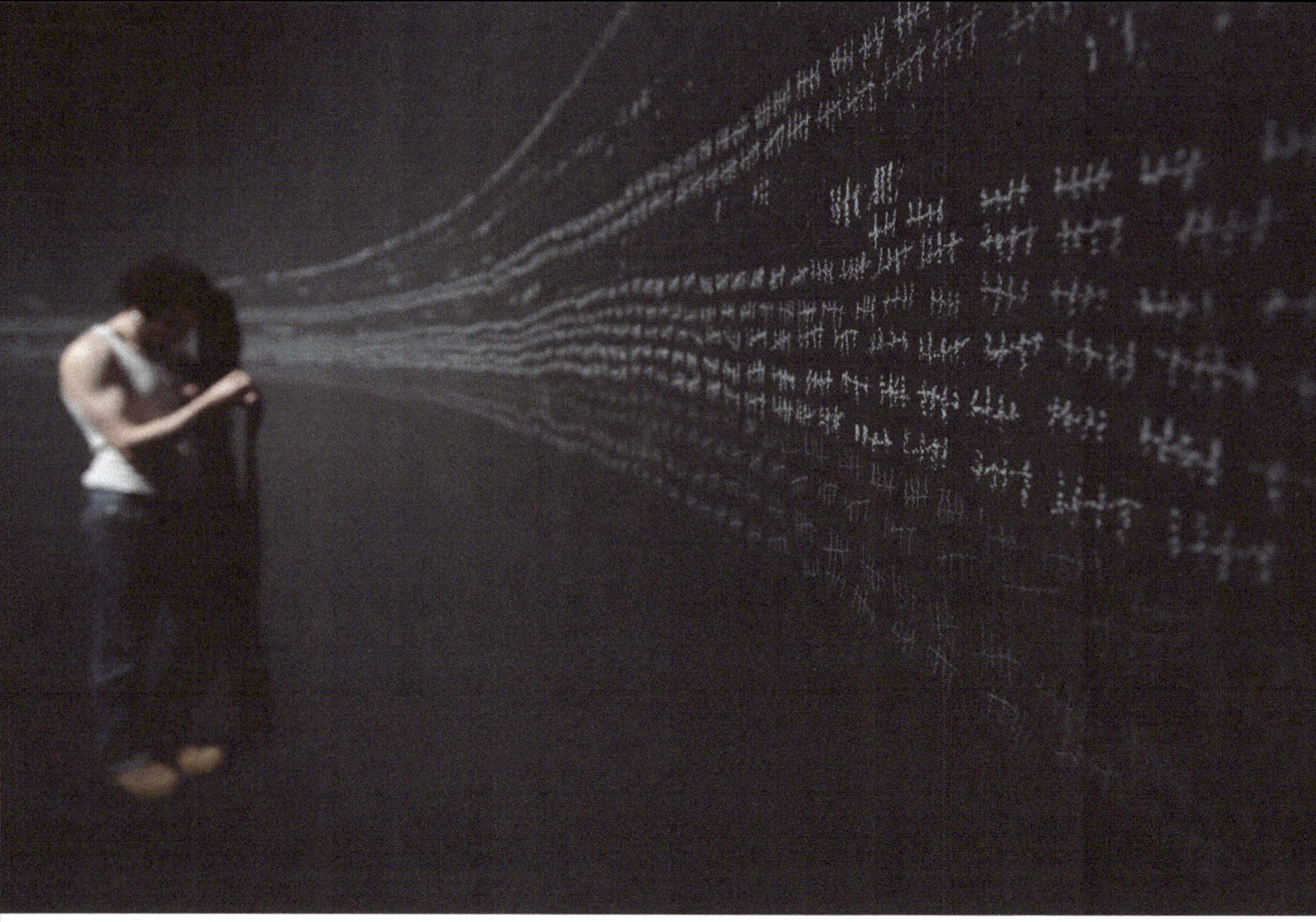

In Our Time (Art and Design Gallery, University of Kansas, Lawrence, KS). 2014. Found local limestone, Masonite, framing, chalk speakers, contact microphones, treadmill, hand-fabricated sterling silver egg, hand-fabricated maple work bench, playing cards, journal, colored lighting gels, furniture, glass cups, other furniture. Photography by Aaron Paden.

where he ritualistically destroyed a silver-plated copper teapot in his first year of graduate school in 2012. By taking a hammer to his own craft, the artist metaphorically breaks his commitment toward the handmade and replaces it with a performative investigation of the body as a schema of behavior, rules, and laws. ***In Our Time*** (2014, University of Kansas Art and Design Gallery, Lawrence)

makes visible institutionalized regimes of sociality. Here, the artist orchestrates how clock time and the human heartbeat regulate experience in different yet interrelated systems of time measure. As he listens to ten thousand of his own heartbeats through a stethoscope, he sets ten thousand white chalk hatch marks onto a room-spanning blackboard equipped with a contact microphone. Four additional

performers, placed behind the wall, follow the rhythm of the amplified marks: playing solitaire suspends time, writing stories preserves the past, biking on a treadmill counteracts bad lifestyle choices, and filing a sterling silver egg echoes the laborious artistry of metalsmithing. ***The Heartbeat Listeners*** (2015) channels the unmediated and unrestrained body as a direct vessel of skin-to-skin contact. In this performance,

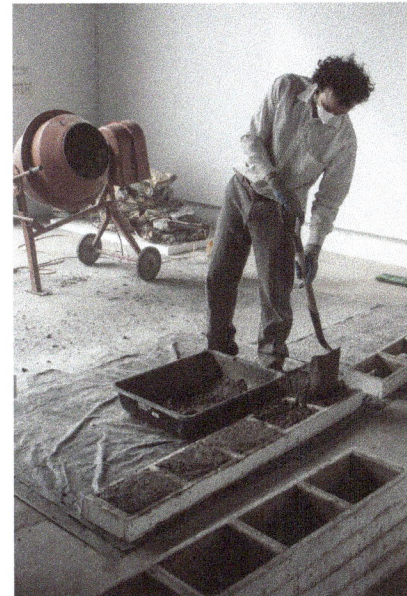

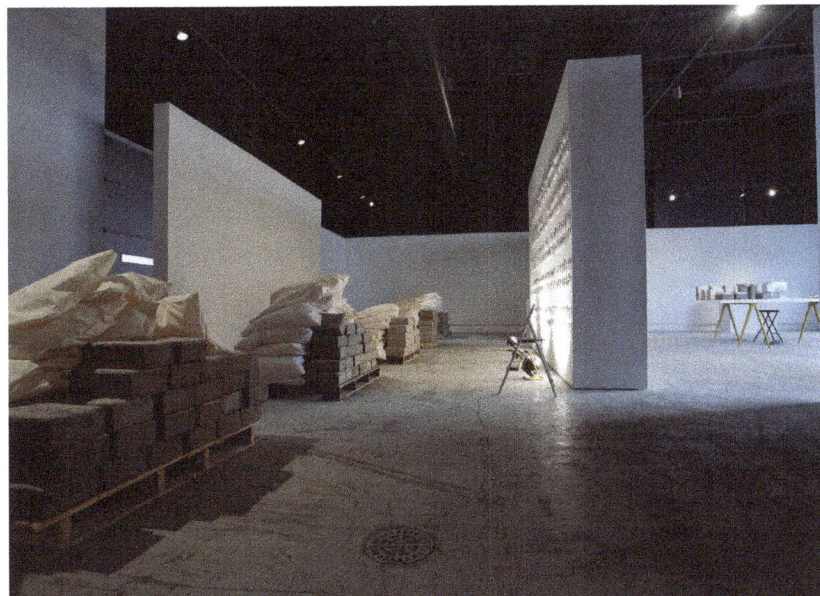

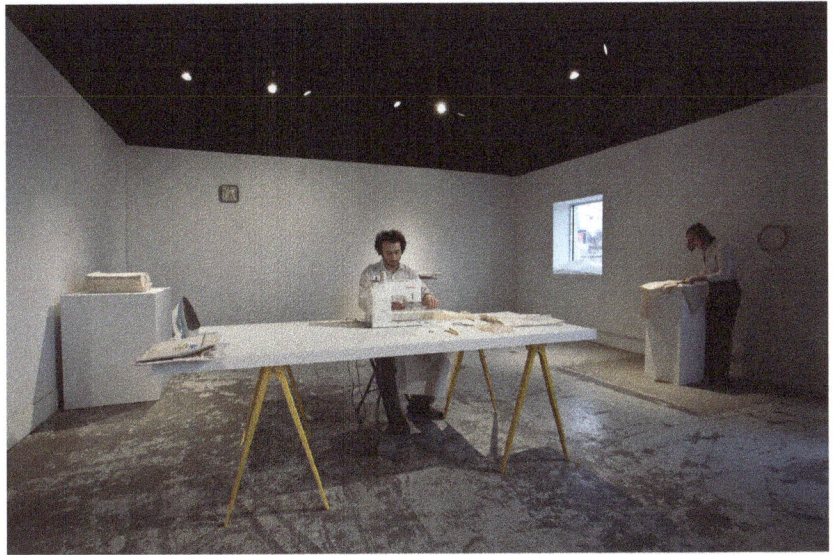

Full Time (La Esquina Gallery, Kansas City, MO). 2015. Concrete, muslin cloth, embroidery thread, plastic trash bags, wooden molds, sewing machine, cement mixer, shovels, palettes, clock, coffee pot, newsprint, other found and fabricated items. Photography by Aaron Paden.

visitors to the Hamtramck Arts Festival allowed the artist (or a coperformer) to listen directly to one hundred of their heartbeats without the aid of device or instrument.

In *Full Time* (2015, La Esquina Gallery, Kansas City), Gold conflates artistic labor with the highly regulated factory labor of the assembly line. He and Rena Detrixhe showcase a forty-hour work week as they sew and cast, time stamp, and inventory thirty white pillow cases and thirty gray concrete blocks to be sold during the opening night. The sale price of each item is $7.85. Simulating a regular office work day from 9 a.m. to 5 p.m. with a lunch break, *The Monkey Chases the Weasel (How Did I Get Here?)* (2016, 9338 Campau Gallery, Hamtramck) similarly indexes time and wage labor. For one day, Gold repeatedly lifts a heavy gray cinder block off a white pedestal, only to place it on a lower white platform at

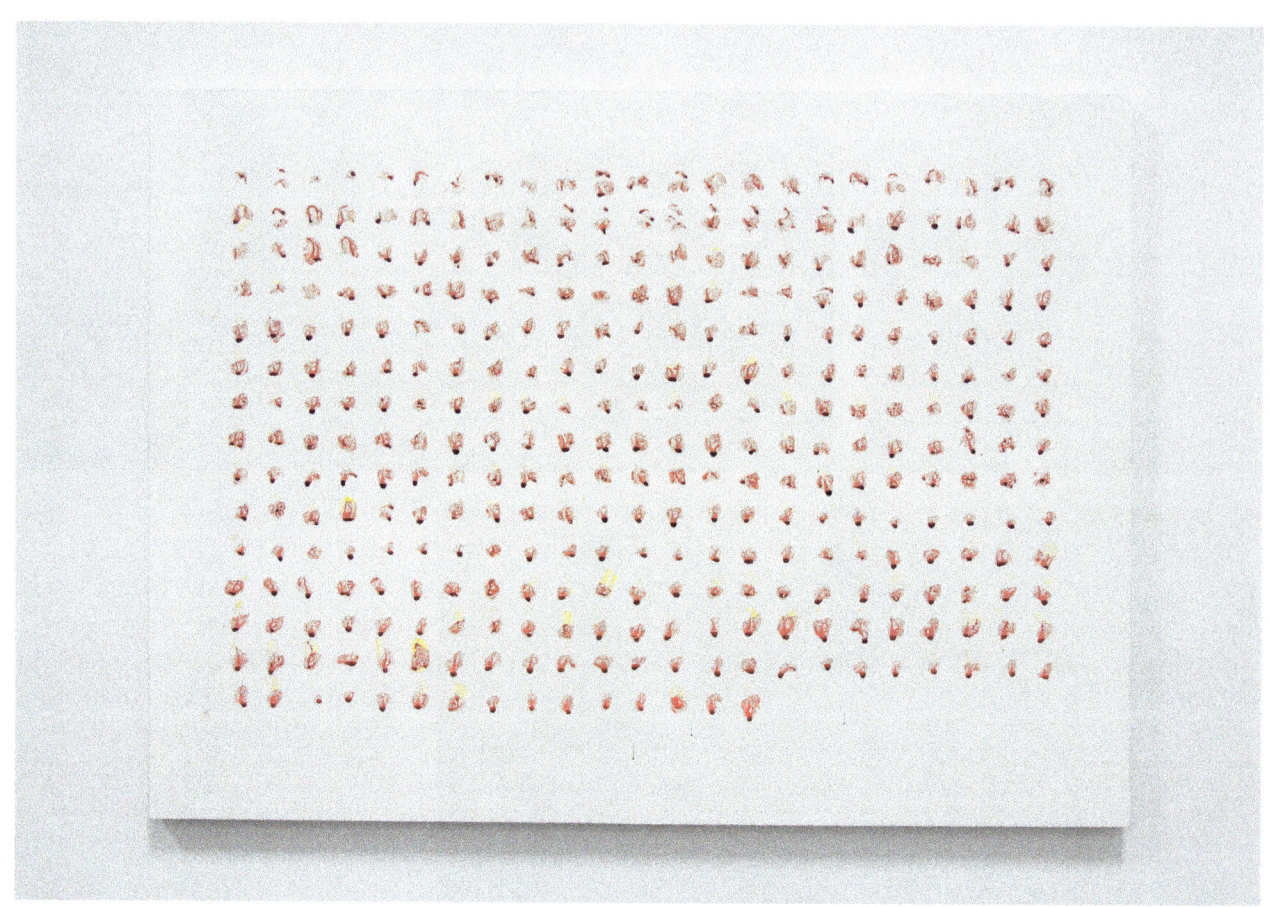

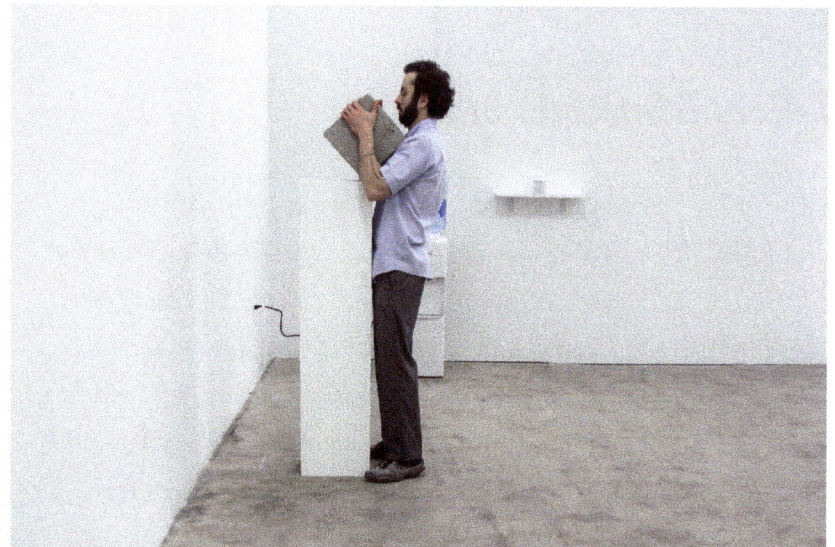

The Monkey Chases the Weasel (How Did I Get Here?) (9338 Campau Gallery, Hamtramck, MI). 2016. Durational performance, concrete block, gessoed panel, blood, sterilized lancets, iodine, water cooler, air freshener. Photography by Melanie Manos.

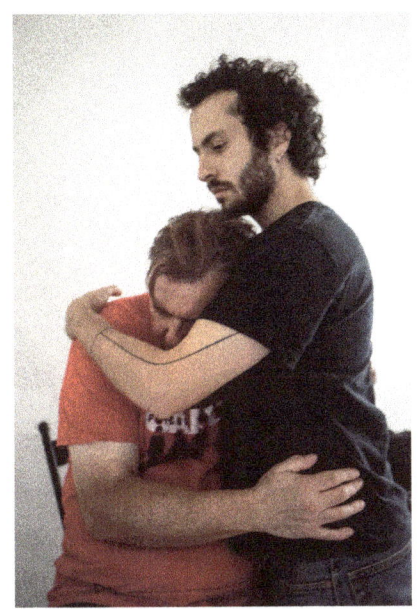

The Heartbeat Listeners (Hamtramck Neighborhood Arts Festival, Detroit, MI). 2015. Performance. Photography by Chris Reilly.

the other end of the gallery, and then moves it back again. He periodically pricks his finger with a steel needle, sterilizes the blood with dark-orange iodine, and after every completed cycle of lifting and carrying, presses it onto a white, gridded sheet with 366 pencil boxes that correlate to the days of a leap year. The drawing and performance serve as a visual trace of the Sisyphean nature of bureaucratic routine. *Braced* (2016, Defibrillator Gallery, Chicago) also presents an endurance test of sorts as the artist supports a three-hundred-pound concrete block—resembling the height and weight of another human being—until he no longer can. The heavy slab then crashes and leaks black motor oil from an inner chamber onto a white sheet beneath it. As a metaphor for the act of working through a burdening relationship (the block's surface holds text from an email correspondence), the act of letting the concrete shatter symbolizes the release of an emotional struggle. Here, Gold visualizes emotional labor as an act of working through a problem (very unlike the literalist spill and scatter process art of the late 1960s). At the same time, struggle and fatigue become intrinsic values of the kind of labor from which creative action emerges.

Gold's process-oriented practice variously explores and implodes the conceptual divisions that ostensibly separate art and labor, art and bureaucracy, and manual and emotional labor in favor of a more holistic worldview of feeling and thinking.

NADJA ROTTNER, DECEMBER 2017